Praise for Kweisi Mfume and *No Free Ride*

"A delight to read . . . How could a young man 'without a
single skill in the world,' who knew only how to 'push bread
through a slicer, shine shoes, and shoot dice' and who was
'broke most of the time and didn't really have a roof to call
my own,' fight his way out of 'the day-in, day-out grind of
poverty' he had known since childhood? This is where Mfume
and co-writer Ron Stodghill show their mettle as biogra-
phers—they relate Mfume's story with such vivacity and
humor that we can't help but root for him."
                                        —*San Francisco Chronicle*

"A candid and moving memoir that reads like the quintessen-
tial all-American success story."
                                        —*The Cincinnati Herald*

"Mfume is a signal figure in politics today: a new kind of
black leader, arisen from outside the civil-rights struggle, and
a new kind of politician, wired to the power source beyond
the traditional structures. . . ."
                                        —*The New Yorker*

NO FREE RIDE

*From the Mean Streets
to the Mainstream*

KWEISI MFUME

WITH RON STODGHILL II

ONE WORLD
BALLANTINE BOOKS • NEW YORK

A One World Book
Published by Ballantine Books

http://www.randomhouse.com

Library of Congress Catalog Card Number: 97-92949

ISBN: 0-345-41364-4

Cover design by Kristine V. Mills-Noble
Cover photo by Ken Schles

Manufactured in the United States of America

First Trade Paperback Edition: April 1997

10 9 8 7 6 5 4 3

I dedicate this book to my beloved mother, Mary, and to my sons . . . Donald, Kevin, Keith, Michael, and Ronald.

I thank the following people who at some point over the course of my life have helped make me a better man:

Sheilah Davenport
Willarda Edwards
Arnette Evans
Angela Foster
Linda Mason
Parren J. Mitchell
Joan Powell
JoAnn Rambaran
Belva Scott
Terry Scott-Stephens
Jim Sears
Ruth Simms
Nydia Velasquez
Lynn Whitfield

CONTENTS

PROLOGUE

I MET him on a hot August afternoon in 1994. I cannot recall his name, but that is not important. He was no different from many other young black men in this country: poor, bright, and troubled. Not so very long ago, that description would have easily fit me. And perhaps it is this, more than anything else, that drew me to this menacing figure with imposing eyes and a slanted pose who ranged like a hawk over this rough West Baltimore street corner, a place legendary for its uncanny ability to dominate generation after generation of black men. Perhaps it was my own history here, the ghosts of a squandered youth and shattered hope, that elicited my empathy for this stranger. Perhaps it was the traces of my own blood that had spilled and dried years ago on that same slab of concrete at the intersection of Robert and Division streets that spurred me to reach out to him.

It is always a difficult thing to gain the trust of a street warrior, and on this day I looked far from trustworthy. I was accompanied by veteran journalist Steve Kroft and his *60 Minutes* news crew. They were trailing me as part of a story they were

1

doing on the growing influence of the Congressional Black Caucus. We had already walked several blocks and filmed in what an outsider might regard as generic urban blight: the buildings boarded up, the laundry hanging above row house stoops, pregnant teenage girls, and old folks peeking out from behind drawn window shades. For most Americans, these are the images of urban decay. For me and hundreds of thousands of African Americans across the nation, these were and are the symbols of home.

My visit this day was both deliberate and contrived. We had come to my old neighborhood to capture a look back in time to my roots. The place had changed drastically from the days when I had walked the streets as a young tough. Poverty held the community in a viselike grip. The buildings, those which were still standing, revealed the deep seriousness of the evil plagues of unemployment, drugs, government neglect, and despair that had seized control of the area. Bands of idle, bitter youth no longer attempted to attend the inferior schools which dotted the community. Here, crime too often was a daily occurrence.

I was chairman of the Congressional Black Caucus and that alone had made me the focus of the story. I suspect that filming me in the midst of this other America was *60 Minutes'* way of underscoring the irony of my ascension. But the media spectacle, the video cameras, the lights, and the bustling technicians clouded me in a shroud of suspicion to those nearby who watched.

In the eyes of this young gang-banger and the others around him I was conspicuously out of my element. Almost catlike, he began to move quickly in the other direction and his posse followed suit. You didn't need a Ph.D. to know what was going on. They thought I was the Man. They probably thought that the camera crew was there to film them dealing drugs or to cast them as an example of the urban problem. The fact that they believed any or all of it upset me.

Moments such as this reminded me that in the eyes of some I have become part of the Establishment that they loathe, a system which stacks statistics and insurmountable odds against them. It's an Establishment of great punishment and little reward, one that many people of color both fear and distrust. On this day, I strangely yearned to set the record straight. To let these young guys know I was not part of any kind of conspiracy that seeks to further bring them down. I was not among the media vultures that thrive and grow fat off the carcasses of poor people crushed under the colossus of urban woes. I was not one of those insincere politicians who make empty promises built on a bunch of false assumptions. I wondered how I could make them realize that I didn't represent that part of the Establishment, that my life, too, is rooted in the same pain and frustration that bonds them together.

"Stay here," I told the camera crew without so much as looking at them. Even in hindsight, I cannot explain the strange mix of emotions that propelled me out into the street that day. As much as I've tried, I can't define the rush of emotion that I felt that sent me running off toward the gang, darting past the row houses of Division Street and around the corner eastward to the opening of an alley. I was not afraid to confront them, though I wasn't fully sure what I would say to them when I did. It was not until I was a good distance away from the news crew, when the pungent scent of marijuana filled my nostrils, that I realized that I had come too close to turn back. The gang, which had slowed into a brisk stride, stopped suddenly in their tracks and looked ready to attack.

My arms held out high and wide, I called out to them in words I hoped would help diffuse suspicion.

"Yo, my man, I don't have a gun, and I don't have a badge. It's just me," I said, as I walked toward them, my hands in full view.

But even as I spoke those words, my eyes quickly canvassed the ground around me for anything that might help defend me against a rush, which I knew was not implausible.

"I don't have a gun, or a badge," I repeated.

A deep silence hung in the air, and in that one long moment of predatory instinct there was no connection between me and the gang. There was just the exaggerated and menacing stare of two generations long since separated by time and space, bound only by the ethics of the street. We both were held captive to a code that demanded, "Watch your back, and cover your ass."

I could feel the tension in the air. They slowly fanned out in a semicircle, as if attempting to secure an even perimeter, much like a pride of lions on the hunt. It didn't matter who I was with down the street and around the corner. Here I was on their turf and subordinate to their rules. I was far enough away now that they could rob me or off me without fear of being caught. They knew it and they had quickly come to realize that I knew it, too.

"Yo, I swear I'm not packing," I said, patting myself down to prove I had no weapons concealed. "I'm from around here, used to live right down the street. I just want to talk with you for a minute."

"Hey G, he ain't packin' nothin' . . . less it's some small shit," said one of them who had slipped up behind me. "He ain't strapped."

I glanced around at the dark, unshaven face leaning over my shoulder, then heard yet another voice in the pack explode angrily, "Punk bitch, you must be outta your muthafuckin' mind. I oughta bust a cap in your ass."

I had been jammed enough before to know that they were now slowly maneuvering into position for a strike. The once neutral faces tightened into menacing, cold masks now as the circle around me closed. With semiautomatics tucked at their waists, they pulled back their baggy shirts, smiled, and flashed their weapons freely. The odds were in their favor and they dared me to move.

"We oughta kick your ass just for runnin' up on us like that," one young gangsta threatened, a thin line of gold glittering in his mouth.

More out of a need to survive and less out of fear, I remained unfazed by a standoff over which I had no control. I had been there before; I knew this scene well. On the street, a brother could see the measure of a man by locking eyes with him. If there was any punk in him, it showed itself in his eyes. It was eyes and body language that were important on the street. Much more than empty words, they were sometimes the only things that made a gang-banger think twice before acting. It was the threat of dealing with someone just as crazy as themselves that served as the common denominator. And it was clear that to a man they all must have thought that I was crazy. Why else would I risk getting robbed and capped, on their turf, and on their terms? Still, the last thing I wanted to do was spook them into violence.

I knew I'd better make my move before something jumped off. "Look, my name is Kweisi . . . Kweisi Mfume," I said, keeping my voice firm and steady. "I just want to talk with you brothers. The film crew is just following me around because they're doing a bit on me and the 'hood I grew up in. No bullshit."

That's when he spoke up—the tall angry one with a baseball cap turned backward and an unlit cigarette slanted across his hardened, boyish dark face. "Don't diss me, muthafucka," he rasped. " 'Cause I ain't your goddamned brother. What you think, I'm some kind of fuckin' fool?"

"No, my man, you can't be a fool," I answered. "You got the drop on me. I know that. You can't be a fool."

My admission about who was in charge eased some of the tension. Even though the group kept me surrounded, the mood lightened a bit and their edgy tempers softened slightly to a kind of nervy curiosity.

"Any of you in school?" I asked.

"Yeah," the head man replied with a hint of sarcasm. "Some of us is, and some of us ain't. I was supposed to graduate last May. So I guess that I is, and I guess that I ain't."

His crew broke out in uncontrollable laughter, dishing out high fives to let me know that I had been chumped. I didn't react one way or another, but continued my spiel.

"So what do you want to do with your life now?"

"I want to have fun," the leader said. "You know what I'm sayin'? Hang out, play the bitches, and keep it real." More guffaws and laughter followed that response.

"You know you can get back in school and still have some fun," I shot back.

Then I knew instinctively that my suggestion had gone too far. Without forethought he pulled a blue steel automatic out of his pants and held it cocked between our faces. My heart pounded faster but my eyes remained steady. He leaned closer, smiled, then put a deep chill into his voice.

"I think I'd rather have fun out here, though," he said.

This time there was no reaction from his posse. Instead, they all turned and looked piercingly at me. As much as brothers on the street respect power or juice, their vision of real manhood has to do more with style, attitude, and the heart to kill. Of these, heart is number one. "Okay, that's cool," I conceded calmly. "But what the fuck do you want to do after you have your fun?"

He sucked his teeth as he thought for a moment, then he spit over my shoulder and said, "I want to go into mortuary science."

My eyes finally blinked and my brow tightened. I admit I was thrown off by his answer, not quite knowing whether to take him seriously or to discount it as another snide joke. I waited for a punch line, but there was none.

"If that's what you really want to do, there's a community college uptown that offers a degree in that field. Maybe I can help you get into the program."

He lowered the gun slowly and looked even deeper into my eyes. His level of interest quickly increased and our sense of confrontation was on hold. I don't think he ever thought he'd get a chance to go to college, and for the moment he allowed the thought to seduce him. All the others were listening now, even though they had absolutely no idea what mortuary science was. We could have just as easily been talking calculus—they didn't know how to respond.

"Why mortuary science?" I asked. He turned even more serious.

"Because I like dealing with dead people," he said. "I like givin' them the kind of dignity when they dead that they couldn't git from the white man when they was alive."

"Dead people," screamed one of the others. "Nigga, you like dealing with dead people?"

Laughter suddenly broke out as embarrassment set in. Now they had caught on to what we were talking about. And, with those few words, his whole demeanor changed. All of a sudden he began to reassert himself as the leader—the meanest and the toughest. He grabbed one of his boys and backhanded him, saying, "Yeah, that's just what I might wanna do, but right now I'm still kickin' ass and takin' names, muthafucka."

And with that he said he didn't want to discuss it anymore. Peer pressure had won and honesty had lost. Just when he got comfortable enough to open up, his friends had reduced his ambition to a joke, and he immediately shrugged it off and reverted to himself. There he was again, the fire-breathing gang-banger spewing forth fear and holding court on his street corner.

I wrote down my home phone number on the back of a card and gave it to him.

"I don't expect you to give me your number," I said, "but I want you to have mine. Call me at home whenever you're ready and I'll work it out with you."

He turned the card over slowly in his hand before dropping it to the ground—just as I knew he would, and I knew he should. The others were still on his case, and to do anything less would have been an invitation to be challenged. Our eyes met for the last time once he had fully regained his dominance. I've seen the stare that he gave me a hundred times before. I, too, have given it and received it. It's the stare of death secretly crying out for life, hoping against hope that someone will decipher it.

"Get the fuck outta here, my man," he said in an almost deathly whisper. "You still standin' on my land."

Then, breaking the stare and with no final words, I turned my back slowly and walked away.

How little things change, I thought, while remaining the same. I asked myself—what will it take to break the cycle of the street? How is it that, despite the odds, there's still the indestructible human desire to hope for the impossible? Even I am struck by the character of change in my own lifetime. For no matter what I might accomplish in public service and beyond, I realize that, like some, I was more than lucky, I was blessed. I still marvel at my own transformation, and at the mysterious divine forces which spared me from becoming another nameless and faceless casualty. How did I survive a rocky adolescence that included an abusive stepfather, the death of my mother in my arms at the age of sixteen, dropping out of high school in the tenth grade, and my own descent into gang-banging, hustling, and adolescent sexual promiscuity. What was it that caused me to rise so high from ashes so deep?

As I left that street corner and returned to the crew of *60 Minutes*, a part of me stayed behind. I couldn't erase the faces of those I had just encountered and confronted. In one quick twist of a moment, life had played a cruel hoax on me. I thought I had been looking into the eyes of young gang members, when in reality I was looking instead into the hazy mirror of an era gone by, and in it I saw myself. Yet because I never gave up on myself I knew that I could not give up on them.

These kids are not beyond rescue or redemption any more than they are beyond hope or help. They are a part of the other America, trapped and lost in every big city and every small town. They are the ones we pass by in our cars as we lock our doors. They are the ones who flirt with death and test our limits. They become teenage parents much too soon, and give up on life much too fast. They are black and white and Latino. And, most of all, they are real. No matter how much we would like to dismiss their existence, they are, and continue to be, among us.

My story, like theirs, is a constant reminder of the fragility of human life, and the divine power that mediates the war between success and failure.

I am a child of the other America, and this is my story of faith.

1

TURNERS STATION

*M*AMA never cared much for doctors. In her mind, only God's touch could truly heal the sick. So I'm not sure how she ever came to call on Dr. Wade that winter morning of 1953. Perhaps desperation and hope drove her to do it.

I don't recall much at all about Dr. Wade, just a blur of a big man wearing a dark suit, and carrying a black leather bag. The old folks who remember him say he was a quiet fellow who exuded an air of authority. They likened him to a wise old owl who, during house calls, would amble about the room, peering curiously over horn-rimmed spectacles. Occasionally, he'd punctuate the silence with an "ah huh," "how does that feel," or "I see." Yet no matter how vague or terse Dr. Wade's mumblings were, people in Turners Station listened as if God himself were speaking.

The truth was, we had little choice. Back in the early 1950s, there were no other black physicians in the town of Turners Station. Dr. Wade was it. Many believed that within the old black leather bag Dr. Wade carried was a healing power that came from the Lord. And so the people of Turners Station came to rely on his support as much as he did on theirs.

On this particular morning, however, Dr. Wade was talking more than usual. He was trying without success to comfort Mama. It seems that I had developed strep throat and Mama had watched my face swell overnight and my body turn red. I'll never forget the pain, the way it twisted like barbed wire up through my little neck, so much so that even swallowing brought forth a lump and a razorlike sting. My lips were parched and blistered, and my head felt so heavy I could barely raise it up off the pillow. Having given me what little medicine he had left in that bag, Dr. Wade was losing hope of curing my sickness.

At age five, I was Mama's oldest child and her only boy. She sat in a chair beside my bed and prayed that I would not die, yet it was clear that Dr. Wade was losing me. My temperature was 106 for the third day in a row, and I was growing weaker with the hours. As Dr. Wade put on his hat and walked slowly toward the door, I imagine he confirmed Mama's belief that modern medicine could not rescue anyone from a deathbed.

The sun had nearly set by the time Mama stood up and began making her way to the kitchen. In the dusk of the twilight she had become a silhouette now, and the silence of the approaching nightfall was deafening. She had prayed long and hard to God for me, but she believed that she had to do more. The angel of death was approaching. Dr. Wade's painful stare hours earlier had confirmed the obvious. Yet it was Mama's unshakable faith that served as the foundation of what was to become the first miracle of my life.

Growing up, Mama had heard all about slavery from her grandfather, who was the last slave in the Willis family, and from her grandmother, who was half-Indian. She had listened closely as a child to the stories they told about slave auctions and plantations, and remembered tears welling up in their eyes whenever they talked about it. But on this evening she remembered something else. She remembered the cures they taught her and the medicines they made. And she believed that God, if asked, could make the cures work, each of them, one by one.

With her firstborn child fading, she turned to an old slave remedy, and blended it with the ritual of prayer.

That night, Mama returned from the kitchen with white rags and white potatoes. The potatoes had been sliced and were still moist, oval, and flat. Slowly, she began wrapping them around my wrists and ankles, tying them securely with shredded cloth. When finished, she took the last few slices, laid them on my neck, and wrapped a white cotton rag around it as well. Legend has it that long ago, during the days of slavery, root doctors used raw potatoes to break the fever of the sick.

I'm not sure what exactly happened over the next few hours, but those African ancestral spirits must have come fluttering down from the heavens above. The power of all those old slaves must have come into my room and communed with Mama that night. They must have gotten down on their leathery ancient knees and sent up a great resounding call for mercy. Mama, I am told, was crying something terrible, her body heaving and shaking as she bent praying on that floor.

"Dear God, let my boy live!" she begged. "Spare my child and I promise to give you the glory and the praise. Precious Lord, please let him live. He's just a little boy. Oh Holy Ghost, have mercy tonight. . . . Sweet Jesus have mercy."

Whatever happened that night between Mama and the Lord surely worked. The next morning, I awoke with the warm rays of sunlight splashing across my face. As I opened my eyes, I couldn't help but think about how bright the sun seemed. I'll never forget that light, the way it was rushing in through my window and seeming warmer than it ever had been before. I was cured. The sickness that Dr. Wade thought was terminal had left my body. My face no longer felt swollen, and my lips, though still parched, now thirsted for water. The fever had broken and the glands in my neck now felt cool. The potatoes, still wrapped around my neck and joints, had turned black and dry.

When I awoke, Mama was still there beside me in the chair where she had been sitting all night. She was weeping quietly now. "Praise God," she whispered with her arm in the air and her hand opened wide, "Praise God. My boy is gonna make it."

The months passed by quickly after the night of Mama's

miracle. Winter soon gave way to spring, and before long school was out and summer had set in. Daffodils dotted the grassy knolls, and the air was alive with the voices of children and the merriment that they bring.

"Peeee Weeee. Peeee Weeee."

"C'mon, Pee Wee. We're gonna leave you."

"Hurry up, sleepyhead."

Though soft enough not to awaken my parents, the voices broke the deep silence enveloping the town of Turners Station. This small, rural hamlet just south of Baltimore was where I spent the first twelve years of my life. As a child, I believed there was no place on earth more peaceful than Turners Station. Perhaps, in retrospect, there wasn't.

Just before the first rays of dawn, my friends would come by to pick me up to go fishing and crabbing. At that hour, all the world's silence seemed to gather above the vast grassy fields and small, frame houses of the community we knew as home. A great spellbinding quiet, it cloaked the winding roads, shallow ponds, marshy plains, and wooded lots. Only the distant chirp of crickets and the whisper of trees swaying in God's morning breeze could be heard for the miles that surrounded us.

Although Turners Station is for me a place of a thousand memories, in many respects it was a town of one. There was one doctor and one dentist, one gas station, and one general store. There was one barbershop and one bar, one movie house and one whore. And while the week had only one Sabbath, at least Turners Station had three churches, with just enough sinners for saving.

I was born on October 24, 1948. As the first of four children born to the former Mary Elizabeth Willis, I came into the world at a time of major change and angst for black people in America. As the nation marched toward the mid-century mark, discontent among "Negroes" in the North and the South was beginning to rumble. I was a post–World War II baby, and some of my first memories are connected to the grief that war had caused my mother. Men in our family had fought in that war. Yet even after distinguishing themselves, often heroically, they returned home to find that the racist structures of Jim Crow were still cemented in our society.

"They wouldn't even let them march in the victory parade," I remember her saying.

Mama told me early on that Negroes couldn't depend on the white man to choose our heroes, but that we had to choose our own. When it came to colored men fighting for dignity, she talked a lot about A. Philip Randolph, the civil rights leader and founder of the Brotherhood of Sleeping Car Porters. She said that when I was no bigger than her thumb, Randolph had organized a mass movement among Negroes to resist going to war unless they could fight right alongside of whites. Like lightning, she said, President Truman signed an executive order giving Randolph what he wanted.

She told the story with such a gleam of pride in her eyes that you'd have thought that she herself was going into battle. But on reflection, I think Mama was simply heartened over the possibility that America might somehow resolve its "Negro Question" and provide social opportunities during the lifetime of her children.

Compared to Mama, my skin is brown. She was a woman of rich and fair complexion, with a hint of the reddish undertones of her half-Indian mother, Mamie. Her hair, Mama said, was as thick and curly as that of her dark-skinned father, Edward Willis, the great-grandson of a Calvert County slave.

Mamie and Willis, I am told, were a hardworking couple who stayed close to the teachings of the Church in raising a tight-knit family of thirteen children (my mother was a middle child in the flock). Mamie toiled as a homemaker while Willis worked locally in the Baltimore area as a brick mason. In that period of the 1920s, Negroes weren't allowed in the brick mason's union, but Grandpa never let that stop him. His reputation for dependable workmanship kept him employed steadily enough to keep his family living with a dignity that the Negro of the 1920s and 1930s held so important. By watching her own parents struggle against disadvantages, my mother came to believe at an early age that education was our people's passport to true freedom.

Over the years, many have observed that I am not a man who is limited by the expectations of others, and I guess my own birth was no exception. Mama used to say that I was so anxious to escape her womb that I forced my way out four weeks and three hours too early. She joked that this must have occurred because she didn't eat the night before, and I, number one son, figured I'd be on hand for breakfast the next day. And so at 7:14 A.M. there I was, crying through the afterbirth and trying to take my first peek at her through my little half-closed eyes.

Being born a little early and without much warning, I was an especially tiny newborn, underweight and frail. Mama quickly named me after her baby brother, Frizzell. But it was Aunt Alice, who came by the hospital that afternoon dressed in her white gloves and church hat, who quickly renamed me.

"He's such a little thing, Mary," she said, planting a kiss on my half-bald head. "Such a cutie wutie, I'm gonna call him Pee Wee."

From that day forward for the next twenty-three years, while everyone else had tough-guy names like Joe and Moe and Butch and Spike, I would be known as Pee Wee.

Turners Station was an all-black, blue-collar town perched quietly on the western shore of the Chesapeake Bay. In many respects, its fate was tied to the iridescent shadows of the nearby steel mills and shipyards of Bethlehem Steel and Sparrows Point. The towering gray smokestacks of those factories loomed on the horizon, standing sentinel and reminding us of the work our futures might hold. The fields of tall grass that grew skyward stretched out infinitely across its unadorned landscape. Only the sight of power lines, draping in straight sequences from utility poles, punctuated the smooth contours of this quaint rural town.

The nostalgic part of me would like to say that Turners Station, along with its three thousand or so residents, was a black utopia of self-contained happiness. That, however, would romanticize the truth. Turners Station was thrust against the shoreline. Its insularity was the result more of Southern segregation than of black cohesion. Settled near the turn of the century, Turners Station was the creation of black settlers wanting to develop a community just outside of a hostile city. The surrounding white community needed nearby colored labor to keep the plants running, yet they wanted nothing of the colored presence.

Railroad tracks were the most visible lines of demarcation separating Turners Station and the adjacent all-white working-class town of Dundalk. Just as visible was the dislike of Negroes that hung heavily on the faces and in the eyes of many of the whites.

We didn't cross into Dundalk any more than was absolutely necessary, which usually meant shopping for items unavailable in Turners Station or riding the back of the bus into Baltimore. Black people weren't always welcome in Dundalk and it was common to see "Whites Only" or "Colored" signs on rest room doors and drinking fountains. It was just as routine to hear the word "nigger" roll freely from the lips of the white men driving by in their cars as we would walk along the roadside.

Folks from Turners Station mostly stayed put, living quietly and independently at the end of the main access road, with the white communities in front of us and the shoreline at our backs. Like soldiers in barracks at some remote outpost, we lived in modest houses running both perpendicular and parallel to the few narrow streets that ribboned the town. An occasional weeping willow shaded the road, and the scent of honeysuckle hung in the air.

Out in back of my house, standing beneath the three pine trees, wearing cut-off shorts and sneakers, were my closest friends: Carl and his brother Kenny, the twins Ronnie and Donnie, and Ulanov, whose odd name was often the subject of our jokes. On the evenings prior to our fishing expeditions, we would pay a visit to old Mr. Hatfield, a retired factory worker and local fishing guru. He was a pleasant old man, slight and stooped, with caramel skin that drooped around his neck like a turkey's. He'd always open the door, rolling those dark brown, deeply set eyes of his as though annoyed by our visit. But we knew he really liked us—Mr. Hatfield liked any youngster with enough patience for fishing and enough will to succeed.

"What y'all boys want, now," he'd say, scratching his gray head as though we'd awakened him from a snooze. "Didn't I tell you to leave me alone?"

"We know you did, sir," I'd pipe in. "But we're goin' crabbing in the morning . . ."

"And you need some gear, right?"

"That's right, sir."

"Well, git around to the backyard and I'll see what I can do," he would say. Then, turning back around slowly, he would snap, "But you'd better bring me back a crab or two for my trouble."

"Yessir," we would say almost in unison. "Yessir!"

Early the following morning, loaded down with all manner of fishing gear, from bamboo rods to buckets, my buddies would be standing outside my bedroom window in the pale predawn light conveying their impatience with loud sighs, grunts, and threats to leave me behind.

"Hurry up, Pee Wee," Carl hissed.

"All right, I'll be right down."

One of life's greatest gifts is having a best friend, and Carl Swann was mine. Living next door and born exactly one month before me, Carl was my first playmate, and our bond was as instant and natural as childbirth itself. As toddlers, we crawled together in the cool, moist grass of our backyards. As children we conspired to lift the dark veil off such grown-up mysteries as matches, cigarettes, and girlie magazines. And as adults we watched our families grow up and our children move on.

Throughout adolescence, we shared secrets, money, and mischief. Sometimes, when our tempers flared, we shared blows. Despite growing up in a house full of sisters, I never once yearned for a brother. I had Carl. Slight, dark-skinned, and with legs as fast as mine, Carl would run with me for miles through the surrounding fields and marshlands. Our similarities and our differences only made us closer. Together, Carl and I redefined loyalty. His fights were mine and my fights were his.

On those early-morning crabbing trips, I'd step into my sneakers and gingerly make my way downstairs, trying hard to avoid the creaky floorboards that might stir my parents out of their sleep. Without fail, my mother's voice would always be the last thing I would hear as I tried to sneak out of the house.

"Pee Wee," she called out this time. "You be careful. And don't get too close to that pond, or the seaweed will grab you." It seemed that nothing escaped my mother's notice, so much so that at times I half wondered whether she was clairvoyant.

We were a poor family, though I didn't know it because everyone in Turners Station seemed just as poor. Life in town was generally good. Each summer the carnival would come and set up big tents on the open field, and every winter there was lots of snow for sledding. There was always something to eat on the table and lots of friends to play with. The days were long and the holidays were special. If this was being poor, I thought at times, then poor wasn't so bad after all.

Our house was small and tidy, its front door opening to a sparsely furnished living room. A sofa sat in the center of the hardwood floor opposite a low wooden table, where the latest *Ebony* or *Life* magazine was always within reach. Against a wall was a Philco television whose big knobs and broad rectangular case belied a viewing screen that was not much larger than a bread slice. The kitchen, with its worn tile and slow-dripping faucet, opened up into the backyard.

Upstairs were two bedrooms; my parents slept in one, while my three sisters and I squeezed into the other. Darlene, LaWana, and Michele were wonderful sisters but terrible roommates. They kept dolls and stuffed animals everywhere, and there was never enough room for me. But I loved my sisters and I soon learned to accept their dominant presence in my environment.

By most standards, Turners Station was a trusting community.

Theft was a rarity, and we were taught that folks were supposed to look after other folks' property. Whether it was clothes hanging to dry on the line out back or coins left lying on a table, stealing almost never occurred. Windows were left open, doors locked only at night, and kitchen staples like flour and sugar were constantly borrowed among neighbors. In spite of the reality that most had little, we all chipped in to help each other out. People, it seemed, didn't worry much about hoarding their belongings. There was a general belief that God would make a way for everyone.

Back then, adults wielded tremendous authority over the young and seemed to spend more social time together. In Turners Station, grown-ups were extremely close-knit. On weekend evenings, the men would gather behind our house in the yard late into the night, drinking beer, playing cards, or listening to a Joe Louis fight or a Jackie Robinson interview on the radio. They burned firewood in a big barrel to ward off insects, and the aroma of smoldering wood wafted up into my window. I can recall lying in bed restless and unable to sleep at night, listening to the sound of grown-ups laughing and talking. I wanted so badly to merely sit near them and listen to their conversation, but I knew they would send me straight back upstairs to bed.

That old African proverb about it takes a village to raise a child was fully enforced in Turners Station. Children were considered the neighborhood's responsibility. That meant discipline was often dispatched quickly and with little negotiation. At school, church, the store, even a friend's backyard, I could never be certain that I wouldn't get a switch or bare hand taken to my backside if my behavior was out of line.

Worse than that, once the news of my acting up got back to my parents, I was sure to get yet another whipping that would make the first one seem gentle. Remarkably, none of this had much influence on my behavior. I still got into trouble, all the time.

"I work too hard to look after you all the time, boy," Mama would yell. "You want me to quit my job so I can baby-sit you?"

Mama worked on the assembly line of Glenn L. Martin Company, an airplane parts manufacturer. Even though the company had been operating in the Baltimore area since 1929, it wasn't until 1941, when World War II siphoned off much of the white labor force, that it began hiring black people. But once its doors were open, Negro applicants flooded the place. They came in hopes of landing one of Martin's sixty-cents-per-hour assembly jobs. My father drove a tractor-trailer rig for Hemingway Transportation, and their combined income was usually enough to keep us fed and clothed.

Throughout most of my childhood, my mother seemed to be working constantly. If she wasn't putting in hours at the factory, or cleaning the houses of the white people on the weekends, she was busy at home cooking, tidying up, and keeping an eye on us. With her hair pushed up and always in place, I thought my mother to be an attractive woman. At five-feet-four, Mama seemed much too fragile to handle the rigors of such hard work.

No matter how weary she was, every Sunday morning she stepped out of the house looking beautiful. Before church I would sit stiffly in my little navy blue suit and watch Mama at the kitchen table using a small file and nail polish to quickly restore her worn fingernails into perfect oval-shaped works of art. Then she would disappear into her bedroom for a while, and moments later emerge in her Sunday-go-to-meeting dress. Her smile would always make her look years younger. Her dark brown and intelligent eyes would look a tad brighter, and her skin somewhat richer. And though her legs must have been tired from being on her feet all week, even in heels she moved with a jaunty bounce, as she readied Darlene, LaWana, and Michele.

I cherished my mother, though I was far from a mama's boy. Even if I'd wanted to be, she wouldn't have permitted it. While she always figured out a way to support me in my endeavors in and away from school, she had little patience for the whining, helpless behavior she saw in some of my peers. As far back as I can remember, she granted me unusual latitude. She trusted that I would make sound decisions based on the Christian judgment she had worked so hard to instill in me and my sisters, the difference between right and wrong.

When Mama was working, and Daddy was on the road trucking, I was charged with looking after Darlene, LaWana, and Michele. My mother showered Darlene, the first-born girl, with attention. Darlene's all-too-frequent challenges to my authority said to me that she clearly did not know who was the oldest and therefore who was in charge.

"I'm the oldest," I'd constantly remind her, but Darlene is as strong-willed as I am, and rarely backed down without first putting up a fight.

"I don't have to listen to you!" she'd yell back. "You are not my father!"

"No, but I am your brother, your big brother."

Of all my sisters, Darlene gave me the most trouble in those years, but I loved her with all my heart. But because LaWana was three years my junior and Michele just a toddler in diapers, she did their bidding when my mother wasn't around.

In fact, Mama did depend on me to help take care of the house and my sisters when she wasn't around. By the time I was seven, I knew how to dust, mop, wash and dry clothes, and change diapers.

Our house had a coal furnace in the cellar, and my job each winter was to keep it going. I was counted on to shovel coal out of a bin into the furnace each morning to make a fire, and then to bank the fire at night. That way the house would be warm when we got up and would remain warm until we fell asleep. The chores didn't bother me much, but I hated being cooped up in the house with my sisters while my friends were outside playing. Girls, I thought. What a terrible way to spend the afternoon.

Mama never complained much about her work, at least not around me and the girls. She loved spending time at home chatting with us about school and entertaining us with stories about our relatives in the city. With twelve other brothers and sisters, she had plenty of stories to tell. She also made sure that we understood the contributions of black people to the struggle for civil rights in America.

"Pee Wee, tell me who Monroe Trotter is," Mama would drill.

"He demanded equal rights for blacks."

"Is that all?"

"No, Mama. He started a newspaper."

"What was it called?"

"*The Boston Guardian,*" I would respond.

"That's good." Mama would smile. "And what else did he do?"

"He teamed up with W.E.B. DuBois and helped start the Niagara Movement."

Looking back, I think that in her own way she was making the best of a bad situation. It was clear to me that my mother would have preferred living in the city, and that it was my father's idea to raise the family in a place far removed from the gritty environs of West Baltimore. I am certain now that it was more than Turners Station's bucolic setting that prompted the move there. By physically separating my mother from her family and all that was familiar, he was able to dominate her attention in a way that would otherwise never have been possible.

If life in Turners Station was mostly good, the bad times began and ended at the steel-shanked boots of my father, Clifton Gray. He was a brooding, hulking man who stood six-foot-two and weighed 220 pounds. As far back as I can remember, he rarely so much as uttered a kind word to me. But that is not why I grew to dislike him. The reason is far more simple than that: he hit my mother. And when he didn't hit her, he abused her verbally. He was constantly yelling and shouting his twisted obscenities.

"Where the hell is my dinner?" He'd come home from work yelling at Mama, "Ain't you got enough sense to know when a man's been on the road two days, he's gonna be hungry?"

His voice was now a snarl. "I'm tired and I ain't in the mood for your foolishness. My dinner should have been ready and that's that. You understand?"

I hated him for the way he treated my mother, and because he sensed this, he hated me in return. I'm really not sure what my father's problem was, but he thrived on the attention that he finally got by intimidating all of those around him.

To this day, my sisters and I view him somewhat differently. I suspect this is because whatever small dose of warmth and affection he had to offer was directed their way rather than mine. Even back then, it was clear that they were his favorites. He would laugh and cuddle them constantly while turning a cold shoulder to me. The only reason I could come up with at the time was that they were just little girls and needed the attention of their father.

Clifton Gray, however, could also be quite cruel. Sometimes when my mother wasn't around, he would grab me by the arm, lean into my ear, and whisper: "Boy, you ain't shit, and you ain't never gonna be shit. You hear me, boy?"

His hands were huge, his grip inescapable; still, I'd struggle to break free. Quickly he would yank me back toward him with his hot breath spewing hateful words into my ear, and I would tremble.

"Don't you run from me, boy. Don't make me have to kick your little ass. I don't know why your mama bothers with you, anyhow."

There were few limits to Clifton's cruelty. He knew, for instance, that I had a phobia about being closed inside any kind of a tight space. I remember once, when I was seven, the joy he got from torturing me with this fear. One summer day, not unlike others, I was playing inside a big cardboard box in the living room. In the happiest and most childish of ways, I was having lots of fun rolling around inside of that box the way so many kids do. That is, until he came toward me and quickly closed the top of the box over my head. He must have also wrapped his body around it, because I couldn't break out, no matter how hard I pushed. He began banging on the sides of the big box. His fists were thunderous when they struck the cardboard sides, his twisted laughter terrifying me.

I started screaming and banging on the lid of the box in hopes that someone might hear me. I actually thought he was trying to kill me, and I screamed as loud as I could. It was an awful moment for me. When you're held in a box, you don't know what's happening outside. You can't see anything, it's dark, and there's not a whole lot of air coming in. In fact, it felt like I was suffocating, and no one would know of my death.

It was pitch dark in there, and every so often my father pushed the box over and laughed like he was enjoying my horror. He would lean his face into the brown cardboard of the box and yell, "Don't be such a little sissy. Be a man, goddammit."

Finally, when he'd gotten his share of laughs at my expense, he pulled back one flap of the lid, and he told me to get out. I could see his large shadow looming over me from where I was crouched down inside the box. But now I decided to stay put. I wiped the tears from my cheeks with the back of my hand and didn't budge an inch. To his surprise, I stayed in the box and wouldn't move. Somehow, even as a child, I instinctively understood that by ending my fear I was beating him at his own game.

"Come on out of there," he coaxed, this time nearly contrite. "It's time to get out. Don't make me hit you, boy. Did you hear me, boy?"

I remained motionless. I had stopped crying because I realized that the box was not some frightening monster with jagged teeth that would hurt me.

I was a boy and it was a box. That was all. It was cardboard and I was bigger and stronger. Crouched in that box, an eerie calm began to settle over me. I had refused to let something so undefined have power over me. My struggle with the box had ceased. The struggle with my father was only beginning.

He kicked the box a couple of times and tipped it on its side; still, I refused to obey him. Even at that age, I reasoned that the best way to defeat my environment was to become part of it. I had become one with the box, and I was beyond the fear created by my father's hoarse shouts. Finally, he became almost crazy with anger.

He tore through the cardboard with his massive hands and snatched me out. Then he tore off his belt and lashed me with it as his voice became almost unrecognizable. All the ranting and raving and wailing at me seemed to slowly take its toll on him. He fell back into a chair, sweating, as he let me go. While the beating hurt, I refused to cry, and when it was over, I knew that I had won. In the end, what had frustrated him had given me my freedom.

From that time on my father and I were separated emotionally as much as we were physically. My detachment, however, didn't seem to bother him a bit. I played Little League baseball for the next four or five years, and he never once showed up to watch me. He didn't come to any of my activities as a Boy Scout or my performances in school plays. Absent fathers might seem common today, but back then it was more unusual not to have one around at special events. It angered me somewhat that while I had a man living in my home, in actuality I didn't have a father at all. When friends asked why my father wasn't there, it became almost second nature to say, "He's working, so he can't make it."

In time, I would come to understand his contempt toward me, as well as his endless crusade to break my spirit.

On many occasions, I would ask my mother why she put up with my father's abuse, why she didn't kick him out or move us away from him. If she was ashamed of how he treated her, I never knew it. Her response was that I didn't understand and that everything would be okay. I think her role, as she saw it, was to make sure we grew up with everything we needed. If that meant that she had to suffer her own lot quietly, then she was prepared to do that.

All those years that my father was getting drunk and hanging out, my mother was out there working to make ends meet. Not wanting to spend extra money for transportation, she would end up walking to and from work, often during the bitter cold months of winter.

Back in those days, it would have been acceptable, if not expected, for her to stay put in her role as a homemaker. I believe that she worked so hard so she could maintain her sanity and retain some independence from a husband who probably loved her in his own insufficient way and did not know how to show it. I remember her coming home in snowstorms with her hands frozen and her coat packed with snow. I often had to help her remove the ice-laden layers of scarves wrapped around her neck and rub her hands with mine until she was finally warm enough to smile.

This situation was ridiculous, because not only did my father have access to a truck, he also had a car. When he was away, the car just sat there, parked behind the house, and when any of us had to go somewhere we weren't driven, we walked.

My aunts Alice and Gloria were both my mother's sisters and her best friends. They spent a lot of time trying to convince her to get

Clifton to move back into the city. They would drop by on weekends and sit laughing at the kitchen table while Mama would entertain them with her small talk and humor. Then without changing a beat, Aunt Gloria would say, "Girl, can't you just stop working for a few hours and come into the city with us?"

"Yeah, Mary," Aunt Alice would chime in. "It'll be good for your spirit to get away for a bit and do some window shopping."

Mama's eyes would brighten at the invitation, but only briefly. "What's best for my spirit is knowing these children are gonna have a good dinner and a clean house," she'd say. "You all just go on and have a good time."

Mama's purpose in life, at least as she saw it, was to keep the family together, to make sure we, her children, developed on a track of good values and a strong sense of pride.

As a fair-skinned black woman, she was sensitive to the politics of color. The divisions between blacks and whites on the issue of skin color, and those same divisions within the black community itself, were not lost on her awareness. She was proud of her race but recognized the perverse obsession some Negroes had with fitting into the white world. Growing up in the 1930s and 1940s, being a few shades lighter than most of her friends had given her a certain cachet in the eyes of many blacks and whites. It was an era of passing, skin-whitening and lightening creams, a time when men were out to marry light-skinned women, who in turn were out to marry light-skinned men. My mother, who resented even the suggestion of any kind of preferential treatment based on her complexion, would often rail against such foolishness.

"My skin could be lighter than these walls," she used to say. "But as far as some white folks are concerned, I'm still not good enough to sit beside 'em on a bus or eat beside 'em at the lunch counter."

My mother was bright enough to realize that as much as she loved me, there were societal limitations on her ability to successfully raise a boy who would be well adjusted in a culture preoccupied with color. She knew that if life was difficult for black women, it was hell for black men. She had watched a society that had tried without success to break her own brothers. She knew the cost they had paid for maintaining their pride and never compromising their dignity. She believed that black men were at risk because they were at the very root of our strength as a race. Poisoned at the root by bigotry and oppression, black men too often died or were deformed by character traits that ate away at their self-esteem.

Mama knew that boys needed to be around men. Since she could not control my father's resentment and the lack of affection he displayed toward me, she exerted control over the things that she could. Mama couldn't provide me with a terrific father, but she did the next best thing. She put me under the influence of the best man she could find in our community—Mr. Smitty—my Little League coach and my first real mentor.

"Playing in the league will be a lot of fun, and it'll be good for you, too," Mama said. "Mr. Smitty will show you how to be a part of a team that likes to win as bad as you do."

Mr. Smitty's lessons reinforced many of the values my mother had worked to instill in me. Philosophical lessons about respect, trust, working together, and depending on others became quite practical out on the baseball diamond because each player had a responsibility to the team. Those who failed to deliver on their responsibility caused the team to lose the game.

Because of my rail-thin arms and legs, as well as my being shorter than most boys my age, I had to work extra hard to win at any sport. Mama knew I envied some kids in the neighborhood who were much bigger and stronger for their years.

One of them was Calvin Hill, who later went on to become a star running back for the Dallas Cowboys. Growing up, Calvin was blessed with the girth and power of a grown man. He had hands the size of baseball mitts and thighs like tree stumps. In the fall, boys from the neighborhood would choose teams and go out in the park to play tackle football. It took nearly the whole defense to pull Calvin down. And in the spring when we played baseball, one leisurely swing of Calvin's bat could send the ball soaring into orbit.

Another Goliath was Larry Middleton. At ten years old, Larry was developing into a man who would be built like an ox. He had broad muscular shoulders, a wide beefy neck, and massive legs. And he was a real bully, too, so much that Mr. Smitty, who ran Little League baseball, kicked him out of the league, because he was constantly beating up his teammates. By the time Larry hit fourteen, Mr. Smitty told him that boxing would suit him better. The advice proved prescient. Larry went on to become a contender for the middleweight championship.

Mr. Smitty always said that what I lacked in size I more than made up for with smarts. He said I had the kind of quick mind that would help me succeed in baseball, or any other sport for that matter. All I needed to do was practice longer and harder than the other boys. Mr. Smitty was a real stickler about practicing to perfection.

I never had a problem with that, and in fact thrived on it because I understood that the discipline of practice would help me improve my skills. I was the kind of kid who wanted to get a hit every time at bat and make every putout on defense. It was on the baseball diamond that I recognized the depths of my own competitive drive.

To me, nothing was more serious than proving myself as the best third baseman and batter in the league. It was not enough to play a good game now and then. I wanted to play a perfect game consistently, with no strikeouts, pop outs, or ground outs, and certainly no fielding errors. That, of course, was unreasonable, but it was my goal.

At practice, I was always the first player on the field, and the last one to leave. Looking back, I think part of my passion for practice was that I have always been tough on myself about making mistakes, so I would do whatever it took to eliminate them. If it meant taking ground balls until my arm was hanging and my butt was dragging, I would do it. Constant repetition and discipline honed my skills and helped me overcome whatever may have been lacking in my physical tools. I also knew that baseball was a team game that depended very much on individual performances. I never wanted to let my teammates down—especially because of a lack of preparation or commitment.

At the same time, it was during those baseball games that I learned that individual victories aren't enough to guarantee a win. The strength and progress that a group makes is dependent on collective, complementary efforts. So even if I went zero for four at the plate, there were other things I could do to contribute to the ultimate goal—a victory by our team.

Looking back now, I realize that much of my motivation in baseball was to change how my father viewed me. As a child, I blamed myself for his mistreatment of me and my family. I thought maybe I wasn't smart, athletic, or tough enough to merit his attention or praise. Maybe if I work harder to improve myself, I thought, then he will treat me like other boys' fathers treated them.

After a while, though, I gradually began to see that nothing I did would ever be good enough to gain Clifton Gray's favor, and I stopped having any expectations from him at all. My anger drove out my pain. When channeled positively, anger can be a potent force, and I vented much of mine on the baseball field.

"That boy knows the game," I remember overhearing Mr. Smitty telling another coach. "He's a little son of a gun but he's got good fundamentals and a whole lot of heart."

I played on the Turners Station Yankees, and we were a terrific team. We had power hitters, steady hitters, talented infielders and outfielders, lots of team spirit, and a brilliant coaching staff. We were so good that after winning in our own league, we went out to compete with the white Little Leagues in places like Dundalk, Essex, and Middle River. These were hardcore, very segregated white communities. These places were so segregated that after we had traveled to go play one of these teams, our bus had to park far away from the other buses.

Playing against these lily-white communities was an eerie experience. From the dugout, I would look over and see the maybe forty people from Turners Station who had taken the trip to cheer us on. On the home team side, a sea of white faces filled the bleachers.

Mr. Smitty may have given me my first lesson on how to overcome injustice. "Now, you can see the umpires are white," he told our team before one of those games. "So, they're gonna be biased to the other boys. Don't expect no favors. If there's a close call to be made, it won't go your way. So just play extra hard and beat 'em fair and square."

He tried to make sure we harbored no malice toward our white rivals. Even though blacks and whites had real differences in how we perceived each other, he explained that respecting our competitors was just as important as outplaying them.

Mr. Smitty also taught us that after the game, whether we won or lost, it was sportsmanlike to walk out into the center of the diamond and congratulate each player of the other team. Of course, when we lost, going through that ritual was much harder. But it was good because it is important that people learn to look those who defeat them in the eye without shame or anger, and confront them, touch them, and say, "Good game." Of course, when we won, there was this extraordinary feeling of euphoria rooted in the pride of the underdog black community's having outperformed its cocksure white rivals.

Still, at the moment the teams came together out on the diamond, we were not focused on the umpires' alleged biases or the bigots we all knew dotted the stands. Each player looked only at the other player, and there was mutual respect that transcended race, but only because we had played the hell out of each other.

We knew we were going back to our separate communities, and probably would never see each other again unless our teams got another chance to play. And I think that each of us, to some degree, felt this to be unfortunate because some of our players could have fit easily onto their team and some of their players onto ours. But each of us knew that the times we were living in wouldn't allow it, that the hope of playing on an integrated team seemed a waste of time.

Still, there were a few black faces in the majors now, a small group of pioneers up from the Negro Leagues. I made it my business to keep up with them all. The old-timers in the neighborhood talked about how Jackie Robinson had become the first black to play on a big-league team, the Brooklyn Dodgers, in 1947.

About three months later that same year, Larry Doby, a strong hitter and outfielder, became the second colored player to wear a major league uniform, making his debut with the Cleveland

Indians. The following year, Satchel Paige, the legendary pitcher who had pitched sixty-four straight scoreless innings during the 1946 season, was also signed by the Indians. Finally, in 1955, the Baltimore Orioles recruited Jehosie Heard as a token on a team of twenty-three whites. To the people of my community, these men were heroes because everyone realized what it took to do your best in a hostile environment. Every time they excelled, their success enabled all black people to walk a little taller.

But we kids weren't even thinking about breaking racial barriers. We knew we weren't going to play on the same team. But if we began the game thinking about our racial differences, it was during competition that we quickly realized that black and white players alike had the same skills, the same enthusiasm, and would fight just as hard to win. And ever since then, it's always seemed strange to me that it's only during athletic contests that black and white men can stand on equal ground.

In time, my friends began looking to me for tips on improving their game. I remember once watching my best friend Carl mope away from the batter's box after striking out two times straight during a game.

"Man, I can't get a hit off that pitcher for nothin'," he complained. "What am I doing wrong?"

"You gotta pay attention," I told him. "He's getting you out the same way every time. He throws a fastball, then a fastball again, and then he switches to a curve."

Carl screwed up his face. "How can you see what that ball's doing, coming so fast?"

I couldn't see the ball's motion any better than Carl could. But I had studied the pitcher enough to realize that he was throwing in fairly predictable sequences. During my turns at bat, I tried using my observations to wrest some control away from the pitcher. Stepping up to the plate, I'd go into a few practice swings, and just as the pitcher looked ready to go into his windup, I'd step out of the batter's box. I wasted time by knocking dirt off my cleats with my bat, gazing around at the position of the players on the diamond. Then I stepped casually back up to the plate.

I'd repeat this routine a couple more times until I could see the frustration on the pitcher's face. With his concentration shattered, he invariably threw more recklessly, and I began connecting for base hits.

Standing on base, I heard a chorus of cheers rise up out of the dugout and bleachers. "Way to go, Pee Wee!"

It was the kind of performance that would have made most any father proud.

2

A MOTHER'S LOVE

*M*Y love for my mother deepens by the year, especially as I reflect on the kind of mothering that many people growing up today will never experience. My greatest champion and fiercest critic, Mama had a wonderful gift for being able to mix love, discipline, and respect in a manner that was as tender as it was firm.

I am in awe of my mother's ability to understand what a boy needed to become a man. Yet most people fail to celebrate the virtues of many black mothers who over the years have functioned—even thrived—in the dual roles of mother and father. Self-sacrifice is a valuable commodity in any human being, and I find it astonishing that so many black women who possessed so little materially were able to give so generously. They have provided generations of black boys with the crucial range of skills essential for survival. My mother's sacrifice enabled me to withstand being targeted by my father. Probably the most valuable lesson Mama ever gave me was teaching me to fight. Muhammad Ali could not have had a tougher trainer.

I'll never forget the time I had the misfortune of crossing a bully known in the neighborhood simply as Big Neal. Neal was the kind of kid we all feared because he picked fights for the sport of it, especially against those smaller than himself. Neal was known to beat up two or three kids at a time. He was so mean-spirited I dreaded the sight of him. To my credit, I was among the few boys around who could proudly claim that I hadn't been pulverized by Big Neal. But when I was eight years old, my luck finally ran out.

As I was walking home from school one day with a crowd of schoolmates, Big Neal blindsided me. I was shocked by the sudden impact that sent me tumbling over into the dirt, and terrified when I rolled over to see Neal's piercing eyes and flared nostrils looming over me. He lunged at me again, but I managed to push myself out of the way and jump to my feet. That's when I started running.

At the time, it didn't dawn on me how cowardly I must have appeared to onlookers as I kicked up dust sprinting away from my attacker. I could only think of escaping what I knew would be painful, humiliating blows by a pair of fists known for blackening eyes, swelling jaws, and caving in chests. Running for my life, I heard shouts, jeers, and laughter erupt behind me as fight-time madness filled the hot afternoon air.

"Don't let me catch you!" Big Neal thundered in an ominous voice. "I'm gonna kick your little ass."

Neal took off after me. My heart was pounding and my legs were pumping like a hot rod's pistons. Racing around the corner of my block, my eyes brightened at the sight of my house just about a hundred feet ahead. To my eight-year-old eyes, our metal screen door sparkled in the sunlight like the gates of paradise.

My relief was short-lived. I must have seriously underestimated Neal's foot speed or his knowledge of the many shortcuts through my neighborhood. He stood waiting for me two doors from my house. I had no choice but to press on into battle. Big Neal pounced right on me. With our bodies entangled, his face directly over mine, Neal rained down brick-solid blows to my ribs and stomach. I tried to force him off of me, but his legs' viselike grip clamped me firmly to the ground.

With the crowd screaming and shouting around us, we

brawled for a long time. I was tired and hurting. The first chance that I had to escape, I bolted directly to the front door of my house. But when I opened that door, my mother was standing there staring at me. A wave of relief washed over me. I'd reached safety.

"If you don't get back out there and fight him, you're going to fight me!" my mother yelled. I'd never seen her so angry before. Her reaction frightened me. The door was wide open and she was screaming loud enough for all the kids on the block to hear her. She grabbed me and shook me fiercely.

"What's the matter with you?" she scolded. "You never just run from a fight."

"But Mama," I managed through swelling lips.

She yanked the door open. "Don't 'but' me. Get back out there!" she commanded. "Go, I said."

Ashamed that I had disappointed my mother and disgraced myself, I staggered back outside and resumed my losing battle with Big Neal. I charged him with all the strength I could muster and knocked him off his feet. He rammed my face down in the dirt hard and thrust his knee several times into my stomach. But I didn't give up. I knew my mother was watching me, and I could never look like a coward in her eyes. I fought Big Neal until the bitter end that afternoon, and he beat me up real bad. The fight broke up only because we were both too tired to go on.

When I looked up, my mother was pulling me up off the ground. I was limp with exhaustion. I had dirt all over my face and in my hair, my lips were bloodied, and my left eye was just about swollen shut. Because my mother had come out, the crowd started breaking up. But they weren't teasing and laughing the way they had when I'd run for cover. They were kind of quiet because although Big Neal had won the fight, he looked as roughed up as I did.

My mother took me home and washed off my wounds, and put a cold pack over my eye. She didn't say much about the fight, but I could tell that she was pleased.

That was the first and last time that I ever tried to quit anything. This lesson was more than a testament to my mother's

wisdom and understanding of how to bring out the young warrior in me. My mother understood that, given my size and the
color of my skin, showing weakness would make me a perma-
nent resident at the bottom of life's heap. She was determined
that I would never let that happen to myself.

Above all, Mama was a realist. She firmly believed that people
should confront the truth rather than escape it or try to compromise with it. That is probably why she was so determined to rid
me of my fears by making me face reality. Like a lot of kids, I
suffered my share of phobias—monsters, snakes, falling off a
cliff—but darkness was my biggest. I was deathly afraid of
rooms and places where I could not see.

I think the spooky side of religion unadhered to had something to do with it. I was a mischievous boy and knew it. One of
my mother's favorite disciplinary lines was: "Be bad if you want
to, but you know the devil will get you for that."

Still, I'd go with Carl to the five-and-dime store, and pick up
two comic books and pay for one. Worse yet would be the times
when we'd stack garbage cans against someone's front door and
ring the doorbell and watch the fun when they would open the
door and get buried in trash. When the lights went out at night,
however, my misdeeds would haunt me like nagging guilt. I
couldn't sleep without at least the glow of the hallway light.
Even when I'd manage to doze off out of sheer exhaustion, the
nightmares would get me.

When I was about eight years old, my mother lost her
patience with me and decided it was time for me to confront my
fear. One day, just before twilight, Mama gathered my sisters
together and prepared to go out. The carnival was in town and
set up on a dirt lot near Dundalk. Although a mile away, the carnival set the horizon ablaze with the lights of its big top and the
rim of a Ferris wheel arching in the distance. As Darlene,
LaWana, and Michele walked outside to the car, my father disappeared quickly into the basement.

Mama came into the darkening living room and sat down
beside me. I hadn't been asked to go along with everyone else. I
was bewildered and upset. I couldn't understand why I was
being punished.

"You're not in any trouble, Pee Wee," said Mama as she placed her right hand on the top of my head and blinked back what was sure to be a tear. "You're not going to the carnival with us because tonight you have something more important to do. Tonight you will learn the mystery of the darkness and you will no longer fear it. Because if you're afraid of the dark," she whispered, "you will be afraid of anything."

When she said this, fear surged through me because I understood a different reality. I instantly knew what was about to happen. I was about to be locked up all by myself in the house awaiting total darkness. I now realized that the reason my father had gone down into the basement was to unscrew all the fuses from the fuse box. Soon he would clean out the candles from the kitchen drawer, thereby removing even the possibility to create light.

"You know Mama loves you," she said, as she hesitantly pulled away from me and withdrew her loving hand. "Mama loves you, but God loves you best."

What my mother understood in that summer of '56 would stay with me for the rest of my life. She knew that a paralyzing fear could prove fatal for a black man in America. Fear could hold you back, hold you in place. Fear would prevent you from taking risks or dealing with challenges. She wanted me to examine my fears and understand that as most fears go, they were irrational and pointless, a trick of the mind if you will, played by the faceless side of our consciousness. Being an innate psychologist of high quality, she knew that any black man who wanted to survive and thrive in this society could not succumb to fear. He must confront his demons and conquer them in order to move forward. I did not understand her wisdom then as I do now.

She pointed to the big picture of Jesus that hung on our living room wall. I will never forget that picture. It was a blond Jesus with the crown of thorns and the blood trickling at his temple. While he wore a serene, placid expression on his face, he had those stare-locked eyes that seemed to follow me all over the house. It was really unsettling because I was always told, "Jesus won't like it if you do that," or "God don't like ugly!" Sometimes simply walking through that room with mischief on my mind would force a sudden change of heart because I didn't want Jesus to know what I was thinking.

One day after doing my chores and heading outside, I got up enough nerve to look into those eyes. I winked at Jesus but he didn't wink back. That's when I decided he must have been really ticked off.

My whole family was religious in a sense. When we'd visit my aunt Annie during the summer, I'd cringe at all these great big pictures of angels with wings standing over somebody or at the edge of clouds. Then we'd go over to my Uncle Percy's house, and he had the same spooky stuff on his walls.

But that evening, for some reason Mama pointed to Jesus and explained that God is looking out for us and protecting his children in both light and darkness. But when she started crying, I knew she was more serious than the moment revealed. With a large tear welling in her eye, she hushed me, told me she loved me, and explained that for my sake she had to leave me.

Still unaware of all that was going on, I didn't fight her at all. I just sat there on the couch and listened to the door lock from outside, and the fading rumble of the car as it rolled off the gravel driveway headed toward the carnival without me.

It was so quiet in that house that the stillness seemed to encircle every object. The figurines on the mantel stood motionless. As I sat on the couch and watched the shadows of twilight move toward me, I knew that I was really alone, and I knew it would soon be dark.

I remember looking up at Jesus and thinking that the devil was waiting nearby to come and get me. And since Jesus hadn't winked back, I knew he was too trapped in that frame to help me. The house seemed to get darker and darker by the second. Soon it was pitch black around me, and I was hearing every sound the house made. Now, no longer in control, I started to cry. I didn't know nor could I imagine why my mother would do such a thing to me. I knew now that the devil was in there with me, lurking, and waiting to get his due.

After a while, though, I felt my fear slowly turning to anger. I figured that if Satan was in the house, he was going to have to deal with me. I remember screaming out loud, daring the devil to come out, daring him to come into the room, and cursing the darkness that surrounded me.

"Come out and fight me!" I cried, running from room to room. "I ain't scared of you! Come out now!"

Through the pitch darkness, I felt my way around to the next room, and then the next room, yelling defiantly, "Come out!" I wanted so much to face the devil now that I screamed at the top of my lungs. I wanted him to see my anger. "Here I am, now come and get me!" I cried.

But nothing happened . . . or maybe it did. Slowly I began to wonder whether the devil was really in the house at all. Maybe the devil was only in my mind, I thought, a manifestation of my fear. Maybe I should become one with the house and the darkness, thereby making the devil become one with me. I went back and sat on the couch. By then I realized that the reason I was afraid of the dark was because I had never before challenged it. I had always accepted it as a formless void full of evil. It was like being in that cardboard box again, alone and confused. By confronting my fear, I had robbed it of its power over me. When I became one with the darkness it could no longer threaten me. I had conquered fear, yet felt no sense of victory. I had grown comfortable in the dark. I lay calmly on the couch that evening and fell asleep, amidst the shadows.

When I awoke, it was to the sound of the car pulling up and my sisters giggling. It was still dark when Mama opened the door and began calling out to me.

"Pee Wee, where are you? Are you all right?"

"Yes, ma'am," I called out, my voice calm. "I'm in here on the couch."

She came in, reached down to hug and kiss me, then handed me a bag of cotton candy. "Mama was worried about you, baby," she said. "I didn't want to leave you but I had to. God knows I didn't want to leave you."

"I was okay," I said quietly. "There ain't nothin' in the dark that ain't here in the light."

"That's right, son, and your mama's proud of you for learnin' that," she said, smiling.

My father, though, was unimpressed. Quietly, he made his way downstairs, put the lights on, and didn't say a word to me for the rest of the night.

When I wasn't outdoors playing with friends, I could usually be found in my bedroom, reading comic books and weightlifting magazines. From first grade through fourth grade, I attended Fleming Elementary. Although quick to learn, I was hardly a model student. Trouble or some kind of mischief always seemed to find me. Some weeks it seemed I spent more time in the principal's office than in class.

This was a sore spot at home because my mother knew that learning came easy to me, and that I should have been earning straight A's. I had a knack for understanding scientific concepts, working with facts and figures, and comprehending the reading material in our textbooks. Don't get me wrong—I was no Einstein. But the truth is that I didn't find school very challenging. Once I understood the subject matter, it was boring. It was bad enough that the day moved at a glacial pace; I also found most of the teachers nice but boring, and the work they assigned mundane.

Many of my classmates would still be scratching their heads long after I'd breezed my way through the day's assignment and begun the homework. "Man, you finished already?" my buddies would ask in disbelief. Sometimes, if they requested it, I'd help them out. Usually, though, I spent the remainder of the period just goofing off. My report cards assessed my performance with such polite phrases as "not meeting potential" or "a fast learner but needs to stay focused" or "inattentive and often displays disruptive behavior."

Unlike in today's public schools, teachers back then practiced corporal punishment. They'd put up with my foolishness just so long before brandishing one of those thick, eighteen-inch rulers and cracking me over the knuckles with it. Those rulers hurt so bad I'd almost cry, if not because of the sharp pain they sent racing up my arm, then for the humiliation of being flogged in front of my classmates. My knuckles were puffy so often that the next time I acted up, teachers would mercifully turn my hand over and whack my palm.

I'd complain to my mother, but my rants rarely drew more than a shrug. "They wouldn't correct you unless you deserved it," she'd say. Usually, she was right.

Rather than submit to quick-eyed teachers who made a living snuffing out fun, I learned to accept the pain of the eighteen-inch ruler as an unfortunate detour on the road to prankish glory. Experience had taught me that a well-executed prank could create a hallway buzz that lasted a whole day, maybe even a week, while a rap on the hand stung for only a few short seconds.

Most of my antics were harmless and quite silly. I did things like sitting in back of the class and inconspicuously throwing spitballs at the blackboard, yanking the chair just as a classmate was sitting down, or slipping out during class and roaming the halls, waving happily at my friends whose eyes were glazing over a lesson.

By the time I reached fourth grade, I had blossomed into one of the several seasoned pranksters in my class. One of my favorite pranks was a little hoax called Adam and Eve. I'd walk up to a classmate, hold one of his arms, and quickly recite a riddle that went like this: "Adam and Eve and Pinchmetight went to the river to spend the night, Adam and Eve came back and who was left?" The person would ponder the rhyme for a quick moment, then respond in a dumbfounded way by saying, "Pinch me tight!" The words were barely out of their mouth when I would pinch their arm real hard until they let out a scream. It was a dumb joke, but everybody fell for it, at least once.

One day, I pulled the joke on Patricia Swindell. Most boys considered Patricia to be the prettiest girl at Fleming Elementary. With her long brown silky hair, deep dimples, and smooth, fair complexion, she was every boy's heartthrob—though most of us were too boyish to admit it. We were also too young to know that we were being raised at a time when color in the Negro community had too much importance. The fact that she was "light" said that she was all right in the minds of the boys who adored her.

The hallway buzz was that Patricia Swindell liked me, and

though I had not yet gotten around to telling her that I liked her too, I figured that playing the Adam and Eve joke might prove me to be a fun, clever, and worthy boyfriend.

On that day, with Carl and Kenny in tow, I walked up to Patricia outside the cafeteria and shyly told her that I liked her. She never even batted an eye, and I never batted so poorly. The girl may have been pretty, but her ignoring me was not. Finally she broke into a broad smile, then covered her mouth and blushed as she looked into my eyes.

"Boy, she's pretty," I thought. Then suddenly my buddies began teasing me with their chant. "Pee Wee's got a girlfriend . . . Pee Wee's got a girlfriend."

Not knowing how to respond and not wanting them to think that I really liked girls *that much*, I quickly changed the subject. "Hey, Patricia . . . wanna hear a riddle?" I asked.

"Yes," she softly replied, still smiling at me.

"Adam and Eve and Pinchmetight went to the river to spend the night. Adam and Eve came back," I concluded. "Who was left?" She thought for a moment and said, "Pinch me tight."

I pinched her arm real hard and the moment I did it, I knew that I had made a terrible mistake. She let out a scream so loud you'd have thought that I had bit her. She dropped her books. Her face turned beet red, and, holding her arm, she ran away crying hysterically. I stood there frightened as my friends cracked up laughing.

I went on to math class, wondering where she had gone. Doodling on my folder, and firing off an occasional spitball into the air, I couldn't concentrate on the teacher. About midway through the class, I heard my classmates gasp, and looked up to see what was going on. Standing in the doorway was Patricia Swindell, teary-eyed and shaking. She was flanked by the school nurse and the principal. She was cradling her left arm, which had swollen up to twice its size. Her light skin was marred by a nasty purple bruise, and her arm was darkening fast.

Patricia ended up having to go to the hospital that day, and I still don't know what condition she had that made her arm swell up like that. I only know that the principal called my mother at work, and she took off and came directly to the school. She showed up furious at my mischief. Mama's soft light complexion had reddened, and she looked almost teary-eyed. The principal had betrayed me, I thought, as I sat outside his office and watched him and Mama talk. When their brief meeting was over, she never said a word to me. She simply grabbed me by the ear, led me out the door, and whipped my butt from the school grounds all the way home.

For the rest of the week, my mother wouldn't let me out of the house, not even for school. Friends would come by my window and yell ominous news about Patricia's condition. I heard all kinds of rumors—from Patricia's arm having to be amputated to rumors that she was in a coma and that she was going to die. I was terrified, could hardly sleep for worrying that I might have killed Patricia Swindell—the most beautiful girl in my school. I imagined that I would have to spend the rest of my life in prison. Or worse yet, suppose they sentenced me to death. I prayed long and hard that she would live.

"You ought to know better than to play rough with girls like that," Mama scolded for days afterward. "You wouldn't treat your sisters like that. You don't treat little girls the same way you treat little boys, Pee Wee. Patricia is a little lady, and you got no business treatin' her like Carl or some other boy out on the football field."

That Friday morning on his way to school, Carl called up to my bedroom window, grinning through his words. "Pee Wee, Patricia's going to live and they're not going to cut her yucky arm off." I was so relieved that I went to school the next week born again and pledging to end my pranks. But it took my mother quite some time to forgive me for what I had done.

That experience hurt me because I was fond of Patricia, but she was no longer fond of me after I hurt her.

One of my favorite memories is that of riding the yellow school bus. Fleming Elementary only went through the fourth grade, and so for grades five and six I rode to Bragg School on the bus. Not only was it a great place to goof off, but it extended to me one of the privileges enjoyed by the white kids who lived over in Dundalk, or so I believed. It wasn't until much later that I learned what was really going on. I wasn't exactly riding the bus to school as much as I was being bused to school. At the time, I probably should have known something was amiss, considering that we traveled past one or two schools each morning to arrive at Bragg Elementary. Bragg, it seems, had great teachers with big hearts but very few materials to work with in a building that was falling apart.

It was not the kind of choice my mother would have made for me, but it was the only one she had. Bragg School was the only one in the county in which colored children were allowed to enroll. This was 1958, four years after the Supreme Court decision of *Brown* v. *Board of Education of Topeka, Kansas*—the ruling that outlawed the separate-but-equal educational practices of Jim Crow. Still, by the late 1950s, I was being bused in a reverse manner because whites simply didn't want us in their schools. The inferior school I was forced to attend was the very thing that the NAACP legal team, headed by Thurgood Marshall, had fought for years to end through long and costly court battles.

"It just doesn't make any sense for you to drive past two white schools every morning just to get to a colored school," my mother would say. "It's just insane how much white folks dislike our kind. They claim to talk to God, but they must not hear God talkin' back to them and speaking to their hearts."

As a kid, I didn't care much about any of this. At the time, all that mattered was the chance to ride a bus after four years of walking to Fleming.

Our bus driver was a guy simply known as Mr. Wynn. We never knew his first name and we never asked. I had been waiting since the third grade to finally see Mr. Wynn, and in some childish way getting a ride on his clanky old bus was almost a rite of passage. You never got to ride the bus until you were a fifth grader, which meant you were no longer a little kid. The bus that I had heard so much about seemed normal, but Mr. Wynn was just as funny-looking as I had heard. With his gray hair sparsely combed over his balding scalp, and his droopy eyes, he looked like a happy old Saint Bernard. His slow, broad smile, which would greet us every morning when he opened the bus door, communicated clearly how much he loved us despite the grief we gave him.

Indeed Mr. Wynn had an unenviable task. We gave him hell every day, yelling and screaming and wrestling on that bus. We threw spitballs at each other and laughed through all kinds of horseplay that drove him crazy. Usually, Mr. Wynn was clueless in pointing out the culprit because the madness was occurring behind his head. Any time he'd quickly stop the bus and get up to investigate, we'd all be sitting there quiet, calm, and angelic. The moment he'd sit back in his driver's seat and pull back onto the road, the ruckus would start up again. Sometimes, to my chagrin, word of my bus behavior would find its way back to my mother, and I would swear it wasn't me. I had a penchant for smuggling rolls of toilet paper from my house and holding them out of the bus window and watching the paper unfurl and stream behind in the distance. When Mr. Wynn would peer over his spectacles to check his rearview mirror, he'd nearly have a stroke.

Midway through my grade-school education, I straightened out a bit because I realized my mother was shouldering most of the heavy burden of the house alone. And I knew it wasn't easy. I realized what she was dealing with, so she didn't have a major discipline problem out of me from that point on. When I did goof off, it was when I really could, like out on the baseball diamond or running through the fields of tall grass, but never around the house.

If most kids loathed being sent to their room, I half enjoyed my quiet times in exile. I could spend hours in there, contented, thumbing through comic books and Charles Atlas magazines. Unlike my schoolbooks, which all seemed to dwell on things that had happened years ago, comic books and magazines offered a different escape. Even a newspaper would occasionally capture my attention.

One article I recall reading in such a way appeared in the *Weekly Reader*, a magazine for elementary and middle-school children. The article focused on the controversy over presidential candidate John F. Kennedy and the fact that he was Catholic.

Kennedy was among the few public figures my mother seemed to like, and this fact, perhaps, led to my own fascination with him. Because he was younger, more dashing, and seemed friendlier than President Eisenhower, he was causing quite a stir. I wanted Kennedy to win the presidency and couldn't understand why his religion could prevent that from happening. Although we were Catholic, too, Mama had taught us that just about any church was good, so long as you went to worship the Lord and not just to be seen.

There seemed to be a lot of grown-up issues that I didn't understand then, and this was just another one. Still, I was changing as I became more curious about life and fearless in my approach to it.

By the time I turned eleven years old, I rarely saw my father at all. He spent most of his time on the road and most of his paycheck on women. Mama knew that her marriage was dying and still tried to remain a proud woman through her sadness and his absences, which sometimes were as long as two weeks. Often he returned nearly broke, with not even enough money to buy groceries. I am not sure where his money was going, and I couldn't have cared less about his follies. All I knew was that with him gone so much of the time, I needed to fill the void as the man of the house and I looked for new ways of doing it.

"Where we goin', Vernon?"

"Five Fingers."

On fishing and crabbing expeditions, Vernon Turner usually took the lead. Because Vernon was a couple of years older than the rest of us, we naturally deferred to him. But Vernon was also bright and adventurous, so he earned our respect by schooling us on matters concerning the outdoors, from street fighting to sports to wildlife.

For me, fishing was often driven more by necessity than recreation. At home, grocery money often dried up and the meals my mother served us reflected it. Once, I remember we went for six straight weeks eating nothing but potatoes. We had mashed potatoes, scalloped potatoes, french-fried potatoes, baked potatoes, potatoes au gratin, and potato salad. We had potatoes with water, potatoes with milk, potatoes with orange juice, and potatoes with tea. I ate so many potato concoctions, I never wanted to see anything that even resembled a spud again.

My mother found new and different ways to feed them to us. Every now and then we'd get a slice of bread added to break the monotony. Mama figured that potatoes and water would fill us up, so we wouldn't go to sleep hungry, and she was right. My sisters and I, later that evening, would eventually stagger to bed, happy and bloated.

Mama took lots of pride in her cooking, so I felt sorry for her when she couldn't feed us the kind of meals we liked, or the kind I knew she enjoyed preparing. She preferred serving up piping hot plates of fried chicken, collard greens, candied yams, and corn on the cob.

Because much of her self-esteem was tied to her cooking, her spirits always seemed highest on those evenings when she was whipping up something special. In a kitchen warm with rolls baking in the oven and corn frying on the stovetop, she'd stand contentedly in the aroma of her good cooking, chopping onions and joking with me and my sisters. But on those dreary nights when money was scarce and the cupboards bare, she was usually quiet and glum. She tried to look pleasant and upbeat, but I could see the sadness all over her face.

Hoping to ease some of Mama's burdens, I'd go fishing on the side of the bay when I could. We were fortunate in that ponds, streams, and the Chesapeake Bay itself were all part of the Turners Station landscape. Just a stone's throw away from my front door was Circle Pond. With tall weeping willow trees draped around its perimeter, Circle Pond carried with it folklore, fantasy, and fun. They called it Circle Pond not just for its shape but also because of its legend. Word had it that in the middle of the pond was a large, bottomless hole that would suck unlucky swimmers into it, never to be seen again. The seaweed that grew underwater and near its shores had been known to wrap around the legs of boys who were wading in it and pull them down into the water. It was easy to see why Mama never liked the idea of me fishing in that pond or sledding across it in the winter when it was frozen over. By night Circle Pond looked like the Legend of Sleepy Hollow, dark, eerie, and evil. But by day it was green, gorgeous, and full of life. Sunbeams bounced off of its waters and green grass encircled it.

Scores of king-size catfish made Circle Pond their home, but it was the Chesapeake Bay, a short hike across town, that offered not only catfish, but also cod, sunfish, bluefish, and crab. Carrying the nets, crab baskets, and old inner tubes we'd borrowed from Mr. Hatfield, Carl and I would go over to a tributary of the bay we called Five Fingers. It had been named after the five smokestacks of a nearby steel mill where men in the community worked. On our inner tubes and homemade wooden rafts we'd float to the other side of a wide channel, where we'd drop our nets in the clear, shoulder-deep water. Bait was usually chicken livers, chicken backs, or a fish head provided from home.

If Vernon noticed one of us having trouble with something, he was quick to lend a hand without making us feel dumb or incompetent. He didn't tolerate put-downs or petty rivalries within the group, nor did he ever pit us against each other through favoritism. He tried to be fair, judicious, and patient with us, and made it his business to see that we treated each other the same way. Vernon earned our trust as a leader because we knew he genuinely looked out for us and not because he wanted to pull rank and hold dominion over us.

Of course, catching crab wasn't exactly brain surgery. You simply dropped your net into the water and waited for the crab to take the bait. Once the crab bit, you just scooped it up into the net and dropped it into a bucket ashore.

The toughest part of crabbing was learning how to pick up the critters. Once, Vernon spotted me struggling to pick up a crab. Each time I reached for the crab, it snapped at me and I'd quickly jerk my hand back. Vernon must have watched for several moments before he came up behind me.

"You'll never get it like that," he said.

"How come?"

" 'Cause, you see those little dots on his shell?"

"Yeah. What about 'em?"

"Those are his eyes. Would you sit there and watch somebody grab you and throw you in a bucket?"

I thought about it for a moment. "I should sneak up on it?"

"Somethin' like that." Putting his arm around my shoulder, Vernon explained the best way to pick up a crab without getting bitten.

"You gotta grab 'em from behind, opposite those two little dots. When you get 'em from his blind side, his claws reach around but can't get at you. Go ahead. Give it a try."

I admired Vernon's smarts, but most of all I appreciated his willingness to share what he knew with others. His attitude was, the more fish and crabs each of us caught, the more fun we'd have as a group. If one of us caught none while the rest of us caught plenty, he'd make each of us give up a catch, and nobody complained about sharing.

I will always be grateful to Vernon for teaching me the value of generosity and providing for others. He viewed life through the clear lens of his own unfolding adolescence. We appreciated and respected him as worldly and wise, and aspired to one day navigate life's course with the same grace and confidence he did.

"Pee Wee, you're becoming quite a crabber," my mother said, her voice filled with gratitude and pride. She'd take the bucket filled with live crabs into the kitchen and promptly dump it into the sink. Then she would pack ice over them and let the crabs chill throughout the day. Around dinnertime, she would put them in a pot of boiling water, vinegar, and beer and let them steam until they were ready for serving, tender and delicious. In Turners Station, you didn't need money to buy crabs; you ate them when you wanted them because you caught them for yourself. I have to admit that they tasted a little sweeter, anyway, since I was consumed with the knowledge that at the age of ten, I had provided for my entire family.

When the sun faded in Turners Station, so would the activity. There wasn't much in the way of entertainment. Some of the men went drinking at Mike & Jitters—that is, if they didn't mind entering through the back door. Others simply bought their liquor at the Old Mill Tavern—which sold Coloreds packaged goods, but didn't allow them to sit there and drink them.

On payday, which came every other Friday, some folks would get spruced up and saunter over to Adams Lounge. A white stucco nightclub reminiscent of a small castle, Adams Lounge not only had live entertainment but was one of the few integrated clubs in Maryland.

At dusk, I knew it was time to head on home, as did my friends, and we all took our curfews seriously. Depending on the season, we'd rush through an extra inning of baseball, or declare the football team that scored the next touchdown an automatic winner.

At our house, there was an evening ritual that began when my sisters and I would come in from outdoors. We'd get out of our play clothes and wash up. Mama placed cleanliness next to godliness and didn't take kindly to us walking around the house dirty. When it was time for dinner, we appeared at the table wearing old but clean clothes and with our hands and faces soap-scrubbed. After dinner, if we behaved, Mama would let us sit on the front steps for a while before sending us upstairs to bed.

There were, of course, those special Sunday afternoons when Mama would have me and my three sisters all starched, ironed, and polished in our best clothes. We'd sit out on the front steps and wait for Daddy's old Pontiac to come pulling up in the gravel driveway after work. When he arrived, we'd all pile into the car and cruise out to the airport. On the way, we'd stop at a little store on the side of the road to buy a big bag of Wise potato chips and a couple of Coca-Colas, the kind in those thick green little bottles that they used to sell. At the airport, we'd pull over off the side of the road and watch the planes as they came roaring down the runway or lifting off into the indigo sky.

It was 1958 and America was wrestling with her conscience on the issue of race. The question of what to do with the Negro had yet to be answered. As white people rode past us with the newer and shinier cars, none of that seemed to matter. I was with my family and we were all happy. Darlene, LaWana, and Michele were all giggling and Mama and Dad were in the front seat talking. The whir of the airplanes with their propellers in gear dominated the afternoon air. This was a good feeling, I thought to myself. I wished I could keep it forever.

•　•　•

One evening shortly after my eleventh birthday, my sisters and I were in our bedroom, laughing and playing and getting ready for bed, when we heard a confrontation break out downstairs. In his usual fit of rage, Daddy was yelling about something and cursing at Mama. All the commotion began to upset my sisters, and they were scared to death. Trembling and staring at the door of the room, they squeezed their hands against their ears, hoping the disturbance would somehow go away. None of us knew if, in his frenzied moment of temper and fury, we would be next in line to bear the weight of his wrath.

I tried to stay put upstairs, hoping that the altercation would die down as it often did. But the noise only got louder and his language harsher. Then I heard the savage smacking of flesh, like an open palm striking a moist face, like the sound of a wrestler being thrown flat on a mat. Mama screamed as if in pain and the scary sound of breaking glass rang through the house. I could hear Mama yelling back at him, shouting that she was sick of his mess, that she wasn't going to take it anymore. Darlene, LaWana, and Michele were all holding each other now, rocking back and forth uncontrollably on the floor, and crying. I heard my father shout, *"I'm the goddamn man of this house and what I say goes!"*

My mother screamed back something that I could not make out. Suddenly, a huge slam against the wall in the room below shook the whole house. The girls wailed as the floor seemed to tremble from the impact.

I had heard enough. I rushed through the door and down the staircase to defend my mother. He grabbed me before I could barely get inside the kitchen.

"Get the fuck outta here!" he screamed. Lifting me off my feet by the back of my pajama top, he shook me as hard as he could, yelling, "I said get the fuck outta here!"

"Lemme go!" I shouted, kicking my feet at him and flailing my arms in the air.

My mother, unconcerned about her own safety, lunged to help me with her arms reaching over his massive shoulders. He angrily shook her off and shoved her hard against the kitchen wall. Dishes fell from the table behind us and shattered. He dragged me to the door, flung it open, and threw me as far as he could outside on the ground. He yelled, *"I said get the fuck outta here and I meant it!"*

My body banged against the ground and I struck my head, tearing the skin off of my forehead. A single flash of hard white light seared my vision, and for an instant I could only lie there. Slowly I got to my knees and knelt on all fours until my head cleared. There was the hot metallic taste of blood in my mouth and my lips were cut and bleeding. My knee, now both bruised and skinned, stuck out through the torn pajamas. From where I was sprawled in the dirt, I could hear him becoming more furious. He was hollering at the top of his lungs, and I heard the crash of furniture hitting the floor.

My mother was crying as I'd never heard her cry before. When I got up off the ground to open the door, I discovered that he had locked me out. Without hesitating, I took my fist and rammed it through the shattered glass pane. I reached in, unlocked the kitchen door, and ran to grab a long steak knife out of the kitchen drawer. His red eyes opened wider with vengeance when he saw me, but for me all fear was gone. I pointed the blade at his huge hulking figure.

"You get the fuck out," I yelled, swallowing some of the blood in my mouth. "If you do anything else to Mama, I'm gonna kill you right now!"

At first, he just stood there, gasping for breath and staring at me in disbelief. "You must be crazy, to pull a damn knife on me, you little shit," he grumbled. His eyes grew tiny and a large vein twitched at his temple. My defiant stare met his and there was no give in me. I knew I would hurt him, kill him, if he didn't leave my mother alone.

He continued peering at me, breathing hard and dripping with sweat. He acted as if he wanted to charge me, and I was hoping it was more than an act. For the first time in my life I wanted to cut his heart out, and he knew it. As we stared at each other in that highly charged moment of standoff, my knife and my will had become the equalizer. No longer would he be free to do as he pleased with us. He now realized that I had the courage to kill him, and he couldn't bring himself to make another move.

"Pee Wee," I heard my mother beg. "Baby, put that knife away!"

"Not till he gets outta here, Mama! Not till he leaves!"

The heavy silence resumed. We continued facing each other, as the seconds flew by. He mumbled something under his breath, growled, and then turned and stormed out of the house. As he slammed the kitchen door behind him, shards of glass from the broken pane scattered across the floor. Mama ran over to me with her face wet with tears.

"Look what you've done to yourself," she cried, reaching gently toward my wrist, and alarmed by what she saw. I hadn't realized it, but my arm had been cut badly on the window I had smashed and blood was dripping freely onto the floor. A strip of glass was still dug into my arm, and beads of sweat ran down my temple.

"I just wish he'd go and never come back. What do we need him for?" I said as Mama stanched my bleeding and bandaged my arm. My anger was still boiling. Inside I was on fire. Silently, I prayed to God to make this man leave us alone. And if God couldn't do that, then I prayed that he would at least make me stronger. Strong enough to protect my family and wise enough to lead them.

Well, God in his wisdom must have heard my prayer. One cold November morning in 1959, my father left for work and never returned again.

3

WEST BALTIMORE

*I*T has happened more times than I can remember: One of the Republican Party's most conservative white members has approached me to exchange stories about growing up hungry and poor. Amid their assaults on America's underclass and their love affair with Big Business, it's easy to forget that a lot of the country's far-right conservatives come from very, very poor backgrounds. Some of the GOP's most prominent foot soldiers can identify with the financial plight of poor black people more than they would ever admit publicly. Indeed, in many cases, right next to the white working-class community in which they grew up was a black community where the residents worked just as hard and weren't much worse off than themselves.

However, today, I am amazed at how many of those, black and white, who benefited from a system that worked in their favor, are aggressively pushing legislation to destroy it. Simultaneously, some are aggressively supporting bills to roll back a number of our basic constitutional protections, while scapegoating immigrants, black people, and other minorities for all of the ills that are plaguing this country.

It's clear to me that some of my contemporaries on the far right are suffering from the same sort of selective memory that often occurs in people from humble beginnings who make a success of themselves. Some are so deeply into denial that they've shut down emotionally to the plight of the poor. Perhaps they fear that recalling their own personal histories would sensitize them to the issues facing America's forgotten, and as a result compromise their new reality.

Such persons are indifferent to the calls to rebuild communities that have been in sharp decline for the past three decades. The worst of them practice a dangerous brand of deception dedicated to trumpeting venomous propaganda that blacks, Asians, and Hispanics are not only unequal, they are inferior to their white counterparts. Rallying their supporters with coded messages that in essence proclaim, "We're tired of taking care of those people's problems," these opinion makers are the chief architects of the wide walls that still separate the races.

The nascent campaign to portray African Americans as inferior and to portray our culture as a national albatross thrives only because its premise has been largely unchallenged. Recognizing the truth would dilute the power of these rationalizations, and jeopardize the swelling populist movement built on scapegoating the underclass for all that ails our society. The truth is that, as black people, we have always taken care of our own problems—there simply was no one else to do it. The War on Poverty, which lasted a mere fifteen years, was a brief skirmish in comparison to the three-hundred-year campaign of Jim Crow and second-class citizenship. The truth is that black and brown people have been no less committed to achieving the American Dream than any other group in this nation—even if it was a dream that could only be fulfilled in "our" part of town.

So many of the naysayers are blind to the autonomy, the community institutions, and the pride that existed within black communities before the devastating riots of the mid- and late 1960s. These leaders refuse to acknowledge that the new kind of inner-city ghettos that are now synonymous with the urban underclass are a recent development, and certainly not created independently by black people. Many of the ghettos they decry are the disastrous outcome of national political and economic policies.

When Ronald Reagan gave his final State of the Union address to government officials and the nation on January 25, 1988, I could only breathe a deep sigh of relief. He had spent the last seven years working relentlessly to request severe budget cuts for programs that benefited the neediest citizens while simultaneously demanding the largest peacetime military buildup in history. He considered his presidency to be one of great promise and renewed hope for the America he envisioned as a "shining city on a hill." During his speech, he boldly, and inaccurately, claimed that "America's poor climbed out of poverty at the fastest rate in ten years" and that "family income has risen in four straight years."

But Reagan's vision of America and his achievements were sadly distorted. As the president waxed proudly from the Capitol that afternoon, there was another America he failed to mention in his remarks. It was an America that was not a shining beacon on a hill, but rather an America in the valley of despair. That America was one cited by the National Urban League study, which found that one-third of black and Hispanic Americans still lived in poverty. It was the same America seen by the United States Conference of Mayors, which reported that poor families were further below the poverty line than at any other time since 1963. It also brought into focus the plight of the working poor—those whose poverty resulted primarily from low wages and who constituted the fastest-growing portion of those living in poverty.

As the president crowed over his administration's success in building "vibrant neighborhoods," I could only wish that he had peered through his limousine window as he rode to the Capitol that night, because he'd have seen too many of his neighbors huddled in the cold and snow, searching for warmth atop a grate or seeking shelter in the doorway of a government building.

Seven years later, in 1995, after the Republicans' sweep of the House and Senate, some in their ranks comfortably spewed antiminority rhetoric and a general disdain of anything urban. I felt duty-bound to remind them that many of them supported the political policies that have contributed to the dismal conditions which imprisoned many black and Latino communities. The West Baltimore I grew up in wasn't a community plagued by hopelessness. It was a place teeming with black professionals and working-class homeowners, active churches, and community centers full of spirited leaders and ambitious children.

This vibrant, self-sustaining community clearly demonstrated what we were capable of doing with our own hard work, values, and resources. Like so many other urban neighborhoods that have been largely abandoned for the last three decades, West Baltimore in the late 1950s and early 1960s was a bustling enclave in a city bound by segregation. I remember being a part of this community, because this is where I came of age.

"Who needs 'em? I got 'em! Any kind you want, any seat in the house."

Beneath the bright glow of the Royal Theatre marquee, I stood watching scalpers hawk tickets to the throngs of people crowding Pennsylvania Avenue. In just a few minutes, the Platters would take the stage, and on this balmy Saturday night it seemed that any Baltimorean who had ever snapped a finger was converging onto the narrow strip of nightclubs and after-hours joints to hear the group that was taking America by storm.

"It's the Platters, folks! Tickets here!"

This hot spot in West Baltimore was a far cry from anything I'd ever witnessed back in sleepy Turners Station. Loud and cantankerous, pulsating with honking horns, droning voices, and raucous laughter, and smelling of cigars, perfume, and roasted peanuts—this was city life. I was mesmerized by its fast, brazen rhythms, its neon lights and taxicabs, its high-heeled women and fancy cars.

It was 1960 and I was only twelve years old. I'd have no more business hanging out on "the Avenue" than a priest at a juke joint. But I'd gotten out of the house that night using the same line I always used. "I'm just going over to Gary's house to sit outside on the steps." Gary Fenwick, who had become my best friend ever since my mother moved our family here from Turners Station a year earlier, fed his mother the same line in reverse. Together, we'd spend hours hanging out, walking the streets and walking the Strip, known back then as the Avenue. It was only a few blocks from my unadorned house, but it was miles from the innocence I had left in Turners Station.

Back in Turners Station, the only places I ever saw so many black folks dressed up at once were church, weddings, and funerals. But the black people pouring into the nightclubs and restaurants on Pennsylvania Avenue were like none I'd ever seen before. They looked rich compared to the folks in Turners Station, where a clean shave and a haircut passed for dressing up.

The black people here were as classy as any whites I'd ever seen in Dundalk, or even on television for that matter. They drove up in fancy fish-tail Cadillacs and handed them over to red-capped valets. The men stepped out sporting black Stetson hats, tailored sharkskin suits, bright silk ties, and shoes so shiny you could see your face in them.

Their women were equally mesmerizing, preening glamorously in their pompadour hairdos, sequined dresses, and feather boas that swayed gently as their high heels clicked purposefully along the Avenue.

Much like Harlem in the 1920s, Baltimore's own history of segregation had spawned this district of flourishing black businesses. Along with the Royal Theatre, there were the New Albert Hall, the Casino nightclub, and the Alhambra Lounge. There were numerous nightspots, and restaurants galore. Live stage shows and even livelier speakeasies covered the twelve-block strip.

Before the turn of the century, affluent whites had once dominated this area's neighborhoods, residing in spacious three-story homes in the areas known as Upton, Sandtown, and Harlem Park. Blacks and Eastern European Jews lived in the city center. But as banking, retail, and commercial interests began to concentrate downtown in the 1930s, black families were displaced. They began moving north and west, occupying the former neighborhoods of their Eastern European counterparts.

Segregation laws on the books since World War I restricted blacks from moving much farther north than Cold Spring Lane. This meant that black migration flowed chiefly into central West Baltimore and central East Baltimore. By midcentury, the city's most prominent middle-class black families were settled there. Those families included the Mitchells, a political dynasty led by Clarence Mitchell of the NAACP and his brother Parren, who would later become the first black congressman to be elected from Maryland. There were also the Murphys, who owned the influential *Baltimore Afro-American* newspaper, and who led a dynasty of lawyers, writers, and thinkers.

In West Baltimore during its heyday, there were some black professionals even moving uptown. In many respects, although their migration took them away from the center of things, these people were considered a rarity. Unlike today, no one begrudged or scorned them for moving uptown and away from the thick of black life. It was understood that they had relocated because they could afford to buy one of the big homes in the predominantly white neighborhoods of Ashburton, Forest Park, or up on Reisterstown Road, where a number of Jewish families had also settled.

Folks on the west side didn't waste time worrying about the flight of one black family because another would move in right behind them. Everyone knew West Baltimore was the home of the black movers and shakers, and people's desire to stake a claim there was real and intense.

In fact, the bravado of the west side has long fueled a rivalry between its residents and those dwelling on the east side. East Baltimoreans thought that people on the west side felt superior because they enjoyed a richer social and cultural history—from the glittery nightclubs on the Strip to such luminous natives as Cab Calloway, Billie Holiday, and Thurgood Marshall. The west side wasn't all bourgeoisie—it was very much working-class. The east side, while a solid and stable community, was much more blue-collar and, to some, much more laid back.

The rivalry is reminiscent of the different points of view held by W.E.B. Du Bois and Booker T. Washington. Du Bois would have lived in West Baltimore, where the intellectuals, business people, and political movers and shakers lived. Washington would have lived in East Baltimore, telling everyone to "Cast your buckets down where you are. Let's learn some skills, make yourself necessary, so we can go on and make some money and take care of ourselves."

The rivalry, in retrospect, really was counterproductive. Our internal clashes only diluted the black power base in the overall community. Whenever progressive whites got involved with the struggles of the larger community, I'm sure they were shocked that two black communities, which seemed to look alike, talk alike, and act alike, had such different views of themselves.

Rivalry aside, there's no denying that in its prime, Pennsylvania Avenue was the cultural hub for black Baltimoreans. Peppered with attractions like the Royal Theatre, the Regent Theatre, and the New Albert Hall, the Strip was the place to be. Big names such as Eubie Blake, Count Basie, Duke Ellington, Nat King Cole, Billie Holiday, Dizzy Gillespie, Ella Fitzgerald, and Redd Foxx regularly appeared on the marquee. After performing, they often dined at the black-owned restaurants or capped the night at one of the many after-hours joints.

Without question the Avenue was a great adult nightspot. I'm not sure, however, that I should have been cruising it at such a young age, but it certainly gave me a fuller sense of myself. West Baltimore was far removed from the dusty country roads of Turners Station, and moving there had immediately enlarged my world. Overnight it had exposed me to a broader range of possibilities for my race, which while still limited, was more than I'd ever known or imagined.

Erosion works quietly, slowly, until it loosens a critical piece of a larger whole and sends an avalanche cascading down a mountainside. Though my mother hadn't wanted to admit it, there had been forces at work for some time undermining her relationship with my father. Since he was a truck driver, we all had been accustomed to his being on the road for several days at a time. But the truth was, even during the times he wasn't working, he often had disappeared for days, and returned without offering an explanation.

Wherever he may have been spending those countless days and nights is still a mystery to us all. Mama assumed his absences involved a woman named Pearl, a temptress who lived on the other side of town who dressed in red and spoke like a geechie. I had seen Ms. Pearl only once, and I'm sure my mama had, also. But the way my mother spoke Pearl's name told me that if she was a friend of my father's, she was certainly no friend of my mama's.

When my father finally did leave, I was torn between happiness that he was gone and anger that he could just abandon us like that. At the time, my sisters were too young to understand the breakup of a marriage, but even small children have a way of sensing trouble. After several days and nights of not seeing or hearing from our father, they realized something was wrong.

They questioned Mama about their daddy's whereabouts and when he was coming home. The answers always came back vague and unsettling. Each evening the girls would wait anxiously at the screen door for him to pull up in his old Pontiac, so they could run outside and be scooped up in his thick muscular arms. Although my father ignored me most of the time, he was always especially affectionate toward them.

When he didn't show up, they'd go upstairs to bed and cry. Mama was devastated, although she tried to cloak her pain in silence. While her relationship with my father had always been far from ideal, I believe she found a certain contentment in simply having a man in the house. Her happiness came from knowing her children would enjoy a life much richer than her own.

She always talked wistfully about wanting us to finish school and have careers. Now, without my father's support, that dream seemed far less certain. Overwhelmed by the prospect of trying to support us as a single parent, she wouldn't eat much and lost a lot of sleep.

Shortly before we moved, I remember waking up in the middle of the night and finding her sitting up alone on the living room sofa. I put my arms around her.

"Don't worry, Mama," I said. "I'll take care of us. We'll be all right. I promise."

"I know we'll be fine, baby," she said in a faraway voice.

I wanted desperately to believe her, but the look on her face that night said otherwise. It was a look of doubt and trepidation. It struck me so hard because I'd never witnessed anything but absolute resolve radiating from her eyes. My mother had never been defeated by anything. Even during my father's drunken tirades, she had always stood her ground. In the wake of conflict or adversity, she always refused to back down, and she worked hard to instill that same fearlessness in me and my sisters.

I was now the only masculine presence in the household. And even at the age of twelve, I had some understanding of what a man was supposed to do. A man protected his family, put food on the table, and offered loving support. I wanted desperately to fill that role, and even fantasized about getting a job so that I could take care of my family. But Mama would never allow me to drop out of school and I knew it. It was important to her that I get an education and, more important, that I made something of it.

My mother possessed a golden inspirational touch, and I could never thank her enough for all of the life lessons she taught me. She had a fearless vision of the world and the role of children in it. She consistently sacrificed her own happiness to provide a stable, loving existence for us. Without her determination, our family would never have stayed together through some very difficult times. She was everything a mother should be. But as I looked at her that night, I realized that the woman who had taught me not to fear was now herself afraid.

Mama's wariness only fired my own desire to prove that we could survive without my father. Although I was only twelve, I was ready to take on the role of caretaker, and more important, I even looked forward to it. So what if he had abandoned us. We'd be fine without him. I'd make sure of that.

On a blustery March morning in 1960, my uncles Stanley and Freddy backed a moving van up to our home in Turners Station. Mama had warned me that this day was approaching. She said that we were moving to West Baltimore to be closer to other relatives. My mother seemed so committed to the idea that I didn't say much at the time. I guess deep down I didn't really believe she'd uproot me and my sisters from the only home we had ever known, but without Clifton there, there was clearly no reason to stay.

Even as I helped fill the many boxes with our belongings, the reality didn't penetrate my denial. I went through the exercise as merely another household chore. But the truth came crashing down on me the moment I saw that moving van roll up on that cold, rainy morning.

To a child, few events are more devastating than moving away from an old, familiar home. Little did I know that that would be the beginning of many such moves. Up to that point, I'd known only one place in my life, and that place was Turners Station. It was the center of my universe, and nothing made sense to me unless it could somehow be connected to it. Filtered through the prism of the people and places that existed there, I could scarcely imagine a world without Carl and my buddies, playing baseball for Mr. Smitty, fishing in Circle Pond.

My family would have never left Turners Station if I'd had anything to do with it. But at twelve, there wasn't much I could say that would have influenced my mother's decision. When Uncle Stanley and Uncle Freddy came in that day without their usual small talk or clamor for a good hot meal, I knew they were there for business.

Sporting tattered jeans and parkas, they barely seemed to notice me as they began pacing the floor, assessing what to load first. Swiftly, they began picking up stacked cardboard boxes and carrying them outside to the truck. With each box I watched them carry out of the house, my heart sank deeper and deeper.

I'd just graduated from Bragg School and been enrolled in Sollers Point Junior and Senior High. I'd already made new friends in this new school and now my mother was taking me away.

Only one thought consoled me: With any luck, I might never see my father again, and that thought alone softened the blow of leaving. No longer would I have to squirm under the glare of his disapproving eyes, or jump at the sound of his voice shouting at me. If most children mourn the loss of a parent, I quietly rejoiced in his absence. Beneath the sadness of watching my uncles clear out chairs, tables, wall hangings, beds, and everything else in the house, I felt a surge of relief that the only person I'd ever hated was gone for good. Or so I believed.

Sometime during the 1920s my mother's father, Edward Willis, Sr., son of a freed slave, purchased a modest house at 529 Robert Street in West Baltimore. It's a small, simple place—a three-story row house consisting of a living room, dining room, and kitchen on the first floor, three bedrooms and a bathroom on the second. Granddad bought the house, I'm told, for family members then and in the future who would need a place to live if they were ever down on their luck. This was also the place where Mama and her brothers and sisters grew up.

Today, I'm impressed by both the foresight and generosity of my grandfather. Long after his death, numerous relatives, including myself, took advantage of this emergency shelter. What has kept his vision both alive and pure is the fact that he forbade selling the house for personal gain. This discouraged anyone from living there any longer than absolutely necessary. In time, my own family would come close to living in this house after being evicted from several others for being unable to pay the rent.

When we first arrived on the west side, Mama was proud to refer to the house on Robert Street as the place of her birth and the family home. The house we moved into was directly around the corner at 1900 Division Street. All of the houses in the neighborhood, it seemed, were practically identical. Block after block after block all you saw were similar two- and three-story brick row houses with white marble steps. If anything distinguished our house from the others lining the block on Division Street, it was that it sat on the corner, somewhat in disrepair.

For the first few weeks, I hoped that my mother would move back to Turners Station. Everything seemed so alien in this new place, so different. I wondered if I'd ever fit into this different neighborhood where so much seemed to be going on at once. It was all so hectic, all so new.

My mother did everything she could to put me at ease. But it took time to adjust to my strange surroundings. Besides missing my friends, I also missed the wide-open spaces and the lush green fields of Turners Station. All my life I'd enjoyed a backyard, and this house had practically no yard at all. There were very few trees amid the concrete streets, and grass didn't seem to grow here.

It wasn't like Turners Station, where I could run out of my house and keep running until I came across a field. There was no pond, beyond which corn and wheat fields stretched to the horizon. Here, it was just concrete on top of more concrete. Our house had an alley beside it, an alley behind it, and cars drove up and down them all day.

Our house, like all the others, sat cheek by jowl with the street. I'd never been in a place where the cars passed by so close to the house. You could hear them when they swooshed by at all times of the day and night. Radios blared, sirens wailed, and every corner was packed with people; I couldn't understand why people would want to live so close together. I felt smothered and torn.

And our new neighbors didn't exactly roll out a red carpet for us, either. The night we moved into the house, I found my mother in the living room holding a piece of paper in her hand and holding tears back in her eyes. The paper was a note that had been nailed to the outside of the front door.

She handed me the paper with the hateful words and let me read it for myself. "Obviously you must be very hard up to move into this house," it read. "But poor or not, the people on this block have rules that we expect you to live by."

It was the first time in my life I'd ever felt poor, but I wasn't embarrassed over it or the note. I was simply angry that a complete stranger could be so mean-spirited to kick a family that had already fallen on hard times. I'd heard and seen white people looking down their noses at us, but never blacks. Back in Turners Station, that kind of intolerance just didn't exist, and if it did, I never saw it.

Looking back on this now, I still can't forgive the cruelty of the note writer, but I do have a better understanding of the note's intent. Back then, the black community had standards that they policed themselves. That note may have been a neighbor's way of letting us know that. Unfortunately, they wrapped their message in hurtful language and damaging insinuation. My mother believed the best about people and, after her initial reaction, she returned to form and told me that our neighbors were probably well-intentioned but lacking a great deal of tact.

For the most part, though, Mama was pleased with our relocation. West Baltimore was home to her. She had grown up in that neighborhood, just around the corner at 529 Robert Street, so it was all refreshingly familiar. Her brothers lived around one corner, her sister Gloria just three blocks away. Her childhood friends were sprinkled across the neighborhood and just a half block away was the dry cleaners where Mama had worked while in high school. It was clear that she was quietly rejoicing over being back on her native turf after an absence of more than ten years.

Once I learned the neighborhood, I made my spending money by selling the *Baltimore Afro-American* newspaper, or as we called it, *The Afro*. Owned by the Murphy family, *The Afro* has been publishing since 1892, and was one of the first black newspapers in the country, if not the largest. *The Afro* was a real trailblazer in the community. Nobody cared much about being on the society page of *The Baltimore Sun* or the *News-American*, they wanted to be on the society page in *The Afro*. It was the authentic source of what was happening in black Baltimore.

The Afro gave us a different sense of the struggles, trials, and travails of people like Jackie Robinson, Willie Mays, and Sugar Ray Robinson because the writers actually interacted with them. *The Afro* also covered our sports heroes when they went abroad, such as the black athletes on the 1960 U.S. Olympic team who won several gold medals. All of us knew their names: Rafer Johnson, Ralph Boston, Wilma Rudolph, John Thomas, and Cassius Clay.

But *The Afro*'s mainstay was letting folks know what was happening locally and day to day through movie reviews, showtime reviews, its clean block campaign, tidbits on Women's Day at Sharp Street Memorial United Methodist Church, and all sorts of news that would have never appeared in the general press. No other publication was going to provide coverage of our people, communities, and issues as comprehensive as *The Afro*'s.

Shortly after my family moved in town, my mother introduced me and my sisters to Mr. Charles, whom she described simply as "a good friend of the family." A tall dapper man with smooth dark chocolate skin and high cheekbones, Mr. Charles acted calm, poised, and very secure about who he was. Above all, he was kind to my mother and made her and all of us feel good. Before long, Mr. Charles really did become like a member of the family. Frequently he'd drop by on weekends after Mama got off work. Often, when times were tight, he'd hand her some money or bring us a big bag of groceries. He took to our house as though it were his own, breezing in comfortably and helping with the chores. He and my mother would spend hours laughing and talking into the night.

At first, I was somewhat leery of my mother's relationship with this stranger who seemed to know her so well. After all, I was becoming accustomed to being the man of our house. But a few months of getting to know him soon wiped out any reservations I might have harbored.

I can think of many reasons that I grew to like Mr. Charles, but none more than the remarkable effect he had on my mother. I'd never seen her as happy or relaxed as she was in the company of this tall, slender, soft-spoken man. Her entire mood seemed to change the moment Mr. Charles walked in.

Mr. Charles also had a particularly soft spot in his heart for children. Nothing made him happier than to see a toddler learning to walk. Sometimes when we were together out on the street, he'd go out of his way to speak to a little kid. Often he'd even give the older ones money to take back to their parents. What I learned later, after many conversations with him, was that he couldn't stand the thought of kids growing up in a life as hard as he'd had. He told me that he felt blessed just to be alive and that every child deserved a chance. That's why he wanted to extend even the smallest gesture of kindness to the kids around him. He thought that he could give them hope for a different kind of life.

I admired Mr. Charles because he was a commanding presence without being loud or bullying. I never once heard him boast, yet it was clear that people held him in high esteem. Anytime he walked along the Strip, people would stop to talk to him or to get his opinion. I found it amazing that he could command such respect from the people on the street. Soon a crowd would gather and people seemed to want his attention and to hear whatever he had to say. Even when he wasn't running the numbers, he seemed to be sought out for counsel. I don't know if everyone liked him, but I do know that everyone respected him.

Mr. Charles became a helpmate of sorts to my mother as well, but it was hard for her to accept favors from anybody. She was a very independent person, and she really didn't like having to feel that she needed a man's help to survive. I remember hearing Mr. Charles and Mama disagree a couple of times, in an affectionate sort of way, about her turning down his gift of grocery money.

We were suffering financially and Mr. Charles knew it. He wanted to help, not because we needed him but because he was beginning to need us. Things were tight in the summer of '63. Mama helped me get an after-school job as a stock boy at the neighboring Dave's Grocery. Among the many Jewish families in our neighborhood, storekeepers David and Inga Pottash had become very friendly with my mother. They sympathized with her predicament of trying to raise four children on her single income as a house cleaner.

"Mary, we know it is not easy for you," Mr. Pottash would say in his thick Jewish accent. "Please, don't be so proud that you won't accept a little help from us now and then. Let your son work here and earn some extra money."

In time, the Pottashes would see my family fall deeper and deeper into a hole. We found ourselves moving from house to house in what was now becoming an all-too-familiar neighborhood. We had fallen so far behind on rent that our landlords had no choice but to threaten to evict us. During a five-year span, we lived in four houses, all within a few blocks of each other.

Mama worked as a maid during the weekends and as an elevator operator during the week, but we were just too many mouths to feed. Our gas and electricity were constantly getting cut off and there were times when candles provided the only light in the house. We cooked our food over the open blue flame of a Sterno can—and slept in bed wearing our coats to stay warm through the night. I longed for summer in a different way and for different reasons than most people. It offered a couple of extra hours of light in the house and a couple of more reasons to be happy. No matter what hardship we were going through, at the time I kept reassuring Mama that I could cope and that I understood our circumstances were only temporary.

During those years, about the only good thing that happened for my mother was Mr. Charles. He would always stop by and spend time with us. Even when we moved from one house to another, he'd drop by with money to take care of the bills and make sure we were settled in. As time passed and Mr. Charles's visits became more frequent, I asked my mother why Mr. Charles was so good to us.

"Mr. Charles is my dear friend," she told me. "I've known him since I wasn't much older than you. A long time ago, he promised me that he'd always keep an eye out for me, make sure that I was always all right. And he always has because he is a man of his word, like I expect you to be.

"Let me make one thing real clear to you, Pee Wee," she said. "Mr. Charles is my friend, but he doesn't owe us anything. What he does for us is a gift, pure and simple. And I wouldn't have it any other way."

My sisters became quite close to Mr. Charles, but the bond I forged was the tightest. He seemed to take an instant liking to me, and after a while, he'd come by now and then and invite me to walk with him through the neighborhood. He'd take me over to Pennsylvania Avenue and we'd walk the Strip for hours. Sometimes we'd talk a lot, and sometimes we wouldn't, but I was never bored. Everybody on the street seemed to know him.

The ladies knew him, the business people knew him, the shop owners and nightclub owners knew him. Even the gangsters on the corner knew him. It wasn't long either before I realized that his name wasn't "Mr. Charles." Everybody addressed him as "Rip." I'd wondered why my mother would introduce him to us by a name that wasn't his. But it really didn't matter at the time. I was walking with a man who cared about us, and I was thrilled at the opportunity to know him.

Mr. Charles made no secret of his disdain for my dad. He thought Clifton was brutal, dishonest, and a chump. "Only a coward would ever hit a woman," he once told me. Witnessing Mr. Charles caring for our family exposed my father as the man he really was. Mr. Charles set a real example of responsibility in our household.

My father didn't come around much after Mr. Charles was on the scene because the contrast between the two of them was too great. When Clifton Gray did come by to give my mother some money, he'd just put it in her hand and keep on going. Or, if he wanted to see Darlene and the other girls, he'd pull up and honk, and they'd get in the car and he'd drive off. Confrontation wasn't Mr. Charles's style, but Clifton understood that his rival was prepared to use it if he had to.

Sometimes, when I went strolling along Pennsylvania Avenue, people would say, "Rip, is that your boy?"

"Yeah, he's my boy," he'd answer proudly.

Even though I knew in my heart that I wasn't, I felt that he said it because it was none of their business. Still, I felt good about his saying it. In some strange way it gave me a level of respect I hadn't yet earned out on the street. Later, when I would walk on the street by myself, I would hear people say, "Yeah, that's Rip's boy. Let him go through."

Sometimes I'd go in pool halls with Mr. Charles, the ones where the real gangsters hung out, betting big money. I knew you didn't go in places like that unless you knew someone. He'd walk right in and I'd walk in behind him. They'd look at me and then just look away. They figured if I was with Rip, I was all right, and I liked being regarded as his boy.

Soon I found myself walking like him and sometimes talking like him. I picked up many of his mannerisms because unconsciously I was emulating him. What was fascinating to me was that I even looked a little like him. Rip was taller than I am, but in a real sense we saw eye to eye. An impeccable dresser, he always wore a black cashmere coat and a brimmed fedora. In the winter of '63, he bought me a coat and a hat just like his. Now we'd walk down the street dressed nearly identically.

When I walked through the streets of West Baltimore basking in Mr. Charles's reflected glory, I held my head a little higher. Of course, I was still a skinny little kid who'd just moved into a tough neighborhood and had yet to prove himself to his peers. I may have earned respect from the kids back in Turners Station, but not in my new neighborhood or my new school. Because I constantly had to prove that I was not just a country bumpkin, I got into more fights than I care to remember.

Mama enrolled me in Booker T. Washington Junior High, and within days I knew that school would never be the same. This was Baltimore in the early 1960s and like it or not, I was caught by its lure. Music by Mary Wells, Curtis Mayfield, Jerry Butler, and the Shirelles filled the grounds around the school. Everybody seemed to be hanging out, holding books, holding conversations, and holding court. Inside, the halls echoed with loud talk and laughter. Booker T. Washington Junior High was some nine blocks away from my house, a fairly long hike through dangerous territory. For a new kid on the block without brothers or friends to pick up his slack, taking that lonely walk sometimes required a leap of faith. I longed many times for the backup of my buddy Carl, who would instinctively watch my back if a fight broke out. Each day, either on the way to school or coming home, it seemed some new bully would jump in my face, hoping to chump me down. Even though I lost a few of those encounters and the fights that went with them, I can honestly say I didn't back down. I had to act as crazy as they did and sometimes be twice as mean. Eventually I started to earn a measure of respect from the predators who sought to break me.

And, of course, it didn't hurt that I started hanging out with Gary Fenwick. With light-brown skin, dark hair, and deep features, Gary was the coolest of the cool. Wild and carefree and full of life, Gary's zest for risk and his disdain for fear made him a candidate for the unpredictable. I don't know what made our friendship click; it just did. In time, with Gary Fenwick as my new best friend, I would come face to face with death, the law, and my own reckless abandon. We learned together, lived together, fought together, and broke the law together. One day, shortly after my thirteenth birthday, Gary and I got into a vicious fight over something extremely important. This time, instead of fighting someone else, we fought each other. After almost a half hour of swinging, punching, and choking each other, we lay tangled on the ground . . . still in a choke lock, winded and sweating and tired.

"Jack-up, my man," I gasped.

"Ain't no jack-up unless you quit," said Gary. "You quit?" he asked.

"Naw, I quit if you quit," I shot back.

"Well, I quit if you quit," he responded. Then we both let go and fell flat on our backs.

I had met Gary in the Falcon Drum and Bugle Corps. My mother had enrolled me in hopes of keeping me off the streets and out of trouble. The Falcons were organized and run by Arnette Evans, a veteran army officer with a vision of creating the city's first young black drum and bugle corps. As the leader of the Falcons, Mr. Evans picked up with us where his military days had left off.

A squat man with light-brown skin and jet-black hair, Mr. Evans rarely uttered a sentence that wasn't laced with a curse word or a put-down. On the day my Mama dropped me off for my first Falcon meeting, I thought Evans was a gentle, even-tempered man. The warm greeting and pleasantries he exchanged with my mother and the parents of the other children made me feel comfortable.

"I just want to thank you for believing in this drum corps," he said charmingly to my mother. "You'll be really proud of your son once we start marching and winning competitions."

But the moment our parents left us alone with Mr. Evans, his brow immediately furrowed and his eyes became cold and steely. "All right," he boomed, pulling a cigar out of his shirt pocket. "Your mommies and daddies are gone now, and you should know that Arnette Evans does not, and will not, baby-sit any of you punks. So all you little sissies shut up, sit down, and try to focus your little pea-sized brains on what I'm about to teach you."

Blustery and passionate, Arnette Evans was unlike anyone I'd ever met. I was stunned by this pit bull masquerading as a man, and I watched and listened nervously as he stalked back and forth across the creaky wooden floor, ranting about the importance of discipline and order.

"If you don't know how to follow directions," he barked, "I don't want you in my corps no more than I want horseshit on my shoes."

He abruptly paused in his tirade and stepped over to me. I was sitting Indian-style on the cold floor of the warehouse where we were to practice.

"This one here," he said, kicking at my sneaker. "I can tell already you don't have what it takes to last one minute under Arnette. You looks like a little sissy. What's your name, boy?"

"Frizzell," I mumbled.

"Ahhh, isn't that a cute name," Arnette Evans taunted in his most girlish voice. "Your mama named you Frizzell. Well, let me tell you somethin', Frizzy. You oughta take your lil' narrow ass home right now, because sissies like you will never survive this corps! You understand, Frizzy?"

I did not answer him. I just stared right back.

"You look like you want to kick my ass or somethin', Frizzy. Is that what you wanna do?"

"No, sir," I lied.

He took the wet, half-chewed cigar out of his mouth, leaned down, and pressed his big fleshy face against mine. My heart was pounding in my chest. My limbs were shaking, and perspiration dotted the skin on my brow. I wanted to cry. "You wanna run home to your mama for some cookies and milk, play with your Barbie dolls, Frizzy?"

"No, sir."

"Well, maybe I'll let you stay here and listen today," he growled. "But don't bother coming back until you learn how to stand up straight and look like a man. And take that pitiful look off your face!"

He straightened up, wheeled around, and began stalking the others who had quivered during his interrogation of me. He moved on one after another and gave them a hard time simply for being present.

Over the coming weeks, Evans proved himself to be one consistent taskmaster, possessed by discipline and obsessed with winning. Those of us who were amused by his colorful language were equally intimidated by his unbridled rage. Like him or not, from that very first day I joined his outfit, Evans began forging a deep sense of dedication to hard work and discipline. His message was drilled so deep in my soul that to this day it prevails as my inspiration to always triumph in the face of adversity. Despite his temper that erupted with all the force of Mount Saint Helens, I learned to appreciate Evans's boundless energy and pursuit of perfection. What I didn't learn to appreciate was his badass attitude, and I longed for the day I could punch him.

While his love for children was camouflaged by his act of unrestrained contempt, many of us who marched in his corps succeeded in understanding how to go beyond our physical abilities and our mortal limitations in ways that neither we nor our parents could have imagined.

Rehearsing us in an old abandoned warehouse, Evans would push us until we would literally fall over with exhaustion. Unsympathetic, he'd just stand over us and push even harder.

"I told you, you wasn't shit, Frizzell," he'd bark at me. "Now get your ass up and show me that you're not as dumb and lazy as I think you are."

Arnette Evans could be rough, cold, ruthless. He pushed us so much that we all wanted to quit, and yet at the same time we wanted to prove him wrong. Without any formal training, he expected us to play our instruments and learn music by ear. And if we missed a note we were pulled out, singled out, and used as an example for his pronouncements on incompetence.

Every parent had signed off on allowing him to train us the way he did. They knew that Evans was the disciplinarian's disciplinarian, and figured we could all benefit from the experience. They never knew that Evans's tutelage meant their children at times were inspired by intimidation. In today's hands-off society, Evans's style might well land him in court. But back in those days, our parents gave Evans carte blanche to kick our butts. And that's exactly what he did.

"What the hell are you doing, Frizzell," he'd bellow at me for failing to turn on my heels on cue. "I've gone over this drill with you at least ten times, and you still keep screwing it up, making the whole corps look bad!"

"But . . ."

"Don't you 'but' me!" he'd snap. "This entire corps is depending on you to get it right, and you keep messing it up. Do you want the corps to look as stupid as you?"

"No, sir."

"Then get it right!!!"

"I will, sir."

"You'd better, or I'll snatch that French horn and make you wear it around your little skinny neck!"

I had learned early in life never to let anyone else's opinion deter me from my goals. For that, I could thank my father, who persisted in bullying me and trying to destroy my spirit. Having survived his abuse, I certainly wasn't going to fold under the likes of Arnette Evans. In fact, it was under his tutelage that I began to learn that I could function under relentless pressure.

There were close to seventy-five of us in the Falcon Drum and Bugle Corps. Evans transformed his group of poor, undisciplined, inner-city kids into a precision, uniformed unit that could march and compete with the best. Little did the all-white marching units know that our precision and instrumentation were orchestrated by a man who never knew the meaning of second best. We could march and perform for hours in the heat or stand at attention in a rainstorm without moving a muscle. Over time, I learned that I was capable of thriving even in an environment in which there was no praise or positive reinforcement for my actions.

Despite my young age, I understood that Arnette Evans was a deeply complex man. He was an extremist by nature, and I suppose his dogged training appealed to the perfectionist in me. There was a part of me that relished this battle of wills. Every time Arnette said I couldn't do something, I vowed to myself that I wouldn't stop until I did it. I was determined to prove him wrong. While I may have been small, I was smart and tenacious, and I refused to buckle under or display a weakness that he could exploit.

I knew that all of Evans's machinations were to measure whether we had what it takes. I knew I had it, and I vowed that Evans would know it, too. By watching the kids around me, many of whom quit under pressure or dissolved into a constant waterfall of tears, I realized that many of my peers simply couldn't tolerate his brand of tough love. Most feared him, while others lost the confidence needed to survive under him. I wasn't a masochist, but I understood that beneath all of his combative bluster, Evans really loved us. He wanted all of us to become survivors, to learn how to achieve no matter what, and he was determined to make this happen even at great personal sacrifice. Learning to function independently of Evans's praise, blame, or doubt taught me to listen to my own inner voice, and that was perhaps the greatest lesson he taught me.

The trials of grueling practice on the French horn and the toll that precision drilling took on my feet taught me how to focus my attention and block out everything else. It is not unlike the discipline practiced in the martial arts, where singular, razor-edge focus enables you to anticipate obstacles and exploit your advantage in the moment. Under Arnette, all I knew was that lack of focus would result in a hailstorm of criticism.

Evans's style of leadership was quite different from that of my Little League coach, Mr. Smitty. While Mr. Smitty's motto was that you always got another chance at bat, Evans believed passionately that there were no guarantees in life. In fact, he preached that you might not get another chance, so you'd better get it right the first time. "You only have one opportunity you can count on," he'd say, "and that's the first one." We had only one shot in a parade at proving to the competition judges that we were the best. If we didn't succeed, it was over. Arnette taught us that we'd better be prepared to be the best, hands down.

As Arnette Evans thundered at us over the years we all learned not to bother saying "I'm sorry." If we made a mistake we already knew what his response would be: "Don't complain, and don't explain. Just get it right, dammit!"

There were times back then when I loathed Evans for being so hard on me. But later, as an adult coaching Little League baseball, I realized what he had been trying to accomplish. He was daring us to come out of ourselves and go far beyond what we believed our own limitations to be.

People are born with a set of innate capabilities and powers, but we tend to put limits on what we can achieve. We are socialized in a way that rewards dependence and punishes initiative. Evans's whole strategy centered around making you so angry at him, so sick of being humiliated in front of everybody else, that you no longer made excuses but rather found a way to overcome them.

Of course, like the rest of us mortals, Arnette Evans had his weaknesses for temptation, too. After all the work was done, Evans liked to sit down with a little shot glass in one hand and his chewed-up cigar in the other. And women found his charm irresistible. But he never lost sight of his goal. He stuck with his tunnel vision and made the Falcon Drum and Bugle Corps reach its fullest potential. We were his mission impossible, his mother of all challenges. The passion that drove him made us believe he had something to prove to his contemporaries. I'm sure that they laughed at the notion of his taking a bunch of underachievers and turning us into fierce competitors. Nothing was going to stop him from achieving his goal— nothing. He spent so much of his own money on the Falcons that he didn't even own a car; yet, in reality, he had more than money could buy.

Gary was one who didn't survive Arnette Evans's boot camp. It wasn't that Gary wimped out, he just said, "To hell with that maniac Evans." Gary was the kind of person who felt he didn't need to prove anything to anyone. Gary's whole life suggested that he didn't have time for that crap. He was somebody who marched to his own drummer, even when we ran in the streets together. He was always different in that regard. On the other hand, I hung in there because I had been challenged and because I didn't know how to quit.

My Little League coach's style in my earlier years was more encouraging. If you made a fielding error or struck out at the plate, Mr. Smitty would tell you not to over-worry. "I made the great players as they came through this league," he'd say, "and I'll do the same with you." Unlike the others who might take the same tack, Smitty did not need validation. He had played in the old Negro Leagues and knew how to overcome adversity. He'd tell tales of the Kansas City Monarchs and the Baltimore Elite Giants and the great Negro players of his day. His advice was: Be patient at the plate and never let them rattle you, because soon you'd get your pitch to hit.

Arnette Evans, though, was just the opposite. He was on your ass twenty-four hours a day and was willing to fight you if it came to that. It was a risky way of dealing with teenagers because there is a thin line between motivating them and destroying them.

Back then, though, I think parents, particularly the few single mothers, were willing to take the risk of trusting a strong man to help build a sense of strength and character in their male children. There was a kind of self-contained pride in our community, and parents had a desire to have discipline be a part of their children's lives, just as it had been a part of their own upbringing.

Our sense of community and trust in role models has eroded over the years. It wasn't that we no longer appreciated what our own community had to offer, it's just that in an era following the passage of civil rights laws in the 1960s, we wanted more. We wanted the full blessings of the "land of the free." We were tired of being held at arm's length, tired of being denied full citizenship. This led to an exploration and desire to experience life beyond the confines of our communities.

There is a painful irony in our dogged pursuit of America's new promises. During the great migration north in the 1920s and 1930s, black people were pouring out of the rural Southern states and flocking to Northern cities for work. There was also a great desire back then to create our own self-contained communities, to have our own banks and our own hospitals and our own businesses.

But in the early 1960s, that ethic was about to change rapidly. Now the Negro wanted to be included in America's mainstream, to be "integrated." "We're just as much Americans as anybody else," we began saying. "What do you mean I can't send my child to this school? What do you mean we're not allowed to try on a hat at a downtown store? Is there something different about black hair? Do you think we have bugs in it or something? You want our business, don't you?"

It was the same message sent by Adam Clayton Powell's campaign in Harlem a decade earlier. His motto was: "Don't buy where you can't work." Black consumers were going into the stores, but were prohibited from trying on a dress or a hat. Adding insult to injury, the same store that accepted our money wouldn't accept our job applications.

That may explain why someone like Arnette Evans was so well respected in our community—there was nothing phony or deceitful about him. His message to parents was clear: "Your kids are just as talented as the white kids, and through discipline and hard work we can prove it." With Arnette, people knew that they were getting everything they bargained for—and sometimes even more.

During my ten years of service in Congress, I constantly drew from the lessons of Arnette Evans. The lessons of being resilient and persistent, and pushing the boundaries of my perceived limitations, gave me an advantage in overcoming new obstacles. Because of him, I was equipped to deal with the tumult of change and challenge and adversity. Sometimes I was amazed at how many of my colleagues were not.

I will never forget my astonishment at the paralysis that gripped the Democratic Party after losing control of the House and Senate in the elections of 1994. For weeks afterward, many of my colleagues were still in denial, and they had a vacant look in their eyes. It was the kind I remember seeing on the streets when a gang fight would break out. You think you're fighting only three or four opponents, then all of a sudden another ten come racing from around the corner with pipes and bats and blades. You look to see who's covering your back, and instead you see surrender and looks of disbelief in your partners' eyes.

The Democratic leadership was walking around in a daze, wearing the same kind of stunned and already-beaten expression after the elections. I was so dismayed by this display of hopelessness that I decided to run for the party leadership with conservatives Charlie Stenholm and Charlie Rose.

Of course, my colleagues said I couldn't win, and tried to convince me not to run, while others criticized me for challenging the leadership. I knew I couldn't win. But winning wasn't the point I was trying to make in this case. My ultimate goal was to get the Democratic leadership off its collective backside, and to move forward aggressively and stop retreating.

For those of us who were black and Hispanic members, being in the minority was par for the course. In the eyes of many that was all we'd ever been. As skilled warhorses accustomed to operating from that position, we knew how to seize the time and use whatever leverage was available. The feeling within the Congressional Black and Hispanic Caucuses was that we'd simply been dealt a new hand of cards and thus had to find a new way to win. So it was very difficult for me to comprehend the shock and denial that was now consuming the party that I loved.

I knew I had no time for sulking because, come January 4, 1995, everything we'd earned, protected, and fought so hard for was going to come under attack by a Republican-dominated Congress. And, in most instances, we wouldn't have enough votes to stop them.

What we did have, however, was our ability to stay in the game. That meant defining and redefining the real issues for the people, and it meant refusing to accept everything the new majority put forth. After redefining the issues, our next move would have to be attack and fight like hell. We had to conduct legislative guerrilla warfare. It meant challenging the Republicans at every little turn, and getting up in their faces if necessary.

I figured that, if nothing else, we could engage in a campaign of tenacity and intimidation. Having enjoyed being in the majority for so long, perhaps we Democrats had forgotten how. Here was our chance to perfect the drill.

Years before, I learned how to deal with real intimidation and challenge by merely hanging out with my buddy Gary. There was never a day when our relationship wasn't tested. My friendship with Gary created more trouble than my mother could have ever imagined. His slightly pudgy frame combined with his thick mustache made Gary look a few years older than the other boys our age. Even at the age of fourteen, Gary knew how to smoke a cigarette and could chug down wine like a grown-up. He shot dice like a seasoned hustler and walked the streets with a rhythmic dip. Without a doubt, I'd never met anyone in my life quite like Gary and I never would again. Hanging around together led to an acceptance among our peers because of our steadfast loyalty to each other.

What I find most curious is that my mother actually liked Gary and let us hang out together. Gary was sort of the Eddie Haskell of *Leave It to Beaver* of his day. In front of my mother, he affected the exceptional manners, polish, and intelligence that were every parent's dream. He'd come over to my house with his choirboy behavior. Everything was "How are you today, Miss Mary?" "No, ma'am." "Yes, ma'am." "Thank you, ma'am." But as soon as we were out of the house, Gary became the wild friend he really was, and I was right there with him.

The first time I got drunk, it was with Gary, and what a terrible feeling it was. We'd convinced some older guy to go into the store and cop a fifth of Richard's Wild Irish Rose. We had seen the older guys sipping it while keeping the bag wrapped around the bottle. Gary and I started out drinking that night in an alley, but preceded our activity with a tradition. Before ever taking a drink, the older guys would start with libations, a moment of remembrance for those who had fallen. Although an African tradition, it had been resurrected in the heart of the ghetto. Libations now were not for great comrades but rather for cats we knew in jail. Gary would pour some of the wine on the ground and say, "This is for Chico," or "This is for June Bug," or "This is for Marty." All of whom were doing time.

It was the middle of July and it must have been ninety degrees, as we stood facing each other under the one lamppost that illuminated the alley. We sipped and waited, sipped and waited. Nothing happened. Soon after we gulped the liquor down, the heat and wine made for instant combustion. All of a sudden it started to hit me, first like a feather, then like a hammer. I remember looking at the row houses and watching them rotate, with one set of houses falling down and then another set coming down on top of them. Then the ground started to move.

I felt like I wanted to die in the heat that night. But God wouldn't let me off that easy. He wanted to make sure I lived through every second of that intoxicated nightmare. I tried to walk but kept falling over. I wanted to go home desperately but knew my mother would kill me, so I finally made it over to a basketball park and managed to lay myself out on a bench. With my head whirling like a spinning top, I leaned over and threw up before passing out.

I awoke a couple of hours later, still drunk, but with enough control over my limbs to make it home. One of the privileges of being the oldest child was that I'd been given a house key. I sneaked in shortly after midnight and collapsed on my bed. I begged God to help me through the night and out of this drunken stupor, and promised never to get this out of control again. I also begged him to find Gary and to scare the hell out of him.

"Hey, honey, hi ya doin' with your young self?"

"You look so cute today, real cute, baby."

I cannot recall the day or moment that I first became acquainted with the three ladies on McCulloh Street. Like many life-altering relationships, this one unfolded gradually, with them waving and speaking to me as I passed their home on the way to school. It's a secret I've kept so long that the details have become hazy even though the

memory has not, even though I was only fourteen years old
at the time.

What I most remember about these women was how beautiful they looked each morning sitting out on their white marble
stoop. They lived together in a regular row house, but they were
definitely not regular folks. I'd never seen such sexy women,
except in the girlie magazines that I could steal a peek at. The
old men who played checkers under the shade trees in Turners
Station would occasionally pull out one of them, before boasting
about the sexual escapades of their youth.

These women had skin brown and smooth as a Hershey bar,
and sex appeal that lit the whole street on fire. They wore long,
tight skirts that contoured with their long slender legs, and
blouses that ballooned at the shoulders and hung low at their
breasts. I loved the way they let their hair cascade onto their
backs and shoulders, and I was intoxicated by the sweet fra-
grance of their perfume. As I walked past their house each
morning on my way to school, I would occasionally catch a
glimpse of one of them looking out beyond the curtain of a half-
shaded window.

I noticed over time that they were extremely friendly, not
just to me but to almost everyone. They reserved their warmest
greetings, however, for men walking or driving past in cars
as the evening fell. Sometimes, they went so far as to step over
to the men, introduce themselves, and invite them inside
their house. This I found to be an unusually nice gesture, even
by the openly hospitable standards of Turners Station. They
didn't say much to the other kids heading to and from school,
but they took a liking to me and went out of their way to
be kind.

After a few months of pleasant hellos and waves, I felt comfortable enough with them to stop and talk in the afternoon on
my way home from school. They'd ask me how I was doing in
class, whether I was staying out of trouble, and tease me about
finding a girlfriend.

"You're such a nice young man," they'd always say as they
would hand me money to run an errand at the store for them. I
didn't know what they did for a living but they gave big tips and

loved to hug and squeeze me. "Come on, sweetheart, and give me a big kiss before you run home," they'd say.

Giving kisses to them didn't take much convincing. Far different from my godmother, Miz Katheryn, who always squeezed me so tight I thought I'd faint, these women simply leaned over and offered me a soft, sweet-smelling cheek. Gratefully, I accepted the honor.

It soon became a ritual for me to stop by on the way home from school to check up on them and to see how they were doing. While most adults I knew seemed only to tolerate kids, these ladies always welcomed me with open arms. It didn't matter that I was at least fifteen years their junior. They were clearly allowing me to become more familiar with them, but not more familiar with their lifestyle. Hanging out on the Strip with Mr. Charles, I'd begun feeling more mature by the day. Yet physically, with my rail-thin arms and legs, I still very much looked fourteen years old.

"Baby, if you were just twenty years older . . ." they would say. Concerned that I'd be late if I stayed too long in the morning, they'd invite me to come back by after school. "Hurry on, and c'mon back later," they'd say. "We'll need you to go to the store and pick us up a few things."

The moment the last school bell rang, I'd run the three blocks to get there. They'd hand me some money to go buy them things like cigarettes, napkins, magazines, and other small items. Any change was always mine to keep. It was the easiest way I had known yet to make a dollar.

Almost a year passed before they finally invited me into their house. Even then I was only allowed into the living room, where I would sit on a sofa and marvel. Before, I had been only as far as the vestibule, but once inside I was dazzled by the beautiful furnishings and dark velvet curtains. Lace doilies adorned the arms of the big cushy sofa, and small chandeliers hung from the ceiling. On the walls hung old black-and-white photographs in oval-shaped frames and on each end table were freshly cut flowers.

I remember being struck by how dark it was in there, the only light being the faint glow of the old-fashioned lamps made of stained glass. Long embroidered curtains trimmed with tassels kept out any sunlight. There were a couple of antique-looking chairs, and a small table in front of the sofa. I was impressed by how clean and elegant the room was. Sitting there in the company of these three gorgeous ladies I couldn't help but notice the silk and satin gowns they wore. God, these were real women, I thought, and here I was with them. Sipping my Kool-Aid and trying not to stare at their bodies, I would just sit there as they laughed and made small talk together.

One day, as usual, I showed up there after school expecting to run an errand. But two of the ladies greeted me at the door and told me there wasn't anything they needed from the store that day. Instead, they needed me to paint a room upstairs.

"You know how to paint, don't you, Pee Wee?"

"Of course," I said proudly. I was lying, but there was no way I was going to turn them down.

"Well, maybe you could come over Saturday and paint a room upstairs for us. Come on up and take a look at it and let me know what you think."

I followed slowly behind them as they walked up the stairs and through a narrow corridor. Part of me was thrilled that I was being trusted enough to enter another part of the house and the other part was scared to be moving so deeply into these dimly lit quarters. We entered the room almost together and I quickly noticed the walls were covered with flowery wallpaper.

"You want me to paint over this wallpaper?" I asked, puzzled.

"No," one of them said, smiling. "Just the trimming around the doors and floor."

As she feebly attempted to explain the job to me, I noticed the other one coming out of the other bedroom. I was breathless. She was wearing nothing but a negligée, her full naked breasts protruding through the sheer fabric. If I'd thought she was beautiful before, she was absolutely heavenly now. For a moment I stared, then was suddenly embarrassed. She came closer, leaned toward me, and unfastened the silk bow in the center of her chest that held the top together. When her breasts fell out in front of me, my eyes popped and I started to run. I felt myself turning away and one of them grabbed me.

"Ahhh, he's a little scared, but it's all right. C'mon over here."

I never feared that these women would hurt me in any way, but I was shocked that they went from consoling me with kisses to caressing my body. Before I knew it they had removed their clothes and mine as well. In an instant we had gone from standing by the door to being in bed together. All sorts of thoughts ran through my head, as my heart raced ahead of my breathing. First I was scared because I didn't know the first thing about how to have sex. Then I was happy because I was about to have sex. Then I was scared again, then happy again. For them, all that mattered was that I was curious and aroused. They took over from there.

We must have spent two hours in that room, lost in avalanches of satin sheets and pillowcases. What I thought I knew about sex from the things I had heard had all gone out the window now. This was what old men under the shade trees meant when they exclaimed, "Good-googa-mooga." Was that the way that I was going to describe these women long after they had passed? As we lay there quietly in the afterglow, a calmness seemed to engulf us. We were now one long knot of arms and torsos. And, although the mirror on the wall failed to glimpse us, the mirror on the ceiling did not. Looking up at it and the image it contained, I realized my innocence was lost, for mine was the sin of greed and theirs was the sin of lust. When they finally led me downstairs afterward, I felt older and wiser, yet perplexed. I knew that I had done something wrong, but I hardly felt ashamed. I glanced at the wallpaper as I walked downstairs by the wooden banister and smiled at the thought of painting over that floral design.

"Are you all right?" I heard one of the ladies asking as I found my way to the sofa. "You're going to keep this as our little secret, right, Pee Wee?"

"Oh, yes, ma'am, I wouldn't tell nobody," I replied.

I assured them that I was just fine, and I don't know that I've ever told a bigger lie.

I'll never forget how weak my knees felt when I got up off that sofa and tried to leave. I wondered how I would find the strength to make it home, but I finally did. When I walked into the house, my mother was waiting to greet me. I didn't tell her about how my day went like I usually did. Instead I headed straight upstairs to my room and closed the door behind me.

That's when the guilt started to set in, and this time it came down hard. I wanted desperately to reveal to someone what had happened, but I'd promised I wouldn't tell a soul. Even more troubling, from a purely male perspective I'd enjoyed what had happened to me, even though I knew I shouldn't have. Fourteen-year-old boys, I'd been taught, aren't supposed to have sex because we weren't responsible enough. But what did responsibility have to do with the fun I'd just had? It all seemed harmless enough to me. Those ladies of McCulloh Street simply liked me a lot and I liked them too. I decided again to keep it secret. It was nobody's business but my own. Not even Gary's.

After that first time, I think I began making a pest of myself. I could hardly concentrate in school, daydreaming over and over again about their wet kisses and grown-up bodies. For the next couple of months, I'd run right over there twice a week after classes and knock anxiously on the door. It was hit or miss. Sometimes they'd let me in for more fun, but most of the time they already had company.

They'd come downstairs in their nightgowns and lace and tell me, "C'mon back tomorrow."

"Yes, ma'am," I'd reply dejectedly, hoping to sneak a peek or smell a whiff of their perfume.

These three exciting women who had taught me how to do it were now preventing me from getting carried away by it.

One Monday morning on the way to school, I noticed they weren't sitting on the stoop as they always did. Walking up to the house, I realized too that the curtains were gone. I peered inside and to my disbelief the furniture was gone too, and the house was completely empty. My ladies had moved out, I thought, without even saying good-bye. My heart sank. I wanted to cry. I thought they were my friends. I couldn't believe that they would leave so abruptly, without even a good-bye kiss. They left no explanation, just far too many memories for a boy at the threshold of his manhood.

I never saw those women again and I would be much older

before I really understood what had gone on in their house and their lives. And every time I would glimpse a brothel or the face of a high-priced hooker strolling the streets, I couldn't avoid thinking of those ladies. I can't help but wonder whether they remember me as well as I remember them, or if the memory of that day in 1962 still haunts them as it does me.

Having my first sexual encounter at such a young age is not something I'm necessarily proud of. But any truthful recounting of my transition from the innocence of Turners Station to the fast track of West Baltimore must include it. For no matter how nice and friendly I considered them back then, the fact is that these women stole my innocence and a part of my heart for good measure.

At the time, it was easy to believe that my sexual initiation signaled my passage into manhood. Nothing could have been further from the truth. The next few years would prove me anything but a man.

4

DISTANT
THUNDER

*O*N a crisp autumn evening in 1962, four Marine Corps helicopters descended on Patterson Park, a few blocks from my home
in West Baltimore. I was in bed when I heard the choppers
whirring in the distance and I sat up immediately, my heart
pounding. The fact that helicopters were nearby was not, in itself,
a particularly special event to me. Back in Turners Station, during
family outings to Glenn L. Martin Airport, I had seen plenty of
helicopters. But I knew these were no ordinary choppers. Aboard
one of them was the President of the United States.

Like most Americans, I was familiar with the myth of
Camelot, superbly concocted by the media and acted with precision by the Kennedy First Family. My mother thought Jackie
Kennedy was a sharp-dressed lady and a nice person as well,
even though we hardly ever heard her say much of anything.
The children, John-John and Caroline, were cute kids and made
the President seem like a regular guy trying to juggle two roles,

one as the father of his young family and the other as the leader of our nation.

Mama followed Kennedy's presidency closely. She was proud when he gave his speech at the Berlin Wall, telling the people in German: "Ich bin ein Berliner." And we were glued to our radios that same fall of 1962 when he called the Russians' bluff in Cuba during the missile crisis. Mama said we came within a breath of seeing the world blown up with atom bombs. There was a big sigh of relief when the news came that the Russians had pulled out their missiles and Kennedy announced that they had backed down.

The year 1962 was busy for Kennedy on the home front as well. Blacks across the country watched to see what he would do when Mississippi governor Ross Barnett vowed that the "nigra" James Meredith would never be allowed to attend the University of Mississippi. Mama, like most of her friends, wondered if JFK would show some of the same backbone with the Dixiecrat as he had with Khrushchev. The President locked up the black vote when he sent twelve thousand federal marshals to escort Meredith to register for classes on the Oxford, Mississippi, campus of Ole Miss. The local whites rioted before federal troops were sent to restore order.

For all these reasons, I was determined to be on hand to witness the President's speech. All week, the streets of West Baltimore had been abuzz with talk that President John F. Kennedy was to deliver a speech at a rally at the Fifth Regiment Armory. Of course, I had never seen a president, nor had I ever met anyone who had. Quite frankly, I had trouble believing that Kennedy, or any other world leader for that matter, was going to appear at that old armory twelve blocks from my house. The very notion seemed ridiculous. In my young mind, a president was like Jesus Christ: you heard about him all the time, but nobody actually saw him in the flesh. Still, I had decided that if the President did show up at the armory, I'd be on hand to witness it.

That Thursday evening, the eleventh of October, I went through my usual bedtime ritual, kissing my mother goodnight after dinner and heading upstairs to my bedroom.

With the faint sound of descending choppers as my cue, I eased myself out of bed and quickly got dressed. Opening the bedroom window, I climbed outside and slid down a pole that ran along the back of our house. To avoid being spotted by neighbors, I cut through back alleys as I made my way toward the armory.

I will never forget the spectacle surrounding the place. It was like nothing I'd ever seen before. Thousands of people swarmed the streets as the presidential motorcade, which had left Patterson Park, moved slowly through the jostling crowds. People waved placards with friendly messages like "Welcome to Baltimore, Mr. President" and "Go Democrats!" Although I recall one that gave me a chill. The placard read: "Impeach President Kennedy. Beware Traitors. Whites will win."

Along the route, people rushed out of bars, cheering the President's arrival and thrusting mugs of beer in the air. I pushed my way through the crowd to keep up with the motorcade, marveling at the endless stream of police cars and long sleek limousines, some sporting government seals, as I followed the route down Eastern Avenue, up Washington Street, to North Avenue, to Howard Street, and then down Howard toward the old armory.

Amid the din of a marching drum and bugle corps, I overheard voices in the crowd saying that way up ahead, beyond our sight, President Kennedy was cruising in a blue Lincoln Continental convertible. Maryland governor John Tawes was at his side.

The Fifth Regiment Armory is a huge gray brick structure, some two blocks wide and four blocks deep. One advantage of being a small black kid was that I could slice my way into the old building undeterred, drawing little more than a curious glance from the sea of white faces around me. Since I was dressed in blue jeans, sneakers, and a T-shirt, they probably assumed I was the child of hired help. That was fine by me because I strolled right into the armory without a ticket. I knew sitting in a seat on the main floor would be pressing my luck, so I made my way up to the top tier and perched on the aisle steps.

As I waited for the President to take the stage below, I gazed at the crowd, wondering why no black people were there. Mine seemed the only black face in a crowd of thousands. My eyes swept the armory, hoping to spot at least one black face, but row upon row, all the faces I saw were those of lily-white men in dark suits and hats, many of them puffing cigars. A couple of men noticed me staring at them, but they just looked right through me and kept on talking and laughing. It was clear that I meant nothing to them.

One man behind me spoke of a woman who'd been injured by a temporary fence that had been blown through the air by a helicopter's windstream. Another talked of a man who'd been arrested earlier that day after telephoning the local newspaper and threatening to kill the President. I couldn't believe that anyone would want to kill the President and wondered whether the man was lying.

After a few short speeches by various men with important government titles, an expectant hush swept across the armory, followed by the brassy melodies of an orchestra filling the air with Baltimore's patriotic song, "The Fighting First." The crowd went wild, roaring to the music as red, white, and blue balloons floated down from the rafters.

Then I saw him, President John F. Kennedy. He was walking out onto the stage, youthful and handsome in a dark suit, waving at the cheering crowd. I sat there awestruck as Kennedy stood behind the podium, smiling at the thousands of people who had come to see him. Flanking Kennedy were three other men, much older than he, beaming in the pandemonium that erupted over and over again, each time more deafening than before. The President stood there graciously and waited for the applause to fade.

"Never have so many Democratic candidates said so much in so little time—and I will join them," the President began. "I'm delighted to come back here to Baltimore. As your distinguished governor said, this state helped nominate me for the office of the presidency . . ."

The President spoke for a few thrilling minutes, the smooth pitch of his voice reverberating through the dozens of loudspeakers across the armory. Long, thunderous applause interrupted him several times, but it didn't bother me a bit. I'd never seen that kind of adoration expressed for anyone, and before I knew it I was joining the ovations. Even though I don't recall much of what Kennedy said in that speech, I remember never wanting that moment to end. I could have sat there all night just letting the sight and sounds of this great event wash over me.

While I was inspired by the sight of President Kennedy, I also recall feeling somewhat like an interloper, certain that a poor black kid like me had no place in that armory, or in John F. Kennedy's world of politics and power. Not a single black person I knew was fortunate enough to have had a ticket to see the President that night. The only reason I was there was because I'd sneaked in.

Nevertheless, being there to see the President meant a great deal to me. I doubt there was a soul in that rally who wanted to be there more than I did, or who was as giddy and excited over Kennedy's vision of hope and progress as I was. Sure, I was barely fourteen years old, but I understood that a president has the power to make life better for people of all colors and creeds. People like my hardworking mother, who was abandoned with four children, and who often didn't earn enough money to pay the electric bill.

Yet in all my enthusiasm for the President, I couldn't shake my sense of alienation. I had a deep sense that all my cheering and foot-stomping that wonderful night in the armory was going unheard, or was less welcomed than the applause of the whites around me.

Still, the experience stayed with me for years. I went home that night, shinnied back up the pipe, crawled through the window, and climbed quietly into bed. With my sisters sound asleep, I lay awake, still exhilarated by the magic inside the armory. Whenever the subject of politics had come up in my classes at school, I'd always yawned. After all, politics was boring adult stuff. But after that stirring experience, I knew I'd been wrong. Politics was not boring. But it certainly was white and exclusive.

I was so excited over having seen President Kennedy that the following morning I risked being punished by telling my mother the whole story—from how I had sneaked out of the house all the way to seeing the President up close and in person. Her reaction surprised me.

"Is that so?" she said with a grin. "So tell me, how was it? It must have been a real sight."

"You mean, I'm not in trouble?"

"No, but you should be for not inviting your mother to go along with you."

My mother had begun working late into the evening in order to make ends meet. Often, she turned to my grandmother to look after me and my sisters. Besides my mother, Viola Gray Johnson was the only other adult I trusted to truly love me. I also respected her a great deal. Even though my grandmother was Clifton's mother, she was a sweet, affectionate woman; she was a tough, no-nonsense disciplinarian as well. A proud, fastidious lady, my grandmother had an elegant air about her. She dressed conservatively, always wearing a knee-length skirt and a simple blouse and hat. She spoke in crisp, deliberate sentences and in her presence insisted that I do the same. "Speaking proper English," she'd always say, "is a sign of intelligence."

For some forty years, she'd earned a menial wage working in the housekeeping department of South Baltimore General Hospital ironing white uniforms, but nothing about her or the way she lived reflected her meager earnings. Her house was immaculate, from the doily-covered living room chairs to the spotless bathrooms to the white marble front steps. My quiet-natured Grandfather Joe, a retired World War I army veteran, scrubbed them daily with Ajax and ammonia.

My grandmother's views on raising a boy differed somewhat from my mother's. As long as I abided by my eight o'clock week-night curfew, my mother's policy was laissez-faire. She trusted me with my own house key, and occasionally allowed me to attend parties—so long as the party was chaperoned by an adult.

I went to those parties as much for the music as to flirt with the girls. My mother was a great music lover, so I had grown up spending hours listening to Ella Fitzgerald and Billy Eckstine singing on those clunky 78 rpm records. By the time she let me go to house parties, the smaller 45s were in and the latest hits by Baby Washington and Sam Cooke were stacked high against the turntable.

I wasn't a great dancer at first, but I was good enough to lure the pretty girls like Peggy Goodwin out on the floor. I had a serious crush on Peggy. But I knew a lot of other guys did, too. I'd spend the whole party monopolizing her time, asking her to dance over and over again.

Reginald Bowman was by far the best dancer in our bunch. Just a fleeting look at the smooth, graceful motions of Reggie's dark, lithe body was enough to wipe out any illusion that I was half as smooth as he was.

Unlike my mother, my grandmother didn't approve of my going to house parties—or anywhere else remotely connected to the streets. To her, such freedom only promised trouble for a boy my age. She made it clear that if I had been her son, she wouldn't have let me out of her sight. Whenever my sisters and I were sent to Grandmother's for a weekend, our play was limited to the house and front stoop. I balked at her restrictions, often pleading with my mother to persuade my grandmother to let me loose. It never worked, though. "Pee Wee doesn't need to get mixed up with these bad boys around here," she'd tell my mother. "He'll only wind up doing something he has no business doing."

Over time, I invariably proved my grandmother correct.

One incident involved the Pottashes, who lived above their grocery store across the street from my house. The Pottashes were good people and had always been kind to my family. My mother's relationship with David and his wife, Inga, had become extremely close. They extended credit to her when times were tight and let me earn money doing stock work and sweeping the floor. Sammy, their son, had become one of my friends.

Around the neighborhood, everyone knew Mr. Pottash loved his car. He pampered that old blue Plymouth, laboring in the hot sun to keep its body waxed and its chrome fenders gleaming. While the car may not have been a late model, it stood out among all the other dusty, dented vehicles on our street. Like a prize trophy, Mr. Pottash's immaculate car was always parked directly in front of his grocery store on Division Street—to be admired but certainly not touched.

It was after dark, past nine or so, and the air was hot and muggy that July night. Unless your house had air conditioning, and none that I recall did, nobody wanted to be cooped up inside because it only made you tired and grumpy. At least outside you could catch an occasional breeze, if only from a passing car. So there were a lot of folks outside that night. The younger ones stayed close to the steps, where their parents could watch over them, and everyone else just wandered about. I was hanging out with Gary and a few guys from the neighborhood. We were standing beneath a street lamp beside that lustrous blue Plymouth.

The Pottashes, having just closed the store for the evening, were taking the day's inventory. The light still glowed inside beyond the grates that went up at night. That's when Jeffrey dared Gary to toss a match inside the half-open window of Mr. Pottash's car. Gary said, "Gimme a match," but I assumed he was bluffing. Along the block, there were just too many adults sitting out to pull such a stunt.

Still, I knew Gary was one of those people you don't dare to do something. He thrived on such a challenge, no matter what the consequences. It was a quality that I detested, feared, and yet admired about him. He had earned a reputation as "crazy," which in my neighborhood was a rare and honorable distinction. Most of us only feigned fearlessness, but true "crazy" folks like Gary had no boundaries—there was no distance between his impulses and his actions.

Usually I served as Gary's voice of reason. I was among the few people who could talk him out of senseless dares such as this one. But tonight, I could tell that Jeffrey's prodding had triggered my friend.

"You ain't nothin' but a pussy," Jeffrey said. "Nigga, you know that man will come out here and whup your ass if you do it."

"Don't do it, man," I told Gary. "It ain't worth it. Mr. Pottash is all right."

But it was too late. Gary's mind was made up, and he was way past listening to my pleas. "Ain't nobody kicking my ass," he announced, his face tight with defiance.

He pulled a pack of matches out of his pants pocket, struck one, and threw it toward the window—and missed.

Few people would ever understand why Gary had suddenly become so crazy. Why he had allowed what seemed to be good-natured ribbing to test him in such a way. Before moving to the west side I would have asked myself the same question. But after two years of living there, I'd come to understand, even admire, Gary's willingness to flirt with danger.

On the streets, nothing was more important than building and preserving respect among your peers. Gary, having been born and raised there, knew this instinctively. He was a master at making sure nobody crossed that fine line between ribbing and disrespect. When Jeffrey taunted him about getting an ass-kicking, he'd crossed that line—at least in Gary's mind. In my neighborhood, Gary won respect by being the champion at doing the unthinkable, and shocking those who believed they were beyond being shocked.

"Don't do it," I pleaded again. "Mr. Pottash . . ."

It was too late. Gary moved toward the partly open driver's side window. I grabbed his arm, trying to pull him away. But he fought me off and threw the second match past the window and into the car. We stood with blank expressions as the tiny flame caught a piece of paper and slowly burned into the clear vinyl seat.

Within ten minutes the fire was smoldering on the big vinyl seats in the front and back, with black smoke curling out the windows and wrapping around the blackening roof. Soon a blaze erupted, brightening the night sky. The flames roared, crackled, and licked hotly at the stunned faces of onlookers. The scene had captured the attention of people sitting in their doorways and looking out their windows. As they began moving in our direction, I panicked. Fearing the car might explode, or even worse, that my mother might come outside and catch me, I barked, "Let's get out of here!" Gary and I bolted toward the alley. As we turned the corner, I saw Mr. Pottash run out of the store to watch helplessly as fire and smoke engulfed his beloved Plymouth.

We ran so fast that within minutes we were standing on a corner half a mile away, our bodies hunched over as we caught our breath. Gary recovered first and broke out into nervous laughter. My heart was beating too fast and my mind whirling with too much confusion to join him.

We, or rather Gary, had burned Mr. Pottash's car, and although I did not want to admit it to Gary, I was afraid of the consequences. I stood there quietly, anticipating the high-pitched wail of sirens I knew would soon fill the night air. I imagined that by now a crowd of people were huddled around the blackened, burned-out car, consoling a dejected Mr. Pottash, as they waited for the police to arrive.

"What's the matter, Pee Wee?" Gary asked. "You all right?"

"Yeah, I'm fine," I lied.

I wanted to go home, but I knew there was no way I could return to Division Street, at least not anytime soon. For the rest of the night, Gary and I would have to walk the darkened west side streets.

It took Gary no time before he was himself again, talkative and ebullient. I didn't say much, mostly worrying about whether my mother had gotten the news yet and what kind of trouble I'd be in once she found out.

My mother learned of my involvement at about 4:30 A.M., when the police knocked on the door with a warrant for my arrest. I was in bed, having sneaked in a couple of hours before, when she came rushing into my room and yanked me up. She was hysterical.

"Did you burn the Pottashes' car?" she screamed. When I didn't answer quickly enough, she snatched me like she had never snatched me before.

Oddly, I didn't resist because I knew I was guilty, even though I hadn't directly performed the act. It was guilt that rendered me passive, made me accept the inevitable punishment. The Pottashes had always been kind to me. I was haunted by that fleeting image of a crestfallen Dave Pottash, watching his car being swallowed in flames.

"How could you do this to them," my mother yelled at me after beating me with a belt strap.

I couldn't answer. It wasn't in me to squeal on my friends, so I took the beating silently. Angrily, she led me down the stairs before her and watched with a mournful look as a policeman put me in handcuffs and into a waiting patrol car.

There were tears in my mother's eyes that night. This was not the future she had envisioned for me. A jailbird. The officer roughly pushed the rest of my body into the car, mumbling, "Get in there, tough guy." Gary was already handcuffed in the backseat with that damn silly grin on his face. I was so angry at Gary I would have slugged him if my hands were free.

"We in trouble now," he said, looking almost proud.

"Shut up," I retorted.

"You mad at me, man?" Gary asked, like he didn't know what he had done.

"What the hell do you think?"

Through the squad car window, I noticed David and Inga Pottash in their nightclothes, standing on the steps and watching us being driven away to the precinct house. The sadness on their bewildered faces was a sight that I will never forget.

In the worst kind of way, it reminded me of how David Pottash would look when he remembered out loud the Holocaust. It was 1963, and he and Inga had emigrated to the United States in the previous decade. I would notice how the other Jewish men would come to visit with them in their apartment over the store, and how they would get that same look on their faces when they told stories about the past. Some of them had numbers tattooed on their forearms and others had history etched in their faces.

David Pottash was a proud and private man. He and Inga worked hard to provide for Samuel and his sister, Hannah, so much so that all they seemed to do was work. Why he took me into the privacy of his people's history one day is still a mystery to me. Sammy and Hannah had heard the history many times but they knew clearly that I had not.

When Mr. Pottash began to tell me about the Jewish people and their history of enslavement and persecution, he began by holding the Torah. He started with the Exodus over three thousand years ago and ended with the Holocaust and Auschwitz.

"Never again," he would shout as he spoke of the horror of the death camps, his English broken and heavily accented. For hours I would listen in anguish because I could see that it pained him to share such recent history with his children. Both his and Mrs. Pottash's eyes would well up with tears as they spoke of America and the new life they had. Here things would be different, they said, as they took me into their family.

And now here they were standing outside their store in night-clothes in front of the smoldering ruins of their car. From the side window of the patrol car my eyes locked with theirs in sadness and in disbelief—as the police car sped hurriedly away.

At the precinct, I watched officers bring in several prisoners, black and handcuffed like us. They were on their way to be processed and fingerprinted. The officers on duty talked to them like dirt, cursing and ordering them around. This was not what I wanted to happen to me, being thrown in jail for something I didn't do. I didn't like being locked up, confined like an animal, without any freedom or privacy. This would be the first of thirteen such run-ins with the law and the last time I bothered to care.

Gary and I eventually ended up going to juvenile court over the matter. My mother, worried that I'd get sent to Sheltonham, the juvenile equivalent of the state penitentiary, made me beg for the Pottashes' forgiveness. She brought a priest from church and Arnette Evans as character witnesses before Judge Breckenridge.

All the kids in the neighborhood had heard about Judge Breckenridge, a notorious scrooge of a white man, who was known not only for the stiff sentences he regularly dished out, but also for the partial paralysis of his upper body that resulted in a hideous hunchback posture.

Because it was my first run-in with the law, I got off with a mere reprimand, consisting of a stiff warning and a slap on the wrist.

"But if you wind up back in here," Judge Breckenridge warned me in that low rumble of a voice, "I'm going to lock you up for a long, long time." From the look in his lifeless blue eyes, I knew in my heart that he meant it.

I have every reason to believe that Judge Breckenridge was on the verge of letting Gary off easy, too. Like me, this was his first offense, and he was a passing student at school. But Gary, who had been gawking at Judge Breckenridge's afflicted arm, sabotaged any goodwill by snickering during the proceedings and chewing loudly on his gum. Gary got two years' probation and an even bigger warning. The judge said if he even missed a report date with his probation officer he was going to go to jail.

The Pottashes' car was insured, and fortunately they were able to buy another one. After that incident they never allowed Gary back in their store again.

Once that incident was over, it was over for me. I was too steeped in my own increasingly reckless adolescence to change my ways—too busy maintaining my rep, swooning girls, and staying on my mother's good side to spend time thinking about the past. I was completely consumed with my present. Although I felt some remorse about the Pottashes, I rationalized that no one was irreversibly hurt. Compared to what was going down in the streets, this, I concluded, was light stuff.

My brush with the law not only embarrassed my mother with her Jewish friends across the street, it also frightened her. Because she was working more hours to keep food on the table, she didn't have time to constantly look after me. Yet it was becoming clear that I needed more supervision, that the transition from Turners Station was affecting me more than she had wanted to believe. She had always treated me as though I were mature beyond my years. Yet in many ways, I was proving to be merely a lost manchild.

I can't really explain what was happening to me, why I started running wild. Some of my rebellion almost certainly had to do with simply being a teenager, and that strange hormonal and psychological shift that goes with it.

But I also believe I desperately wanted to prove to my new city friends that even though I was from what they considered the country, I could more than handle myself—that I could fight, talk stuff, and hang out with the best of them, and even better. It didn't matter that my performance at school was slipping, or that Mama was breathing down my neck harder than ever. The most important thing was that I was making a name for myself, in the streets that would soon consume me. I knew those streets were full of life, but they were full of death, too. I never saw a man killed until I was fifteen years old, and I knew I never wanted to see it again.

I always thought Marshall Braxton and his brother Louie were pretty tight. Whenever Gary and I were hanging out, we'd always run into the two of them and they would be laughing and talking stuff to each other. From far away, they even looked about the same—tall, broad-shouldered, with bushy afros and jet-black complexions. They were a couple of years older than I, and pretty tight with the gang in the neighborhood.

Sometimes Gary and I would stop when we saw them smoking a joint or downing a fifth of Thunderbird. They would talk stuff about who got paid big in what crap game, what chicks were sleeping with what guys, who got their asses kicked over what beef.

But on this day, I was coming up Division when I saw Marshall yelling and pointing his finger in Louie's face. They were standing in front of Hankin's liquor store and everybody was crowded around and watching. I ran up to see what was going down, and I could tell right off it was serious. I had never seen Marshall go off like he did that day.

"Gimme my goddamn money right now, muthafucka!" Marshall was shouting at the top of his lungs. "Nobody's gonna smoke my money up but me."

While Marshall was having a total meltdown, Louie barely seemed to notice. He was high, red-eyed, and delirious.

"Nigga, you gon' get your money back," Louie slurred. "You act like five dollars is a lot of money. That ain't shit."

"Muthafucka, you said you needed bus fare to look for a job," Marshall went on. "Why you gotta lie to me, man?"

" 'Cause it ain't none of your business what I need the money for," Louie shot back. "You ain't my muthafuckin' father, bitch."

That remark made everybody chuckle. That's when Marshall swung on Louie and cracked him across the jaw. Louie went down on the concrete and Marshall was all over him, kicking, whaling on him like a madman, with hard blows. Louie's blood was gushing all over Marshall's black fists.

"You played me for a fool, muthafucka! You don't play me!"

Louie struggled to get up, but Marshall overpowered him and was on his back, with his forearms pulling against Louie's throat. Louie was gasping for air as he struggled to break free.

"Lemme . . . go," he said, with his eyes bulging and blood running out of his mouth.

"You lied to me like I was a bitch!" Marshall yelled, tightening his grip around his brother's throat. "I'll show you who the bitch is!"

By now, people were getting scared. Louie was choking to death. His face was flushed bright red, and his eyes were bulging more as though they were going to pop out of his head. He needed air bad.

"Man, you're gonna kill 'im," somebody called from the crowd. "Ease up, man!"

But Marshall had already crossed over the edge. That edge where fury and insanity meet. I could see in his eyes he was no longer fighting his brother—he was gripped by the frenzy of death. He'd gone too far now to turn back or even find his way. Locking his forearms tighter and tighter around his brother's neck, Marshall's body convulsed as he crushed Louie's windpipe. When I saw Louie's arms flailing, I ran up to Marshall and tried to pull him off.

"That's enough, man!" I yelled. "Ease up! Let him go!"

But I was too late. As I grabbed Marshall to pull him off, he loosened his grip on Louie, letting him drop limply onto the concrete. A woman in the crowd cried hysterically as she got down on her knees and put her head against Louie's chest. All of us who stood there were frozen with shock. Louie was dead, and we all instinctively knew that. He lay alone on a street corner with a circle of faces looking down on him. His head jerked quickly in one last muscular reflex as the blood that trickled out of his mouth formed a pool in which his face rested. I had never seen a man killed before. I felt sick and weak and hot and cold all at once. I looked intently at the stillness now in Louie's face and watched his eyes, glazed and wide open.

Marshall Braxton had fled the scene long before the paramedics arrived. Louie's body had gone cold by then. After they placed him inside their ambulance and drove away, those left on the corner began to disperse. A light rain began to fall now on Hankin's Corner. Wet from earlier perspiration and the new falling mist, I turned and left by way of a nearby alley. Walking alone and looking straight ahead, I was expressionless as I thought of what I had seen. The only thing worse, I thought, was to have been Louie. The passing of time would soon teach me that the only thing worse was to have been Marshall.

The courts ruled later that the death was accidental manslaughter and that there was no intent. Marshall Braxton was released, though his soul was not. From time to time over the next few years I would run into him on the street. He was never the same person after choking his brother to death. Neither was I after watching him do it.

If there was one saving grace that kept me from sinking as low as many of the cats on the corner, it was my steady commitment to the Falcon Drum and Bugle Corps and the desire to kick Mr. Evans's ass. For fifteen months, we drilled under the stern guidance of his majesty, holding practice four nights a week and once on the weekend. During that time, Evans organized us into a drum corps, a bugle corps, a drill team, and a color guard. He taught us how to march in lockstep with perfect posture, timing, and precision.

Arnette Evans also single-handedly taught each of us to play an instrument, from xylophones to drums, and we were taught music by ear. I learned to play the French horn. We held bake sales, car washes, and everything else to raise money for more instruments and, later, for more uniforms.

Even though we worked hard to perfect our skills, we wondered aloud whether the day would ever come when we'd compete or whether we were wasting our time on a pipe dream. Arnette, however, didn't indulge defeatism. "If you can't believe and trust in yourself and each other to make this happen," he'd yell, "then please excuse yourself. We don't need jackasses like you polluting our vision! If you can't see your fuckin' self as the best, then goddammit, you never will be!"

After calming down, he'd tell us to keep our heads high, and that soon we'd have enough money to buy not only instruments but also uniforms that would make us all proud.

Even while I dodged the danger of the streets with one foot, my other foot was still marching on through the arduous drilling of the Falcon Drum and Bugle Corps. No one was more surprised than cats like Gary when one bright spring morning in 1962, the Falcons went marching down Division Street. Mr. Evans's vision of creating Baltimore's newest and sharpest drum and bugle corps was finally realized.

It was a glorious day. Everything he'd prophesied had come true. A little over a year after my mother enlisted me, we had mushroomed from a ragtag group of twenty kids rehearsing in a tiny, dank basement on Etting Street into a well-organized unit of 150 members filling the second floor of an abandoned warehouse.

The day before we were to march publicly for the first time, Mr. Evans handed out our uniforms. They were even snazzier than we'd ever imagined. Mexican-inspired, our hats were black with a wide, flat brim, decorated with a red satin band. We wore baggy red silk shirts with wide collars, and balloon sleeves that buttoned at the wrists. At the waist was a cummerbund with a sash that dangled alongside the blue tuxedo pants, which were vented and bell-bottomed to expose an inlay of red silk.

It was a moment of great joy and pride for the entire community. As we stood in straight formations, preparing to step our way out of the old warehouse on Lawrence Street, we began playing "Moon River" to an uptempo marching beat. We could hear cheering erupting from the crowded streets below. Many people in the neighborhood had donated to our cause, and as we came strutting purposefully into their sight in our dazzling new uniforms and playing our instruments, their mouths nearly dropped open in amazement. With my shoulders squared and cheeks swelled with air, I blew my French horn with passion and fury as I marched in the middle of the procession amid some thirty other horns.

"Pee Wee! Pee Wee!" Recognizing the voice instantly as my mother's, I gave her and my sisters a dignified glance and a happy wink and kept on strutting.

From the looks on people's faces in the crowd, I could see that we were impressive, that they'd never witnessed anything quite like this. Of course, back then marching bands and parades were a big deal. However, they were accustomed to watching white drum and bugle corps and black groups like the Elks, Masons, and Daughters of the Eastern Star. But we were younger, more vibrant, and different. We had a sense of flair they couldn't match, and we were more disciplined. We high-stepped, swaggered, fanned out in formations that opened and closed with razor-sharp precision. Mr. Evans had worked hard to get us to this point, cursing, screaming, and cajoling. But we had endured the tirades, and now we knew it had all been worth it. As we marched on that day, playing tunes like "Lady of Spain" and Sam Cooke's "Cupid," not one of us missed a note, beat, or step.

The Falcon Drum and Bugle Corps went on from that day to win a ton of awards. We also earned the respect and admiration of our white rivals, who had never seen a black group like us. Sure, we had the sense of style and rhythm expected of black people, but we also had the precision, discipline, and focus that are paramount in competing.

Over the next three years we traveled by bus throughout Maryland, Delaware, Pennsylvania, Virginia, and New Jersey. To this day, you can walk through my old neighborhood and find people who remember the Falcons. There wasn't one of us who didn't appreciate how the leadership of one passionate and focused man had lifted us above the limited possibilities we saw for ourselves.

I'll never forget the pride in Arnette Evans's face when we won a regional competition in McSherrystown, Pennsylvania. The Falcons were the only black team competing in the huge event, and we stole the show that afternoon before a crowd of hundreds. During the weeks prior, we had practiced so hard that our performance was flawless. We marched as one, and played our instruments with a clarity that our rivals listened to in awe.

During the awards ceremony, Arnette swaggered out onto the field and accepted our first-place trophy. He wore a grin so wide we all chuckled, wondering aloud whether this was the same SOB who had made us ride several hours on the bus to McSherrystown in absolute silence. Now, with his eyes bright as he embraced his assistant, Mr. McKnight, Evans assembled us all at the big yellow school bus and looked out approvingly at his young champions.

"You know, it hurts the shit out of me to say this," he said, smiling. "But I'm really proud of all of you. Today, you showed what can be achieved when you put your minds and hearts toward winning, toward believing in yourself and not letting others define what you can or cannot do.

"You came here and showed these folks what you're made of. You showed them that pride, discipline, and order exist in the Negro community just like in white ones. You have proved that a person can do anything he wants in life if he's got the heart and the perseverance to outlast those who doubt them. These folks were not expecting us to go home with this trophy today. They thought they were gonna kick our little asses back to Baltimore. I hoped you would prove them wrong, that you would show them that the Falcons don't settle for second best. And goddammit, that's exactly what you did. Ain't that right?" he barked.

"Yes, sir!" we all shouted.

"What do we do?" Evans barked again.

"We kick ass!" we chanted back.

"And when they count us out, what do we do?"

"We rise!"

"So we can what?"

"Win!"

"I can't hear you!" he shouted.

"Win!"

"You said it!"

Generally, after competition, the Corps simply piled on the bus with sandwiches and card games for the ride back to Baltimore. But that afternoon, as a reward for our performance, Arnette Evans surprised us all by allowing us to hang out at a nearby county fair. Half-afraid he might change his mind, we sprinted away and fanned out across the grassy field. We had a ball that day, eating hot dogs, drinking soda, and riding a towering Ferris wheel until we were ready to drop from exhaustion. The white people of McSherrystown didn't seem to mind us at all. When we returned to the bus hours later, Arnette Evans was chomping on half a cigar and peacefully sipping a beer.

"All right, champs," he said quietly. "It's time for us to take the prize on home where it belongs."

As I grew older, I was becoming increasingly aware of world events unfolding around me. So much was going on during that fateful year of 1963. The newspapers heralded the fact that Russia had sent the first woman into space, Valentina Tereshkova. Everywhere I turned, there was something being said or written about the Beatles, the mop-top group from England. But while the white kids of the day were possessed with Beatlemania, we wanted generous helpings of the Motown sound.

On a morning in August of 1963, I awoke to the sound of my mother praying quietly in her bedroom. I went to sit beside her, as I often did when she would talk to God. When she had finished and after saying Amen, she told me that thousands of people, black and white alike, were going to Washington, D.C., that afternoon to hold a demonstration against the government for its terrible treatment of black people. She wanted very much for us to be there. Talk of the march had dominated the community as well as much of the media for some time. But she was flat broke, and couldn't afford the bus fare for herself and four kids.

"It's all right, Mom," I said consolingly. "Maybe we can go some other time."

"No, Pee," she said, shaking her head and holding her rosary. "This won't happen again. This country won't ever experience anything like what's going to happen today."

It didn't take long for me to understand why Mama wanted to march with the crowd. Even as a child, I had begun to realize there were forces much greater than she, my teachers, coaches, or friends, and that these forces influenced the way my family and others like us lived.

My eyes had been gradually opening to the fact that many people in Turners Station and on Division Street lived there not because they wanted to, but because they were trapped there, victims of circumstances far beyond their control, and powerless to do anything about it. I had seen such powerlessness when Mama pleaded with utility companies not to cut off our heat and lights. I had felt myself in the powerlessness of my invisibility in the armory that night, and the icy presence of Judge Breckenridge, who seemed dedicated to incarcerating black boys like me and Gary.

More and more, I began listening to adults as they recounted stories about black people who were beaten or killed by racist whites. The elders in my neighborhood talked about the Birmingham, Alabama, police commissioner, Eugene "Bull" Connor, and his shock troops attacking and arresting Dr. King and his supporters during the civil rights marches.

The pictures on the television showed whites turning high-powered water hoses and vicious dogs on the protesters, some of whom were women and children. Others were just clubbed and arrested. One man told my mother that the home of Dr. King's brother had been bombed in Atlanta, and that a riot had followed.

There were so many horrible stories. Like that of a young man in Houston who had been beaten with a tire iron and hung from a tree, with the letters KKK carved on his chest. Then some whites set off a bomb in a church in Birmingham, killing four young girls. Finally, just two months before the March on Washington, Medgar Evers, who had led several protests against prejudice in Jackson, Mississippi, the state's capital, was killed, shot in the back outside his home by white racists on a drive-by.

Each story I heard left me more angry and confused. Why were they killing us like this? What had we done to them? Why did they hate us so? Could hate really make people act like animals this way?

"Why are some of the white people trying to kill us?" I asked Mama one night while we were watching the TV news. In it a burly white officer was dragging a black woman by the hair to a police van, and again I turned and asked, "What's wrong with them?"

She turned off the television, touched my face, and said quietly, "Some of them are sick in their hearts. Some of the others are afraid of us, of what we might do if we get a taste of real freedom."

The morning of the march, as my mother prayed, I thought about all those tragedies, and I connected her own misfortune to them. Why was it that my mother, who had worked so hard all her life, couldn't even afford five bus tickets to ride thirty miles to Washington?

"Maybe somebody could drive us to the march," I suggested.

"There's too many of us and we'd still have to pay them," she said. "How about we sit down together and watch the newsreel on television tonight?"

That August evening, my family huddled together on the living room floor to witness an event I would never forget. In the looming shadow of the Washington Monument, thousands of people crowded on both sides of the half-mile reflecting pool and spilled out to surround the base of the Lincoln Memorial. It was an awesome, mind-numbing, and joyful sight. As we watched this massive crowd gathered so peacefully in the clear summer air of the nation's capital, waving placards and swaying to the soulful a cappella of Mahalia Jackson crooning the spiritual "I've Been 'Buked and I've Been Scorned," Mama closed her eyes and rocked. I sat mesmerized, listening to the song, which had been a part of my growing up, sung by a woman Mama loved.

We sat quietly, our eyes riveted to each image the camera brought to our tiny black-and-white screen. But if we were quiet before, we became breathless as the dark, dignified face of Dr. Martin Luther King, Jr., appeared. Introduced as "the moral leader of our nation," Dr. King stood before the cheering multitudes, his shoulders squared and his voice crisp and eloquent.

"Five score years ago," he said, "a great American, in whose symbolic shadow we stand today, signed the Emancipation Proclamation . . ."

King went on to state how the promises of America's fore-fathers, as far as black folks were concerned, had amounted to little more than a "bad check." That we, one hundred years later, were still suffering and fighting for our basic freedoms and civil liberties. With each of his statements, my mother nodded passionately, mumbling an occasional "Amen."

King spoke with a fiery conviction that sizzled beneath his deep, baritone voice. I remember leaning closer to the small, oval screen to take in each detail of his fervent and powerful message. He continued, the pitch of his voice rising, falling, and echoing across that sea of people.

"There are those who are asking the devotees of civil rights, 'When will you be satisfied?' " he boomed. "We can never be satisfied as long as the Negro is the victim of the unspeakable horrors of police brutality. We can never be satisfied as long as our bodies, heavy with the fatigue of travel, cannot gain lodging in the motels of the highways and the hotels of the cities. . . . We cannot be satisfied as long as a Negro in Mississippi cannot vote and a Negro in New York believes he has nothing for which to vote. No, we are not satisfied, and we will not be satisfied, until justice rolls down like waters and righteousness like a mighty stream."

My mother was now up on her feet. It was as though Dr. King had transported us from our living room into the hot muggy pews of a Baptist church in the Deep South, where the sweat-drenched preacher was lifting his congregation into a spiritual high of shouting and hand-clapping and foot-pounding. The call and response dialogue and the syncopated cadence of his voice had begun calling forth a spiritual reaffirmation even among the most disconnected.

"I say to you today, my friends, that even though we must face the frustrations of today and tomorrow, I still have a dream, and it is a dream deeply rooted in the American dream . . ."

I sat savoring the majestic power in Dr. King's voice as it resonated off the stage and spread out across the gathered multitudes of Washington. "One day this nation will rise up and live out the true meaning of its creed—We hold these truths to be self-evident, that all men are created equal. . . ."

And then King said something that made my mother break down with tears streaming down her face:

"I have a dream," he said. "My four little children will one day live in a nation where they will not be judged by the color of their skin but by the content of their character. . . .

"I have a dream today!"

As his speech drew to a close, we sat listening with a mixture of joy and sadness, hope and sorrow.

"When we allow freedom to ring," King said, "when we let it ring from every village and hamlet, from every state and city, we will be able to speed up that day when all God's children—black and white men, Jews and Gentiles, Catholics and Protestants, will be able to join hands and to sing in the words of the old Negro spiritual, 'Free at last, Free at last, thank God Almighty, we are free at last!' "

Soon after those words and the thunderous applause that followed, a television commentator began describing the obvious. Mama got up, walked over to the tiny knob on the TV, and turned it off. We sat there in the sudden and hollow quiet of our tiny living room, and watched while twilight gave way to night.

Later that year, not long after the march, we were stunned at school one day when the principal announced that somebody had shot President Kennedy. A hush fell over the classroom as we, like millions of others, waited to hear if he was alive. I couldn't believe it. The halls were filled with teachers crying and students walking around in a trance. I put my head down on a desk and hurt as if a big wound had been ripped open inside me. The image of the young, smiling President making that speech in the armory flashed into my mind and a tear rolled down my cheek. I had actually seen him, I thought to myself. And now, as with Louie, I was trying to understand his death. At home, my mother shook her head sadly, saying, "They always kill the ones who try to do some good."

5

DEATH AND THE NEW REALITY

IN the winter of 1964, Mama began her gradual retreat out of my life. It was a retreat that I refused to accept, believing that acknowledging what was happening to her might somehow confirm or validate it. And for a while, she encouraged my ignorance.

A couple of times, I hinted some concern to her, but came away feeling paranoid. "I'm fine," she'd insist. "Just a little tired, that's all. Doesn't Mama have the right to be tired sometimes?" I could only accept her denial as truth.

I should have known otherwise. The signs were too numerous. The nagging pain and stiffness in her limbs that kept her awake through the night. The fatigue that drained her ability to work so often that she eventually lost her job. The abrupt and uncharacteristic drinking of liquor to help dull her pain. The considerable weight loss and darkening below her eyes.

But I went on telling myself that Mama would be fine. And I continued believing that lie even after her legs weakened to the point where she had to sleep on the sofa because she could no longer make it up the steps to her bedroom. Perhaps I believed her because I had no choice. And what sixteen-year-old boy wouldn't dive-bomb into denial at the thought of losing the only person in the world he could really count on.

Then one night, shortly after Christmas, my mother called me downstairs to sit beside her on the living room sofa.

"Pee Wee," she said calmly. "I know what I'm about to tell you is going to hurt. God knows, I'm hurting, too. But there are times when a person has to be strong. And now I need you to be strong for Mama, more than any time before. You're a big boy now, growing up to be a man, and there are things I need you to start thinking about."

The conversation that ensued still grips me. In the living room of 1834 Division Street, with my sisters asleep upstairs, Mama confirmed my worst fears. She told me that she was dying of cancer, and had less than six months to live.

That was the night that my childhood ended. A rush of emotion surged through my body. For the first time in a long time I really wanted to cry. I felt that another curse had been deliberately thrown my way. Didn't God have enough without punishing our family and the woman who believed dearly in his word? And yet, in spite of it, here we were, facing another twist, another turn, another test.

My mother was not afraid to die. In fact, her faith in God was helping her create a serene passage out of this life. But she did harbor a strong fear of hospitals, and it was because of this fear that she'd put off seeking treatment.

Two years before, her younger brother, Freddy, had committed suicide; he spent his last moments in the hospital before finally dying. Back then, Provident Hospital was one of only two in the city that accepted black patients who were poor. It was the only black hospital in the state, and the atmosphere was hardly inviting. It was nothing but long, dimly lit halls, cramped rooms, steel cots, and the nauseating smell of ether that ran throughout the building. Unlike Johns Hopkins Hospital on the other side of town, Provident had a simple mission in that era of segregation: service the poor and keep them healthy. After sitting for hours at the bedside of a friend, my mother would return home vowing never to spend so much as one night in any hospital.

When Mama finally did pay a visit to Provident, which was just four blocks from our house, the doctors told her that she had waited too long. There was nothing they could do to help her and very little she could do to help herself. Accepting her fate, she never went back there again.

"I want to die in the comfort of my own home," she'd say. "I want to be with my family."

My mother's greatest concern was for the four young children she was leaving behind. I was sixteen years old. Darlene was fourteen, LaWana thirteen, and Michele only nine. At that time, my sisters and I had very little contact with our father. Mama worried that her death might leave us to be parceled out into foster homes. She'd talked about planning to make arrangements so that, after she passed, I would go and live with my uncles, and my sisters would move in with our grandmother, Viola.

In the months before she died, she would religiously call me downstairs at night and I would spend hours on the sofa listening to her talk about what life would be like for us after she was gone. The conversations always occurred after my sisters had gone to sleep, and at Mama's request. I would listen quietly and politely, but the subject of her dying was never one I was comfortable with. I just couldn't fathom the idea of waking up or returning from school and her not being there. In our first conversations, I spoke wistfully of a miraculous recovery, about us getting back to our normal lives.

"I don't think that will happen," she'd say. "But let's pray on it."

During those talks, my mother mostly drilled into me a sense of responsibility for myself and my sisters. "You've got to stay out of trouble," she said. "Don't go giving in to the way of the world. I won't be here to help you out. And your sisters will need you to look after them."

She went so far as to make me promise that I wouldn't let anything bad ever happen to my sisters, but my nodding that I understood wasn't enough.

"No, I want you to say it," she pushed. "Promise me right here and now that you will not let anything happen to your sisters, as long as you can help it."

"I promise, Mama," I said firmly, yet sadly—still trying to distance myself from the rapidly approaching reality.

Through repetition and simple phrasing Mama made sure she didn't leave this world without giving me what she believed were life's most important lessons for survival.

"Your word is your bond, and don't ever forget that," she told me one of those nights. "Your word, what you promise to people, is all that you got that's worth anything. Once folks stop believing what you say, you ain't got nothing. That's why you always gotta tell the truth, and don't promise people what you can't do.

"And remember, always let God guide your life, and nobody else. Only he knows what's good for you, what the right path is for you—not any of your lil' buddies runnin' around out there on the street, or them girls you so busy chasing around these days. Not even Grandma or Mr. Charles. Only God knows, so you have to listen closely to your heart and watch for the direction his light is shining. That's where you should always walk.

"Petey, you're special and don't you ever forget that," she said. "God spared your life when you were just a baby. Ain't no sense denying your destiny. I could see that something special was coming down your life's path. Mama knows that the road ahead won't be easy for you. Without me here to help, you have to be a man a lot sooner than all your friends. You'll have to take on responsibilities that are beyond your years. But no matter how hard things get, promise Mama you'll never give up, that you'll never settle for second best. Promise me that."

"I won't do that," I said, filled with sadness and disbelief over the thought of my mother's absence.

"I need a better response than that, Frizzell," she said firmly. "I said, promise your mama you won't."

"I promise you, Mama, I won't."

"God gave you a good head and good heart. He's made you strong where others are weak. And when God gives you blessings, you've gotta give some of what he gave you back to help others."

Mama's homilies were repeated frequently over the next four months. Given her delicate state of health, I'm certain that it took tremendous stamina to hold a family together during the day and then to prepare me for my future at night.

I knew that we'd hit upon a serious topic when Mama switched her address of me from the more familiar and affectionate Pee Wee to the more serious and adultlike Frizzell.

"Frizzell, I want you to listen to me real close," she murmured, propping herself up on one arm to angle her increasingly thin body over the double ring of pillows I'd retrieved to support her more comfortably.

"I want you to grow up to be a great man, a man like your granddad or a man like Dr. King. And even though I won't be here to see it happen, I promise you that I'll always help you find a way. I promise I will always be with you. Even when you cannot see me, know that I am there. I will always be there."

Then, as now, black parents everywhere were encouraging their children to do something more with their lives. For those of us then, it seemed like a new day. Yet the racial conflicts continued throughout the South. Three civil rights workers—Michael Schwerner, Andrew Goodman, and James Chaney—were killed by local whites in Mississippi.

Malcolm X quit the Black Muslims that same year and started his own group, the Organization of African-American Unity. However, he was gunned down shortly after that during a rally in Harlem's Audubon Ballroom. As Mama and I watched the TV footage of the police carrying his body out, she said, "They killed a real man but not his message. He knew too much, and had come so far."

Nearly every night during those four months, Mama talked to me about my life, my goals, my future. Then one night in April her condition worsened. I was sitting there on the sofa beside her when her pains grew sharp. She wasn't saying much that night; she was in a great deal of discomfort. I remember hoping that my presence was providing some comfort during her suffering.

Something else, however, was even more unusual about that night. In our neighborhood, there was a stray dog that always showed up at our back door in the evening. Mama, who loved animals, felt sorry for the mutt. She'd named him Prince and quickly decided that he was more than welcome on a daily basis to a bone or whatever table scraps she could assemble. Her adopted Prince would quickly devour the food and disappear down the alley.

On this night, however, my mother and I heard loud barking outside. I went to the window and looked out. Prince had made his usual appearance. But tonight, instead of going to the kitchen door, he showed up at the front of the house and continued barking from the concrete sidewalk.

"What's Prince doing here this time of night?" I remember asking my mother. Still in pain, she didn't say much.

Her face appeared more drawn than usual and etched with fresh lines of fatigue. She'd lost a lot of weight in recent weeks, and felt tired a great deal of the time. Often, she seemed to drift off, doubled over and just staring out at nothing or no one in particular. I sometimes wondered what she was thinking during those long moments. Sometimes I couldn't tell if she was in pain or not, but tonight was different.

As we sat there on the sofa, Prince continued to stand in front of our house, barking and howling like he was going mad. It was very annoying and very unusual. I went outside a couple of times and chased the dog away. Within minutes, Prince would return and resume his bloodcurdling howling, which became increasingly intense. After a half hour he finally left.

Mama instinctively knew what his strange behavior foretold, but for me it was a lesson about to be learned. Not long afterward, she squeezed my hand tightly and looked helplessly into my eyes. Her mouth fell open, and she let out a strange gasping sound and fell over into my arms. I had never heard a sound like that before and have never heard one since. The dark room suddenly seemed to be filled with the soft sound of wings. It was the Death Angel, I thought, coming as Mama said he would, riding the crest of an eerie cool draft that blew through the room, icy, soulless, and vacant of life. The next few moments became an eternity for me. Like a page unturned or a book unread, I would be left forever to wonder what if. That night in April 1965 my life ended, began, and ended again.

"Mama . . . Mama . . . Mama!" I screamed frantically, hugging her unconscious body against me. "Oh, no . . . Mama!"

I shook her, rocked her, my wet tears falling down onto her motionless face. "Mama, I love you, please don't leave me. Wake up, Mama, wake up." But nothing I could do would revive her.

For the rest of my life I would live with that night and the rush of feelings that went with it. "You only got one mother," Mama would often say to us, and now the weight of her words had sunk in. Even now I cannot describe how terrifying those moments were as my mother lay dying in my arms.

Beyond that point, the events of that April evening blur. Somehow, I managed to get to the phone to call the hospital for an ambulance. My sisters heard me crying and came running downstairs, but I ordered them back up to the bedroom. With trembling hands, I called my aunts and uncles and told them what had happened. After what seemed to be a lifetime, an ambulance finally came. With its siren and red lights flashing, it illuminated the street in front of our house. The attendants took one look at my mother and immediately took her out on a stretcher.

It seemed like the whole neighborhood had crowded in front of our house. The nameless, faceless stares of those who had quickly gathered were mixed now with curiosity and sadness. I

rode with Mama in the ambulance, holding her hand as paramedics worked to revive her with electric stimuli. They banged
on her chest and breathed into her mouth, but it was not
enough. One of the paramedics looked at me and then turned
away slowly, unable to speak.

"I'm sorry, kid," the other one whispered, perspiration beaded
on his face. I could feel the warmth leaving her body by the time
they rolled her through the emergency room door.

As I sat in the tiny, brightly lit room with Mama lying flat on
the white paper cover of a small single bed, the attending
physician pronounced her dead. He pulled the sheet that covered her slowly over her still face as tears began to well up all
over again in my eyes. He gritted his teeth slowly, stared
without expression in my direction, then turned and left,
leaving her and me alone.

I uncovered her face, kissed her on her forehead, and as if she
could hear me, told Mama I would be right back. That quickly, I
was beginning to accept the unacceptable. Mama had crossed
over to the other side; now I had to move quickly to fulfill her
wish for last rites. Uncle Bootsie had witnessed to Mama long
ago about the power of the Gospel, and once saved she never
wavered in her belief. She wanted her priest present in the hour
of her death and I instinctively knew I had to get him.

I walked quickly out of the emergency room with my eyes red
and my vision blurred. Uncle Ed, Aunt Gloria, and Uncle
Stanley were rushing into the emergency room as I was rushing
out. We didn't speak in that one quick moment, but we didn't
have to. They read my face and knew.

In just a few moments I arrived at Saint Peter's Catholic
Church. Mama's priest met me at the door, and when told of
her death he quickly grabbed his Bible and a rosary. As we
walked together back to the hospital, he tried his best to make
clear the mystery of life. But for me, at age sixteen, it was
all lost on the moment. When we got back to the hospital,
Mama's sisters and brothers had gathered and were sobbing at
her bedside.

One shock after another hit me in those manic hours after my mother's death. Later that night, Mr. Charles came by the house, his eyes red and swollen as if he had been crying. He hugged me for a long time, and that comforted me.

"You know how your mother was, how she kept things to herself," Mr. Charles said. "She was the kind of person who always tried to handle everything herself. Never wanted to burden nobody."

Sitting there that night listening to Mr. Charles, I could tell that a part of him had died as well. The pain was etched deeply in his face. Each mournful word he spoke seemed to choke him as it worked its way out of his mouth into the stillness of the room. His shoulders tight and hunched as though his bones were chilled, he sat beside me and took long drags off a cigarette. At times, he hung his head back in disbelief and whispered incoherently. Then he would drift away into himself, mumbling and staring, first at the ceiling, and then at the floor.

I had cried so much that night, I couldn't cry anymore. I was too numb. I couldn't feel anything, think anything. I just sat there staring at the wall, half hearing Mr. Charles ramble on through his hurt, drifting in and out. His voice got quieter, his tone sadder the longer we sat. I could sense that he was working his way toward something, as if he had more to say but was holding back. But I didn't push him. I was too ripped up inside to push for anything. All I wanted was for my mama to come back. I wanted all this to be a bad dream, to wake up and find her sitting there quietly beside me.

I sat there numbly in the same darkened room where earlier that evening Mama and I had talked. Mr. Charles's words were still tumbling out as we sat there together. Then, haltingly, he stood up and randomly paced the floor. He lit another cigarette and blew smoke at the ceiling.

Mr. Charles turned and looked at me. Then he told me that he was my real father.

Although only a few hours had passed, my whole world had changed. Bittersweet now was my new reality. Losing a mother and gaining a father almost simultaneously had proven too much for me to bear. I was drained and dazed.

• • •

I don't recall much at all about the days or nights following my mother's death. Even though I had held her as she took her last breath, I was unwilling to believe that Mama had actually left me forever. The thought of seeing her in a casket, eyes closed eternally, was too much for me to bear. Darlene, LaWana, and Michele, who were still quite young, hadn't the faintest notion of how radically our lives were about to change. Later in life, they would tell me that they can only remember the strange sadness that surrounded them. Because they were girls and much younger than I, I knew they would be taken care of, that someone in the family would always look out for them. I wasn't so sure about how I would fare. The thought of being left alone in the world without Mama frightened me. The fact that I had no choice would make me survive.

In a zombielike state, I sat beside my sisters through the funeral and let my mind drift off to anywhere that blunted the sharp pain that pierced through me each time I looked at Mama lying there in her casket. I tried hard not to cry, but I could not control my tears. They were streaming down my face as I sat there with my sisters. Clifton Gray, whom I now knew was my stepfather, was there, but we barely glanced at each other. Not wanting to let my mother down, I held my head high and wrapped my arms around my sisters. I made a decision that no matter what happened to me from that point forward, I would not succumb to my feelings of pain and abandonment. I vowed to myself that I would never dishonor my mother with weakness or fear.

I didn't see much of my father, Rip, after the funeral. My inability to maintain an even closer relationship with him, especially on the heels of Mama's death, was a profound loss in my life. There are those who've asked me why Rip, after returning to my life, didn't help me more in the immediate period after that. I think I knew the answer even if he didn't. He loved Mama so much that he was devastated. It would take eight years, a period of drug abuse and a trip to prison, before he would finally begin getting his own life back together. During that period my fourth sister, also named Michele, would be born.

My father's life was obviously a complex one, and he too had to survive out there on the streets. His life was totally unpredictable, and he knew it. I'm certain he loved me, but we both understood that he couldn't be there for me.

But if my father gave me nothing else, his life in the world we knew demonstrated for me what it meant for a black man to command respect and possess influence. To me, as a young boy, Mr. Charles had what young people today call "juice." Because I identified with him, I believed that I could have that kind of power, too.

This is why my own relationship with my sons has been so important to me, because I knew what it was like to have two fathers and still have no father at all.

But back then, on the streets, I was so scrambled inside and filled with so much pain and confusion that all I could do was keep running. With Mama gone, I literally had no one in the world but myself.

A boy wants his father to be something special. A father wants his son to be all of the things he could never be. I was still stunned from learning the truth about my lineage, and yet I had always felt a deep closeness for this man who was now my father. I looked at him in an entirely different way after his admission to me. I knew I had always loved him and now I knew why.

His revelation explained so many things. I thought back to those wonderful times when we walked together along the Strip on Pennsylvania Avenue. I remembered especially the times when he'd tell people I was his boy.

Life, I thought, had been simpler after Clifton Gray left us, when Mr. Charles and I had each other, and Mama loved us both.

A few days after the funeral, I went to visit Arnette Evans in the warehouse to tell him that I had to quit the Falcons. I needed to find work to support myself and my sisters and would not have any time anymore to be in a band. Arnette had known my mother fairly well, and I could see in his eyes that he was hurting for me.

"You don't need to tell me why you're here," he said. "I know why. I'm real sorry to hear about your mother."

He didn't look at me while he spoke. He just stared out the window.

"Your mother was a good woman, a damn good woman," he said. "And let me tell you something—she loved you. She loved you more than you know."

I had never heard Arnette Evans speak so softly. His lip quivered as he talked and stared out of the window.

"You have to realize that things like this happen, and you can't do anything about it now. I understand if you can't make it here anymore. Don't feel bad about it."

"I'm sorry that . . ." I began to say, but he cut me off.

"I said not to feel bad about it, boy. It's all right. You've got things you need to do, and nobody's gonna hold that against you."

I nodded, feeling relieved that Mr. Evans was not angry at me for leaving, that he understood I wasn't quitting to escape, but rather to survive.

"Keep the uniform, okay?" he said. "And even the horn if you want it. And if there's anything I can do for you, just call and I'll see to it that things get worked out."

For a few moments, there was only an awkward silence as we stood there across from one another. Then I noticed with surprise that Arnette Evans was fighting back tears as he wiped a hand over his glassy eyes.

"When your mother brought you to me, she asked me to help make a man out of you. God knows I tried," he said. "Now, get on out of here and do what you gotta do to take care of your sisters. And make your mama proud of you."

Unable to bring myself to say good-bye to the man who had challenged my courage and tested my resolve, I just stood there frozen, groping for a word to say.

"Get the fuck out of here," he politely grumbled.

We didn't shake hands or anything. I just said, "Yes, sir," then turned and marched away.

Within two weeks after the funeral, a new reality had taken hold of my life. It was the stark truth of survival. Basic matters of food, clothing, and shelter had suddenly become complex, open-ended questions that aroused more doubt than hope.

My sisters and I would eventually be split up. Still bobby-socked and girlishly young, Darlene, LaWana, and Michele would be moved in to live with our grandmother. My aunts had too many children of their own to care for and could only help by sharing the load with Grandmother. Viola Gray Johnson believed that under her guidance, my sisters might receive at least a quotient of the feminine nurturing and upbringing that Mama would have offered them.

On the other hand, since I was a cocky, beyond-my-years sixteen-year-old, I was viewed as being at least marginally ready to stumble toward whatever fate would be mine. So I would be placed in the custody of my two divorced uncles, who lived on Robert Street in the house Mama's dad had bought. This whole transition, of course, was all a great shock to me. While absolute freedom is something that most young boys yearn for, I was scarcely ready to live it out in spades. What I remember most, though, is how quickly both my physical and emotional worlds shrank to a stranglehold.

The fact was that I could no longer depend on others to provide for me and my sisters. My grandmother had long been retired from her job as a laundry room maid and was living meagerly on a pension. My uncles could barely feed and clothe themselves on their modest pay and could do little to provide for me. It was painfully clear that a formal education had suddenly become a luxury I could no longer afford. With little choice but to help chip away at the financial burdens of those who were caring for me and my sisters, I dropped out of high school in the spring of 1965 and immediately went to work.

My decision to drop out of school in the tenth grade shattered the very foundation of my mother's dream for me. "The black man will never get ahead in this country without an education," she'd always said. "You've got to go to school in order to come up from under the control of others."

While dropping out seemed in defiance of Mama's expectations for me, I saw no clear options if I was also to honor my pact with her to take care of my sisters. I was torn between building my own future and helping to keep afloat the only family that I had. Since Mama had sacrificed for us, I believed she would understand my choice to give up school for the well-being of my sisters.

Still, at the time, most of my friends were living what I considered to be charmed lives. They were not wealthy by any stretch of the imagination. They lived frugal, penny-pinching lives, where hand-me-down clothes were the norm, and second helpings of dinner were not. But they all had mothers at home, and many even had fathers. Their stable homes allowed them to enjoy lives overflowing with everything from house parties to homecomings, from junior and senior proms to movie matinees. They seemed to have it all: the bake-offs and bandstands, the cookouts and the bijous that left a buzz lingering in the air longer than that first French kiss.

But while my friends were savoring every sweet drop of their youth, frolicking and carefree, I was chained to the sidelines. My life had been reduced to a blur of odd jobs and paltry paychecks.

I was working three jobs now. One of them was in the slicing room at Pariser's Bakery. I'd take my place at the conveyor belt at about eleven at night and work until seven in the morning. It was monotonous, exhausting work because that conveyor belt never stopped moving. Hard, crusted, and seeded, the loaves of bread kept coming down the belt one after another and I'd grab each one, turn it over, put it through the slicer, slide it down into a wrapper, and put the whole thing into a machine that would fold and seal the wrapper. After grabbing a few hundred of those loaves, my fingertips were so raw and sore that it hurt to even pick up my timecard to clock out.

When I wasn't working there, I was at the Lafayette Market,

selling poultry in a stall and packing chicken, fish, and rabbits in ice for display. On Sunday mornings, I shined shoes on the street corner for the people walking to church.

In my neighborhood, it was rare for a boy my age to be working a full-time job. I knew it was just a matter of time before word spread that my pockets contained more than lint. It happened one night as I was headed to work at the bakery. I was alone and I'd let my guard down just long enough to be dumbfounded when, out of nowhere, I felt a slab of wood land heavily across the back of my head. My knees buckled, and I went down face first on the concrete. As I pushed myself up, a burly forearm seized my neck and locked me so hard in a chokehold that I could barely breathe. Warm blood ran freely from my nose and mouth and I was too dazed and shaken to respond.

"You're gonna break his fuckin' neck," I heard a voice call out.

"You think I give a shit," a voice shot back as the arm squeezed even tighter. "Just take his fuckin' money, okay?"

I used my waning strength to jab my elbow into his ribs, and his grip loosened long enough for me to break free. Dizzy and breathless, I tried to stagger forward, and fell against a wall. I still managed a blow that connected squarely on the jaw of one of those who were coming toward me. But that was my only shot. The four punks who wanted to kick a little ass began whaling on me until I dropped down on the ground. One kicked me in the mouth and the ribs, while another clubbed me mercilessly with the bottom half of a pool stick. I instinctively tried to cover my head from the blows but I was too dizzy and off-balance. They beat me so bad I thought I was going to die right there in the street.

"Just take the fuckin' money," I said, blood frothing between my swollen lips.

"We want more than your money, you smart muthafucka," one of them said.

Ripping the pockets off my pants, they took the few dollars I had. Worse, though, they stole the shoes right off my feet. I felt completely powerless, a feeling made all the worse by the fact that instead of running away, they walked away and left me lying there, twisting and bleeding in the street.

After that night, I vowed never to be caught off guard and defenseless again. I called Gary, who knew a dude who peddled guns. Later that week, we met him in an abandoned garage and I bought a .32 caliber revolver. Never again would I be a helpless victim. The next time somebody jumped me, he would pay with his life.

By the time I was eighteen, I'd discovered a quicker, more profitable way of making money than working in a bread factory and shining shoes on the street corner. I had learned that my father, Rip, earned most of his living running numbers and lending money. In a strange way I felt that hustling came naturally to me. If I'd been forced to choose a career, it would have been as a numbers runner.

Running numbers gave you instant status. Nobody enjoyed more respect or popularity on the Strip than the numbers man. Before the lottery, the numbers were big in black neighborhoods. If you put down as little as a buck on a number, you could hit and rake in five hundred. It was such a good deal that everybody played, whether they could afford to or not. Even some ministers who preached against the numbers played them on the side.

But the numbers racket was also illegal, and getting caught with numbers slips on you was tantamount to a sentence. It might have been a victimless crime and perhaps even an economic benefit to the community, but judges came down hard on numbers runners. So the runners would hire guys like me to go out and collect the slips.

As jobs go, this one was a cinch. I'd walk into a barber shop and pretend to be conversing with the barber or a customer, write down their number (always in pencil), collect the money with a handshake, and move on down the block. This was how I learned to cover the whole neighborhood, from beauty salons to liquor stores to pool halls to gas stations. I'd even make house calls on the sick and shut-in just so they could get their numbers in.

I'd walk for three or four hours, writing numbers and taking money. The best runners were the older guys who had done it for years. They were so good that they memorized every number they took a bet on. That way, if they ever got jammed by the police there never was any evidence. The rookies like myself were taught to write on small slips of paper and, if caught, put them in our mouths right away and swallow them. The police took special pleasure in locking up a numbers runner because they would turn in the slips as evidence but keep the money. At the end of my route, I'd turn over the cash from my route and get paid fifty bucks or so right on the spot.

The allure of the street life was strong, very strong. For a young black man, then as now, there was a sense of powerlessness that threatened to consume you unless you embraced the power of the street. To get respect in the neighborhood, you had to earn it on the street. When you had the power of the street, people got out of your way. People feared you. Out there, as in the straight world, power was about getting money, about getting paid. I did a lot of growing up on the streets of West Baltimore. And I got paid.

When I wasn't working, I'd hook up with Gary Fenwick and we'd hang out on the corner of Robert and Division streets. That's where the toughest of the neighborhood held court— talking loud, fighting, gambling, and getting high. That's where you'd find those who ruled, like Sam Cherry, Ghost, Icing, Vaughn Chase, and Chief. And then there was Country, who was by far the most feared of the group. Country was big, brawny, black, and bad. You never knew what to expect from him. He'd just be sitting on the steps playing the dozens, when all of a sudden he'd be up on his feet barreling down the street. The next thing you know, he'd have some guy on the ground who wasn't supposed to be in the neighborhood anyway, pimp-slapping him upside his head.

"Nigga, I said gimme some money!" Country would be hollering as his swift fists came down across the victim's face. "I'll piss on you right here in this street. Gimme your money, and quit cryin' like a bitch!"

The poor guy would pull out his money, hand it to Country, and haul ass away. Country was so feared that nobody even dared look at him when he returned, counting his cash and talking his trash.

Country and the others were in their mid-twenties, much older than Gary and I. I'm not sure why they let us hang around with them, but we earned our way. Being spotted with such ruthless cats put Gary and me in a different league from our peers. We didn't do much talking when we were around Country and his crowd, we just listened and laughed. For us it was important to mimic that air of barely hidden insanity that won you respect.

Half the time, we were scared to death that one of them might beat us up just for kicks. They punched so hard that your whole chest would cave in when they hit you, and hitting you was just a sign of affection. I'd watch them drink four or five bottles of Wild Irish Rose or Thunderbird until they were raging drunk.

One night, Vaughn Chase took a sip of his wine and looked woozily over at Sam Cherry. "Man, I never really noticed before," Vaughn slurred, "but you one ugly muthafucka." Twisting his face, he shook his head sadly. "I don't know who your mother screwed to make yo' ugly ass." Everybody erupted with laughter. I was laughing so hard I was crying. Sam jumped up with rage in his bloodshot eyes and said to me, "What's so funny, young boy?" I was still laughing so hard with the others that I couldn't get a word out. And then came his fist. He hit me so hard it felt like he had put a hole in my chest, but I never laughed at big Sam Cherry again.

After a while, Gary and I were accepted as part of the crew, but it wasn't without a stiff price. We got into a lot of fights at their instigation but we loved every moment of it. If an outsider from across town came over to hang out, the others might challenge me to take his money. If I didn't, they'd threaten to take mine, so I'd have no choice but to kick ass.

These guys were so treacherous that this was entertainment for them. Even the police were afraid to deal with them. Whenever they were all standing on the corner, the police rarely stopped to tell them to break it up or cut down the noise. They'd just stay in their car, flash their floodlight, and continue to cruise slowly on by.

Hanging out on the corner I learned how to shoot dice, bet money, and talk trash. Back then, there were crap games on nearly every third or fourth street corner. Some folks played for big money in the four or five crap houses on the Avenue, but too many dudes got killed in there. You could be shooting dice and winning when somebody might accuse you of putting weighted dice in the game, or a loser who didn't want to pay up might tell you to kiss his ass, and it would all be over. I saw too many bodies being carried out of crap houses to ever think about playing in them, no matter how much money was involved.

I stuck mostly to shooting craps on corners and in alleys, where it was almost as dangerous, but at least I didn't have to check my gun. There, at least, I'd have room to run if the police raided the area. You'd be out there on the corner and all of a sudden one of the dudes standing on the side would pull a sawed-off shotgun out of his pants. "Give me all your fuckin' money or get ready to see Jesus in the morning." Before you knew it, everybody'd be on the ground, taking out their money, pulling off their watches, shoes, and whatever else had some street value. I learned quickly to gamble around people that I knew or to have someone packing heat to stand there and watch my back.

I learned to shoot dice from one of the best in the neighborhood, a cat we called Michael Pink Lips. With his bronze face, high-pitched voice, and huge, fleshy pink lips, Michael was a respected hustler. He spent his days and nights on the Avenue, beating folks out of their hard-earned pay or the winnings they'd hustled in the street.

Michael Pink Lips liked me because he could sense my hunger to get ahead, and one day he decided it was time for me to learn one of the finer points of hustling.

"The game is simple as hell," he told me. "That's why you see so many niggas out here playin' it."

He handed me a pair of red dice. "Roll 'em," he said. "If you hit seven or eleven right off the bat, you win."

I twirled the dice on the concrete. The combination came up two sixes. "You lose," Pink Lips said. "Two or twelve, you lose. If you hit any of the other numbers, that number is what you call your point. So, you shoot the dice to make your point. If you roll a seven before you hit your point, you lose."

I listened closely, watching the intensity in Michael Pink Lips' face as he instructed me. He was one of the best, so it was no small favor that he was taking the time to show me the ropes.

"The ones who win understand a couple of things," he said. "You gotta know odds and you gotta read probabilities. It's a game of chance, yours versus somebody else's, so the more you understand the better you're gonna be.

"Look," he said. "Every time you roll the dice, the number that you have the best chance of hitting is seven. You got three combinations, two and five, four and three, and six and one."

"Yeah," I said, nodding, "I get it . . . yeah."

Michael Pink Lips taught me how to place side bets that help even up the odds when they're stacked against you. He taught me how to be fearless in games, and how to, as he put it, "talk shit, kick ass, and take money." He also showed me how to spot bad dice and how to throw them myself.

"Some niggas like to do what's called paddin' and twirlin'," where they lock up the dice and don't really shake 'em up like you're supposed to," Pink Lips warned. "On a soft, flat surface like a pool table, you don't get a true roll, that's why people lose, 'cause they can't pop the numbers. I don't play on nothin' but hard surfaces because when the dice hit it they jump."

Under the tutelage of Michael Pink Lips I began shooting dice and winning. It amazed me how fast the game was played, how much money flowed back and forth through the crowd from side bets. It was hard to keep track of it all. Yet by playing so many games I began to understand the element of hot luck that Michael Pink Lips referred to as "feel"—the true driving force of knowing how to bet, what to bet, and when to back off.

"Most people are more concerned with their 'feel' than they are with the probabilities of the bet," he told me. "Gambling's an emotional thang—and that's where we get our advantage, we fuck with their emotions, mess with their head."

The more I played, the more I realized that while most people knew the odds were against them, they'd still bet on feeling. I began learning how to exploit that fact without letting on that, like them, I knew that the odds were against my winning, but unlike them, I went with the odds and not against them, as Pink Lips taught me. With epithets flowing and emotions running high in the crowd, I always appeared just as cocky as the next guy. But in truth, my mind was always focused on the odds and locked on the probabilities.

After a while, I became a sort of expert at the game. I knew how to twirl dice, spin dice, set dice, and shave dice. I was eighteen, slick, and streetwise, learning my way in the school of hard knocks.

6

BATTLEGROUNDS

*I*T was 1966, and a new spirit of black militancy had taken root throughout the restive streets of West Baltimore. Swept up by the fiery passion of Stokely Carmichael, chairman of the Student Nonviolent Coordinating Committee, and the strong defiance of Floyd McKissick, executive director of the Congress of Racial Equality, the young brothers of my community adopted their closed-fist salute and rallying cry for Black Power. Every militant speech delivered by the angry men fell on fertile ground with us, while we watched the death toll of blacks murdered by whites in the South grow. Our fury simmered and boiled at each injustice perpetrated against the black race, including the highly publicized killings of civil rights leader Vernon Dahmer and Sammy Yonge, Jr., a college student. It was a rage that was becoming uncontainable, spilling out of inner-city streets and into small towns across the nation, with massive rioting occurring in many areas.

During that year, I had fallen into the full-blown habit of spending most of my waking hours in the streets. It was not that

I loved the streets so much—I simply hated being home. My cramped, shuttered room in my uncles' house had become its own kind of prison. It measured eight feet by six feet and it required stepping down to get into. I avoided being there as much as possible, using the house sparingly, almost like a homeless person who makes camp for a night, knowing the next day he will move on. Some have asked me whether during that time I felt a sense of gratitude that I wasn't homeless, but I felt no gratitude at all. What I did feel was a bitterness that, at sixteen years old, I had been cast from my mother's nest of support and affection into a dingy, second-floor room of cracked walls and linoleum floors. I harbored no ill feelings toward my two uncles who allowed me to live there. I loved them, and in their own way I guess they loved me. After all, they were Mama's brothers and she loved us all. But I barely even saw them, and what little contact we had was so casual it might as well have been nonexistent.

"Everything all right, Petey?" my uncle Ed might ask me on his way out the door. I would always nod and respond, "Yessir," not wanting to bother him with the truth or burden him with a lie.

The fact was, I felt terribly alone. I was angry and confused about everything that was supposed to matter in my life. And with each passing day, my separation from my mother and all the values she had tried to instill in me was growing wider.

I could hardly sleep nights as images of Mama slipped hauntingly into my dreams, when I could hear her soft, clear words as though she were lying there beside me.

"I need you to be strong. Don't give up. Don't let me down," her words would beg into my ear until I awakened with tears in my eyes, clinging to sheets damp and cold with sweat.

It frightened me how my mother, even in death, was so alive in my thoughts. I could see flashes of her loving eyes beaming down on me in the darkness, feel her warm breath against my cheek as she spoke desperately from that place to which she had gone, which I was certain was heaven.

Still, those same words of wisdom and encouragement of Mama's that once had a levitating effect had become nothing less than a burden as I tried to forge my own life in the streets. I tried hard to block her out, and her vision of a clean-cut kid with choirboy values and a Puritan work ethic. That vision didn't fit at all into my new reality. Even though I was street hustling, I kept my jobs, both of them. I would have made a career of shooting dice and running numbers, but the risk kept increasing and the cash flow was too sporadic.

Despite the action and excitement of street life, anyone who has truly lived it can testify that it's a sordid, nonstop B-movie drama that often gets stale quick. You can lose your direction and your life in a heartbeat and often over nothing. I understood better now why my mother had always preached that the streets were a dead end and a fool's game at best.

In hindsight, I certainly could have benefited from sorting out my feelings with someone other than myself. However, that didn't even seem an option. Back then, I managed the best I could with the resources I had. Quite frankly, I don't believe there were many folks who'd have been willing to sit through my venting.

I never doubted that I would survive. But what was important to me beyond mere survival was that I didn't end up on the bottom of the heap. Outside of my own family, many of my buddies were too busy dealing with their own issues and problems to take on any of my burdens. With their troubles, ranging from siblings strung out on dope, to run-ins with the law, to neighborhood scores yet to be settled, their capacity for hearing other people's problems was limited.

I learned very quickly that I didn't have the luxury of indulging my feelings. My mother had taught me the importance of being able to contain my emotions—"to suck it up and hold it in." And if that was not sufficient, Arnette Evans had reinforced that same world view. If you didn't learn how to contain and repress your feelings and keep moving forward, you were going to get stepped on or left back. So, I mostly kept my feelings to myself.

I think because I was ashamed that I was falling so far off track, I avoided people like the Pottashes, Arnette Evans, my father Rip, and anyone else who had known my mother well. I didn't want to hear another lecture on how disappointed she would have been.

Had Mama seen me in those days, she would have been heart-broken—I didn't need them telling me so. She had spent her life sweating in factories and cleaning up the homes of rich white folks in order to open doors for her own children. Her greatest hope was that my sisters and I would have a life that surpassed anything the Negro of her generation had ever imagined. She prayed I would become more than some street-running hustler who passed his time hanging on corners and betting in pool halls. It had been the fate of too many men she knew, including my own father, whom we both loved dearly. Yes, she wanted more for me, and now I was failing her miserably.

I would never have been able to articulate this at the time, but I knew that the part of my mother that I let live inside me would never have tolerated the feeble excuses I could muster about what I had become. This wasn't the life my mother and I had talked about and dreamed about. She wanted me to be somebody and to make a contribution. Settling for second best was not acceptable. She knew I could do better. I knew I could do better. And to do anything less might mean that I wasn't worthy of being her son.

Not only was Mama concerned about what I would do with my life, she was just as concerned about who I'd do it with.

"There is a world of pretty girls out there ready to tempt a young man," she said. "But I always want you to remember that a great girlfriend doesn't always make the best wife. Some men think a pretty face is all it takes, but it never is, it never is."

I grew up in the 1950s and '60s and in many ways, I was fairly naive about sex. I wasn't fast, like many of the other boys my age who had older brothers they had to measure up to. I knew then that a double standard existed regarding sex. According to the tenets of the time, we knew without a doubt that if a relationship survived its early courtship stage and grew serious, we would be expected to marry and have children. I recognized that if you were intimate with a lot of girls, you were respected by the other guys. But if a girl was intimate with several boys, she was seen as easy and whorish. Loose females willing to have sex with anyone were never to be taken seriously as legitimate girlfriends and certainly not as future wives. Back then, girls sleeping around at sixteen were definitely the exception.

During my formative years, boys were never socialized—even in the worst of circles—to go out and exploit women or girls. But while we weren't socialized that way, we witnessed it through the goings-on in the larger adult community. We experienced it through the gossip and our own observations, even though we were never taught that at home. What we learned at home was that marriage was special and that life was sacred.

Of course, making sense of these conflicting messages wasn't always so simple. Often, the dating and sex didn't lead to marriage. But if this was the case and the girl got pregnant, we were taught that the child would be our responsibility. The idea of abortion was never even considered. My extended family always frowned on abortion because to them all life was precious. Out-of-wedlock births reflected on the transgression of the parents rather than on the legal status of the child. The baby was seen as a new life to be loved and nurtured. And it was the man's responsibility to give that new life all the emotional and financial support it needed.

When it came to relationships with women, I'd been socialized largely by my mother, and my aunts Gloria and Alice. They taught me what they believed was appropriate. I did have male role models as well. Mr. Smitty and Arnette Evans were strong pillars of the community whose lives carried no hint of shadow or scandal. But their lessons revolved mostly around achievement, teamwork, and discipline. Girls and sex were rarely part of the discussion. At home, though, such socialization took on a decidedly different slant. It included near-redundant discussions about respecting my three sisters and treating them with love and care, which I heard from the first day each of them was born. I was taught that I was responsible for them, in a sense. The message was clear: Love and respect your sisters and treat all women with respect. "Never hit a woman and never curse a woman," Mama would repeat. "And never date a woman you wouldn't be proud to marry." The issue of having sex never came up.

This message was a stark contrast to the message of the streets, where the issue of sex came up more frequently than the sun. Power on the street carried with it a certain kind of sexual appeal. Either it attracted people to you or it attracted you back to them.The power of the street led to what every guy my age wanted: sex.

In my neighborhood, sex came the easiest to the players, the guys who had some juice on the block and a strong image and rap. If you could talk a good game and back it up, then girls, it seemed, swarmed around you. At that age and despite popular beliefs, scoring didn't always matter. It was the chase we relished, simple and complete.

Compared with teens today, though, we were far from the sexual conquistadors we thought we were. While my first sexual experience was at age fourteen, it was a definite aberration for the '60s. During my initiation into sexuality I was christened with a feast, then cursed with subsequent years of bitter famine.

From the moment I hit puberty, I realized that sex was a coveted perk—it was a fringe benefit of being one of the cats. Everybody thought it was cool to have sex, and none of the guys I knew ever turned it down. When a girl gave it up to you, you began walking differently, talking differently. I wouldn't say we were obsessed by it—but we were overjoyed at getting it.

In many respects, your currency with girls was deeply linked to your reputation and your heart, to your courage and to your bravado. What held value for them was who you knew, who you ran with, what you'd done, and how fearless you were. All the girls loved a bad boy, and sex became a by-product of that respect. Born of being feared, being independent, and controlling your turf, sex was something that would just come along.

And boy, did it ever come along. At least it did for some of the guys I knew. Vanetta Keys and Roxie and Delores Trotter were my closest female friends, but they were the nice girls of the neighborhood. It was all I could do to sneak a kiss with Roxie or Delores while rolling around in their vestibule or sitting on their stoops. I wanted more but they wanted less.

My hormones were jumping by age seventeen and I knew it. It had been three years since the women on McCulloh Street had suddenly moved away, and I had no simple way to connect with ecstasy.

In my frustration and confusion, I turned to women, especially older women, for comfort. In their own way, they were all special to me because they threw me a lifeline and filled the enormous void that threatened to consume me with attention, affection, and care. That was as close as I dared come to love.

Looking back, these liaisons offered the only quiet escape I had from the daily pain of bitter poverty and profound loss. At the time, I thought that these relations were fitting confirmation of my manhood—certainly there was no one in my life to challenge my twisted notions of conquest. I was virtually incapable of opening up and trusting people my own age, but with older women it was different. Unlike those my age, these women seemed to understand that I was a person almost impossible to know. They didn't insist on anything except unblinking honesty and an appreciation of their years.

I was so terribly confused back then that I'm not sure why any woman even bothered dating me, why they didn't go running in the opposite direction the moment I approached them. I had nothing much to offer and I wasn't considered handsome. In the hood, I was just another high school dropout, working at menial jobs, living in a small room, and wasting my time.

My world on its best day was a mixture of scheming, gaming, hustling, and brawling. I was going nowhere fast and chasing after things that would never last.

If my own life had undergone radical change, Clifton Gray's had not. One day after coming home from work, I called over to my grandmother's house to check on my sisters. Darlene answered the phone, and as we were talking, I sensed that she was on edge about something. When she wouldn't tell me what the problem was, I asked to speak with LaWana, who picked up the phone sounding similarly upset. I told LaWana to put Michele on the phone, and there was only silence.

"What the hell is going on?" I asked. No one would say anything.

Darlene came back on the line and I pressed her hard about what was happening there.

"We don't want you to do anything," Darlene pleaded. "Don't get crazy, Pee Wee."

That's when I knew something had happened. "What did Clifton do to you?" I asked, trying to keep the anger out of my voice.

It turned out that Clifton had gone to my grandmother's and for some reason had hit Michele. I thought of Clifton, this six-foot-two, 240-pound man, hitting my little sister. No way. I hung up the phone and rushed over there to check on her. Her entire face was swollen from the blows, one eye puffed up and both cheeks bruised. She was crying hysterically. There was no way that I would allow this to happen again to someone I loved. I picked up the phone and called Gary.

"Meet me on the corner of Presstman and Etting," I said. "Put the gun in the car, the baseball bat, everything."

That was the kind of call Gary usually made to me, so he knew I was serious. Against my sisters' protests, I ran outside, hopped in my car, and sped across town, running red lights and everything to meet Gary, who was already waiting for me when I arrived.

Always the extremist, Gary had in his car about four baseball bats, face masks, a couple of lead pipes, brass knuckles, a shotgun, and a pistol. He also had stolen license plates. We unloaded it all into my car, changed the plates, and zoomed off to make Clifton pay for what he had done.

At the time, Clifton was living with his girlfriend, Ms. Pearl, the woman with whom he had cheated on my mother. Gary and I drove up the street and saw the flicker of television glowing on the second floor of the house where they resided.

We rang the doorbell several times, and when he pulled the curtains back and saw me, Gary and I walked over to his car and started smashing the windows with our pipes. We knocked out the front windshield and the back window and were about to begin on the sides when Clifton came storming out of the house wearing only a T-shirt, shorts, and socks. I was waiting for him to run at me, so I could bash his skull in, but he stopped on the front porch and started hollering and cursing me.

"You just wait, you little no-good muthafucka," he yelled. "I'm going to get your little punk ass put away for this. You ain't shit. You never was shit and you ain't ever going to be shit."

That's when I pulled the automatic from my waistline and popped a bullet in the chamber. Clifton scurried back into the house. I darted off after him, and suddenly heard the piercing wail of sirens in the distance. Gary grabbed me and I broke away. I ran up to the vestibule door and kicked out the windows. Leaning my body through the shattered glass, I pointed the revolver up the stairs and fired off a couple of shots.

"The cops, man!" I heard Gary calling out frantically from the street. "The fuckin' pigs are comin'!" I slipped the gun back in my belt and darted to the car, and Gary drove off.

The following morning the police showed up at my house and arrested me. After a day and night in jail, I was brought before the court commissioner at the district courthouse. Clifton was there in the courtroom, angry as hell. I was charged with destruction of property and assault by threatening. The judge found me guilty, hit me with a fine, and threatened to lock me up for a long time if I went anywhere near my stepfather again.

I never regretted the incident because after that, we didn't have a problem with Clifton Gray ever again. We barely even saw him. He just drifted aimlessly, and a few years later, he died.

Back in those days, I wavered precariously between two very different obsessions: women and war. Both would end up teaching me lessons; women demonstrated how quickly life could be brought into the world and war showed me how quickly life can be taken away.

By 1967, the Vietnam War was raging and the weight of the military burden seemed to land disproportionately on the black community. In sheer numbers, our casualties were alarmingly high. Dr. Martin Luther King, Jr., drew increasing criticism by proclaiming that he would campaign against the controversial war because it had become a major obstacle in advancing the cause of civil rights in America. In more of his speeches, he spoke out not only against the moral cost of the conflict but about its mounting financial burden for the nation. He noted that the government spent $500,000 a year for every Vietcong soldier killed, while only $53 a year was allocated for each person living below the poverty line during the War on Poverty. His words, like the much-publicized statement that "no Vietcong ever called me nigger," caught our attention.

We listened closely to Dr. King's pronouncements, his booming voice cracking with emotion: "I oppose the war in Vietnam because I love America. I speak out against it not in anger but with anxiety and sorrow in my heart, and above all with a passionate desire to see our beloved country stand as a moral example to the world."

In the black community, we knew that the government was spending an exorbitant sum on the war and military defense at a time when so many poor American families were just surviving on the tiny salaries they earned. Most African Americans were still trapped in low-paying jobs, with very few working in skilled or white-collar professions. At that time, only two percent of American doctors and dentists were black, and the median income of blacks was one-third less than that of whites.

Extensive TV coverage brought the barbarity of the war into our homes nightly. The rampant killing of Vietnamese civilians combined with the wanton waste of young American lives left a bitter taste in the mouths of many back home. As the Vietnam conflict continued, more men were needed to maintain troop strength. The mandate from the Selective Service, which administered the draft, found scores of reluctant yet capable conscripts in the nation's ghettos. However, many young black men resisted the draft despite the lack of work to be found in the cities. It was not our war over there—our war was here.

Meanwhile, the domestic war for black people had ignited on the streets of the urban centers as we watched the assaults by white supremacists on civil rights activists in the South. Church bombings, night shootings of black men, Klan attacks on organizers, and police brutality against marchers only heightened the militancy of ghetto residents. Dr. King and his followers may not have struck back, but many people did. It had started four years earlier with a growing wave of race riots throughout the country in places like Rochester, Jersey City, Chicago, and

Philadelphia. In most cases, the National Guard was called out to quell the disturbances. That same year, Harlem residents battled with police in the streets following the shooting of a fifteen-year-old boy. One person was killed, 140 injured, and another 500 arrested. Tensions diminished only when President Johnson sent the FBI to the scene to probe the shooting.

The riots continued, increasing in intensity. It seemed all of the black neighborhoods were powder kegs, just waiting to explode. The more militant young voices of Stokely Carmichael and H. Rap Brown tightened their grip on us. They fed the growing distrust of whites among many in the black community. With pride, young black men and women were growing Afros and wearing dashikis. We were proud of the Black Panthers for standing up to the police reactionaries. Tapes of Malcolm X condemning the more moderate civil rights leaders and their white counterparts were in vogue. Those of us who had survived the streets had a problem with King's impassioned plea to America's conscience in the wake of the bloodstained campaigns of Montgomery, Selma, and Birmingham. Our optimism was eroded by the government's conspiracy against black leaders and organizations, designed to destroy the civil rights struggle.

In this volatile atmosphere, the riots erupted with more frequency. A riot in Cleveland's poor Hough area in July 1966, with black residents firing at police, resulted in four deaths, 50 injuries, and 160 arrests. Another disturbance occurred shortly thereafter in Chicago. Dr. King went there, but was stoned by whites in the suburb of Cicero. The following year, Detroit was devastated by one of the worst riots in America's history, with 43 killed, more than 2,000 arrested, and 5,000 left homeless.

America appeared on the brink of total chaos. The yippies Abbie Hoffman and Jerry Rubin were pushing the antiwar movement further into the pop culture. The 1968 Chicago Democratic Convention became a bloodbath. Peaceniks and the police gave the nation's TV viewers a clear look at homegrown violence.

The widespread rioting in America's cities prompted President Johnson to form a special advisory commission on civil disorders. He tapped Illinois governor Otto Kerner to head it. Between 1964 and 1968 there had been 329 major riots in 257 cities, causing 220 deaths, 8,371 injuries, and 52,629 arrests. The Kerner Commission concluded that "white racism was the principal cause for the disturbances," noting that "our nation is moving toward two societies: one black, one white—separate and unequal."

With all of this going on, the country seemed to be coming apart at the seams over two issues: racism and Vietnam.

Both of those issues profoundly affected me and many other young black men. The specter of bloody Vietnam hung over all of us. The Vietnam conflict was the first war where African Americans were completely integrated into combat units. However, black soldiers were dying at a much higher rate than whites. In fact, in the early years of the war, our soldiers comprised over 23 percent of the fatalities suffered by American troops. This inequity was not lost on me. If you were eighteen and healthy, the one thing that woke you up in the middle of the night was the thought of being drafted, because you had no control over it. There was no escape.

This was a strange time to be a young black man in America. On the one hand, we felt that things were finally going to change for our community, that all things were possible essentially because we possessed more rights than our forebears ever imagined. On the other hand, the forces of repression were raging with renewed vehemence. By 1970, Richard Nixon and his conservative regime were in power. The compassionate spirit of JFK's New Frontier and Lyndon Johnson's Great Society were over and a new self-serving spirit prevailed. Less money was earmarked for programs of social uplift. Less time and energy were spent on revitalizing the blighted inner cities, and the job markets in those areas almost completely dried up as small black businesses went under in record numbers. By 1971, the unemployment rate for blacks was twice that of whites and about 32 percent of black teens were out of work. The only option many young black men possessed was to enlist in the military and take their chances facing the perils of Vietnam.

Some whites were going to Canada to live, while some were

going to graduate school to get a deferment. But in the black community, there were always flashes of the war in your head. You knew that eventually you were going to get called. Each day, its invisible hand seemed to reach down into my neighborhood, pluck out another young black man, and send him off to die in combat.

Reginald Bowman was one of them. If ever there was a gifted soul among us, Reggie was it. Smooth and dapper, he was full of life, as we all were at the age of nineteen. He had pearly white teeth, a thick Afro as round and perfect as a full moon, and an infectious grin contrasted against smooth brown skin. Reggie was the one guy in the neighborhood the girls craved, and all the other guys understood why. You name it and Reggie had it, from a gold tooth and gold chains to pleated sharkskin slacks and colorful Ban-Lon shirts. Nobody could outdance him, or outtalk him with the ladies. He could merely show up on the scene and every girl was instantly goofy and dreamy-eyed for the rest of the day.

Reggie Bowman was everything. Most of all, though, he was my friend. And because he was, it seemed without a doubt that even the world outside our ghetto would have to one day make room for Reggie. As discouraged as I was about my own future, even I knew that about his.

What I didn't know at the time was that this other world, the white world, didn't give a damn about Reginald Bowman or anyone else on my corner. Consumed by its own interests, this world placed no real value on our lives. As long as we stayed out of their neighborhoods, away from their daughters, we were considered inconsequential. Even though both our pain and our existence were invisible to some, we found importance with one another. And Reggie was important to all of us.

When we went down to register for the draft, Reggie took that military office by storm. Even the hardened veterans in the room were taken by his charm.

"You keep your nose clean and your ass to the wall and you can be a good soldier one day, boy," barked a sergeant.

"Yessir," Reggie shot back. "I can be better than good, sir—I can be the best."

Well, we all knew damn well Reggie wasn't into being a soldier, but we fairly blushed because no matter what the situation, our buddy always knew exactly what to say and how to say it.

I will never forget that warm Friday afternoon I went by his house and sat with him on the porch. His draft number had come up and he was leaving for Fort Meade the next morning, and after that to boot camp. Reggie was generally a talkative and jovial guy, but that day he was quiet and somber.

We had just watched a grim President Johnson on television announce that he was sending more U.S. troops into war. Reggie had the look of a doomed man awaiting a date with the gallows. I wanted to know my buddy's thoughts about possibly going to Vietnam to fight.

"You scared, man?" I asked, watching his face.

"Hell, yeah," he replied solemnly. " 'Nam is no joke. You can get wasted over there in a heartbeat."

"You ever think about not going, maybe running off to someplace?"

"I'm not a coward. I'll do what I have to do. I just don't want to die for nothin'. Dig what I'm sayin'?"

Then he gave me the oddest look. There was something churning in his mind that he dared not think, dared not say. "What if I get killed," he murmured. Wearily, he swallowed hard and closed his eyes.

Two months after Reggie went away to Vietnam, he returned home in a body bag. It seems that he had stepped on a land mine while on patrol.

With Reggie dead, and the death toll steadily rising, many of us grew to question our government for sending troops to Vietnam for slaughter. Reggie's death turned me totally against the war. What was the point of it? This was a war that nobody seemed to want. It came when African Americans still were fighting for their right to equal opportunity. Even in Vietnam, black men were unable to avoid the blight of racism. There were reports on the news of Confederate flags flying, cross burnings, and clashes between black and white soldiers. Yet blacks were fighting and dying valiantly for this country in a jungle war ten thousand miles away. They comprised nearly 15 percent of the total combat fatalities, or 50,000 dead. Those who could not get a deferment by going to college prayed that their number did not come up in the draft lottery. Most of the brothers in my community were unlucky.

On campuses around the country, the hippies and peaceniks felt that no one should go. In fact, by 1969, about half of all college students were opposed to the war and the draft, and those numbers continued to climb. That year, violating the draft was the third-ranking crime in the country, and of the 37 million registered for the draft, one in 1,600 was considered delinquent. Thousands left for Canada or Sweden, mostly white youth who could afford the mobility. Nearly 2,000 went to prison rather than go to war.

"No Vietcong ever called me a nigger," we'd say defiantly, knowing that if our draft numbers were called we'd have no choice. We'd have to go to war as the others before us had done. Because I was classified as 1-A by the draft board, I was more than eligible for military service. It was clear that on this point I had little control, but it was equally clear that others did. The pop culture of the day began to reflect a steady protest. The lyrics of songs were changing and simultaneously the messages they sent. Just a few years after the end of the civil rights era, the nation and its people were remarkably being tested again. I, like so many others, was unsuspectingly thrust into the debate. We questioned authority while others redefined loyalty. American patriotism and the Constitution were now on display for the whole world to see. "America, love it or leave it" became the rallying call for "hard hats," a coalition of blue-collar workers, Jaycees, and Veterans of Foreign Wars. They demanded unflinching loyalty to the flag, while the young and the rebellious thirsted for reason. I was certain that my time to "serve and protect" was just around the corner.

Years would pass before I finally realized just how much the war had taken out of my community. When I saw scores of physically maimed, psychologically damaged, and drug-addicted veterans who had returned to a country that offered them little for the sacrifice they had made, I understood their pain in a different way. My friend Dewey came back home missing an arm and addicted to heroin. Blinking at me with his watery eyes, he told me, "I gave this country all I had and turned around and got shit in return. They drafted us, sent us over there, and then forgot all about us. America hated the war but she hated us more. I came back and people acted like I was a criminal or something, like I napalmed villages or killed children. Well, fuck America, and fuck you too." Dewey didn't mean it, but his dignity and soul had been raped.

I looked at the tattered military insignias on his jacket and the dog tags he never stopped wearing. I gave him the last few bucks I had and turned to walk away. He spit on the ground and thanked me. I felt sad as hell for him and all the other vets who had come home to this.

In the end, I was lucky. My draft number never came up. I had no way of knowing that would happen back then, so I adopted a philosophy that later became a shield: "Live for today because tomorrow isn't guaranteed." Indeed, for me tomorrow held little value anyway. I was poor, black, and in real trouble.

What did hold value were here and now, and I pushed both to their limits. When I wasn't working, I spent a lot of time getting decked out and going to parties where the mood was usually light. Nobody was mourning about friends who had been drafted or had been recently killed in the war.

I wanted nothing more than a big reputation, or a "rep," as we called it back then. I certainly didn't want to kill anyone. But I wanted the gang in the neighborhood to know that I was one of the baddest, toughest, and slickest among them. I wanted them to respect me for what they saw me do to others, and to fear me for what they believed I would do to them. I didn't pack a pistol every day yet, so I was prepared to use bricks, bottles, baseball bats, and even switchblades to prove my point.

For the most part, the streets were devoid of ethics. Nobody looked at things from a higher moral ground. That kind of reasoning just didn't exist. Everything was based on instinct and survival. It was all about earning your rep and hanging on to it no matter what the price. Right and wrong had no place in the equation.

Gary and I always hung out together whenever there was a party. We wanted to make sure we had each other's back covered just in case things got out of hand.

One night we were at a party on the east side and away from our turf. Looking back, we probably shouldn't have been there in the first place because we didn't know the neighborhood that well at all. It was just that I'd met this rather fine lady earlier that week and she had invited me to come hang out with her at this set.

As it turned out, the party was jumping. Beer, wine, and reefer were flowing all over the house and fine mamas were packing the place to the gills. The music was thumping hard when we arrived a little past midnight, and the room was rocking with Sam and Dave's "Hold On! I'm a Comin' " and music by the Temptations and Smokey Robinson. Folks were out on the dance floor, grooving and sweating under the blue lights. Damn, they sure know how to party over here on the east side, I thought. After a few more 45s had spun on the turntable, the mood switched when the slow music started. "Love, love, love makes me do foolish things . . ." It was Martha and the Vandellas, and in no time I was back out on the dance floor with a girl. Gary was over in the corner, leaning suavely into the face of some fine mama. I was dancing slowly, sweating, and trying to dip while the woman I held was digging in. "What's your name, baby?" she asked while smiling up at me. "Pee Wee," I said through my heavy breathing as I inhaled her perfume. I pressed my lips against her soft brown cheek.

"Pee Wee," she softly exclaimed. "You're too big to be a Pee Wee."

"Well, that's who I am," I said weakly.

"You must not be from around here, huh, baby?"

"No," I said, "I'm from the west side."

"Well, I tell you what, Pee Wee. I'm gonna call you 'Coffee,' 'cause you grind so fine."

Well, as soon as she said that I got an erection that wouldn't stop. It was harder than eighty dollars' worth of jawbreakers.

But by the time the music faded and James Brown began screaming, "This is a man's world," another girl had grabbed me for a slow drag. I was having a ball. From the look on Gary's face as he slid his arms around his new lady's slender waist, he certainly was too.

But then, from the corner of my eye, I saw trouble brewing. Some rough dudes were peering over at Gary, who was too busy running down his line to notice their stare. I didn't stop dancing, but I watched the situation closely. I saw Gary lower his arm from around the girl's waist when she handed him her glass for a refill. As Gary walked in the direction of the bloods, I caught his eye and beckoned him over my way.

"What's up, man?" he asked.

"You cool?"

"I'm straight."

"But watch your back," I whispered. "I think some bloods here got a problem with you pushin' up on the lady."

"Well, fuck 'em," he said. "She's all over me, man. I don't give a fuck if they are jealous."

"Yeah, but . . ."

Gary cut me off and walked away toward the steps, heading upstairs. I spotted one of the guys moving in his direction, released the young lady I was dancing with, and walked toward him and stopped. Slowly withdrawing the .32 caliber snub-nose pistol I had strapped to my leg, I then cut my way through the throng. When the guy's pace quickened I moved faster.

"Yo, look out, Gary," I yelled.

Gary turned around just as the dude dove on him, and a fight broke out on the steps. I saw the guy's crew moving toward the brawl, and I fired three shots into the ceiling. His boys stopped in their tracks and looked at me with absolute fear in their eyes as I waved my pistol in their direction. The fight on the steps stopped, too, when they heard the shots. Then screams and cries erupted. Everyone scrambled to get as far away from me as possible. The music went off. The crowd panicked.

"Go ahead," I yelled. "I dare you to jump him!"

I walked over to one of them, a big, dark dude, and got right up in his face. "Try it!" I hollered, as I busted him upside the head with the gun. His head bleeding, he cowered away with his face in his hands.

I stepped up in another one's face and pointed the barrel to his temple. "I should snuff your ass right here," I said. Then I cracked him across the face with the side of the gun even harder than the first cat.

"Gary," I called out. "You cool?"

"Yeah, man," his voice came back.

"Let's get outta here," I said. "It ain't nothin' but a bunch of lame-ass punks here!"

The room was at a complete standstill. Gary got up off the steps, dusted himself off. I slid my piece into my belt and we made our way up the steps, waiting for someone else to move, but they didn't. I felt a huge rush of power surge through me. With a pistol and one fit of rage I had tilted the balance of power in my direction. As we rushed out the door with the sound of sirens starting to blur, Gary turned to me and stopped.

"Damn," he said. "I forgot something back there."

"What?"

"That chick's phone number!"

"You're crazy," I said. "You are out of your damn mind."

"Nigga, you're the one who's crazy." Gary laughed. "Even I ain't never shot up no party."

I went home that night feeling numb and carefree. For the first time since I'd met him, Gary Fenwick had honored me as "crazy." From him, that was the ultimate compliment.

I met my first love, Pauline, on one of those blue-light party nights in June of 1966. I was hangin' out at a small dance hall over on Lafayette Avenue. A jukebox was blaring and party streamers were looped across the ceiling. The warm, un-air-conditioned room seemed to sway slowly in the heat of the crowd. Even in a room full of pretty women, Pauline stood out in the throng of black teenagers. I was with Gary that night, and I remember spotting her across the room, sipping punch and chatting with a group of friends.

"Good Lord," I whispered. "Do you see what I see? Check

her out." I nudged Gary and glanced in her direction. "Now, that's what I call fine." On the next take, I quickly recanted. "No, that's what I call superfine." By now, my mouth was gaping open and I stood there in a daze.

Half girl and half woman, Pauline was beautiful. She was unadorned by makeup or trinkets, and her virginal demeanor was completely enchanting. For a few long moments that night, I stood there in the midst of the crowd admiring her mane of black hair that cascaded and curled down to her shoulders. Her moist, light-brown skin was radiant, and her soft curves revealed a youthful innocence beneath a form-fitting dress. Part of me was intimidated by her beauty and part of me couldn't take my eyes off of her. She reminded me of the older girls I'd swooned over back in Turners Station when puppy love was a way of life. Pauline had a wholesome manner that suggested a good upbringing. I liked that.

As the Impressions sang "Gypsy Woman," I found myself gliding in her direction. I greeted her with a smile and extended my hand. She looked up shyly and offered me an innocent smile of her own.

"Wanna dance?"

"Yes." She nodded, and gave me her hand.

Through what seemed to be an invisible crowd, I ushered her slowly onto the dance floor. We danced and smiled at each other all night long. When we weren't dancing, I was busy leaning into her pretty face. By the time the last song was playing—Percy Sledge singing "When a Man Loves a Woman"—I was smitten. As the crowd slowly filed out of the dance hall, Gary shook his head in disbelief but never said a word.

After the party, I walked Pauline home. Sauntering slowly past the line of row houses with their lighted windows, we made small talk and blushed until we reached her door. We stood outside on the steps for a while. The house windows were open and propped up by summer screens, so we couldn't be too sure that her parents weren't just on the other side awaiting her return. We talked and laughed in whispers until, finally, after ten minutes or so, she ended the night.

"It's very nice meeting you," she said. "Thank you for walking me home."

"It's nice meeting you too," I muttered. "Would you like maybe to go to a movie next week?"

"I think so," she said. "If I can get out of the house."

Then she brushed my hand lightly with her fingers and walked up the steps and through the door.

That's how it all began with Pauline and me. Three months later, we were moving blissfully, if not haplessly, into our first sexual encounter, an encounter we would both soon regret. In the fall of 1967, Pauline called me to her home and broke the news. "I'm pregnant," she said.

I was devastated. The announcement of Pauline's pregnancy sent me straight into orbit. I was eighteen years old and couldn't imagine how I'd ended up in this fix. If Pauline was upset, her parents were furious. My financial prospects were bleak. And without my mother there to guide me, I simply felt as though I were drowning in a sea of troubles. How could I possibly take care of a wife and baby when I was barely able to take care of myself?

Unfortunately, instead of bringing me to my senses, Pauline's pregnancy had the opposite effect. With renewed vigor, I devoted myself to being a manchild running wild. I never fully considered the ramifications of my behavior. I figured I was as safe as most of the guys I knew who were having sex, but I wound up feeling cursed. It seemed that every time I did it someone else became pregnant. Every time—it never failed!

The subsequent overlapping births of my other sons within such a short period of time only added to the insanity of my life. I never knew the results of my tom catting around until I got the news of each forthcoming baby.

I gave new meaning to the phrase "sowing wild oats." Consider: In May 1968, Pauline gave birth to Donald. Later that year in August, Yvonne gave birth to Kevin. A year later, in October 1969, Brenda had my son Keith. In January 1970, Carlitta gave birth to Michael. And three weeks later, in January 1970, Pauline gave birth to our second child, a boy we named Ronald.

I often think back to what was going on in my head in the first place that would compel me to be intimate with so many young women in such a short period of time. Certainly, none of this could have happened if I hadn't sought sex to begin with.

As a teenager, I could never understand why I was paying such a high price for my promiscuity. Why was I being singled out? I knew guys in the neighborhood who went through girls like a bee going from flower to flower, but they never got anyone pregnant. And I knew girls in the neighborhood who slept with countless dudes and never got pregnant. All of these pregnancies wiped me out emotionally and twisted my head around for a while.

Having sex began feeling like a trip to the casino. And because I knew the odds were stacked against me, I placed my bets cautiously, and I became wary and nervous whenever the mood hit. Fathering five sons in two and a half years was a testament to my promiscuity. I was out of control and didn't know it. I was on a roller coaster headed straight down. Life, I thought, had always been cruel to me, so why should I expect anything else? Hadn't I been the one born into poverty, who suffered illness and near-death before the age of six? Wasn't it the man whom I thought to be my father who reminded me daily that I would never be anything? Didn't God snatch my mother away when I was but sixteen and my youngest sister was only ten? And shouldn't I recognize that, try as I might, I had become another statistic of America's underclass? Those and other questions I would one day answer for myself, but for now a new reality was settling in.

Becoming a father before my time brought with it many pressures, and among them was the pressure to marry. I felt as though it was the right thing to do, but I had absolutely nothing to offer.

I was a high school dropout without a single skill in the world. All I knew how to do was push bread through a slicer, shine shoes, and shoot dice. I was completely broke most of the time and didn't really have a roof to call my own. I was still living in a room at my uncles' house, and without any assets or the prospect of acquiring any, getting married seemed forever out of reach and distant for me.

Pauline, Brenda, Carlitta, and Yvonne were wonderful young women whom I cared for deeply, but I was now twenty-two and clueless. I was skeptical about whether our young love could withstand the day-in, day-out grind of poverty. They had never experienced the everyday hardships that I'd watched my mother go through and it was my prayer that they never would. I couldn't bear the thought of any of my sons' mothers scuffling in menial jobs while trying to raise a family, and growing old before their time the way my mother had. I had to find a way to guarantee that they'd never go hungry or get evicted from an apartment because we couldn't pay the rent. I wanted things to be better for us and better for my children. I was intent on trying to break the cycle of near-poverty in my life.

At the same time, though, I realized that my relationship with my children was no laughing matter. Donald, Kevin, Keith, Michael, and Ronald would soon become and forever remain the purpose of my life. My love for them far exceeded my love for myself, and I became a child again each moment we spent together. As I watched them learn how to walk and talk, I saw myself all over again. I understood what my father must have felt looking at me as a child, and what his father before him felt. They became my reasons to stay alive, the reasons that wouldn't let me ever give up.

On the night of April 4, 1968, I returned home from a long shift at the automotive repair factory where I had just found work. After washing a day's worth of grease and gook from my hands and face, I flung myself across the tiny bed that took up most of my room and reached to turn on my transistor radio. It was then that I heard the news.

Frantically, the voice on the radio cried out that Dr. Martin Luther King, Jr., the man of peace, had been shot and killed by a white man. I was both stunned and dazed, frozen without words. King had been standing on the balcony of the Lorraine Motel in Memphis when he was hit. Jesus Christ, I thought, this can't be happening again. First Kennedy, then Malcolm, now Martin. The image of the photo with Dr. King dying on the motel walkway and the others pointing at some unseen killer still haunts me. Twenty-eight years later I would go there myself and stand where he stood on that balcony. Dr. King was killed by some white bigot, I thought, like so many others who hated anything black. And all of white America was holding its breath, and all of black America erupted.

With my body still numb, I really did not know what to do with myself. They had killed him. They had finally killed Dr. King. I could hear his voice in my head as my anger seethed. That his booming, heartfelt voice was now stilled forever was more than I could comprehend.

Like so many others who heard the news that night, I felt a strange compulsion to run outside to be out in the open air. I jumped up quickly and darted into the streets. The chilling news had begun to spread as mobs of screaming people emerged from their homes. Some stood stock-still. A few cried uncontrollably. Others cursed the white hate that had snuffed out the life of our brightest hope. I had never seen a group of people so angry. Any white person, anything connected with white people, was fair game for this collective rage.

Everywhere I turned, I heard the same questions asked: How could they do this? How could they have killed such a man? The murder of Dr. King struck a massive blow at the very soul of the black community in a way that the shooting of Malcolm X never did. Dr. King was a man of nonviolence; he never raised his voice in anger against those who had cursed, beat, and jailed him.

Everyone remembered how he had refused to retaliate when he was stoned in Cicero. He was obviously hurt, but he didn't answer hate with hate. He was our saint, our Nobel prize winner, and now he had been cut down. The whole neighborhood was out in the streets that night. Traffic was blocked off and nothing was moving. Nobody used the sidewalks—we walked in the streets. Everyone was crazed with anger and needed to vent it fast. The anger had spread through them like fire in their bones.

Then came the sound of shattering glass as the crowd moved over to Pennsylvania Avenue. They went on a rampage, overturning cars, shattering their windows, and setting them afire. Then they turned their attention to the shops along the Strip.

Almost everyone seemed consumed by this fever, this need to smash, to destroy, to obliterate something tangible with their pent-up rage. Glass from the stores dotting the community lay in jagged shards as crowd after crowd moved in a frenzy down the street. Desperate store owners put up makeshift signs proclaiming "Soul Brother" on their doors and stood out in front, begging the throng not to vandalize their businesses. Others hung red, black, and green flags in their windows, hoping that this show of allegiance would convince the crowds to spare them. It was a remarkable scene and yet a regrettable one. We were blind with rage, and collectively were destroying our community. From a curb on Pennsylvania Avenue, I watched the chaos with a bewildering mixture of horror and amazement.

Dark clouds of smoke billowed into the night sky from dozens of fires throughout the city as the sound of wailing sirens approached. The police arrived and fanned out in a feeble attempt to contain the disturbance. They were clearly outnumbered—and they knew it. This was mayhem without rhyme or reason, the most dangerous kind. Outfitted with riot gear, with hands placed firmly on their guns, the police stood by their cars and watched the mobs go about their destructive spree. When their precinct captains ordered them into the melee, they hesitated, fearing for their own lives. They knew they represented everything that the rioters hated at that very moment. And none of them wanted to die. But quite a few of the people in the crowd were prepared to die that night, if need be. They hurled bricks and rocks at the officers. The police, oddly, held back, maybe because they understood our profound loss, or maybe because they understood that we were only hurting ourselves by destroying what little we had.

That night, virtually the whole neighborhood was burned down. Businesses, buildings, cars, and houses were on fire everywhere I looked. The tragedy was that it was our own community that was being reduced to ashes. Just as it was happening in the core of West Baltimore, it was also happening uptown in Park Heights and Reisterstown Road. On the east side, businesses all along Gay Street, East North Avenue, and

Broadway were torched completely. Whether it was an auto dealer or a grocery store, it burned that night.

I couldn't believe what was happening but couldn't imagine a world without Martin Luther King either. In my eyes, Dr. King *was* the civil rights movement. I was aware of other leaders, though none could compare to Dr. King.

In the months prior, Dr. King and his safety had been on my mind. I knew if they could kill a president, then those with sick minds would think nothing of killing a black man. Dr. King had been changing in those final years just before his assassination, expanding his strategy to include economic and political issues as well as moral ones. He addressed the need for equal access to housing and employment and challenged the government to live up to the true meaning of its creed. In one speech, he countered his critics by asking, "What good does it do to be able to eat at a lunch counter if you can't buy a hamburger?" When he spoke out against the Vietnam War, many black and white leaders attacked him, saying he should stick to civil rights issues, with some of them accusing him of being un-American. Rednecks openly remarked that he was sticking his nose in where it didn't belong. In many white communities, the thinking was: "Wait a minute, boy, it's all right as long as you're talking about black people. But don't start talking about America and what it should not be doing globally." Many of his closest friends backed away, especially once J. Edgar Hoover turned up the heat in a full-scale effort to discredit him.

Toward the end, as the FBI plan to bring him down increased, Dr. King stepped up his activism, working harder, sometimes twenty-four hours a day. He seemed to be everywhere. He understood that our community was running out of time.

In one of his last writings, the prophetic 1966 "Where Do We Go From Here: Chaos or Community?", Dr. King warned both white America and the African American community to get our house in order before our time ran out. "We are now faced with the fact that tomorrow is today," and "we are confronted with the fierce urgency of now. In this unfolding conundrum of life and history, there is such a thing as being too late. Procrastination is still the thief of time. Life often leaves us standing bare, naked, and dejected with a lost opportunity. . . . [We] may cry out desperately for time to pause in her passage, but time is deaf to every plea and rushes on. Over the bleached bones and jumbled residues of numerous civilizations are written the prophetic words 'Too late.' There is an invisible book of life that faithfully records our vigilance or neglect. . . . [We] still have a choice today: nonviolent coexistence or violent co-annihilation. This may well be mankind's last chance to choose between chaos and community." Prophetic words indeed.

Dr. King understood that fundamental change, not just the right to vote, was needed to improve the living conditions of all Americans. That was why he returned in his final days to his moral fight for the grass roots, those too often overlooked and left out. The Memphis protest for the garbage workers was the last example of that mission.

I walked block after block that night, dazed by the destruction around me. When I returned to my street, I saw the Pottashes' store being ransacked and looted. The glass had been kicked out and the doors ripped off and people were running out of the store with handfuls of merchandise and throwing it into the street. It hurt me to watch that, but everyone was powerless to stop it. Sheer rage had boiled over like a volcano erupting. David Pottash and his wife and kids hadn't done anything to deserve this. Their only crime was that they were white and Jewish in a sea of black pain. I knew they believed in Dr. King and his vision, and had done whatever they could in the community to gain the trust of black people. But, like a lot of Jewish shop owners who lived above their stores, they had become a target of the collective rage exploding in the streets that night. The only thing that prevented the Pottashes' store from being torched was the police who parked there on Robert and Division.

By eleven o'clock, the police department had called in all available personnel, even those who were off duty, and the arrests began. By the following morning, the jails were packed to the gills at every station and precinct in the city.

It was a sad, ugly night. The almost intolerable suffering and pain of our loss was too much for us to bear, so we hurt ourselves. Cut away in the process were many of the vital supports of our own communities. Martin Luther King was dead, and with that loss came the realization that our best and brightest hope for renewal and redemption had been taken. Something died in our neighborhood that night. Dr. King had been our moral compass, and the fortunes of so many of our communities seemed to evaporate that April evening. So much went through my mind as I watched my people burn their future.

The wanton destruction born of rage and despair affected not less than 125 major cities, where full-scale rioting had occurred. A week after Dr. King's death, President Johnson signed a comprehensive civil rights bill into law, but it was too little too late.

I stepped outside the next morning to the blaring of police bullhorns calling for an end to the riots. It was the same desperate call being sounded by law enforcement officials across the country as they struggled to tame the unruly mobs rampaging through cities from Los Angeles to Detroit to Newark. In the hood, weary-eyed politicians stood on street corners, vainly crying out for order.

"Stay in your homes! Don't destroy your community!" voices bellowed. "We'll get through this! Don't get arrested! Don't burn anything! Don't steal anything!"

Nobody listened to the cops or the politicians. Some of them had rocks hurled at them. Nobody wanted to hear their message. People only wanted to unleash their anger out in the streets. Nobody was at work that day. Everybody was in the street—some seething quietly, while others exploded with rage. Sidewalks became useless as people swarmed the streets, daring anybody—even police—to hit them. For those hours, at least, we had claimed the streets as our own.

On this second day of rioting, it was clear that the upheaval was not going to subside. The President declared a national emergency and ordered the National Guard into Baltimore. The Guard was marshaled because of the fear that with our own streets now burned, we would move into neighboring communities and wreak similar destruction. The mobs, which had started spilling uptown, across town, and downtown, had only white neighborhoods to move into and torch. The Guards were brought in to ensure that didn't happen.

Before long, the streets were teeming with army personnel carriers cutting through the thick crowd. Soldiers were everywhere, sitting grim-faced in trucks, twenty deep at times, holding their weapons, riding along waiting to stop and be deployed, at which point they would run off the truck and assume a position on the street with fixed bayonets and a mission to protect property. I didn't know if the orders were shoot to kill or what, but these soldiers looked scared and yet ready to kill. The guards were all over the streets for blocks. The few black ones caught hell because they were black.

"You're not a soul brother! You're here to do the white man's bidding!" folks yelled out at them.

But they were standing at attention or they were in fixed positions. They never said anything, never blinked, never sneered, never smiled. They knew what their orders were, and were prepared to carry them out.

By nightfall, the community was an armed camp, occupied by the National Guard, with a dusk-to-dawn curfew imposed on residents. Later, Gary said it was as if white folks were saying, "Well, you've had your time to grieve, but enough is enough." Because there was no facility large enough to jail all the rioters, the mayor and the governor authorized the use of the Fifth Regiment Armory.

That night I ventured back out into the smoldering, wreckage-strewn streets. The looting had been heaviest at night, and I wanted to see what was going on in the streets for myself. According to the news, rioting was still going on in cities across the nation. This was history, in a sense. I wanted to witness it firsthand. More, I was desperate to know what was happening to black people in my community, to my neighbors. I didn't violate the curfew to toss a Molotov cocktail or smash a window. I just wanted to see what was happening. Suddenly, I felt my arm seized roughly, and turned to face the steely glare of a white officer. Using his weight, he pushed me swiftly toward a nearby armored truck. I lunged away from him but was wrestled to the ground by another officer from my blind side.

"Let me loose!" I yelled, struggling to break free. But they were all over me, yanking my arms around my back. "I live in this block," I protested.

"I don't give a damn where you live," I heard one of them snort as handcuffs went around my wrists. "You got no business out here."

Just a few years ago I had swooned to Kennedy's vision of hope in the Fifth Regiment Armory, but that night I was jailed there with hundreds of other black men and women. My head was throbbing with anger as I stood in the hot, musty armory where we were packed like sardines. It was a big, cavernous facility but there were very few rest rooms in the place and the stench of urine was unbearable, along with the maddening feeling of claustrophobia that gripped me after several hours of being trapped. But just as I had found a way to sneak in years before, I decided I would find a way to sneak out that night.

As a kid, I used to climb up wire and poles to go steal pigeons out of the church's belfry. I'd climb up about fifty feet onto a pole and swing myself into the belfry, where I could grab pigeons to take home to raise. That night, in the back of the armory outside a window, I spotted a long black electrical wire wrapped in a dark plastic sheet, and plotted a simple escape plan. There were plenty of police and guards around. But I was patient, and careful not to draw attention to myself. I waited and waited, walked around and walked around, and the first time I found an opening I slipped through, got out a window, and climbed down the wire onto the street, where I safely took the back alleys to go home.

For the next two nights, the riots continued throughout the city. The strict curfews and the National Guard's policing managed to restore the semblance of order to the streets. Still, when the smoke lifted and the Guard finally left, it was clear that West Baltimore would never be the same.

The Pottashes, nor any of the other Jewish store owners for that matter, never returned to my neighborhood, which was now littered with vacant stores. Singed and burned-down buildings now hung over the landscape. The City of Baltimore, in its so-called restoration effort, spent the three weeks following the riots merely boarding up buildings. Soon, it seemed that nearly every building on the Avenue was boarded and shut.

It's been said that once you kill the head, the body has to die. Dr. King was the head, and it wasn't long until the anger over his assassination turned to confusion. And our disillusionment and anger were only heightened by the fact that a white man, an ex-convict named James Earl Ray, had killed our leader. People were searching for a sense of direction but there was none, in large part because King had represented our bridge to the white community, and was perhaps the only leader whose intelligence and charisma had a galvanizing effect on both the races. Even though we hurt for our community, many of us now wanted to escape it and could not. We knew even then that the city would never be the same. In thirty years, failed efforts to rehabilitate and renovate have confirmed that fear. But a big part of that failure is the result of a trend nobody can legislate against: After the riots, those who could afford to get out fled my community en masse and never returned.

My first son would be born less than a month after the riots ended. It's a good thing in many respects that my children didn't have to live through that upheaval—in their lifetime they would have upheaval of their own. While this country has a long and bitter history of social unrest, nothing has come close to the riots. The level of rage, spontaneity, or pain has never been as far-reaching as in those days following King's death.

Not long after the riots, on a bright day in June, I was standing on the corner waiting for Gary when I noticed a man dressed crisply in a suit and tie walking up and down the street, handing out fliers and introducing himself as Parren Mitchell.

I recognized his name instantly—at least the Mitchell half of it. In my neighborhood, everybody knew who the Mitchells were. They were famous and they were powerful. My mother used to speak admiringly about Clarence and Juanita Mitchell. "Right here in our neighborhood is one of the most respected political black families in this whole state," she'd say when we first moved to West Baltimore, and later she spoke of how their fight for civil rights was even gaining them national attention. Not long after she died, I'd read in *The Afro-American* that Mr. Mitchell's brother Parren was working with the Community Action Agencies, in Lyndon Baines Johnson's War on Poverty. Every big city had a similar program, and Parren ran the one in Baltimore. On this day, he was asking people to support him in his run for the United States Congress.

Johnson's War on Poverty programs, which started in 1964 in response to earlier urban rioting, offered millions of dollars to hard-hit areas for education, housing, job training, and recreation. These Great Society programs were later criticized by many conservatives, but many poor people, especially the young, were greatly aided by their implementation. Originally put into place to quell the possibility of unrest during long, hot summers, they allowed local communities to create positive outlets for all of the restless young people.

No matter what my mother's feelings were, I honestly could not have cared less about the clean-cut fellow campaigning up and down Division Street. I was thinking about my own troubled life. I was thinking about possibly going to Vietnam and coming back in a body bag. I was thinking about the ladies and how I was already a father. I was thinking about my future and how I didn't seem to have one. I was thinking about how pissed off I was at this square-looking dude passing out bullshit on my turf. All I knew was that he had to have some heart to be working my corner. He was handing out some lame flier about his running for some stupid public office. Even though a camera crew followed closely behind him, it was dangerous for him to be here. What had politicians done for me, or any of us down here anyway? All they did was talk, talk, talk. I waited for him to walk over my way, and when he did, I called him out.

Taking a long drag off my cigarette, I stepped up in his face and let the smoke out. "Look, my man, you need to move on outta here with that bullshit you're handin' out. This is my ground, and you're standin' on it."

My words didn't faze him. Parren was, and still is, a very

engaging person and not prone to intimidation of any sort, especially from a young trash-talking street tough like I was. Surprised that he seemed to warm up to my challenge, I moved up on him so close that I was looking dead in his eye.

"Young brother," he said sharply. "This isn't your corner, and if it is you're just wasting your life standin' on it."

His words washed over me like ice water. I was stunned that this old man was fronting me off like this. I was nineteen at the time and could only think of how good it might feel to be kicking a member of the first family's ass. But that seemed too easy, and perhaps too risky as well. I bit down hard and sold another wolf ticket as I let the heat I was packing show, stuck in my belt. "First of all, I ain't your fuckin' brother. Like I said, old man," with the gun now more evident than ever, "you're standing on my ground. You lucky I haven't kicked your ass or robbed you. So why don't you just keep on steppin'?"

"No, why don't you tell me what your problem is?"

"My problem is that you or nobody else can't do nothin' to change things for black people. And I don't like you comin' around here lyin' and actin' like you can."

"Then tell me, young man, what are you doing to help black people, or even yourself for that matter?"

"I work."

"And I suppose you think working is enough. We've been working for hundreds of years in this country. Nothin' new about that."

"Just get on up outta my face, old man. That con game you're runnin' ain't gonna work here."

"The only con game being played is the one you're playing on yourself. You actually think standin' on that corner will get you respect. Well, I don't respect you because you're wasting your life away. And the white man doesn't respect you either. You tell me who respects you."

"Look, Dr. King already tried what you're doin' and look what happened to him. Look at what happened to this neighborhood."

Parren laughed. "Please, young man, don't talk to me about Dr. King or this neighborhood until you're ready to become part of the solution and not the problem.

"Brother, I can't help anyone who doesn't want to help themselves. When you understand that you need to be involved in a system much bigger than this street corner, then we can talk."

He reached in his jacket pocket and handed me a card, saying that if I ever managed to change my mindset to give him a call. And he left.

Over the next few weeks, I couldn't shake off my exchange with Parren Mitchell. For all my bluster, I knew I was walking a kind of tightwire and that my ability to sustain such a precarious balance was no more predictable than the wind itself. While I had never wanted to concede to the harsh possibility of falling, believing that second guesses only hasten defeat, I was burdened with a gnawing inner voice that I could not silence. It was a voice that hailed from deep within and spoke gloomily of prison, death, and damnation.

I had long squelched this spiritual voice by turning up the volume of my own voice, but shortly after my encounter with Parren I listened to it and reflected on it. I wondered whether this other self had in fact provided the gravity that had kept me alive on the tightwire. I wondered why all these years after my mother's death, I had essentially been living two lives: one that was obscure and remote and streetwise which I kept hidden from my family, and the other that was grounded in the values with which I was raised. One part of me thrived on being cunning and vicious, while the other was quietly going off to work, giving money to my grandmother for my sisters.

Now and then, my buddies had all wondered aloud why I even bothered working a regular job, considering I was pulling down enough cash from hustling to make my minimum-wage gigs look like peanuts. Sometimes I even wondered the same thing, and yet I could never answer that.

I can only reason that I kept my jobs because my family has always been hardworking. My mother worked at the assembly plant, and when she got off, she went to work for white folks in their kitchens. My stepfather worked, sometimes fifteen hours a day, out with his rig, running cargo all over the place. All my uncles worked and my aunts worked. So for me, keeping a job always seemed natural, no matter what else I was up to.

Shortly after my confrontation with Parren Mitchell, I found myself thinking a lot about my dueling identities, and how Mitchell had dismissed both sides of me as irrelevant. I also thought about how it would have hurt my mother to know that a member of the Mitchell family regarded her only son as a problem for black folks rather than a solution. But in my heart, I knew I was far from ready to give up my life on the street. I was too connected to it, and it to me.

Still, with all these thoughts swirling in my head, I decided to at least give Parren Mitchell a call. Maybe, somehow, there was something positive in it for me. He, like Hubert Humphrey, who was running for President, at least seemed to be true to his convictions. A day later, I began working as a volunteer in his campaign headquarters. My role was not much more than walking the neighborhood and putting fliers in doors, or approaching people to ask if I could put a Parren Mitchell bumper sticker on their car. The work didn't make me feel much better, but it did make me feel involved.

Both Parren and Humphrey lost that year, but I won something in the process. I saw two men with courage and compassion stand up to the odds and fight for what they believed in.

Looking back, I know that something was kindled in me in that seemingly inconsequential face-off with Parren Mitchell. Sometimes a chance meeting can alter your life, and this was one of those times. Although three years would pass before I experienced my epiphany, who knows what would have happened to me if I had not met Parren that day. I began to consider the reason for my being alive, the reason I was spared from the hell of Vietnam. Back then, I couldn't know what that reason was; I only had a vague sense that there was a reason. But this moment of introspection quickly vanished when I faced my reality and the urgency of making it on the streets. I began running harder and faster from myself, and from my mother's voice.

7

NOWHERE TO RUN, NOWHERE TO HIDE

*O*NE of the most fascinating aspects of human life is its unpredictable nature, the seemingly arbitrary manner in which events unfold. Some people find the volume of life's uncertainties so unsettling that they remain frozen in a state of perpetual indecision. They feel powerless and view themselves as floating aimlessly toward some unknown destiny. But I don't believe that all people spend their lives merely floating. Many walk a spiritual path revealed to them by a force much greater than themselves. These epiphanies, these moments of spiritual transformation, are a gift of the Divine. They bring revelation, clarity, and purpose to lives that had once seemed mired in chaos.

I'm not suggesting that we can define, categorize, or explain every single event that occurs during our lifetime. I am saying that from time to time on our life's path we come upon pivotal events that defy description or analysis, events that lead to a greater understanding of ourselves. Sometimes if we are lucky they offer a life-altering message. Some people see these events as gateways, signposts, or moments of revelation. Others describe them as mysteries or blessings, absent of explanation. I choose to call them miracles.

It is easy to believe that these strange and powerful moments, as inexplicable as they are, might be figments of a vivid imagination. Many have listened skeptically to the recovering alcoholic who swears to have heard angel wings at the moment of his lowest depth, or the hapless sinner who comes crying for grace after holding the cold hand of death. While such testimonials might stretch the boundaries of what we know as reality, we must confess that our realities are limited. When we acknowledge that our human understanding is woefully inadequate to explain spiritual epiphanies, we have taken an important first step. I believe, based on my own personal experience, that what may sound like a far-fetched tale or episode often turns out to be a precious glimpse into how God steps in at times to save us from ourselves. Was it not Saul of Tarsus who was struck blind on the road to Damascus before being transformed into Paul, the disciple of Jesus?

Over the years, many people have asked me how I was able to tear myself away from the strong lure of the streets in West Baltimore. And, try as I might, I have never been able to provide the one-size-fits-all answer that many of them are seeking. I do know that my transformation was not by design or deep introspection. I wasn't that conscious at the time. Many people trapped in the declining spiral of a dismal life have been redeemed without the call of the heavenly trumpet. It's precisely because of this that I continue to marvel over the mysterious event that occurred in my life in the summer of 1972—a mystery that ultimately became my miracle. Just as I've never been able to comprehend the strange howling of that dog on the night my mother died, neither will I ever understand my own epiphany. Nor will I ever forget the spiritual emergency that brought it to be.

The city had been steaming hot that Friday afternoon. The rows of marble stoops that lined the sidewalks of West Baltimore seemed to be nothing more than a progression of right angles as dusk began to cool the humid air. The July heat was still lingering in the thick evening haze, but with slightly less intensity. Those who had gone inside their homes to escape the sweltering afternoon sun were starting to come back outside. Some sat on their stoops, while others leaned headfirst out their windows, hoping to catch a rare breeze.

From my bedroom window, I could hear the banter of children laughing and talking down on the street, and the firm beckoning of mothers calling them inside. For a moment, the streets grew calm and peaceful and I, in my youth, grew restless.

Before long, though, the air was filled with the deep, raucous voices of the men who'd begun to congregate. The corner of Laurens and Division streets was now converting to its night shift, with boys in the hood wanting to be men, shooting dice and talking trash. This was the sound that beckoned me that evening, a sound that told me night had truly fallen over the city.

Sweating despite the furious whirring of an electric fan, I pulled on a red silk shirt and black gabardine pants and readied myself for the action outdoors. Maybe I'd smoke some weed, drink some brew, and if my hand was hot, make a little money as well. I reached inside my dresser and grabbed some cash from the bottom drawer. I put the tens and twenties in my back pocket, ones and fives in my front, and tucked a pack of Kools in my socks. With a few round strokes, I rubbed some Dixie Peach pomade in my hair, brushed it back, and pulled the collar up on my shirt. After a final check in the mirror, I left and headed down to the street to the corner I loved.

We called it Hankin's Corner, a testament to our affinity with Hankin's liquor store, which straddled the intersection of Laurens and Division just a block down the street from my house. Hankin's was a run-down store in an even more run-down building whose crumbling stone facade seemed on the brink of collapse. This corner that I loved so well existed in a different solar system from the white world that helped create it. If the segregated housing patterns of the '30s and '40s had spawned the ghetto, then surely corners like Hankin's secured it. Even though it was an eyesore to many, we were the loyal patrons who supported the store. Its wide windows were filthy, blackened with dirt. The corners and sills were encrusted with dead flies from summers past. But Hankin's wine and whiskey kept us so high and disconnected that none of it ever mattered.

Several cardboard posters stood faded in the window—pictures of smiling white people hoisting a glass of booze. A cigarette was always dangling carelessly from their other hand, with a pack of Lucky Strikes or Camels lying clearly within reach. Smaller signs taped to the windows pictured bottles of Wild Irish Rose, Jack Daniel's, and Thunderbird wine. Ironically or deliberately, these potions or products seemed to always be on sale. I often wondered why the white people on those posters always seemed to be so happy. It was obvious that they were trapped in a neighborhood they couldn't get out of, held in the grip of Hankin's Corner, just like me.

By now the corner was bustling with the young and brash of the neighborhood—the hoodlums, slickers, and wanna-be's. Their bodies and black skin, backlit by the red and yellow glow of neon lights, glistened in the nighttime heat. But no illumination could soften the haunted expressions of age etched deeply in their young ebony faces. All the better-known members of the group were out that night. As I walked toward the corner I saw Mumbles, his burly arms folded against his barrel chest and a freshly rolled joint clamped between his thick, dark lips. Beside him was Noxie, sitting on the curb. His long twitchy fingers held a bottle of Thunderbird, and the butt of a pearl-handled revolver peeked out from his waistband. Hovering over him, waiting for the action to start, was Slim the taskmaster. His tall, lanky frame and white teeth gave him the look of a crazed predator whenever he laughed heartily. Lawrence, a dark-skinned, broad-shouldered cat who was usually gregarious, looked withdrawn as he stood staring blankly into the night, talking to Gary in his halting stammer.

As I approached, I could hear their laughter starting to erupt as they deadpanned each other and played the dozens.

"You big buffalo head, coyote breath, teeny dick muthafucka. Your mother's eyes are so crooked, when she cries, tears roll down her back," Noxie cracked to Mumbles as he laughed uncontrollably.

"Fuck you!" Mumbles shouted back. "Your mother's so ugly she make blind rats run. She's so old she was bustin' dishes at the Last Supper."

By now, everyone was laughing, their pearly white grins a striking contrast to their ebony skin. This was the best part of the life on Hankin's Corner. It was a chance to laugh squeezed in between too many chances to die.

It was also a chance to be our age again. For just a moment, we could forget the real possibility that many of us would die near this corner, just as so many of us before had done. This was the place where I had watched my friend Chico drown in his own blood after being shot. The corner where I'd seen Marshall Braxton strangle his own brother to death in a fight over five dollars. This was also the corner where Michael Pink Lips taught me to twirl dice, and the corner where I first saw a cop kill somebody in cold blood. Laughing took my mind off all that, and playing the dozens was the way to start the action.

Before I knew it, two hours of hanging out had passed by and the dice game was well under way, but for some reason I wasn't able to focus on it. Even as I talked shit with the gang, my mind just kept drifting off. Then suddenly I felt a sharp nudge that jarred me out of the spell.

"C'mon, muthafucka, throw down," Bibbs yelled at me. "You in the game, nigga, or are you here to watch a muthafuckin' pro in action?"

Each time I tried to focus, something seemed to be pulling me back into a daze. I felt weak, breathless. My arms and legs were going numb. But still I tried to shake off the feeling and get back to laying bets.

"Fuck 'em," barked Mumbles. "I got you covered for twenty dollars, muthafucka. Throw the fuckin' dice, and I bet you don't make your point."

Money was being tossed onto the ground at the feet of the bet makers. The crumpled bills lay there in a large circular web, as Slim grabbed the dice, blew on them, and shook them in his fist in an almost religious ritual.

"C'mon, sweet Jesus," he muttered with his eyes closed, "help me make a blind man see and a crippled man walk."

The red dice went spilling onto the concrete, and it was clear that Jesus didn't hear him. The first of the pair stopped with a one showing, and the second finished its spin and rested the same way. "Snake eyes!" screamed Mumbles as he feverishly scooped up a handful of greenbacks. "I swear to God and four other white folks I'm gonna break your black ass tonight."

Despite all the noise around me, I was slowly being engulfed in an eerie, all-enveloping stillness that seemed to be swallowing up Hankin's Corner. It felt like being trapped inside an invisible cocoon, and I couldn't shake it off. Noxie pushed a joint at me and urged, "Go ahead. Take a hit, nigga. You ready to git a piece of this action now?"

We were all huddled together. But Noxie's voice and everyone else's all seemed to be fading in and out. Soon I could hear nothing but the pounding of my own heart thudding in my ears. Everything appeared to be shrinking around me, as if the world were folding in on itself. I was scared. I wanted to scream, but my lips were parched and my tongue was dry. I couldn't yell and I couldn't swallow.

My eyes quickly cut back and forth across the faces of the dark figures around me. Their movements seemed somehow distorted and exaggerated, as if I were looking at them through a fun-house mirror. I could see them talking—their lips moved, and the veins strained in their necks. But the pounding in my ears was so loud I couldn't hear a word they were saying. There was a slow-motion quality to everything. Whenever I went to move, it was like pushing against some unseen force, like trying to swim underwater against the tide.

I blinked my eyes hard, trying to find something to focus on—anything that would help me snap back. I was filled with a terrible sense of panic. It may have been a hot humid night in the middle of July but that brick wall I leaned on felt like a glacier against my back. A bone-deep chill had come from nowhere and wrapped itself around me like a sheet of ice. The cold kept getting worse, and I felt like I was freezing to death. Suddenly my legs went all rubbery. Unable to support my weight a minute longer, I began a slow slide down the brick wall.

It was at this moment that something came over me that if I live to be a hundred I will never be able to adequately explain. It was an experience that defied logic, but would be stamped indelibly in my mind and soul for the rest of my life. I could only accept the truth of it on the strength of my faith in God.

As I crouched there on Hankin's Corner on that hot, muggy night, all I could feel was the icy chill of the brick and mortar against my back. The stillness that surrounded me now seemed to muffle even the pounding of my heart. The silence seemed to become a living thing, reaching deep into my soul, and calling me to attention in a way I've never felt before or since. My fear began to melt away—all I felt in its wake was a tremendous sense of anticipation. I knew that something was about to happen, but I had no idea what.

Every nerve ending was straining to hear, to see, to sense what was coming. A haze, a halo of golden light was taking shape, getting bigger, coming closer. It was like a cloud, but it was more real than that, more tangible. It had a vibration to it, almost like music, like the air on a stormy night just after lightning strikes and before the rain begins to fall. That cloud of golden light felt soft, like melted honey, yet it was more powerful than anything I'd ever felt before. It kept moving toward me, moving through me. Filling me with something so familiar, something that felt so good, it was like I was six years old again. What was it, that feeling? I could almost remember.

Love! It was love! I'd been shut down for so long, I'd almost forgotten what it felt like. I could feel tears welling up behind my eyes, but I blinked hard to keep them back. I didn't want to miss a moment of what was happening. I kept staring into the center of that golden haze; it kept pulling me back again and again. Then I began to see something else taking shape deep in the heart of the cloud in which I found myself. It got more solid, clearer, until, at last, I saw!

It was my mother's face, bright as a midsummer's day. There she was, looking straight at me, and I was blinking and looking at her. How had she found me six years after her death, and how could this be at all? I was astounded, ashamed, overjoyed—all at the same time. I knew that she, too, recognized me. I could see it in her eyes, all the loving and the caring I hadn't allowed myself to miss. But there was something else in her eyes. It was like a great sadness overtook her as she watched me out here on Hankin's Corner, a parasite now feeding off the streets and consuming my future. Here on the street where she'd grown up and spent her last days, I watched her eyes close slowly now, as though the pain of seeing what I had become was too much for her.

Then she looked at me again and this time smiled her old familiar smile. There was no disappointment, no judgment, just total love and acceptance. I felt safe and protected, as though we were back home in Turners Station. She never said a word, but I felt her presence powerfully. I felt cradled in an unconditional love. In the light of her clarity I felt washed and clean. For the first time, I could see that I had locked myself away in a prison of darkness. I had to let go, once and for all.

Suddenly I was filled with such a sharp, sweet pain that it took my breath away. The golden fire of Mama's love was burning away all the rage and confusion that had filled me, burning away everything I'd done to dull the pain of her loss, the pain of my present life. "Mama, I didn't know," I said silently to her. "I didn't know. I couldn't see."

Another wave of energy flooded through my body, filling me with the most perfect peace I have ever known. I felt newborn, vulnerable—completely open to the possibilities that lay within me. I felt . . . forgiven. In this one powerful moment I knew I had been completely transformed.

Mama's face slowly began receding back into a golden haze, and I leaned toward her, reaching out to her protective spirit. I wanted to keep her with me forever. But somehow I knew this wasn't to be. As mysteriously and swiftly as she had come, she was gone. The bright haze melted away like the mist at sunrise, and I found myself back in the action on Hankin's Corner.

"Muthafucka," I heard Slim call out to me. "I don't know what you been smokin' but give me some of that shit *now!*"

I looked up and saw their faces again coming into focus. As I staggered to my feet, still leaning against the wall for support, I saw them all staring at me as though I'd lost my mind. But any expression of concern dissolved into indifference as the noise of the street quickly filled my ears.

"Kiss my ass," I quietly mumbled at Slim.

I knew that my mother had seen the emptiness in my life, and I vowed that I would make it up to her. I knew I had to prove to myself that her hopes for me had not been in vain. She'd realized that I needed help, and she'd reached out to let me know that help had come. I had cursed God that night at the moment of her death and spit on the crucifix with anger. As I did not understand the will of God, neither did I understand his redemption. Now it was up to me to accept it.

All those late-night talks we'd had, all the life lessons she repeated to me again and again, how many times she told me that I was supposed to make it if anyone did. I had to make it out of here, out of poverty, off the streets, because if I could break free, Mama could break free. And this was as true for her now as it had been in life.

"God will make a way out of no way," she would say. "A way out of no way." And God had, on this very night, on this blood-soaked corner, made a way for me.

I quickly realized that I had to change, and that I had already been profoundly changed. God had given me a second chance that night. He'd ripped my insides out and shaken me to the core. I knew I'd never, ever, go back to the life I'd been leading. I didn't know how I was going to do it, but I knew that I had to start all over again—and I had to do it now!

At that moment I was flooded with new strength, and a new purpose in life. As on the night in Turners Station when I was left at home alone, I knew I had the courage to face the darkness and to conquer it! The first step was walking away from Hankin's Corner. I stood strong and whole and proudly took it.

The crap game raged on behind me as I got up and began to walk to my house. Over my shoulder I caught a glimpse of those familiar white people on the posters in Hankin's dusty glass window. They were still smiling as they had been for years, holding up their glasses of Jack Daniel's and puffing on their

Lucky Strikes. But now, for the first time, I could smile back. I knew that, unlike them, I was on my way out of here. I had broken free of the grip of Hankin's Corner.

That night, when I got back to my room, I fell on my knees and prayed like I'd never prayed before. I prayed and cried all night long. But these were tears of joy as I asked for God's forgiveness. And I asked Mama to please forgive me this one last time for letting her down.

I realized now that I wasn't alone, and that I'd never been alone. And as I knelt and cried on the floor of my room that night, I made a very real promise to myself, and to God. I promised that I would never go back to the life I had known. Now that I had one more chance, I would do everything in my power to make a real difference—not only in my own life, but in the lives of my people.

I learned a powerful lesson that night on Hankin's Corner. Sometimes you have to take a fall to ultimately take a stand.

And I had to keep falling for months afterward. I had to fight for my life to get off that corner. The gangs in the hood were not about to just let me walk away. Every time we crossed, they'd call my bluff, pick a fight, or beat me bloody. But even that didn't change my mind. I'd just fight back as hard as I could, pick myself up again, and head back into my new life. At some point they sensed that I was filled with a new energy, a new resolve, and new insights. After a while, they just gave up on me as a lost cause and left me alone.

I may have been a lost cause to them. But I had found myself and I was never going to get lost again. One door had closed and another had opened as the mystery of life worked its will. If I had ever doubted God's presence in my life, I knew I'd never doubt it again.

Perhaps there's a parallel side to our existence on earth—a sort of way station between life and death. Maybe this is the place the Almighty allows us brief passage at moments of great need, a place where God gives us a sign and offers a second chance for salvation.

Or, perhaps, as some would suggest to me later, my memories or perceptions became distorted that night, when I crossed for a moment into another place. Maybe, they would say, things didn't actually happen the way I thought they had at the time. Maybe, and maybe not. But I know what I know. I'm not a clairvoyant nor an accomplished interpreter of visions or dreams. But that amazing experience made me question the whole direction of my life and changed me in a special way.

I was one person when I walked out to the corner that night. And I was a whole other person when I left it. I had learned the lesson of the wise man and the lesson of the fool. I got a piece of my soul back that night and knew what price I had paid for losing it. What I'd won with that final roll of the dice was the knowledge that life could never be a free ride.

8

FIGHT THE POWER

*I*T was a late Friday afternoon in August of 1973 and I was sitting behind the microphone in the glass-encased studio of radio station WEBB. As Marvin Gaye crooned over the airwaves, I sipped a tall glass of ice water and used my free moments off-air to rest my eyes. I had just broken into radio as a rip-and-read reporter and part-time announcer. I was bushed, having worked earlier that morning only to return hours later to fill in for Curtis Anderson, who usually did the drive-time slot, a peak time for listeners commuting to and from work. Curtis was our star jock, and it was rare for him to be out sick. And while I pounced on the opportunity to work the coveted drive-time hours, my body was starting to slump and wane from near-exhaustion.

Looking out through the huge plate-glass window before me, I watched the blazing July sun as it slowly retreated behind the downtown skyline. The day had been a scorcher. By noon, the temperature had already hit ninety-seven degrees, and had risen relentlessly throughout the day. Now, with the air beginning to cool, the streets of West Baltimore looked almost inviting.

Scattered across my desk were several books, from Frantz Fanon's *Wretched of the Earth* to Maya Angelou's *I Know Why the Caged Bird Sings*. As the music played on, I grabbed an anthology containing Paul Laurence Dunbar's "We Wear the Mask," which I planned to read aloud at the end of my broadcast. It was then that I noticed the station manager, Diamond Jim Sears, standing outside the control room frantically waving his arms at me. Though I couldn't hear him through the soundproof glass, I knew he was shouting. I could see the veins straining in the thickness of his neck.

Marvin Gaye was only halfway through the tune when I began fading out the volume. Diamond Jim had rattled my nerves but I knew I had to keep my cool.

I leaned into the microphone. "Well, brothers and sisters of B'more, it's time to be more aware," I intoned casually. "I'm afraid my time is up, and I'm gonna have to get on out of here. Parting is such sweet sorrow, but sweeter still is a chance to meet again. Here's a last word from a brother long since departed to help you deal diligently with The Man." My voice now breathy and deep, I potted down the music as I rode the mike, to officially sign off. "This has been Kweisi Mfume, and I'll be back at you real soon with more in store from 'Ebony Reflections.' Peace, and more power to the people."

I quickly popped in a tape of Malcolm X's speech at Harvard University. While I realized that playing Malcolm would only worsen my predicament, there was principle at stake. It was just a matter of time before the station succeeded in censoring me anyway, but I'd be damned if I'd do it for them. This was a battle I planned to fight to the end.

As I scurried out of the studio, Diamond Jim collared me at the door. "Bad news," he bellowed. "Mr. Brown is in town and heard some of your show. He called a few minutes ago, and he's pissed. Says he's on his way over here."

"What should I—"

We heard the lobby door slam. Diamond Jim's eyes widened.

"That might be him now. I'll take care of him. You . . . you get lost somewhere."

Diamond Jim disappeared down the corridor. Flustered, I just stood there for a few moments, not quite knowing where to turn. But I suddenly heard the unforgettable, raspy voice greet Diamond Jim curtly as he made his way to the door.

"Tell that deejay I wanna see him right now," the voice barked.

"He's already left for the day, Mr. Brown," said Diamond Jim, grinning and lying through his teeth.

"C'mon, I just heard him on the radio not even a few minutes ago. Where the hell could he have gone that fast?"

"Goddamn if I know, Mr. Brown," Diamond Jim said. "He gone already."

With my back pressed against the cold wall of the supply room, I tried to keep as still as possible. When I heard the door to Diamond Jim's office slam, I knew Mr. Brown was drawing near. Slowly, I crept to the rear of the room, and crouched behind a tall shelf crammed with dusty audio reels, headsets, and microphones. It was hot as an oven back there. Drenched in sweat, I mopped my face with my dashiki.

"You sure he took off already?" croaked Mr. Brown. "Let's just take a walk around here and see."

The voice came from the corridor outside, and I heard footsteps moving in my direction. This was it. But as I crouched in the darkness of the supply room, I couldn't help feeling a little foolish and a bit discouraged. My freedom-fighting buddies on campus and in the street had been fighting the opposing forces of armies and the police, dissident political factions, and bounty hunters. Me? I was hiding from James Brown.

It seems rather funny now that my first black employer was the "Godfather of Soul." But in the years after the strange occurrence in front of Hankin's liquor store, I was determined to knock down—or outmaneuver—all the obstacles blocking my way. Many have asked me whether my street-corner revelation pointed me to the road of public service or politics that I would pursue years later. Certainly, that would have made for a smooth transition. But the truth is that I walked away from

Laurens and Division streets that night with only one ambition—to turn my life around. At the time, that was enough. A
destination would have been meaningless to me back then. For I
was a man on fire, burning with a real desire to charge head-on
wherever my God-given talents were leading me. Most of the
views I was airing at WEBB in 1973 were rooted in my experiences on the college campus and in the lecture halls. It was the
early 1970s, and I was like so many other students of the time
who really believed we were the genesis of change. It was a general and unquestioned assumption that the stances on issues
taken on campuses reverberated throughout the country in a
way that was direct and consequential. Unlike many students
today, we didn't enroll in college back then to merely gain a pro-
fession. We enrolled in college to try to change the world.

It was a shock to me how much I enjoyed being back in
school and involved in academic activism. While the Community College of Baltimore was only a community college, it
unveiled a whole new world to me. I learned quickly that education was the best vehicle to begin overturning a status quo that
historically repressed and marginalized our race.

Many positive changes had occurred in my life since that
strange night in front of Hankin's liquor store. My prayers had
been fulfilled in a way that was beyond anything I could have
expected. In what felt like an instant, my vow to pull away from
the streets and follow the righteous path of higher principles
was transforming me from a wayward street hustler into a
person I could look at proudly in the mirror.

I always wondered what my mother would have said if she
could have seen me then. From volunteering in a couple of local
political campaigns, I'd moved on to become a top student at
CCB, where I was a popular activist and leader. I was also
proving to be a natural organizer, as editor of the school's paper
and cofounder of the Black Student Union. I was still far away,
however, from the level of discipline I would eventually acquire,
but college was proving to be an apprenticeship for things yet to
come. One of the other major changes that occurred was my
falling in love with and subsequent marriage to Linda Shields.

Our romance could hardly have been considered whirlwind.

In fact, I first met Linda in late 1970, months before I began straightening out my life. Still deeply entrenched in street life, I became acquainted with Linda only because my best friend, Gary, was dating her sister Sandra. Without that connection, I doubt that Linda and I would have ever spoken a word to each other. She was three years younger than I, a studious girl, very much involved in church and the activities of her sorority. Quite the opposite of me, she wasn't the least bit interested in my hustling lifestyle, nor I in her straitlaced pursuits. Familiarity was our only bonding factor. Since Gary and I were always together, during his frequent trips to visit Sandra, Linda and I were often thrust into each other's company.

"Nice day, huh?" I'd strain with politeness.

"Sure is," she'd say, staring into her schoolbook.

The Shieldses were a good, hardworking, religious family who lived in a tidy West Baltimore row house on Pulaski Street just across the street from Frederick Douglass High School. While my rapport was slow with Linda, I clicked instantly with her father, Buster, a friendly, jovial man who made his living as a factory worker at Bethlehem Steel, as well as her mother, Willeen, a kindhearted lady who has recently retired after spending years in domestic work. Always warm and hospitable toward me, her parents, as well as her siblings, did their best to make me feel at home, even as they were aware of my irregular lifestyle.

Gary always expressed surprise that I hadn't shown an interest in trying to date Linda. After all, not only was she bright and unspoken-for at the time, she was quite pretty, with a smooth, almond-colored complexion, deep brown eyes, and big sunny smile.

"You're crazy," Gary would say. "Most cats would be on that in a heartbeat."

"That's most cats," I'd always deadpan. "I'm not interested in chasing another skirt. I got enough of them and the trouble they bring."

Indeed, when it came to women, I had become far less prone to pursuing the next pretty face in the crowd. I already had five sons, and wasn't looking for any more trouble. Besides, Pauline, the mother of my sons Donald and Ronald, and I were back together in an on-again, off-again relationship that had continued for years. At the time I met Linda, Pauline and I were on again. And the fact that Pauline and Sandra were best friends made Linda truly off-limits.

But shortly after I had gone back to night school and earned my GED, things began to change between Linda and me. I started looking forward to my visits with Gary, just so I could sit out on the front porch and spend time with Linda, who I was discovering had a great sense of humor, an energetic attitude, and a good ear for music. I had a collection of eight-track tapes in my car at the time, and sometimes we'd go cruising along the avenues and streets of Baltimore listening to Nancy Wilson, the Dells, or the Chi-Lites, laughing and talking and learning to become friends. While our relationship hadn't moved beyond platonic, I was becoming fonder of her by the day.

Linda had every reason to believe I was sincere about wanting to date her exclusively. In the time since we'd first met, I was showing real signs of change. While the women, hustlers, and rough cats in the neighborhood still knew me, they had all but lost their ties to me. Life following my transformation was now an ever-spinning top whirling around in an evolutionary spiral of change, discipline, and commitment.

By now it was late 1971. Pauline and I had decided that our relationship wasn't headed anywhere, and after several last-ditch attempts to reconcile, we broke up. Just as it had with Brenda, Yvonne, and Carlitta, my relationship with her from that point on would be as parents to our children only. They all became my best friends, but I had blown another opportunity for stability in my life. Donald, Kevin, Keith, Ronald, and Michael were still very young, and I was still very lost. I had a High School Equivalency Certificate but few skills, and five mouths to feed but few dollars.

Linda had seen the quiet agony that I suffered, but instead of running away, she stood with me. Against the wishes of her friends and against the urgings of her family, she saw something in me that would make her stay. She knew that Pauline, Yvonne, Carlitta, and Brenda were quickly proving to be wonderful

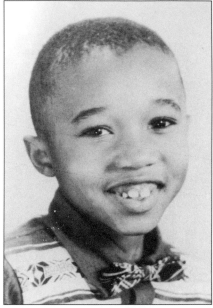

My first day of school at Fleming Elementary, 1954. Bow ties were optional.

With my sisters LaWana and Darlene in 1956.

In a wagon with my sister Darlene, Christmas 1952.

All photos, unless otherwise identified, are courtesy of the author.

Mama, Mary Willis, out for a
Sunday stroll in 1959.

My father, Mr. Rufus "Rip"
Tate (Mr. Charles),at a
club in West Baltimore.

Mama and her sister Gloria
out in front of their home on
Robert Street.

Waiting patiently for a date to come downstairs.

Street corner life, West Baltimore style, circa 1969. That's Gary Fenwick on the far left.

Gary Fenwick and I making a fashion statement at a local dance club in 1967.

In 1967, Pauline and I on our way to a party.

Linda Shields and I on our
wedding day in 1972.

My official WEAA publicity
photo as program director, 1977.

Going door to door during my
1979 campaign for City Council.

Addressing the City Council
at a meeting in 1979. Frank
Gallagher is seated to my left.

Posing with my aunt Marie and
my sister Michelle on my first
day in office as a Baltimore city
councilman.

Posing with "The Greatest," Muhammud Ali, in 1977.

With my former colleague, Councilman Mimi Dipietro (center),
and Congressman Ben Cardin at a 1989 fund-raiser.

It's a family affair. Watching the 1986 elections with my five sons. From left to right that's Kevin, Donald, Keith, Michael, and Ronald. Behind them are William Murphy, Jr., Joan Powell, and George Buntin.

The heart of any campaign—its volunteers—celebrate with my campaign manager, Belva Scott, and me in 1983.

A veteran of over thirty years in public life, former congressman Parren J. Mitchell attends a 1986 fund-raiser.

Victorine Adams and local volunteers from my district help me celebrate my fortieth birthday.

The Baltimore Sun

In 1993, out on the streets in the Fourth
District, taking my message to the people.

Tom Wolff

Oodles Mines, my barber since I was sixteen,
prepares to take a little off the sides.

On my way to
a committee meeting.

Jason Lee/Patuxent Publishing Company

At a campaign rally in
Baltimore's Fourth District.

Baltimore Afro-American Newspaper

Louis Myrie

With my long-time friend Carl Swann and former Speaker of the House Tom Foley in 1993.

Courtesy of the CBC

At a 1993 Congressional Black Caucus press conference. I'm flanked by Representatives Maxine Waters and Ron Dellums, both of California.

Courtesy of the CBC

Judge Leon Higginbotham administering the oath to the 1993 Congressional Black Caucus members.

The CBC convenes a 1993 strategy session with Attorney General nominee Lani Guinier.

At a 1989 CBC press conference we expressed our opposition to the U.S. policy toward Haiti. Deposed Haitian President Jean Bertrand Aristide stands to my right.

Being arrested at a 1994 White House protest in support of Haiti.

Support
Haitian
Democracy
not Words

HAITIANS
ㅗㅐㅅㄷ
DEMOCRACY
the
UNITED STATES
BETRAYED
them

Facing the press with fellow members of Congress while protesting the U.S. policy toward Haiti.

A 1993 meeting with former head of the NAACP, Ben Chavis.

General Colin Powell with members of the Congressional Black Caucus in 1989.

South African president Nelson Mandela acknowledging the audience's warm reception after his 1994 meeting with the CBC. (From left to right: Barbara-Rose Collins, President Mandela, Bobby Rush, Kweisi Mfume.)

The NAACP meets with Anti-Defamation League national director Abraham Foxman, and Arnold Aberman (second from left) in April of 1996.

Earl Graves was instrumental in helping me make the transition from Congress to the NAACP. Here he joins me at December '95 press conference in New York.

Being sworn in on February 20, 1996, as the chief executive officer and president of the NAACP. Chief Judge Emeritus Harry Edwards administers the oath.

President Clinton, Myrlie-Evers Williams, and I pause for a moment of reflection during the swearing-in ceremony at the Justice Department.

At home with three of my sisters (from left to right) Darlene, LaWana, and Michele.

My sons Donald, Keith, and Michael join me at a gallery opening in Baltimore.

At the NAACP Image Awards with Joe Madison, Whitney Houston, Denzell Washington, Myrlie-Evers Williams, and Lynn Whitfield.

Nelson Mandela's indomitable spirit has been a source of inspiration for millions and the symbol of a hopeful future for all. I am privileged to call him my friend.

Taking time out during a busy day in 1994 to deal with the most
important issue we face today—the future of our young people.

mothers, and that the bond between them and me, and my children and me, was something she could do little to change. Nonetheless, she believed that I really was a different person, intent and focused on changing my life.

We were now falling hopelessly in love with each other. Uncontrollably and without fear of disappointment, both of us let down our guards and opened our hearts. For two people who never set out to be anything but friends, we found ourselves intensely attracted to one another, and at the delicate age of twenty-one, Linda came to know me as no woman to that point ever had. My warts and fears were in full view now, but for some reason, with her, I didn't care. The only thing that mattered to me was to make sure I did the right thing. Don't make the same mistake again, I thought, and don't be afraid to fall in love.

On the first day of July 1972, Linda and I got married. I stood anxiously that afternoon in Brown's Memorial Baptist Church with Gary and Carl amid a hopeful throng of well-wishers. Dressed in a black tuxedo that bell-bottomed at the ankles and sporting a large Afro bush, I waited at the altar for Linda and her processional to follow me through the church door.

Then, a moment later, Linda appeared, radiant and glowing in a white lace gown. She looked almost angelic, lifting her eyes almost shyly as she walked slowly toward me.

"Man, she looks gorgeous, PeeWee," my best man Gary whispered in my ear, as the organist gently played "Here Comes the Bride."

Breathless, I could only nod in agreement. She moved gracefully down the aisle with her beaming father, Buster, beside her.

Ecstatic that this long-awaited moment had arrived, I was scarcely aware of the 150 or so guests that had come to witness our wedding. After we had exchanged vows, Rev. Paul J. Harris's voice echoed and reverberated, "What God hath joined together, let no man put asunder." I don't quite remember all of the feelings that ran through me at that moment, but I do remember some.

I thought of my sons and then of their mothers. I thought again of Linda and then of myself. I wished quietly that my mother could have been there, and then wondered blankly if I was there myself. Darlene, LaWana, and Michele were there with my grandmother proudly in tow. My youngest sister, Michelle, who was born in 1968, was too young to attend.

Just months earlier I had caught Linda off guard with a short but dramatic proposal. One night before dropping her off at home after dinner and a movie, I swallowed hard and asked her to marry me. Words that had, to that point, never come out of my mouth, now flowed freely and effortlessly. Linda just looked into my eyes softly and didn't speak. As the new moonlight of the evening fell gently across her smooth brown face, I knew more than ever why I had been so smitten by her and trapped hopelessly in her glow.

"Yes, I will marry you," she whispered back. Then with tears in our eyes we both smiled, embraced, and kissed. I smiled again as I remembered that night, then turned my attention quickly back to the Reverend Harris. "You may now salute your bride," he said. "And may God bless both of you." I lifted the veil over her face and gave her a big kiss, as people cheered.

Just like that, it was over, or maybe it had just begun.

As a married man, both happy and content, I ended up with two jobs, selling life insurance and working as a reporter at WEBB. Juggling two jobs while attending school left me dog-tired most of the time, but I was so determined to break away from hardship that I hardly ever noticed. I spent those precious few free hours I did have with my sons or Linda, each providing an energy that kept me focused and moving ahead.

At CCB, I proved an especially motivated student. I don't think you could have found anyone on campus more serious or committed to learning than I was. Having been a competitive pupil back in elementary and junior high school, I was on a mission to prove to myself and others that I could still be among the best and brightest. The fact that I had been on the sidelines of academia for seven years slowed me down some; I got fair to mediocre scores on the first exams of the semester. But once I learned the lay of the land, I began to hit my stride with high scores and well-written term papers.

I also recognized that I was part of a wave of black students nationwide with our first opportunity to attend colleges, many of which were formerly all-white institutions. This was not something to be taken lightly or for granted. At predominantly white CCB, we thought of ourselves as the new breed of black thinkers who would propel our generation by challenging the institutions of government. America, we believed, had to honor the hard-fought civil rights laws enacted just a few years prior, or we would be this nation's worst nightmare.

Of course, the stakes were much higher for me than for most students. I had children to help feed and clothe, not to mention three sisters I was still occasionally sending money to. I couldn't afford to waste time and simply go through the motions. For me, college was a ticket to fulfilling my dreams and my promise to my mother. In and out of class, I gravitated to the serious students who seemed truly devoted to learning as an intellectual pursuit.

My change in attitude brought a decision to change my name. More than ever, I needed a way to reconnect with my cultural ancestry, and Kweisi Mfume became it.

I viewed my name change as one of necessity and survival. Frizzell Gray had lived and died. From his spirit was born a new person.

I would often think back to my days in Turners Station and how Mr. Smitty would pull me aside on the baseball field to tell a story and teach a lesson. "A change of name," he once said, "is nothing new or unusual. Forty generations before Christ, Abraham and Sarah's names were changed when God decided to make them father and mother of great nations. Jacob's name was changed from Jacob to Israel, when it became his mission to carry on the tradition of his forefathers. Saul of Tarsus, who was the persecutor of the early Christians, became Paul, an apostle of Christ." Although many years had passed, Mr. Smitty's story made sense now. A true elder in my family, my great-aunt had brought back, at my request, an indigenous name from the coast of West Africa. She would later explain that it was the only name she felt appropriate and the only one I would ever need. "It doesn't say what you were, child, it says what you will be.

"Kweisi, that means conquering," she said. "Mfume . . . son of kings.

"The vibrations in the name will help you to be what you must be. Always be true to yourself and your name will carry you," she uttered. "But if you bring dishonor to your new name it will forsake you. You are Kweisi now . . . Kweisi Mfume."

Most of my best friends in college turned out to be veterans of the Vietnam War. They, like me, were older students, as bright and politically aware as any men I've ever met. I ran with a group of six veterans, Sweetpea, Partlow, Junie Carter, J.T., George Buntin, and Jerry De Shields. Fresh out of the war, they were among an influx of veterans taking advantage of the GI Bill at CCB.

The "vets," as we called them, congregated up on a grassy knoll on campus we used to call "the Hill." They'd sit up there with their dog tags on, smoking reefer and listening to the loud music of Jimi Hendrix or Parliament and Funkadelic. Sometimes between classes, I would go hang out on the Hill. Easily distinguished from other students, the vets dressed mostly in green army fatigues and pretty much hung out by themselves. They greeted each other almost religiously with a special handshake called "dap." It was what the brothers who served in 'Nam did as an expression of kinship and solidarity. When they eventually took the time to teach it to me and to explain the bond of trust it sealed, I felt a part of their circle.

I remember being awed by the closeness shared among them. The only thing that comes near that is the kinship we had on the streets, where you gave your running partners your absolute trust. You instinctively knew that your gang partner was your greatest asset because your life was in his hands, and vice versa. You had to believe in each other, know each other, and come to think like each other because that was the only way you would survive the streets. Gary and I did that effortlessly back in the old neighborhood. The vets displayed that kind of bond. They knew that from moment to moment in the jungles and mud of Vietnam their survival depended on each other. They never forgot that when they returned from war.

Although I hadn't fought in the war, something about my ability to survive clicked with the vets, and they treated me as if I had. Part of our rapport had to do with my strident rhetoric that dared to question authority. Anyone who spent more than a moment with me knew that I believed that a terrible hoax was being played on black people in this country. I believed that most of us were going to live and die without ever having experienced anything near what was promised in the Declaration of Independence about life, liberty, and the pursuit of happiness. We weren't at all protected under the laws of the land—black people were citizens in name only. We were a people chronically and institutionally disenfranchised, feeding off the scraps of the educational system, the job market, and any other channels leading to a life of dignity.

We were cannon fodder for war, a dumping ground for drugs, and chattel for the penal system. We spent money for products made by companies that wouldn't hire us, and were exposed daily to media images that defamed us. Police harassed us, employers denied us, the media exploited us, and white communities shunned us.

Yet, black people were expected to believe in the American Dream as much as white people did. Why should we? The very notion was obscenely cynical, and any black man or woman who thought differently was living in a fool's paradise. My disdain for the system was evident as a new wave of militancy engulfed my persona. I didn't just *wear* a bush, I *was* a bush that burned with revolutionary fervor, from the wildfires of racism and prejudice that smoldered around me.

Beyond my and the vets' similar disdain for the system, I also empathized with their unspoken frustration. They'd put their lives on the line for their country, in a dirty war that nobody wanted to fight, only to return home to prejudices and rabid anti-Vietnam sentiment. I recalled stories I'd heard about the black soldiers in World War I. Even after liberating France, they were forced to fight in segregated units and never allowed to wear their uniforms in the ticker-tape parades. So I understood the Vietnam vets' bitterness at the system. I hated it, too, and threw bricks at it every chance I got.

On campus I became involved in a Black Student Union movement to boycott Gulf Oil, which was allegedly plowing money into South African investments that were being used to prop up the military there. Each day, we marched in opposition to such companies. The symbol of our campaign was a large poster showing police brutalizing black South Africans, its bold orange letters bannered across the top urging Americans to "Boycott Gulf Oil."

As a result of the campaign, my desire to learn more about South Africa became almost an obsession. I spent hours in the campus library and at black bookstores, studying the country's history and its inhumane system of Apartheid. I spent countless nights reading about the racist Vorster Apartheid regime, which oppressed the 16 million blacks living under the terror of the white police state. It was mind-boggling to read that four million whites reigned supreme in a land where blacks needed identity cards and passbooks to travel freely. In the library, I learned of the 1956 "treason" trials, when over a hundred blacks and sympathetic whites were arrested on false charges. I read of the shocking 1960 Sharpeville massacre, in which more than sixty men, women, and children were gunned down by police. I learned of the courageous African National Congress leader, Nelson Mandela, and his long imprisonment. Even more, I learned of our nation's financial involvement with the white racist government. Armed with all this information, I wanted to do something to help bring about change there.

It was only through my own research that I began to truly understand the vicious nature of Apartheid, as well as discover the heroism of the man named Nelson Mandela.

"Fifteen years in prison with no sign of getting out!" I'd marvel to my friend George Buntin. "That's a real leader, somebody willing to die in jail for what he believes in."

The more I read about Mandela, the more I realized that he was the embodiment of the struggle for liberation in South Africa. As a young boy, he tended cattle while hoping for a future that would be as exciting as the "good old days" described by village elders. The times longed for by Mandela's mentors were the decades before political and economic domination by the white man. With deep pride, he spoke of peace and prosperity under the leadership of African kings. These tales served as the seeds of Mandela's political involvement and created a thirst for more knowledge that he hoped would be quenched by getting an education.

I made it my business to become an expert on Mandela's life. I learned everything I could about the man, and the more I studied his life, the more I felt a strange sense of empathy and brotherhood with him. I was impressed that during his years at the renowned University College of Fort Hare, Mandela became an outspoken student leader—regardless of personal consequences. For example, after the South African government passed a series of segregationist laws during the late 1930s, he was expelled from the institution for participating in a strike against the government's actions. He later went on to study law at the University of Witwatersrand, and was certified as an attorney in 1952.

It was during his stay at the two universities that Mandela met the two men—Oliver Tambo and Walter Sisulu—who would help sharpen his political convictions and philosophies. The African National Congress (ANC) was the organization through which they would map out strategies to force the South African government to repeal the pass system, the Land Act (which gave whites control of 87 percent of the territories), and other discriminatory laws.

Mandela joined the ANC in 1944 and became the National President of its Youth League in 1951. In 1952, he headed the Defiance Campaign, which resulted in 8,577 nonviolent protesters against racial discrimination going to jail. Shortly after he was elected president of the Transvaal ANC, the government banned him from public meetings for two years, and reimposed those restrictions for five more years in 1956. His public voice may have been silenced, but he remained a key behind-the-scenes spokesman and organizer for ANC activities.

Realizing that the government considered him to be a major threat to its demonic system of apartheid, Nelson Mandela spent the months leading up to his 1962 arrest in hiding, but secretly sharing his views on human rights with African nationalists in neighboring countries. Once captured, he was sentenced to five years' imprisonment—three for incitement to strike and two for illegal exit from the country. While serving the term, he and seven others were charged with plotting violent revolution in the famous Rivonia sabotage trial. On April 20, 1964, Mandela delivered a riveting four-and-one-half-hour speech in his own defense.

"During my lifetime I dedicated myself to this struggle of the African people," he said. "I have fought against white domination and I have fought against black domination. I have cherished the ideal of a democratic and free society in which all persons live together in harmony and with equal opportunities. It is an ideal which I hope to live for and to achieve. But if need be, it is an ideal for which I am prepared to die."

Mandela was found guilty and sentenced to life in prison. Despite pleas from every corner of the world, the South African government refused to release him. In studying the life of Mandela, not only was I inspired by his courage and his determination to go to jail for what he believed in, but I also grew to despise the whole system of Apartheid. It was a system that reminded me so much of what historian John Hope Franklin said about slavery in America when he called it that "peculiar institution." Because it set out to define a person's humanity based on skin color and lineage, it was no better than and certainly no different from Apartheid. On a couple of occasions, I wrote to Mr. Mandela, to express my support for his cause, though I doubt that my letters got through to him. Little did I ever imagine that nineteen years later we would meet and become friends, or that he would be President of South Africa.

My outrage over the cruelties of Apartheid and Mandela's imprisonment spurred me deeper into the movement. I became involved in several local organizing meetings where small groups of college students, progressives, and Pan-Africanists discussed the issues and planned protest marches. Many of the organizers were members of the Black Panther Party. One of them was Paul Coates, a slim, coffee-brown fellow who had organized several bookstores with Pan-Africanist literature and other books with a revolutionary message. Paul, who was about six years older than I, spoke at many of the meetings, and I came to regard him as a real visionary in the movement. Although he was regarded as a militant in those days, Paul was a brilliant thinker who spoke with great compassion about the black family unit. Like me, he believed that information had to precede liberation, and that people needed knowledge to be able to make rational decisions.

During these years, 1972 and 1973, there wasn't much national interest in Apartheid, and those who were interested were considered on the fringe. The collective mindset had mellowed somewhat in the years since Dr. King's assassination. Upheaval across the nation had just begun to subside following the Vietnam War, and the remnants of a Black Power movement were lingering, but had less force.

Meanwhile, our campus activism was clearly bothering the administration of the college. I believed that in order for us to be more effective it was more necessary than ever to control the flow of information. That, of course, meant controlling the college's newspaper, which was easier said than done. Although student dues paid for the printing of the paper, the problem was that the administration generally controlled the newspaper by controlling the choice of the editor. Not just anyone could become editor of the *College Crier*. You practically had to be anointed by the faculty, even though they held elections for the position. The administration knew that as long as they controlled the newspaper on campus, they could put out a lot of fires.

I persuaded Sweetpea, Junie Carter, George, and Jerry to help me get enough votes to get me elected as editor of the paper. We mapped out a tight guerrilla campaign of false illusions. Our strategy was to make sure that the administration knew nothing about what was going on until the last minute, so they wouldn't have any reason to void the election. To do that, we had to get commitments—almost blood commitments—from a lot of students that they'd show up on election day and vote for me. But just as important, they would have to keep quiet about their plans. We also got three nondescript freshmen to file for the position. When it came time to elect a new editor of the newspaper, they all withdrew their candidacies just hours before the election, and I was the only one running. The administration was shocked. They knew they'd been had and they wanted to keep nominations open for one more day, figuring they could find someone else to step up and run. But nobody else offered a nomination, and the job became mine. Our plan to control the flow of information and propaganda had worked, but the process to force meaningful change still awaited us.

As editor, I knew I now had the clout to galvanize real grassroots support to shake things up at the college. In September of my second year we decided we needed to control funding in order to pay for the creation of a black studies program in history, so we locked down some buildings a couple of times and demanded change. By December, we wanted Stokely Carmichael to come and address the student body. When the administration refused, we took over the administration building one night, removed the American flag, and hung red, black, and green liberation flags across campus. The next day we organized picket lines in front of the school and tied up vehicular traffic.

Soon, I'd distinguished myself at CCB as a smart and committed leader. When I wasn't in class or out working, I was all over the city in the areas most people had forgotten, giving speeches and passing out literature. Places like the Timbuktu Center, Soul School, and the Black Panther headquarters were where I continually spent my time. "Watch out, brother," my friend Kazi would warn. "The pigs got their eye on you. They fixin' to plant some dope on you and give you a crime or they just might bust a cap in your ass and say they thought you had a gun." Kazi was concerned for good cause. The police didn't care what you did on campus; but organizing in the community was a more serious matter. They had informants everywhere and didn't care for our militancy.

The risks were clear, but the problems in our community ran too deep to ignore. Heroin, illiteracy, and low self-esteem had a choke hold on the ghetto. While some were making it out, most others were trapped for life. The vets, the BSU, the Pan-Africanists, the Panthers, and the Black Muslims were joined together at the hip by a cause—to help the black community understand who we were and where we were headed as a race.

During my last year at the community college, I worked ever more actively as editor and vice president of the Black Student Union. Our biggest push was to broaden the black studies curriculum. Our argument to white faculty was that conventional history courses merely offered "his story" rather than "ours." We wanted to expand and broaden the offerings of the history department. We also pressed for a guarantee to all students of their First Amendment rights regarding which speakers visited campus.

When we weren't challenging, defying, or serving notice on the administration, we were prodding our fellow students into action. Apathy was an issue the BSU really homed in on, trying to convert what we derisively labeled "commuter students" into more involved, vocal participants in campus life. Our argument was that if you didn't stand up and get involved here, you were definitely not going to get involved once you graduated. After all, no environment was safer or more comfortable than a college campus.

9

RADIO DAYS: "EBONY REFLECTIONS"

*T*HE power of mass communication, particularly my love of radio, would fuel my involvement in campus politics. As a boy growing up in Turners Station and later West Baltimore, I would spend hours in my bedroom listening to my transistor radio. Even as the batteries weakened, I would press my ear against the speaker and take in the music until the sound faded completely.

As I got closer to graduation, I began envisioning myself behind the microphone in a radio station control booth. Just as in the early days of radio talk show host Michael Jackson, I gave some thought to this medium's huge potential as a political tool for raising consciousness, shaping opinions, and fueling debates in the community. Unlike Gus Adiar and Parren Mitchell, my first political mentors, and other black elected officials in Baltimore, I didn't believe that real power lay in how much legislation you got passed. I felt that the real potential power lay in the hands of black disc jockeys as de facto leaders who could communicate political ideas creatively and compellingly over the airwaves. I knew that shaping public opinion and galvanizing people into action was what really created social change.

In radio, as in most professions, getting a foot in the door requires some serious paying of dues. My first jobs in radio didn't earn me a penny. I was a gofer in every sense. But if anything distinguished me from other gofers, it was my enthusiasm and dedication. I willingly performed thankless duties with a smile, constantly reassuring myself that it was merely a matter of time before my "time" would come. And when it did, I vowed to be ready.

Back then, the popular radio jocks supplemented their incomes by spinning records at dances and parties known as "hops." Held at places like the YMCA or little recreational centers around the city, these hops were where young people flocked if for no other reason than to get a real-life look at their favorite jock. It would be years before lightweight cassettes and compact discs hit the market—innovations that offer immeasurable ease to a jock's life. Back in the '70s, pop music was played on 45s or 78s, and the jocks had to lug heavy cases of records to the hops. Realizing that such heavy lifting was the least favorite part of a jock's work, I began offering to do the job for them—for free. So my first job in radio was toting the music for the jocks as they went into the hops, and then lugging the heavy cases back to their cars. Some jocks would do two or three parties a night, and I'd haul the music to and from each destination.

This volunteer labor was my way of getting an inside track on announcing. There was a guy who lived on my block named Champ Hagins, and another guy by the name of Sam Beasley who lived uptown. Both Champ and Sam were teenagers when they went on the air. I was envious, and figured if they could announce, so could I.

One jock I fetched for was Eddie Morrison. Eddie worked at WSID and had cut a record back in the 1960s called "The Madison," which inspired a dance that over the years has evolved into what is now called the Electric Slide. When I hung out at hops with Eddie, he introduced me to a lot of folks in radio, and soon I found myself volunteering at WWIN. Of course it was another gofer job, but at least I was inside a radio station. For me, this was paradise. I'd go for newspapers and cigarettes, jot down phone messages, and do anything else that needed to be done around the station, including fending off girlfriends and groupies vying for jocks' attention. I may have been a mere gofer, but I was a damn good gofer because I was observant and independent and didn't require any hand-holding. After a while, I knew the lay of the land, and my superiors came to trust and depend on me more and more.

That trust brought me my first break in radio: answering the request line. It was a late-night job—I'd go in around eleven or midnight and simply field phone calls all night, writing down musical requests from the audience and handing them off to the jock. That's when I really started thirsting for my turn in the jock's seat. They always looked so cool and completely under control sitting in the sound booth wearing headphones, and manipulating all these buttons and switches. Outside in the lobby, beautiful women would sit and wait for them to get off work. And recording artists would breeze in and out, promoting their latest records and doing interviews.

The biggest advantage of handling requests at WWIN was that the jocks would let me work with the equipment in the production studio. A production studio is just like the master studio. It has all the same equipment; it's just that whatever you're doing there is not going out directly over the air. It's where you produce "actualities" for the news department, make commercials, and create almost everything else that goes out over the air. It was in the production studio that I began learning the equipment and developing my motor skills, which is critical because radio is all about quick reflexes and your hand movements, and how you operate equipment.

Once I learned the basics of the control board, I started producing demo tapes of myself with incoming and outgoing music, and doing commercials. Even though I secretly harbored other ideas about radio being more than merely entertainment, I made demos that mimicked the official tradition of "personality radio." Because I hadn't yet developed my own "handle," I honed a style that was a blend of all the hottest jocks.

It was around that time, 1970, that I heard about an opening for a weekend slot at WWIN. The program manager was a guy named Al Jefferson, then known as "Big Al." Al was a much older guy with an easy way about him. I liked him a lot, and we had become fairly friendly with each other while I was volunteering.

Al also knew how badly I wanted to go on-air, and that I was in the pecking order for a shot at becoming the station's next jock. Ahead of me was Guy Brodie, and ahead of Guy was Curtis Anderson. After learning about the jock job, I immediately went into Al's office and gave him my demo tapes. This really wasn't necessary because he'd heard me practicing for months in the production studio. With me sitting right there, Al put in the tapes and he listened for a while. Then he leaned back in his chair.

"Let me tell you something, man," he said finally. "I'm not going to hire you."

"I don't understand what you mean," I said.

"I'm not going to hire you because you don't have your own style, your own personality," he continued. "You simply don't have what it takes to be on the air, and I really don't think you're going to do good in this business. Maybe you ought to try looking at something else."

I was floored. "But Al, this is all I want to do," I protested. "I've done just about everything there is to do here for three years. I've been a gofer, I've taken requests, I've carried records, I've worked in the production studio, I've done everything. It's only a weekend slot. It's my one shot, that's how you get in. How come you're not going to hire me?"

"I don't think you have the voice," he went on. "You just don't have a voice, you don't have your own personality yet. I can look at people and tell when they're going to make it in this business and when they're not. So I'm being honest with you."

I was in a state of total shock and disbelief. Of course, I would have conceded that I needed to tighten this up and work on that. But I knew I had talent and that I could do the job. I was really furious and disappointed with Al Jefferson. I felt that he'd always been fair with me, and that he was a nice guy—but he was dead wrong in my mind on this decision.

I left WWIN the next day and I never went back.

For the next couple of years, I'm sure there were a lot of people who assumed that I'd given up on ever becoming a jock. On the street and at parties, I would encounter radio personalities like Sir Johnny O, Johnny B., and others who worked at the station, and they'd ask about what happened and why I'd left. I never said much to them about what transpired, though, because I was too embarrassed and too angry.

But every night, I was planning my comeback. When I wasn't working, I was at home in front of a mirror, reading copy, working on my voice inflection, and trying to hear myself as someone else would actually hear me, not as I ideally wanted to sound. I practiced speaking over and over again.

After a while, I didn't think I had much more improving to do with my voice. The more I practiced, the more I realized I could control my voice as well as any jock on the airwaves. But a part of me kept harking back to Al Jefferson's criticism—that I didn't have my own personality, my own unique style of delivery that would make me successful.

In the fall of 1973, I went to see Diamond Jim Sears, the station manager at WEBB. He'd known my family back in Turners Station, and was pleased that I'd stopped by. I told him I was there to apply for a job, that I needed the job, and that I'd like the opportunity to audition for him.

Diamond Jim ended up offering me a job as a news reporter, which in the business was known as "rip and read" because there were no rewrites unless you had a rare free moment. You just got it off the Associated Press or U.P.I. feed, and assembled it by region. Then you grabbed the tiny bit of time they gave you in radio in those days, and you did your news at the top and the bottom of the hour.

Diamond Jim started me at two dollars an hour—and when I left the station four years later, I was still making two dollars an hour. I started as the noon broadcaster coming on after Moon Man and before a lineup that included Naomi Durant, Eddie

Tee, and their hotshot jock, Curtis Anderson, whom Diamond
Jim had lured away from WWIN.

To us staffers at WEBB, Jim Sears was a grumpy but lovable
father figure. This, of course, is something Diamond himself
would never have admitted. A barrel-chested man standing six
foot six and weighing 250 pounds, Diamond projected the image
of a tough and hard-driving manager. When he came to work,
the walls shook because he was always slamming doors. His
iron-fisted persona was understandable, considering how hard it
was keeping James Brown happy. However, when Brown was
around, Diamond made sure he got the respect he deserved.

I remember the way Diamond Jim would pound the desk in
his spartan office, chain-smoking and complaining about this,
that, and the other. He spoke in a language that was hardly the
king's English. Every word that tumbled across his lips was delivered with a twang as thick as the lapels on his countrified suits.

Once, after one of my more politically loaded shows, Diamond summoned me to his office.

"Get your shit, and let the door knob hit your ass," he erupted.

"But, Mr. Sears—"

"Don't give me that Mr. Sears shit," he snapped. "I'm sick of
protectin' your ass from Brown."

I figured there was no use arguing, so I got up and walked out.
As I was heading for my car, I heard Diamond scream after me.
"Get your goddamn ass back in here!"

Not many people know it, but back in the sixties, besides making
such hits as "Papa's Got a Brand New Bag" and "Say It Loud—I'm
Black and I'm Proud," James Brown was the owner of Baltimore's
only black-owned radio station, WEBB. He also headed stations in
Atlanta and in his home town of Augusta, Georgia. But WEBB was
his crown jewel. A steady moneymaker, WEBB helped him
finance his lavish, high-rolling lifestyle of fancy cars, expensive
clothes, and all-night parties among the jet set. While it was
rumored that Brown's operation suffered from poor financial
management, you'd be hard-pressed in those heady days following
the civil rights movement to find anyone, black or white, who

didn't admire the man. Not only was he known as the hardest-working man in show business, he dressed like the best-paid, too.

I was among the millions mesmerized by Brown and his dazzling dance steps, the way he'd glide rhythmically across the floor as though it were a sheet of ice, drop into a split, and rise up spinning like a top. Like other blacks, my adoration for Brown stretched far beyond his music or his dancing abilities. James Brown seemed to be breaking all the rules of white America while simultaneously succeeding within it. Jet black, and flamboyant, Brown was the least likely type of black man to make it big in America. He'd not only succeeded as a performer, but was bold enough to make a foray into the world of business.

Back then—and still today to some extent—black radio was black in name rather than in ownership. Because a radio station's chief source of revenue is through advertising bought by companies, it is always looking to expand its base of listeners. Until the early to mid-1950s, the black consumer audience was largely overlooked. It wasn't until then that white-owned stations began to recognize the financial bonanza that lay untapped in the black community. Realizing that white announcers would lack credibility and perhaps fall short in capturing the attention of black listeners, these stations hired the most colorful, talkative, persuasive black folks they could find and made them the jocks. By the time WERD in Atlanta began winning black listeners in the early 1950s, other similar stations throughout the South and in some northern cities began hitting the airwaves with such colorful black jocks as Jack the Rapper, Long Tall Lean Larry Dean, Paul Fat Daddy Johnson, the Moon Man, Eddie Morrison, Johnny 'O, Rockin' Robin, Hot Rod, and, of course, Diamond Jim.

As was often the case with black celebrities back then, many of these pioneer black jocks would die poor. The problem was that while they were raking in the bucks for the white station owners, they themselves didn't have a stake in the prosperity. So when James Brown came along and purchased WEBB in the early 1970s, black Baltimore rejoiced. It was a big deal for us because we knew Brown had a special affinity for the city. Not only could he always count on drawing sellout crowds when performing at the Royal Theater, but he had also fallen in love with a woman in town and, as fate would have it, married her. No question about it, Brown was a big name in Baltimore and personality radio was his thing.

But by the time I arrived at WEBB in 1973, most of us younger jocks sensed that personality radio had begun to decline.

"I swear, as much as I love them cats," I remember a young deejay named Guy Brodie musing quietly, "I think those older guys need to move over and let the young blood take over."

While respect prevented us from protesting, Guy, Johnny B., Curtis Anderson, and I knew in our heart of hearts that radio was shifting into a more polished, refined kind of science, where the groove was rooted in cadence, rhythm, and beat. We understood that programming schedules were cutting into the boundless chatter, and technology was eclipsing the power of personality.

I always felt somewhat like an oddball at WEBB. Unlike my colleagues, I was enrolled in school—at the Community College of Baltimore. My consciousness was blossoming, understanding the world better and, more important, who controlled it. I recognized that WEBB's black ownership was an exception, that most jocks worked for white folks and wielded no control whatsoever. We didn't produce or own any of the products we advertised, but if we said to buy them, black folks would buy them.

No matter how much I admired personality jocks, I couldn't somehow bring myself to be one. They were far too gifted in their craft, and I was too focused now on the new world I found around me. Radio offered many things, but liberation was not among them. It offered wall-to-wall music, and perhaps a minute of news at the top or the bottom of the hour. Of more concern to me was the fact that black radio in Baltimore provided no commentary or analysis of the news—and that was the vacuum I wanted to fill. With the nation still reeling from seismic shifts in attitudes and perceptions caused by the civil rights movement of the 1960s, I believed radio was a treasure chest waiting to be opened. At the very least it could offer a forum for listeners to discuss and debate urgent issues affecting our community. I believed then, and still do, that black radio had a great responsibility to its listeners. That meant more than merely broadcasting news sound bites, liquor ads, and hip out-takes; it meant taking something we didn't own and making it work for us. So while other jocks mastered the art of spinning records, I pushed to find new ways to air the truth. The forces shaping life in the black community were powerful, and after coming back from the edge, I was on a mission.

My answer to the dearth of black cultural expression was a Sunday afternoon show called "Ebony Reflections." By design, "Reflections" was vastly different from other programming on the air. It avoided safe, generic be-happy themes whose sole focus was playing just the music of the day. Oh, there were the hits, to be sure, from the Isley Brothers and Funkadelic, to Donna Summer—but there was also more.

I'd gotten into the habit of reading through three or four newspapers each morning, and I'd also been reading a number of books. From W.E.B. Du Bois's *The Souls of Black Folk*, to John Hope Franklin's *From Slavery to Freedom*, to Carter G. Woodson's *The Mis-education of the Negro*, I had found a missing link to my African past.

"Ebony Reflections" was based on a simple premise: Having just come through a decade of tremendous social change and upheaval, black people were hungry for something more than just a good time. I sensed that they also wanted programming that focused on the real issues and struggles in their lives, and I made it my business to provide it. Sure, I played some Top 40 music, but my show consisted mostly of songs that carried a social message. Revolutionary music by the Last Poets, Marvin Gaye's "What's Going On," and tunes by Gil Scott-Heron and others. In between, I'd slip in the poetry of Nikki Giovanni or a speech by Malcolm X. The voice of Marcus Garvey or Martin Luther King could be heard riding in over the sax of Pharoah Sanders or Gary Bartz. "Ebony Reflections" was clearly dif-ferent, but so was I. Frizzell Gray and PeeWee were no more. Though still not yet fully defined, something new was forming inside me out of something old, and every day brought a sense of awakening. I needed a vehicle to mobilize the community, and James Brown's station became it.

I challenged listeners to call in to discuss social issues, which was pretty unusual in those days. Did listeners feel that the Black Panther Party was a legitimate tool in our community, or should we accept the negative image the media had given it? Why aren't we helping each other instead of waiting for the government to step in? And why aren't we challenging the disproportionate slaughter of black men in Vietnam? Sometimes, if there was a major national issue, such as the impending impeachment of President Nixon, I'd open the lines up to callers on those subjects, too. But "Ebony Reflections" was primarily driven by issues that went to the heart of the black experience. I tried to give those living in the hood the rare opportunity to air their political views without negative consequences.

"It's been a long time coming—and unfortunately many of the bloods did not live to see this day because they came home instead in body bags," I said. "But a Vietnam peace agreement was signed today in Paris by representatives of the United States, North and South Vietnam, and the Vietcong."

"That's right, it's been a long time comin'," a caller chimed in. "Too damn long, if you ask me. Black folks didn't have no business fightin' that war in the first place, Kweisi. My brother came home last year from the war all messed up in the head. He worked all his life and now he can't even find a job."

"Sister, you may recall me predicting that black unemployment would become the scourge of our veterans. Well, black unemployment among vets is twice the rate of that for whites. The so-called Great Society isn't looking so great these days."

"Kweisi, I work as an assemblyman over at . . . well, I won't say the name, but they just hired a white guy to be my supervisor and he's got no training whatsoever. I've been with this company thirteen years and only had one promotion in that entire time." Someone else would call in about the dope man recruiting in their neighborhood or about truancy in the schools.

Because "Ebony Reflections" was a completely experimental and new concept for black radio in Baltimore, it scared the hell out of Diamond Jim. He had a heart of gold and loved organizing the community, but now I had taken it one step further by raising the ante, challenging the system and biting the hand that fed us. Diamond was positive that my show would bring heat to the station. He knew that the IRS, the local police, the urban klan would soon react to my fight-back message, but he worried more about the reaction from Mr. Brown. At the very least, he reasoned that I would run off advertisers.

That was stress Diamond didn't need. The station was already on shaky ground because Brown strained money from it to help support the other two stations. We turned a profit, but it vanished quickly. But his robbing Peter to pay Paul decisions weren't done with any malice, it was just his style of business. He simply assumed that his long run of musical hits would continue, and he'd plow the earnings from them back into the station. But things never did improve for Mr. Brown, because times were changing, and a new generation was slowly taking over the charts.

As someone making only two dollars an hour, I couldn't understand why Brown kept borrowing against assets. At WEBB, I had gotten used to wearing secondhand clothes that I bought from the thrift shop. For some reason I did not feel embarrassed, as I would have while hanging out on the street. The only thing that mattered was that I was doing something I believed in and that my boys had what they needed. I loved them dearly and worried that they, like me, would grow up in a society alive and well with racism.

Once, after one of my more politically loaded shows, Diamond summoned me to his office. My kids were piled in the front and back seats of the car. I had brought them to the station with me as I occasionally did, and now we were headed to the zoo. Donald, Kevin, Keith, Michael, and Ronald were becoming more a part of my life as time moved on. Linda had willingly become like a second mother to each of them and often went without as I took what little I had and put it toward their support.

Diamond didn't have the heart to fire me. Beside the fact that he liked me, he knew I was top-notch at my job. Back in the early 1950s, Diamond himself had worked as a disc jockey. Around the station, it was well known that Diamond still longed to be on-air. But radio had changed too much since his heyday. Diamond had come up during the fifties and sixties, in the throes of "personality radio," when stations won listeners through the colorful personalities of their deejays. By the seventies, though, a different kind of jock was beginning to emerge, one who promoted himself less and the station more. Diamond's trademark of syrupy Southern charm and one-line wisecracks had become extinct.

But to the chagrin of all who worked at WEBB, Diamond would occasionally impose himself on the airwaves. His massive frame dwarfing the turntable, Diamond would announce: "It's two o'clock in this man's city." By "this man," he meant the all-powerful white man, something old-timers naturally picked up on. Then he would launch into a monologue of corny one-liners, like "My father was a pistol. That makes me a son of a gun." It was sad and humorous.

Diamond Jim was the last of a dying breed of old turks. But what I learned from him was how powerful radio could be as a catalyst to influence behavior in the community. While Diamond wasn't political, he was quick to assert himself as a caretaker of the community. If he heard that a family had been burned out of their home, Diamond made sure we immediately went on the air with a food drive. If some people were being evicted or kids didn't have clothes to start to school, Diamond would preempt all programming and put in tapes of minister James Cleveland or gospel music by Mahalia Jackson, and start preaching. Just a step away from being a preacher, Diamond would deliver sermons about these families' woes that made tears roll down your cheeks. At times like those he wasn't considering James Brown's wishes at all. His only focus was helping, and for that we came to love and respect him.

Brown, like Diamond Jim Sears, was slowly becoming an icon of a passing era. New groups and solo artists were coming on the scene, and the early stages of rap music were less than a decade away. The hot new acts were the Ohio Players, Kool and the Gang, War, the Emotions, Earth, Wind and Fire, and the Isley Brothers. People were clamoring less for James Brown and more for Funkadelic and Rufus, featuring Chaka Khan.

Mr. Brown wasn't alone in his criticism of me. Many of WEBB's listeners also wanted wall-to-wall music and would turn the dial when I was on-air. They didn't want to discuss what was happening in our community, nor did they want to hear about their responsibility as citizens. Nobody talks about it much now, but back then there were lots of people who weren't receptive to the message of Dr. King or the civil rights movement. They were happy focusing on having a good time and going along to get along. That crowd was much more interested in hearing Curtis Anderson and Moon Man than in my sober discussions and commentary.

At the young age of twenty, Curtis was our franchise—WEBB's one real star. Blessed with all the gifts of a superjock—a silky-smooth voice, razor-sharp timing, and a hip, self-assured manner, Curtis was the envy of Baltimore radio. Our station may not have had a big ad budget, but we had Curtis Anderson. Curtis worked the prime shift, afternoon drive-time, and emceed all the high-profile, extracurricular gigs like concerts and celebrity interviews.

With his roundish head, bulging eyes, and almost rotund frame, Curtis was not a particularly striking man. But women loved him anyway, swept up by a presence that shifted from quietly self-confident to downright cocky. A self-proclaimed party animal, Curtis lived his life in the fast lane, often showing up at work after just a wink of sleep. Because he was such a professional, his performance never suffered. Curtis could go on-air blindfolded and suffering with laryngitis and still work his magic. Johnny B., Eddie T., I, and all the other jocks admired Curtis because everything seemed to come so easily to him. But I never tried to imitate him or diminish him. He was my friend and I knew it would have been impossible.

He'd grown up without a stabilizing force in his life. For a father figure and role model, he looked to Diamond Jim, who protected, nurtured, and counseled him like his very own blood. Diamond was often tougher on Curtis than he was on the rest of us, trying to keep his young head on straight. It worried him deeply that Curtis lacked self-discipline and liked to live on the edge. But Diamond worked hard keeping his "adopted son" on the straight and narrow. And, for a while at least, Curtis never lost his balance.

Even in the face of Curtis's shining star, I still received enough favorable response to know that my "Ebony Reflections" was a worthwhile show. "Brother, I just called to tell you how much I appreciate what you're doing," I'd often hear. "Nobody else is doing it," others would say.

Yet, I could understand why Brown had trouble accepting my critical views of Nixon's America. His reluctance was typical and history has largely validated my thinking. As much as some whites hate admitting it, there's a strong correlation between a black person's political stand and his ability to amass wealth in this country. Success in a capitalist system is deeply rooted in crossover market economics, where a premium is placed on appealing to the broadest possible audience.

Back then, I faulted James Brown for bending to such pressures. I felt he, as the sole owner of WEBB, had a responsibility to those who kept his empire flourishing. Unlike most, he didn't depend on the paycheck of a white-owned company to maintain his livelihood. He was accountable only to WEBB's advertisers and listeners, most of whom were black and supportive.

During those infrequent occasions when he'd drop by, getting the station back to wall-to-wall music ranked high on his agenda. The only buffer between me and the unemployment line was Diamond Jim. Usually, Diamond Jim knew ahead of time when Mr. Brown was coming to the station and would tell me not to come to work. Brown had been known to show up at any one of his stations and fire employees on impulse. If I wasn't around, I might be spared. But today, his visit had caught us off guard. So when he arrived, I hid.

"Well, I want his ass to be like the other jocks on the air. If you ain't gonna fire him, dammit, I'll fire him myself," Brown barked at Diamond Jim, rasping at the top of his lungs.

At WEBB, the spectacle of a James Brown tantrum had become as familiar as the shiny puff of permed hair that lay matted to his brow. His polyester bell-bottomed slacks flapping above his clunky platform shoes seemed to make a music of their own as he worked his way around the station.

I listened through the door as Diamond Jim explained to Mr. Brown my importance to WEBB, how the ratings were up, how popular my show had become. I even heard him lie for me, telling Mr. Brown that I'd toned down the revolutionary stuff, and was playing less Malcolm X and so forth. None of this, of course, was enough to persuade him, and nothing frustrated James Brown more than not being heard.

"Look," he said, his voice feigning calm, "I want him outta here, off the air, the Oom-foo-mee dude." He paused. "What's his name?" It always tickled me that, despite his obsession with changing me, James Brown could still not pronounce my name.

"It's Kwah-EE-see Oom-Foo-may," Diamond Jim corrected.

"Whatever his damn name is," Brown shot back.

Graduating from the Community College of Baltimore was bittersweet for me in many ways. I had grown attached to many of the students and professors at the school during those two years, but was looking forward to attending Morgan State University.

Although our group in the Black Student Union was being forced by circumstances to break up, most of us tried to stay in touch. Several had transferred into Morgan State with me, while the rest enrolled in other nearby four-year colleges. This included my Vietnam vet friends, who had rented a small house off campus on Fairview Avenue. They lived a kind of anything-goes bohemian lifestyle over there, with few rules and fewer problems. Each had his own little sacred bedroom. The rest of the house was pretty much public domain, and there was always plenty of traffic coming and going at all hours of the day and night. Whenever I hung out with them there, the scene was always refreshingly familiar, with the acrid aroma of marijuana mingling with blaring music of Funkadelic and Jimi Hendrix. At Morgan, we remained a tight bunch. At CCB we had fought to make sure that Stokely Carmichael's messages would be heard on campus. In our new school we would eventually bring in such speakers as Jesse Jackson and James Baldwin, Haki Madhubuti, and Angela Davis. Baldwin, a friend of mine named Kip Branch, and I once spent four hours at the Pimlico restaurant talking well into the night about race relations in America. As a writer, Baldwin was among the best. As a thinker, he was brilliant.

I was extremely proud of being a student at Morgan State University, and tried to make sure I got the most out of the experience. Considered one of the nation's leading historically black universities, Morgan boasted some of America's brightest and most influential black professionals among its alumni. Because I would be there only two years, it was important to me to make my mark quickly and not squander an opportunity. To that end, I spent the first few weeks attending orientation meetings for every student association on campus.

I had assumed that going into Morgan as a junior would put me at a disadvantage compared to the more plugged-in students, at least in terms of running an organization. But barely a month into my first semester there, I attended an Urban Studies Association meeting and impressed my colleagues with my views on the importance of mass communications in the black community.

Many students at the meeting told me that they were familiar with my "Ebony Reflections" broadcast on WEBB and agreed with some of my ideas. I'd heard that the university had put in a bid for an FCC license to launch a campus radio station, and one of my suggestions that night was to develop a committee that would push for it. The group liked the idea, and ended up electing me president of the association. This qualified me to serve as liaison to the Student Government Association. For the next year, both groups petitioned the FCC and lobbied and harangued Morgan's administrators until we were able to launch our own radio station—WEAA.

The most unfortunate aspect of my transition to Morgan State was that Linda and I were slowly drifting apart. My social activism and community involvement were taking a toll on our marriage. Shortly after I began at Morgan, Linda enrolled in the University of Baltimore. With both of us now juggling work and school schedules, there wasn't much time for each other—or at least we failed to make the time.

"The only time I get to hear your voice is when I cut on the radio," she once snapped at me sarcastically. "It's like we don't know each other."

On a few occasions, we tried to reconnect by sorting out our feelings and talking things over, but the chasm between us was taking on a life of its own. Even the times we spent together were marred by awkwardness, a sense that our common ground had slipped away from us. I was focused on changing the world and she was focused on other things. It was a formula that spelled disaster. At one point, we considered seeking counseling from our church's pastor, but we never got around to it. We were facing our first tough period and it showed.

In truth, we didn't give the issue of our conflicting interests the attention it deserved. It wasn't until years later that Linda expressed to me how she felt during this time of our unraveling marriage. "I wasn't angry at you for drifting away from me, because I was at fault too," she'd say. "Sometimes things happen before you realize they happen. We were both consumed with so many things, and evolving in our own ways, that when I looked up we had simply lost our bond. The worst part was that I didn't know how to get it back and neither did you." In hindsight and with precision, she was right.

The one time I recall seeing Linda's pain over what was happening to us was during my first year at Morgan. I was on an organizing committee that brought poet Nikki Giovanni and the Last Poets to a recital on campus. I was so excited and busy with planning it that I neglected to mention the event to Linda. Even more, I didn't tell her that I was among a handful of students chosen to recite our own revolutionary poetry. Linda discovered what was going on when a member of the organizing committee called our apartment to confirm a few last-minute details for the event that evening. I wasn't home, but Linda took the message and without comment, decided on her own to show up at the event. The irony was that one of my readings was a love poem dedicated to her. I had written it shortly after we married and wanted to share it with the large crowd that had turned out.

When the program ended, she walked up to me angrily. We had drifted so far apart, I didn't realize I had forgotten to tell her about the event until she appeared there, standing before me. I could see the hurt etched in her face. "How could you leave me out of something so special," she wanted to know, planting herself in front of me.

There was no good excuse, and so I offered none. Quite simply, we had seemingly reached a point where we were married merely by law and living arrangement. But in the most important ways, we had lost touch with each other and moved in our separate venues. She had become interested in someone else, and I knew in my heart it was over between us.

"What should we do about this?" I asked Linda. "What's happened to the love we had? We never fought like this . . . mistrusted like this, or left each other out of what we do. What is happening?"

When I graduated from Morgan, I was offered a job as program director of WEAA—the station I'd founded. Station manager Al Stewart, along with Doris Hawks, Carry Dean, and I were nearly the entire staff in the beginning. A close friend, Debyi Sababu, helped to cover for us on air. It was a job with a frenetic and demanding pace, and I scarcely recall all the wheelers and dealers who came through my office. But there was one appointment I will never forget—the meeting I had with my one-time idol, Big Al Jefferson, the man who assured me I could never succeed in radio.

On the day of Al's appointment to see me, I looked out of my office and saw him in the lobby waiting his turn with all the other record promoters. I was sincerely glad to see him after all these years, because basically I always considered him a nice guy—though dead wrong about me.

I called him in and we greeted each other with a firm handshake.

"So what's happening, Big Al," I asked amiably, certain that this wasn't a social call, but one of pure necessity. "It's been a long time," I said, extending my hand toward his shoulder.

He held up two 45s. "I want to talk to you about these records. Just like the old days," he said, and smiled.

"Oh, is this your new label?" I knew that Al hadn't been in radio for several years, and I assumed he'd moved on to running his own company.

"No," he said. "I'm a regional promoter working the mid-Atlantic region."

I was somewhat startled by his announcement. To some, it may seem unfair to characterize his position as hitting hard times, but anyone in radio knows that it's no step up to go from being program director for the hottest station in the city to being a regional record promoter for a label no one had heard of.

"You know, things just happen," he explained, looking dead in my eye.

I nodded. "Anyway, what can I do for you?"

"Well, we're really trying to get this record moving, and we need some chart action," Al Jefferson went on. "If we can get your station to spin it, we know that we can force some other stations on it."

"What's it sound like?"

"It's not a dog. It's got a good rhythm section, good vocals."

I listened to Big Al Jefferson's sales pitch for a few moments, then he fell silent. "Look," he said finally. "I'm also here because I want to apologize to you, whether or not you give these records some chart action."

He looked me directly in the eyes. "I was wrong," Al Jefferson said. "I was really wrong about you."

He didn't have to explain what he was wrong about. We both knew. Al Jefferson had made the wrong call about me, and at the time it had been a tremendous setback. I'd volunteered at WWIN for three years in a row, wedging my dream in between college courses, five sons, and countless other demands. I had many problems and issues affecting my life, and I'd used up every ounce of my precious time waiting for this shot—and then to be told after a too-brief audition that I wouldn't be hired because I didn't have the talent felt really unfair, and as if Al Jefferson had made a totally wrong call.

But it was his call. And his opinion.

He continued to apologize until I finally waved it off. In the end, I'd made it without him. Maybe his call had given me the single-minded drive I'd needed to innovate and get my vision on the air.

"It's all right," I said. "Really, it's okay."

I took the records from him, asked about his family and the old crowd that hung out at our former station, and wished him well. As Al Jefferson stepped out of my office that day, I had only one regret. I should have thanked him for constructing an obstacle that, in the end, helped me as I set out on a very different journey: running for City Council.

With no real political base or campaign war chest, getting elected to public office would be even tougher than getting on the airwaves.

10

IS THIS SEAT TAKEN?

*D*URING the summer of 1978, you could hardly walk down the streets of West Baltimore without hearing a car radio blaring the music of Grover Washington, Jr., or the Isley Brothers' hit record "Take It to the Next Phase." For me, those words transcended the song's simple message of a hot romance. In so many other ways it seemed that all Americans, especially blacks and Hispanics, were pushing to reach the next phase in our lives. We were striving for higher goals in this post–civil rights era when opportunity was finally penetrating the secure fiefdoms that had been dominated so long by white males.

In 1978, a forty-seven-year-old woman named Margaret A. Brewer was appointed as the first female Marine Corps general. And in April 1978, Jill E. Brown, a twenty-seven-year-old Baltimorean, became the first black woman pilot for a major U.S. airline when she began working for Texas International Airlines. On the other hand, black advancement was also stoking a

216

growing debate over racial quotas. Later that year, the Supreme Court ruled that the University of California had to admit a white man named Allan P. Bakke to its medical school. Bakke had sued the school, saying his civil rights had been violated because of racial quotas designed to boost the minority enrollment in the medical school.

If it was an ambitious time, it was also a bizarre time. It seemed that every day a new oddity of some sort occurred at home or abroad that got people talking. From late summer into the fall, folks were bemoaning the national gasoline shortage that had resulted in a frustrating rationing system across several states. Maryland motorists grumbled over a requirement that we purchase at least five dollars' worth of gas if we owned a car with fewer than six cylinders and seven dollars' worth if we had a larger engine. It seemed ridiculous, too, that because my license plate ended in an even number I could only buy gasoline on even-numbered days, while those with odd-numbered plates bought gas on odd days.

This strange situation had barely passed before tropical storm David came raging through the mid-Atlantic region during the first week in September, flooding several local counties, displacing residents, and damaging housing and farmland to such a degree that President Carter had to declare Maryland a major disaster area. Later that winter, hundreds of lost souls unwittingly followed a religious demagogue named the Reverend Jim Jones to a death ceremony in Jonestown, Guyana. At Jones's persuasion, more than 900 of his People's Temple disciples, most of them black—and nearly 250 of them children—drank poison and died in a tragic ritual. Strange and bad news, it seemed, just kept on coming. The worst news came in late summer of that year. My father, Rufus "Rip" Tate, had died. The facts surrounding his death were something of a mystery. Rip had been a diabetic, and, after several delays, the coroner determined that he'd died from an insulin reaction. On an unseasonably cool day, I boarded a plane to Milwaukee to identify my father's body and bring him home for a proper burial. What I could not bury was my lingering sense of regret and sadness over the time and opportunities we had lost.

• • •

As far back as I can remember, I have always harbored a deep love of sports, and no athlete fascinated me more than Muhammad Ali. Muhammad Ali is among the truly great athletes in history, not only because he possessed the physical attributes that enabled him to outperform his rivals in the ring, but because he was also a sharp, analytical thinker. Ali's mind, not his fists, was his most powerful weapon. It was only a year earlier that Ali and I had staged a fund-raising set of exhibition fights to raise money for the Sister Clara Muhammah Elementary School. During the match Ali forgot it was an exhibition, and accidentally knocked me out. But it was all in fun and we raised money.

No matter the sport, the greats know that the real contest always begins long before the official clock starts ticking. Ali made exceptional use of his days before a big fight, seizing them as opportunities to size up his opponents, probe for weaknesses, and design a plan to exploit those shortcomings in a way that would lead to victory. Throughout his boxing career, he had proved himself a master strategist. I'd started following his career during his early days as a young champion boxer, then named Cassius Clay, and rooted for him when he fought for the United States in the 1960 Olympics in Rome, Italy. I felt his pain when he came home to Louisville, Kentucky, and was refused service at a local lunch counter. My respect only grew when he beat Sonny Liston right out of his championship belt in 1964. Joe Louis used to jar an opponent with one hand and knock him out with the other, but Liston could flatten you with either hand.

Nobody expected Muhammad Ali to last a round with Sonny Liston. Critics chided him for not having the physical skills of a great champion boxer. They said he lacked the punching power of Joe Louis, Rocky Marciano, Jersey Joe Walcott, or Ezzard Charles. They also claimed that Ali, or the "Louisville Lip" as he was sometimes called, never punched to the body. Marciano advised Ali to call off the fight because he didn't think the young boxer had enough ring experience to battle Liston.

Ali first premiered his winning strategy at the weigh-in in Miami: taunt the big man endlessly and make him unravel. He jumped up in Liston's face, shouting, "You're ugly, you're a bear and I'm going to whup you bad." Liston was visibly shaken by Ali's performance.

Ali knew how to make his opponent blind with anger. At every press conference, in every public appearance, at every Howard Cosell interview, Ali kept taunting Liston with a blistering verbal firestorm of bravado, bluster, and poetic put-downs. Ali had realized something important: if you can get a bear angry enough and disrupt its psyche, the bear will make mistakes it would normally not make in the course of hunting its prey. Ali's trap worked wonderfully. In the weeks prior to the fight, Liston became so angry over Ali's constant trash talking that he completely lost focus. The moment he stepped into the ring, he was frayed psychologically. Ali's taunting had gotten the best of him. By the seventh round, Liston was hurting so bad he couldn't even answer the bell to start the round.

As I launched my campaign for a seat on the City Council that year, I realized the lesson in Ali's tactics. I also knew that it was crucial for the underdog to deliver the punch in the right spot and at the right time, or it wouldn't have any impact on the outcome.

I needed an inspiration like Ali for my campaign because gaining a seat on the Council was a long shot in almost every way imaginable. Not only had I not been anointed by the Baltimore political machine, but I had very few connections among the city's power brokers. And my reputation throughout black Baltimore was as a disc jockey, not as a political mover and shaker.

But even though I had all that working against me, I was unshakable in my belief that it was time for a change. And I believed, insanely or not, that I was the man who could make that change happen. Much of my motivation to run for office was fueled by a singular desire to oust Councilman Emerson R. Julian, who I believed epitomized an old-fashioned, elite, out-of-touch brand of politics in Baltimore. Serving his third term on the Council as one of the three representatives of the city's Fourth District, Julian was a prominent physician in the community and considered by many to be an independent political voice. However, I believed that much of this image as a free-thinker wasn't based so much on the substance of his ideas, but

on the fact that Julian, although black, was intolerant of the
racial dogma that permeated many political debates. When it
came to voting on issues affecting the black community, this
silver-haired son of an Indiana railway clerk—often referred to
as "Doc"—prided himself on not being a knee-jerk emotionalist
but a color-blind pragmatist.

Back in 1970, when then Mayor Thomas L. D'Alesandro was
under fire to put more blacks on the school board, Julian derided
the idea as foolish and unnecessary. Later, when it was popular
among blacks and many liberal whites to support antipoverty programs, Julian blasted such efforts as a waste of taxpayers' money.

While Julian's views were winning him credibility among the
city's white power elite, some of the poorer blacks in his own
district had taken to calling him an Uncle Tom. I didn't so much
agree with that characterization as I believed Julian's approach
was generally wrongheaded and damaging to many of those
who had voted him into office.

The truth was, the black community was suffering from a kind
of benign neglect. The most glaring example of this at the time
was that virtually all the city's resources were being plowed into
the downtown Inner Harbor—a sparkling glass, steel, and concrete development of hotels, offices, shops, and restaurants
designed to symbolize the renaissance of the city and be a lure for
tourists. While the downtowns of most major cities had become
little more than ghost towns, in those days of expanding suburban
malls, the City of Baltimore could boast a blossoming skyline of
new architecture, including a World Trade Center, the National
Aquarium, the Maryland Science Center, a Hyatt Regency Hotel,
and several elegant promenades and other glitzy developments.

But as the city doled out hundreds of millions of dollars to the
armies of construction workers who toiled daily in cranes and
tractors to erect this colossal tourist attraction on the Chesapeake
Bay, the adjacent neighborhoods were being largely ignored and
left to decay. Streets riddled with potholes, cracked sidewalks, and
broken curbs lined block after block of abandoned, dilapidated,
and burned-out housing. Blacks made up 55 percent of the city's
nearly 800,000 residents, yet the waterfront development made
crystal clear our stark lack of political and economic power.

Equally atrocious was our income and housing situation. Black unemployment in the city hovered above 12 percent while white unemployment was only half that. The poverty rate was a chilling 55 percent. Those who were able to find work were twice as likely as whites to be stuck in dead-end, blue-collar jobs. Unable to afford to buy a house or to get a bank loan for a mortgage, blacks were twice as likely as whites to rent housing. In fact, some 90 percent of public housing residents in the city were black. With 30 percent of black households headed by women, the economic pressure was clearly placing even more stresses on the black family structure.

The situation was dire, and it wasn't going to get better without new leadership in local government. One problem was that the Inner Harbor was the brainchild of Mayor William Donald Schaefer. A respected Democrat nationally, Schaefer was also a master of hardball city politics in the tradition of Chicago's late (and infamous) Mayor Richard Daley. Schaefer said of Daley admiringly, "He had temporary employees for eighteen years. When he wanted something done, they didn't have to monkey around. It was just done."

A portly man with brooding eyes and boundless energy, Schaefer spun a fine "man-of-the-people" image with such photo-ops as cruising around town on weekends in his 1975 Pontiac, pointing at potholes and uncollected garbage, and dispatching the proper city agency on Monday morning to correct the problem. The truth was that for a decade, Schaefer had been building a power base by steamrolling adversaries and hardballing critics, and now he was enjoying the fruits of his labors. Known for his temper and dogmatic style of leadership, Schaefer reigned supreme over a remarkably docile and deferential Council that would further his own agenda. When it came to his major pet initiatives like the Inner Harbor, few outside of me dared challenge him.

In addition, to cut through red tape and bureaucratic hassles, Schaefer had created special troubleshooting agencies that reported directly to him and always got the job done. Cynically referred to by some as "shadow governments," this complex, byzantine network of quasipublic corporations that were financed through mayorally appointed trustees carried out the management and economic development projects that in most cities would have been the domain of municipal agencies. The trick here was that because they weren't legal extensions of the government, they weren't burdened with any of the bureaucracy and red tape that might render them ineffective. Whenever the mayor was attacked over these shadow governments, he got defensive.

Many middle-class Baltimoreans cheered the mayor on because of his ability to win big money from Washington. President Ronald Reagan liked Schaefer's pro-business bent, and during those years more than half of the city's annual budget came from federal and state grants. Schaefer basked in enthusiastic support from the business community. There was nary a project that he backed that failed to draw the rallying support of the well-heeled business people in the Greater Baltimore Committee.

To get his way, Schaefer shouted, yelled, and cajoled—and he certainly didn't hesitate to wield his extraordinary power when necessary. Many Baltimoreans bitterly recalled the time back in the early 1970s when the City Council axed $10.5 million from his budget. The mayor responded by cutting off the air-conditioning in the Council chambers and having their cars ticketed for parking violations. Suspending city funds and services was also part of Don Schaefer's bag of tricks for pressuring local organizations to bring their position more in line with his agenda.

Because of Schaefer's power, nobody, including "Doc" Julian, was willing to fight the mayor on the critical issues affecting black people—whether it was the lack of minority contracting, our absence from local government boards and commissions, and especially on his grand vision of developing the harbor. It was my belief that Julian, like most of his Council colleagues, simply yielded to the mayor. This fact, coupled with Julian's cavalier attitude toward some blacks, only bolstered my desire to take his seat.

It was common knowledge throughout the city, at least among radio listeners, that I was fed up with Schaefer, the

Council, and the whole range of clubby politics across the state of Maryland. As station director and talk-show host at WEAA, I spent countless hours on the air venting my frustrations to my audience about all the mayor's clever manipulations that allowed him to rule with runaway authority.

"You can build up the central business district of any city and make it a tourist attraction!" I ranted constantly over the airwaves. "You can go to New York and get a good ad agency to run a slick campaign to increase public awareness. But at some point you have to stop and look at the peripheral areas just outside the central business district and deal with the human suffering that's going on!"

Listeners were equally outraged. The phone lines were always lit up with callers spouting their anger, frustration, and downright fury over what they considered to be spineless representation by some black Council members.

"We've got nothing but a go-along, get-along Council down there," I said. "They're all afraid of getting on the wrong side of the mayor."

"Somebody with a backbone oughta go down there and tell 'em like it is," a caller chimed in. "If they can clean up and build up downtown, then they sho' oughta be able to do the same thing to these neighborhoods."

"You're absolutely right," I agreed.

Then one caller caught me totally by surprise. "I hear you're considering running for office, Kweisi," the woman said. "I hear you're gonna take on Emerson Julian. That true?"

I laughed. "Now, where did you hear a thing like that?"

"I get around, Kweisi," she deadpanned.

"Well if things don't change soon, I just might," I allowed.

"I sure hope you do," the woman said. "Black folks around here need somebody who's not gonna sell 'em down the Chesapeake to keep the mayor happy."

There was a steady flow of such remarks that fueled my belief that Julian's seat wasn't as secure as many believed. I was discovering that disenchantment over his leadership in the Fourth District had risen. Even an outsider and political neophyte like me might stand a chance running against the black Democratic machine. Because Baltimore was solidly Democratic, the winner of the primary election was virtually a guaranteed shoo-in for assuming office. For this reason, I knew I would have to exert myself full-out during this primary.

Like my campus activism, my decision to run for public office grew out of a simple desire to fight a system that much of the time exploited its weakest citizens and took the acquiescence for granted. Ever since I'd campaigned for Parren Mitchell following Dr. King's assassination April 4, 1968, I'd developed a growing appreciation for the role politics played in society.

I watched in admiration as Mitchell dusted himself off after his first losing attempt at a congressional seat and campaigned even more tenaciously to successfully win office in 1970. Since then, the World War II veteran had become a strong, uncompromising voice in the Congressional Black Caucus—many called him the "conscience of the Congress." He was well on his way to becoming one of the most influential black leaders in the country.

A fierce advocate for the rights of the poor and minorities, Parren Mitchell was most widely recognized for his effective leadership in protecting and promoting the interests of minority small business developers. In 1976, using his position as a member of the House Budget Committee, Mitchell attached an amendment to President Carter's $4 billion Public Works Bill compelling state and local governments receiving federal dollars to set aside 10 percent of the funds for minority contractors and suppliers. Upheld as constitutional by the Supreme Court in 1980, this amendment was one of the strongest pieces of affirmative action legislation ever enacted until its demise during the Bush era.

Parren's nephew, Michael B. Mitchell, was maintaining his family's community activist tradition by serving as a Fourth District councilman. Michael once boasted of his uncle, "For the first time we had a black guy standing up to Nixon and telling him to go to hell. We're in the big leagues now."

I remember watching proudly as such local black leaders as

Mitchell, State Senator Verda F. Welcome, and real estate and land developer William L. Adams joined forces to wrest funds from the government to rebuild East and West Baltimore following the riots that destroyed over a thousand city businesses. Progress was slow, but during the ten years since, more than half a billion dollars in federal, state, and local funds were used to restore the burned-out area.

Developments like this had changed my views markedly since my street-corner clash with Parren—a time when all I'd felt was hopelessness over the plight of black people. It was becoming increasingly clear to me that unless the community shared in the decision-making process at all levels of government, we would forever be doomed to scraping the bottom of Baltimore's barrel in areas of employment, housing, and education. To be sure, compared to other cities, Baltimore's blacks were making significant inroads into the local and state political structure. In the late seventies, the Seventh Congressional District, which encompassed more than half of Baltimore, could boast the greatest concentration of African American elected officials in the country.

But much of the hard work still lay ahead. While minorities had accounted for most of the city's population since the mid-1960s, only two had ever held citywide political office. Deeply disturbed by the absence of our people in broad positions of influence, I'd volunteered to work in Milton B. Allen's 1970 campaign for state's attorney. That same year, I cheered on Paul L. Chester, who shocked voters when he was elected clerk of the Common Pleas Court, one of only a half dozen clerkships open that year.

True, I was quite busy working at WEAA, as well as trying to keep my five growing boys on the right track, but the aspect of social activism still energized me. It was at times like this that the words of my ex-wife, Linda, would ring clearly and hauntingly in my mind. It had been five years since that night at Morgan State University when she walked up to me at the Nikki Giovanni program. Frustrated at the level of passion I was bringing to my newfound social activism, she said, "You just have never found a cause you would walk away from, have you? Don't worry," she continued. "You can't help yourself, it's in your blood." And maybe she was right. Whatever spare time I had was invested in volunteering in the campaigns of those candidates I believed to be courageous and bright enough to make a positive change in government. I worked on Saundra Banks's campaign when she became the first black clerk of the court in 1978, and helped to work for others who ran for the State House. Always working on somebody's campaign, I hoped my own high energy and commitment might help pave the way for others seeking elected offices that minorities had long been blocked out of.

However, by 1979, I was growing extremely restless in my role as an outsider. Simply supporting others no longer seemed enough. I wanted to hold office, to take my best shot at pushing through programs and policies that would benefit the lower end of the economic spectrum. But as in the case of my hero Ali, the odds were not in my favor. The first strike against me was that I was only twenty-nine years old, and many said I looked even younger than that. The fact that most of my adult working life had been spent in radio was also a negative—no matter how effective my show was in emphasizing local and national political issues. Most people still saw me as a disc jockey. This perception saddled me with a significant image problem and people simply didn't take me seriously. It didn't help either that my name was so nontraditional, a fact I knew was bound to confound or turn off certain voters. All of these issues were exacerbated by the fact that I had no money.

Although the obstacles were mountainous, my determination loomed even higher. Tearing a page right out of Ali's golden handbook of psychological warfare, I marched down to City Hall one afternoon in December, where the City Council was holding its weekly meeting. I don't recall what the Council was voting on, but the galleries were full of people. The TV cameras were there, along with a full complement of the print media. I quickly sized up the situation and decided to make my move. Often, politics is nothing but good theater, which is something the great politicians have understood very clearly. Brash and purposeful, I pushed past the security guards and walked out onto the floor of the Council.

I realized what a formidable force Doc Julian was in the community. But I boosted my adrenaline level with thoughts of how, compared to me, Julian had it all going for him, how he was a doctor with considerable wealth and influence, and because of this he was considered an upstanding public servant. Yet, I believed him to be a man with a cavalier attitude topped off by a sense of unassailable entitlement because of the political clout that he'd accumulated. Julian had to go! That's all there was to it. And I was the man to replace him. I was young, brash, full of ideas, and determined to make a change. Julian represented the Old Guard, the Establishment, the traditional barriers to change and progress.

"I'm here," I called out as I sat down in Julian's empty Council seat. "This is my seat and I'm here to claim it for the people. I can't wait until Election Day because Emerson Julian is through! T-H-R-O-U-G-H. All power to the people."

There was an audible gasp in the room. City Council President Walter S. Orlinsky and the Council members were all staring at me in disbelief as the cameras flashed and my face grew more serious. I needed free publicity to beat a good campaigner like Julian. I realized that in order to win I needed to distract him, confuse him with a series of unexpected jolts. I had to keep him off balance, to keep him angry at this young upstart. With a blitz of Mfume antics in the press, Julian would forget to do a lot of things, and I would take advantage of his lapses.

"Yes," I continued. "I came here tonight to claim this seat and the best way to claim it is to sit in it. And now that I'm in it, I think I like it!"

As the guards began to grab me, I belted out a final pronouncement. "So somebody go find Emerson Julian right now and tell him that I'm the person that he has to deal with. Kweisi Mfume, that's who he has to deal with now! And there will not be politics as usual in this city anymore."

I managed to put on a real show that evening before the guards promptly threw me out of the building. I guess they figured there was no sense arresting me, because I wasn't crazy—I knew exactly what I was doing. Predictably, the scene was reported on local radio and TV that night, and was carried by newspapers the next day.

Word got back to me that Julian was outraged that I'd been photographed in his Council seat. That's when I knew I was getting the best of him. I called a press conference and went after him again. Julian was so furious that he pretended to ignore me. He thought if he didn't acknowledge me, then perhaps I wouldn't exist. In just a matter of weeks I had become his worst nightmare, and talk that he might retire began to surface. If he could deny me the satisfaction of defeating him by leaving office graciously, why not? Knowing that with a vacant seat, a flood of candidates would run, Julian believed that he would get the final laugh. Then, two months later, the bad news came: the sixty-one-year-old Julian had suffered a heart attack at his home and died just thirty minutes after arriving at Lutheran Hospital.

It was a tragic turn of events and I felt horrible. I wondered how much I had contributed to his stress. Had my chiding pushed him further toward cardiac arrest? I also wondered how many others were blaming me for Doc Julian's sudden death. My goal was simply to win, but this was not the way I wanted it. Each day I picked up the newspaper there seemed to be more praise recalling Julian's good works for the city. "He was able to voice concerns of the black community and wasn't speaking from any organizational bias," grieved Walter S. Orlinsky, president of the City Council. "Doc wasn't shy about being black but didn't necessarily play the traditional black games," Orlinsky continued. "He brought perspective to the Council."

Now somewhat guilt-stricken and paranoid about how people would perceive me, I stayed off the campaign trail for a few weeks. Julian was succeeded on the Council by his son, Dr. Emerson R. Julian, Jr., who had made it clear early on that he wouldn't seek a term of his own. I decided to use this time of citywide mourning to adjust and to develop a new strategy. My campaign was based on unseating Julian, the weakest of three incumbents in my district. But the elder Julian's death had brought nine new contenders into the race. Doc, I thought, had succeeded in the end, denying me the chance to defeat him.

I'd learned from volunteering in other campaigns that the

more crowded a political race becomes, the more critical it is to develop a sharply focused message that distinguishes you from the pack.

"People can sense when you're running on ego rather than principle," Parren Mitchell once told me. "That's why it's never enough to simply know the issues in your district. You can't gain the trust of voters until you can explain quickly and specifically why your positions are the right positions. It's never enough to just bash your opponent."

Recalling Parren's words, and considering Julian's unfortunate death, it was clear that I needed to revamp my strategy. My narrow anti-Julian platform from which I'd launched my candidacy had suddenly lost its relevance.

Such was the beginning of my strange, tenuous debut into the world of politics. Young, naive, and idealistic, I would stumble my way through a rather rocky apprenticeship in the rough and tumble of Baltimore's most visible power circle. In all honesty, it's only in hindsight that I can now look back on my campaign or the seven years I spent in city government with fond amusement. At the time, I was too busy scraping for mere survival to enjoy anything about the experience. It was baptism by fire from the start. Much later, during my years as an elected official, people would often ask me why I was still such a frenetic and aggressive campaigner—despite the fact that my margin of victory was widening with each election. My response has always been fairly simple: When your first campaign was as rough as mine, you learn to take nothing for granted.

I may call my first run for public office a campaign, but it was really more like a crusade. A campaign implies a kind of formal and highly organized group that galvanizes its energy for a common purpose, and then dissolves once that purpose is achieved. But my team was a collection of loyal friends who knew that, despite everything working against me, I'd fight tooth and nail for what I believed in and never sell them out. More than anything else, this emotional backup system compensated for my shortcomings in that first race.

As I began studying the issues facing the city, I quickly understood why Schaefer had been able to amass such control. Rather than having neighborhood-sized wards, political Baltimore is made up of six large districts, each of which elects three representatives to the City Council. You'd think that these eighteen Council members would act as an equalizing force for a dominant mayor. However, the longstanding and peculiar city charter is slanted heavily in favor of centralized government control. In most cities, such functions as welfare and waste disposal are typically administered by county authorities, but in Baltimore, those roles fall to the city government. This unusual arrangement served to bolster Mayor Schaefer's high-handed rule, while dooming most grassroots protests to futile gestures. The sad irony in Baltimore's reputation as a city of strong, vital, eclectic neighborhoods was that virtually all of its strength flowed out of the mayor's City Hall office.

I wanted to wrest some of that control away from the city government and channel it into the neighborhoods, where I felt it belonged. It took some convincing to persuade my buddies that I was serious, though. While I had a background of political activism, I was just a few years out of college, and some of them wondered whether I might be getting in over my head. Carl Swann, my old buddy from Turners Station, was married then and not looking for mission impossible when I dropped by unannounced one day to see him. Carl was exhausted, having just come home from his shift at a local steel mill, but he was visibly happy to see me. However, when I told him of my plan to run for office, he stared at me in disbelief.

"Man, have you lost your goddamn mind?" he bellowed.

"I'm serious, Carl."

He cracked up laughing. "That's the craziest shit I done heard all day," he said, taking two beers out of the refrigerator and sliding one across the kitchen table to me. "You got it made over there at the radio station. Why would you want to go and run for some damn elected office?"

"Because what's happening downtown is nothin' but a joke, and you know it."

"Yeah, I know," he said soberly. "But you don't want to get

involved in that stuff. It ain't nothin' but a bunch of cheats, suits, and sellouts over there suckin' up to the mayor, bro."

"That's right. That's why I want to run. All that's gotta change."

"You're really serious about this shit, aren't you."

"Damn straight I am. I just wanna know whether you'll help me get in there."

"You raised any money yet?"

"No."

"You got any volunteers yet?"

"No."

"You got a platform yet?"

"Uh-uh."

Carl sipped his beer and flashed a mischievous grin. "What the hell you waitin' on, Pee Wee? Ain't nothin to it, but to do it."

Once I had Carl on board, I began calling some of my college friends and asking them if they'd come together one more time and help me win this election. Some of them I practically begged, admitting that without their support I wouldn't be able to run because my resources were so scarce. I managed to persuade about fifteen volunteers, including George Buntin, Jackie Johnson, Terry Scott, Cynthia Chase, Rodney Orange, and Rosetta Kerr. Buntin served as my campaign manager for a year. Kerr was my co-campaign manager for field operations. They were a bright and energetic team, and we held our meetings in the annex of Brown's Memorial Baptist Church, where seven years earlier Linda and I were married.

It was there, in our makeshift headquarters, that we came up with our campaign slogan of "Beat the Bosses." It was the perfect theme, not only because it was catchy, but because it made a powerful connection with our community's frustration over being disenfranchised from the local power base. Folks didn't have to scratch their heads about what bosses we were referring to. Everybody knew we meant those who controlled City Hall and Mayor Schaefer.

The mission of our campaign was to instill a new sense of empowerment in the Fourth District. To achieve this, though, we knew my greatest challenge would be gaining rapport and credibility on the very streets in which I'd grown up. My radio shows had given me some celebrity, but to campaign success-fully meant that I had to reinvent myself as a serious and appealing contender for public office.

Baltimore businessman Raymond V. Haysbert, president of Parks Sausage Co., was a real player in the business and po-litical arena and one of the first persons I sought out. Haysbert was a tall, imposing man who exuded that easy, self-assured manner often displayed by people of wealth and influence. He had bright eyes and a jovial face, neither of which should be mistaken for meekness. Back then, Haysbert was fast becoming known throughout the country as a shrewd and forceful figure with a knack for winning the necessary political and business battles to keep Parks Sausage flourishing. With annual sales pushing $20 million at the time, his company was well on its way to becoming one of the largest black-owned businesses in the nation.

Nevertheless, Haysbert's success was the exception for black businesses in Baltimore and around the nation. At the time, there were some 3,093 black-owned businesses in the city, em-ploying just 2,642 people. Many of them were so small, the owners ran them themselves with no other workers. Black entrepreneurs had largely missed their opportunity to expand when white businesses abandoned the city's black com-munity following the 1968 riots. Instead, an influx of smart Korean entrepreneurs opened stores and created even stiffer competition.

Because Haysbert was successfully navigating through these tough conditions, he was admired as a keen strategic thinker. People trusted him for his counsel and advice in arenas far beyond his main forte of business.

When I called Ray to make an appointment, I figured he'd probably turn me down flat. After all, his calendar was filled with meetings of the movers and shakers. For him, meeting with a local disc jockey fell under the heading of charity work. But if there was anything Haysbert disliked, it was being out of the loop. Perhaps it was sheer curiosity that made him agree to meet with me that day and offer his views on local politics.

Sitting amid the flowering plants in the sunroom of his home in 1979, Haysbert was far warmer and more receptive to me than I'd anticipated. In fact, he spent hours with me discussing winning and losing in politics, and how issues and image influenced both. He even shared his discouragement with the pace and breadth of black entrepreneurship in the city.

"It's really sad how little black economic activity there is in this city," he lamented. "A few people are breaking loose and doing their own kind of mom 'n' pop things. But not nearly enough is happening in terms of major economic development for black people. I meet a lot of people with desire, but most of them lack the determination to get the job done."

Haysbert spoke to me for two hours about the state of business development and politics. Surprised and flattered that a mover and shaker like Haysbert was sharing his thoughts with me, I sat there absorbing his every word and offering my opinions when appropriate.

At one point, I began airing my views about the need for rent control in Baltimore to counter the growing problem of rent gouging. I told him I believed that rent increases should be limited to between four and seven percent, depending on whether the landlord pays the cost of some or all of the utilities.

"It's really putting a burden on low-income tenants," I said. "Many people in my district are being forced to move out of their homes because they can't afford their rent any longer."

I don't think Haysbert agreed with my view. He said he was saddened to hear that poor people were being evicted, but went on to say that in these times of high inflation, rent control might hurt the local economy.

"I'm not sure, but it seems to me that investors and apartment owners might start putting their money into real estate in neighboring counties that don't have rent control," Haysbert said. "The city's trying to build up the tax base, and those kind of laws tend to cripple property ownership."

It surprised me that I didn't challenge Haysbert's conservative pro-business thinking on the matter. I realized that it was clear that we had at least one thing in common—a desire to see more people from our community in positions of political influence.

Finally, as our meeting drew to a close, Haysbert folded his long arms and peered at me.

"Because you're a bright young man with some interesting ideas, I will do what I can to help you," he said. "But you have to take my advice, all of it, and without questions or reservations."

I winced internally, wondering just what kind of compromise I'd have to make. "What are you advising?" I asked.

"Well, first, you've got to change your image—the way you dress. That look is fine for the entertainment business, but it's all wrong for politics."

"What do you mean?" I asked defensively. "I think I dress fairly well."

"Yeah, but what you have on reflects where you are. Instead, it should reflect where you are going."

Haysbert then recited a litany of image-enhancing recommendations. "Cut your hair—your bush is way too high. And take off all your jewelry, and don't ever wear any again. Get rid of those bright suits—buy only dark ones. And don't wear colored shirts. Make sure they're all white. Shave off that facial hair because the more you have, the less people trust you. Psychologically it's just the way it tends to affect people's thinking."

Haysbert also told me to develop a list of ten issues on the things people are the most interested in. "Know those issues backward and forward, inside and out," he said. "Repeat them over and over in your head so you can always draw on them. You should never need a notepad, or need prodding or pumping. Be able to just rattle them off in detail like you own them."

Finally, Haysbert suggested that my nontraditional name could be a stumbling block to voters, and that I should work to make them comfortable with it. "It might help to go to people's doors directly—let them see and hear you," he said. "Talk with them and ask them for their votes. If you knock on enough doors and speak to enough people, you can overcome the name problem. The best thing about your name is that it could work to your advantage. No one can run another candidate for the office with the same last name unless they create an Mfume overnight."

The straightforward advice of a heavyweight like Haysbert would prove to be invaluable. What it didn't solve was the other pressing matter at the time: money. "You're on your own in that regard," he told me as he ushered me toward the door.

For the next few months, my campaign team fanned out across the district. Our goal was to knock on no less than ten thousand doors. I could always depend on my team to be the eyes and ears that kept me tuned to my rivals' activities.

"Earlier today, I saw people campaigning all over Pennsylvania Avenue," George Buntin would invariably pipe up at meetings.

"Well, we need to be there, too," I'd shoot back. "I know we're running low on leaflets, but Rosetta and George should probably go out today and work the neighborhoods between Upton and Sandtown. Shake some hands and get the word out that we're taking back our share of power from the bosses down there at City Hall."

"Which area do you want me to work?" Jackie would ask.

"Hit some churches and drop off some bumper stickers, especially Bethel AME, Union Baptist, and New Shiloh Baptist. Feel them out and see who their members plan to support.

"And Terry, you and I will go and drop some more posters off at Masjid Ul Haqq Mosque, then meet me in a couple of hours over at the New Fellowship Ministry in Sandtown. They're renovating some town houses from the ground up, and they're real proud of their efforts. Let's go over there and check it out."

The pace of campaigning is as frenetic as it is exhilarating. I spent hour after hour on my feet walking the blocks, introducing myself to virtually anyone who would stop and listen, and knocking on the doors of absolute strangers.

"Good evening, sir, my name is Kweisi Mfume."

"Your name is what?"

"Kwah-EE-see Oom-FOO-may, sir," I'd repeat. "It's African."

"Well, it's mighty odd, that's for damn sure. Anyway, what do you want, kee-see?"

"Well, sir, as you know, the primary elections are approaching and I'm running for a seat on City Council. I plan to win this race, sir, so I can be a strong voice in City Hall for your interests.

I grew up in this neighborhood, right around the block on Division Street. If you have a moment, I'd really appreciate hearing some of your thoughts on what kind of leadership you think we need to bring some positive change to this district."

I had never been a salesman like this before, and felt somewhat out of my league. But now I was selling the power of an idea, and the people I encountered saw my passion. I found that most residents would at least listen politely even if I sensed their lack of interest. It took me a while to realize which issues sparked the greatest enthusiasm among voters, but when I did I made a point to learn them inside out.

It was a rigorous but immensely valuable routine. Day in and day out, we would be on the street corners at 7 A.M. greeting potential voters on their way to work. At 5 P.M. my team would reassemble and begin canvassing various neighborhoods until sundown. Then everyone would go home for the night, while George, Rosetta, and I went back to the office to plan which area we'd canvass the following day. We'd continue our discussion of how to raise money, how to draw media coverage, and how to gain endorsements as well as organizational support in the district.

We worked the district feverishly, despite the fact that throughout weeks of campaigning it was becoming clearer that Baltimore was sliding toward yet another status-quo government. By all indications, Mayor Schaefer was expected to get a strong renomination vote in the Democratic primary. A win for Schaefer would put him in the esteemed company of the two other third-term Baltimore mayors, Howard W. Jackson and Thomas "Big Tommy" D'Alesandro. Schaefer was largely benefiting from the weak opposition put up by Delegate Patrick L. McDonough and Clarence "Tiger" Davis, a community organizer. Both were out hurling bland and roundly ignored criticisms of Schaefer, saying he favored bricks and mortar over poor people and blue-collar city residents. It didn't hurt either that Schaefer had doled out $1.8 million to Council incumbents. The cash was allegedly for street repairs, but everyone knew it was to put those members back in the voters' good graces.

Still, my team and I understood just how much was at stake in this primary election. It offered our community the chance not only to increase its representation on the City Council, but also to elect the first black city comptroller.

Social activist Norman V.A. Reeves was vying to become the Fifth District's first black councilman. Reeves, who was crippled by Lou Gehrig's disease, had lost the primary unfairly four years prior due to a "name's-the-same" ploy. An unemployed truck driver also named Reeves had thrown his name into the race at the last minute. The guy didn't spend one day campaigning and walked away with about 1,500 votes, while Norman Reeves lost to the white incumbent by a similarly narrow margin. We were all hoping he'd win this time around and strike a blow for fairness and courage.

In the other big race, Democratic State Delegate John W. Douglass was embarking on his second attempt to unseat Hyman A. Pressman, the incumbent four-term city comptroller. If he won, Douglass would be the first black city comptroller in Baltimore's history.

Because there were such high stakes involved, we were all baffled over forecasts that the primary would draw one of the lowest voter turnouts in recent memory. Citing a sluggish mayoral race, the lack of a Democratic contest for City Council president, and little excitement in other races, the Baltimore *Sun* reported that only 32 percent of the city's 380,062 registered voters were expected to cast ballots in the September 11, 1979, primary, and even that estimate was optimistic. The city's television stations had decided not to broadcast any of its usual early evening election specials, afraid that pre-empting regular programming would hurt their ratings that night.

Indeed, the races in several of the city's districts may have lacked intrigue, but the race for Emerson Julian's now vacant Fourth District City Council seat was shaping up as the hottest contest in the city. Two of the city's most formidable black leaders, State Senator Verda F. Welcome and businessman William L. "Little Willie" Adams, each supporting a different candidate, were embroiled in close battle for control of the district.

With nine contestants battling for Julian's seat, it was tough to deliver a clear message through the clutter of ideas. And with the primary heading into its final months, the newspapers were starting to make their endorsements, and the political clubs were stepping up their efforts for their chosen candidates. I was still essentially an unknown, with no real political ties. Then, one day, good fortune smiled my way.

Hoping that the fractious political landscape in the Fourth District might work in my favor, I decided to pay a visit to Verda Welcome, who had earned the distinction of being America's first black female state senator. She was a beautiful, matronly woman with walnut skin and lively eyes that peered intelligently through big, oval-framed glasses. An amazing lady whose long, impressive political career had made her an icon in Baltimore's black community, Verda had served in the state legislature since 1963. Before that, she had been a respected member of the House of Delegates. A graduate of both Morgan State University and New York University, and a member of Delta Sigma Theta sorority, Verda boasted plenty of high-profile friends and solid connections throughout the city.

In much the same manner as my cold call to Haysbert, I contacted her and asked to meet for some advice. Although we had never met personally, she invited me to her home for afternoon tea with her and her husband, Dr. Henry C. Welcome, a well-known physician in the city. The couple lived elegantly in a large red-brick home on the west side.

I was instantly struck by the luxurious fashion in which Senator Welcome lived, from the uniformed maid who greeted me at the door to the antiques-filled splendor of the well-appointed living room where Verda was sitting, casually sipping tea. While in her late sixties at the time, she had an air that was disarmingly alert. "Now, young man," she said. "Please sit down and tell me again, how do you pronounce that name?"

"It's Kwah-EE-see Oom-FOO-may," I politely replied.

"I see," she said, pausing. "And tell me, why is it you want that name?"

There was no judgment in her voice, only curiosity. I explained to her that I was a product of the '60s, and that I'd discovered a degree of liberation and pride in shedding the name of my forebears' slave master for one of African origins. I told her that it had been a gift from my great-aunt Lizzy, and that it meant "Conquering Son of Kings."

"I see," she said quietly, peering ever so softly over her glasses. "Well, Kweisi, this is my husband, Dr. Welcome. He wanted to come see who it was insisting on meeting his wife. Dr. Henry C. Welcome is his name, but from this point on, you can call him Palie."

"Yes, ma'am," I said, as respectfully as I could, as Dr. Welcome smiled and shook my hand.

"I understand nobody has endorsed you, is that right?"

"Not as of yet, ma'am, but I'm hoping for one any day now."

"I see." She glanced over at Dr. Welcome, and then back at me. "And, why do you want to do something like this?"

I went through my whole explanation about why I believed that the district—although she was a part of the district—needed some new ideas and fresh leadership. I also began explaining that I wasn't being disrespectful of Dr. Julian in the weeks before his death and that I'd only been trying to win. She cut me off in midsentence.

"You don't have to apologize for that," she said. "You didn't have anything to do with it. We knew Emerson and his family well, but that was God's work. You didn't have anything to do with it."

She asked me how much money I had in my campaign fund. When I told her that we probably had about $600 left in the account, she shook her head sadly, then turned again to her husband.

"Palie, I asked this young man over here because he picked up the phone and called me for advice. We had a long conversation, and I liked the sound of him," she said. "Of course, I don't know why anybody would want a name like that, and I'm not sure I'll ever be able to know how to pronounce it, but I like his honesty, and I wanted you to be here for this meeting."

She turned back to me and smiled softly. "Well now, young man, tell me something about your mother."

"My mother is dead, ma'am. She passed when I was sixteen."

Her face clouded for a moment, and brightened again. "Well then, tell me about your father."

- "My father is in jail."

"Oh," she said, as her brow arched suspiciously. "He didn't shoot anyone, did he?"

"No ma'am. He's there for running numbers."

"I see. May I ask who, then, taught you to become the fine young gentleman that's sitting here before me?"

"My mother," I said. "Before she died."

I told Verda Welcome a lot about myself that day, how after my mother died I'd fallen off the right path and had to spend years picking myself up. That I'd pushed and gotten my GED, and pushed more through the Community College and Morgan State University, where I was a student organizer and activist. That I'd worked even harder and made a name for myself on radio, and had even helped launch a station where I was now the program director.

But Senator Welcome seemed the most moved when I told her that my mother had always wanted me to make a contribution in life. I also revealed to her that I felt in my heart that winning this election would be only the start of a long life of serving people.

Strangely and without explanation, a level of comfort filled the room, and I felt a powerful change. I don't remember all my words that day, but whatever I said sealed our relationship. Perhaps she could see the hands rubbed raw on the bootstraps of my life. Or maybe she could sense my years of personal and private struggle. She knew that I hadn't been softened or distracted by a life full of promise or privilege. Whatever it was and whyever it was, her whole demeanor seemed to warm toward me from that moment on. And in the end, she told me that not only would she offer her own endorsement, but she was going to put the whole weight of her political club behind me.

"I think you might just be committed enough to make a real and lasting difference," she said.

Verda's endorsement proved to be critical because it offered me a legitimacy among older black women that I hadn't had before. Although the younger crowd was familiar with me from radio, our research had shown that the real power group, the ones who voted consistently year after year, were black women homeowners, ages thirty-five to sixty-five. That was Verda's group, and her membership in Delta Sigma Theta, the Continentals, the Links, and other social organizations helped immeasurably in boosting my name recognition. Then, finally, after failing to snare any other major support, I won an endorsement from the *News-American*, one of the two daily newspapers in town.

I was using phantom campaign funds and was in need of a campaign headquarters. Rev. Douglass Miles, the pastor of Brown's Memorial Baptist Church (the church I'd been married in), came to my aid by loaning me the use of the building's annex for the stretch. As with many others seeking public office in the black community, it wasn't unusual for my first campaign to have its roots in a neighborhood church. Because of my outreach to the clergy, I began getting more endorsements from the larger ministerial community. Help came quickly, especially from the younger ministers, many of whom signed on to work with me.

The essence of my campaign, though, remained getting out in the street and meeting the voters. Door-to-door campaigning is rough and exhausting work, but it has always been the lifeblood of activist campaigns, and I knew it. When you're running on tight funds and lack the support of a major political organization, you can only hope that voters will recognize your commitment and passion for making a difference in government. Back in 1971, Barbara A. Mikulski had shown how powerful face-to-face campaigning can be when she trumpeted her impressive record of grassroots advocacy to win a harrowing battle for a seat on the City Council, before moving on to the Congress.

Out on the stump, I noticed that my message of empowerment, change, and renewal was gaining supporters. I was elated by the sound of the swelling applause, the hope on their faces, the steady flow of words of encouragement from would-be voters. People now walked up to me at appearances, saying that they'd been following my campaign, and that I seemed to be the only one saying anything worthwhile. Their positive responses offset the hardship of running the whole campaign on a shoestring of about $11,000. Though we were scrimping on everything from radio ads to bumper stickers to leaflets, my message of empowering the masses was sinking in and building momentum on the street. At the last moment, I even won the coveted endorsement of *The Baltimore Afro-American* newspaper. As we came into the final stretch of the campaign, all of these developments were helping to buoy my spirits.

11

NOT POLITICS AS USUAL

*O*N Tuesday, September 11, the moment of truth had arrived, candidate Mfume's campaign was drawing to a close. All that day, I remember trying to convey an air of calm and confidence for volunteer workers who were nervous and anxious. I would soon discover that after every campaign you always hit a moment of second-guessing yourself. You wonder what it was that you could have done better. Did you get your message out to the right people? How many who said they'd vote for you in the end actually would? What eleventh-hour political favors have your rivals promised in order to woo away some of your supporters?

These questions were nagging at me furiously that day, and it was all I could do to stay upbeat. More than anything, I had to reassure myself of the many things I had done right that in the end would help me win. When I thought of all I'd gone through, from taking the advice of Ray Haysbert and later Ken Wilson, to walking the neighborhood streets and knocking on thousands of doors, to gaining the support of Verda Welcome and some local churches as well, a brief surge of reassurance bolstered my confidence.

That night we watched news flashes of the various races across the city on a small portable black-and-white TV that sat conspicuously in the headquarters that had become home.

As expected, with nearly all of the city's 486 precincts reporting, Schaefer had pummeled his closest challengers with margins as wide as six to one. It was shortly before 10 P.M. when we watched the ebullient Schaefer arriving at his South Calvert Street campaign headquarters to modestly declare his victory over Patrick L. McDonough and Clarence "Tiger" Davis. Although the general election would pit Schaefer against Republican Samuel Culotta, in Baltimore, winning the Democratic primary was tantamount to a shoo-in victory.

"I am very, very happy tonight," beamed Schaefer, looking exhausted. "When you run in an election, you're happy if you win. If people didn't think I'd done a good job, I wouldn't have been reelected."

Each of my sons seemed more jittery that night than anyone else. They had been aware of Dad's preoccupation with winning, so much so that they knew how much was at stake. After tagging along behind me from one speaking engagement to another, it was clear how much they, too, wanted to win. Dressed crisply in suit jackets and slacks, when they weren't gobbling down ice cream and cake, they were pulling at my sleeve anxiously.

"Are you winning, Daddy?" Donald must have asked me a thousand times.

"Dad, how many votes do you have?" Michael invariably chimed in.

"How many more votes do you need to win?" asked Keith.

"I'm not sure, fellas," I told them. "All I can say is that it's looking good." By 9 P.M. I had dropped them all at home and prepared for what I believed would be a long night to come. By the time I got back to the campaign headquarters, only four of the nine candidates were left in the race. The others trailed far behind.

Indeed, according to my own calculations I was faring better than most had expected. By 11:45 P.M., with 100 percent of the voting precincts reporting, my unofficial tally showed me ahead of Mary B. Adams by about a hundred votes for the remaining seat in the Fourth District, while incumbents Michael B. Mitchell and Victorine Q. Adams had strongly secured their reelection. But just as my staff and I began to believe that I was on my way to winning the district's remaining seat, the news flashed to a celebration at Mary Adams's headquarters. Silently I stood there and listened to a report declaring her the winner with 5,900 votes compared to my 5,854.

As I stood there, numb with disbelief, reporters were cutting through the shocked crowd toward me. With cameras, note-books, and microphones in tow and faces of unspoken condolence, they formed a loose perimeter around me.

"It was a hard-fought primary," one of them said, sticking her mike up to my face. "Can I get a concession remark, sir?"

"Absolutely not!" I quickly replied. "There is absolutely nothing to concede."

There is a point in every campaign for public office where the physical and emotional stress takes its toll and people begin to break under the pressure. That point was reached with reporters' requests for my concession speech and my refusal to oblige. Like an erupting volcano, the room became engulfed by the quiet sobbing of volunteers and their looks of despair. It was almost like being at a wake. Exhausted and dragged down by what was feeling more and more like defeat, people began consoling one another and flailing about miserably in the room. This went on for several minutes and was followed by a steady file of people putting on their coats, patting me on the back, and walking off slowly into the night.

"Don't worry," they were saying. "It's all right, you fought a good fight. You should be proud of yourself."

"Something is wrong!" I snapped. "The numbers are wrong! We won this election."

Apparently, I wasn't the only skeptic in the room. One old man known only as Mr. Glenn sat there firmly in his seat and pounded the wooden table. A deeply religious hulk of a man who stood about six-foot-six, Mr. Glenn crashed his stump-sized fists down on the table, bringing the mournful buzz to complete quiet.

"I don't feel it in my bones!" Mr. Glenn boomed. "God hasn't said anything to me! Don't concede, because it's not over. It's not over!"

"That's right," I broke in. "By our own count, we're ahead of Adams by about thirty votes."

My revisionist math was enough to keep some supporters on hand for a while longer, but was hardly enough to spark a celebration. And as more and more radio and television stations reported my defeat, my headquarters began to empty, as people were streaming out one by one.

"Take care of yourself," they told me. "Stay in touch. It was a good campaign."

"It's not over," I insisted. "Really, it's not over."

For hours into the morning, I sat there quietly with Carl, Pete Rawlings, George, and Rosetta Kerr. In a room littered with campaign hats and other paraphernalia, we had turned off the television because we didn't want to see any more bad news. Finally, we turned off the lights in the place and wearily headed out into the streets that I so desperately wanted to change.

"Something is just not right about this," I said to them as I got into my car. "Let's meet in the morning. Maybe then things will be clearer. I know our numbers are correct."

The following morning, I awoke to a banner headline in the Baltimore *Sun*: "Schaefer easily wins nomination; Pressman halts bid by Douglass; activist Reeves wins Council seat." And there I was as a postscript in the fourth paragraph, which read, "Another vacancy in the Fourth District produced such a close contest last night that it apparently will be decided by the absentee votes. Mary B. Adams, a former Councilwoman, clung to a slim lead for the third seat over Kweisi Mfume, a local radio station director."

As expected, incumbents Michael B. Mitchell, the nephew of Parren Mitchell, and Victorine Q. Adams won decisively in the district. But because my own race was so close, I was worried that if the election had not been stolen from me yet, somebody was certainly trying to do it now. I decided to turn to a backup plan, a plan that was admittedly rather dicey and one I hoped to never have to use. But considering the circumstances, I had little choice but to protect the election tallies until the official canvass took place.

In Baltimore, after votes are cast, the polling machines are unlocked with a code and key. A long sheet listing all candidates and every vote cast for them is removed from the machine. This official evidence is then transported to a warehouse on Franklintown Road, where they also house the voting machines for the entire city.

We knew that if the election was going to be stolen, it would be stolen in this warehouse, where someone would slip in with bogus sheets and substitute them for the real ones. From observing the warehouse in the weeks leading to the election, we also knew that there was only one guard on duty there, while there were several windows through which someone could break in.

For the next couple of days, Carl assembled a group of committed volunteers to go down to the warehouse, prepared to sleep out on the roof and along the perimeter of the building if necessary. Their sole task was to make sure that the power brokers didn't steal the election from us.

Two days later, on September 14, a newspaper headline proclaimed, "Mary Adams' edge holds up." The news account reported that Adams had maintained her narrow lead over me as absentee ballots were counted in our battle for the Democratic nomination for the Fourth District Council seat. "According to Gene M. Raynor, Mrs. Adams had received 25 votes in absentee ballots against Mr. Mfume's 24," the article noted. "That widened the former Councilwoman's lead over the radio program director to 47 votes. The election board will start checking the printouts from various polling machines today in an effort to make sure that the election judges' initial reporting of the vote was correct."

That evening, my suspicions were confirmed. After seven hours of tedious rechecking, election officials uncovered several tallying errors. Just to be sure there were no dirty tricks about to be played, I had two teams of supporters on hand as observers, recording the corrected vote as it was being read from the printouts. It was quiet and tense as the tape rolled out of the machine. And after Raynor read off the votes, I had the two teams separately add their totals. After about a half hour, they each came up with an identical result—5,882 votes for me, and 5,879 votes for Mary Adams—a far cry from the 47-vote loss initially counted.

"You've won by three votes!" one of my supporters shouted joyously. "You beat her by three votes! Praise the Lord!"

I was almost at the point of exhaustion. It had been a long, relentless struggle, but I had prevailed. My only wish was that Mama were there to celebrate with me. I would have loved to see the pride in her eyes.

I was thinking of her later at home that evening when the phone rang. It was my grandmother, offering a prayerful and tearful congratulations. She was the granddaughter of a slave, who had lived in a different era and had come through a different struggle. Politics in her day was something reserved for whites only. Thus, the thought of her grandson beating the system that had denied her was almost more than she could bear.

"Before you start any celebrating, fall on your knees, and don't be shy to give God the glory. He has brought you a mighty long way, child. . . . A mighty long way."

Then, with her voice reduced to a cautious whisper, she warned, "Just remember who those three votes came from."

"Who?" I asked back.

"The Father, the Son, and the Holy Ghost," she said convincingly. "As long as you're black, don't you ever forget that, boy."

"I sure won't, Grandma," I promised her. "Don't you worry, I won't."

In what remains the closest election in Maryland's history, the September 15 Baltimore *Sun* declared my victory with this memorable headline: "Fourth Recount puts Mfume over Adams."

That year, I was one of two freshman councilmen to be sworn in, while the other was Norman Reeves. Because of his Lou

Gehrig's disease, Norman arrived late in his wheelchair. This was before the days of access ramps for physically challenged people. Thus, for the swearing-in ceremony, Norman had to be carried up on stage. Rev. John R. Bryant, who is now an AME bishop, offered the invocation as Mayor Schaefer presided over the inaugural. As we watched Norman being hoisted up for his oath of office, the Reverend Bryant admonished the elected Council:

"All of you should forever be reminded," he said, "of the example of Norman Reeves. For each one of you is carried this day into office on the backs of others. If you ever forget this, you need not ever serve."

Rev. John Bryant's invocation was very moving and one that I would forever take seriously. I have never forgotten his words. I try to keep them in front of me as I move forward in life, because public service is founded on the trust of the people, and my strength as a leader is only as strong as the backs of the people who helped me get here.

Ironically, adhering to this philosophy put me instantly at odds with many of my new colleagues. I was there representing the 120,000 people in my district, not the mayor or other City Council members. Much of my campaign had been fueled by direct attacks on Schaefer, and the fact that black people were not represented on the city's boards and commissions. Those denunciations carried a high price because I was greeted with ill will and hostility once I took office.

Up close, I began to see for myself the punitive rather than conciliatory nature of Schaefer's style, what a powerfully strong and intimidating political force he really was. Things were done his way, or not done at all. Among the eighteen Council members, he enjoyed a solid ten-vote majority anytime he wanted it, and those who dared to dissent wound up on his hit list.

I spent every one of my seven years as a councilman on the mayor's hit list. I didn't care about his legendary power or temper—I wasn't about to have him bossing me around and telling me what to do, nor was I going to surrender in order to gain acceptance. I let him know where I was coming from on my very first day in office.

"There are two cities here—a black one and a white one—and

there is too much disparity between the races," I declared. "There needs to be some sharing. The last book on American history I read said that slavery ended with the Emancipation Proclamation. There has to be a mutual respect!"

That was my opening salvo in what I knew was going to be a war between me and the mayor. Nobody had ever gone after him as aggressively and undiplomatically as I did throughout my years on Council. In my self-appointed role as maverick and loyal opposition, I got under Schaefer's skin to such an extent that we became the worst of enemies. I constantly challenged him, demanding to be heard. He would throw me out of his office, refusing to let me be part of meetings and discussions. On a couple of occasions, he literally ordered the water to my district turned off, making it harder for me to deliver basic services to my constituents. We had many nasty fights, and at times were close to exchanging blows. Years would pass before we could carry on a civilized discussion.

It's easier to refect on this now, considering that today Schaefer and I are friends and political allies. He would go on to become an influential governor of Maryland, and I would become a member of Congress. Sometimes we talk about my early days in the Council and how the earth would shake whenever we'd rumble. He admits that I often got under his skin, and I admit that he has gotten under mine.

However, when Schaefer's mother died several years later, I identified with his sense of loss and pain. Some people just scribbled a note of condolence, but I went to the funeral service and then on to the grave site. I knew what it was like to lose your mother, no matter what your age or station in life. In what seemed, for me, all too familiar a setting, there was no animosity between us that day. Standing there at the edge of that grave, I saw a side of him that I'd never seen before. He wept uncontrollably before the flower-draped coffin as it rested on the struts over the freshly dug hole. My mind, for an instant, darted backward in time, to when I stood where he stood. Although long since closed, that chapter of pain was now unfolding on pages before me. I discovered we had come from similar backgrounds, with mothers who had been strong influences in our lives. His personal sense of loss was now reminding me of my own. Although we occasionally clashed in the Council after that, the level of our anger was never the same. That day in the cemetery something intangible had changed between us, and brought with it a mutual respect.

Schaefer ruled the City Council with an iron fist. I'll never forget the time I was pushing the Council to declare Martin Luther King, Jr.'s birthday a legal holiday. For years, I'd gone to Washington to join Stevie Wonder, Diana Ross, and Jesse Jackson and the thousands of others who were fighting for the same cause. Shortly after taking my seat on the Council, I drafted a resolution that proposed King's birthday as a legal holiday in the city, and that the City Council would not hold its regularly scheduled meeting on that Monday.

It was 1980, and many other cities had adopted similar resolutions. But in this case, my resolution died because nobody would second it. Instead, a deep silence came over the chamber. It was quite embarrassing because generally, at least out of courtesy, an amendment is seconded, and then just left to die on the vote. Not even one of my black colleagues supported me because everyone knew that not only did the mayor not like me, he didn't support the idea of another holiday. They were all afraid. The risk of aiding and abetting me meant they might end up in the doghouse with me. I was dejected that day. It was now very clear to me that I was not serving with independent thinkers, and my sense of alienation would only increase as time wore on.

During my years on the Council, many of my best times were spent on-air. Shortly after being sworn into office, I'd restructured the format of the radio station and become the host of a talk show five nights a week. Although the old program was popular, I didn't feel it was appropriate for an elected official to be out spinning music. Besides, I really wanted to broaden my horizons with the community using the power of WEAA.

The talk show became an instant hit, and I enjoyed it more than anything else I've ever done in radio. I liked the show because I could be completely open and frank, with no facades to maintain and no pressure to entertain. I had constant dialogue with my audience. People called me at their most joyous moments, and they called at their weakest. With personal confessions, or out of sheer loneliness, they felt open and welcome to speak. Some called on a regular basis simply to challenge me, and some never called at all. It was an extremely interesting experience each night because every call was unpredictable.

It was 1980 and Ronald Reagan had just been elected President. That alone created endless discussion for my show. Through my dialogue with the listeners, they began to see who I was and what I stood for. Every evening, the show took me into the homes of fifty or sixty thousand people. Few had to wonder about my views on a particular subject. You can't fool a microphone, just as you can't fool a camera. Through a microphone, people can hear sincerity and they can hear deceit.

I also continued to plan ahead for my future. In 1982, I enrolled in a master's degree program at Johns Hopkins University. Even in graduate school, I tried to avoid the more narrow, specialized programs. I wanted to learn more about the broad spectrum of human endeavors. I wanted to learn more about early civilizations, foreign affairs, and the global community. I wanted to study the great writers of our times, and develop my own writing skills as well. I wanted to understand the environment, how cities arose, and the role of politics that shaped them.

Education gave me a more proactive approach in my life, and I never ceased to wonder at how it freed me. I felt that I was again taking greater initiative in molding my destiny, unafraid of where it might lead. My choices, my actions would now decide the future of my life, rather than the circumstance of my conception or the color of my skin. Education was my unshakable cornerstone of growth and hope and change.

Ironically, my classroom experiences at Hopkins also had the effect of raising the level of my frustration on the City Council. Now I began to draft resolutions that dealt with national issues, directing the President to do such and such, or to take into account the citizens of Baltimore on this issue or that. Each time, I was admonished by my colleagues, whose attitude was, "Look, if you want to be in Congress, you need to run for it. This is the City Council, thank you, and we like filling potholes. And we were doing just fine until you got here."

Although I never stopped raising those national issues, I began to realize that I needed to learn the ropes of being an elected official. I needed to figure out how to change things. After all, that's the only reason I'd gotten into politics in the first place. I began to learn that you can change things when you're able to win on issues, when you can get people to do what they ordinarily wouldn't do, and when you're able to influence a process so that in the end that change takes place. For me to sit there and not master the environment would have been against everything I had ever learned.

While I wasn't very effective during my first few years on the Council, my constituents cheered me on as the lone renegade. There was one particular situation, the downfall of City Council President Walter S. Orlinsky, where I stood out starkly from my colleagues.

With his longish hair, dark features, and middle-age paunch bulging at his waistline, Orlinsky was perhaps second only to Schaefer as the most colorful politician in Baltimore in those days. But where Schaefer was gruff and direct, the three-term Council president exuded a lofty, professorial air that always seemed out of sync with realities of local government.

Nonetheless, Orlinsky was exceptionally bright, and his supporters and detractors alike fell under the spell of his lofty proclamations and high-minded witticisms. In newspapers and public hearings, Orlinsky could delight or anger citizens with his snappy responses to some of the city's most pressing issues. When asked about progress on the construction of a subway, Orlinsky quipped, "I don't think anyone should have to wait a decade for a subway that goes from nowhere to nowhere." He once put himself in charge of a commission to investigate the police force, and defended appointing himself by saying, "I looked around for the person I trusted most." He railed against the public's not-in-my-backyard stance on landfills and prisons, arguing that "Everybody wants to send people to prison, but nobody wants a jail. Nobody likes garbage, but nobody wants landfills. We're either going to eat garbage and get shot—or grow up."

Orlinsky seemed to revel in his gadfly reputation, though it was never clear to me whether he was more committed to disarming his assorted detractors or to proving his own cleverness. In the spring of 1982, my suspicions were confirmed by a federal investigation of Orlinsky for his suspected role in extorting thousands of dollars from garbage-hauling companies seeking contracts with the city.

Throughout the investigation, Wally steadfastly denied any wrongdoing, although new revelations about his role in the scandal seemed to arise almost daily. For nearly nine months, Wally extolled his own honesty and virtue and said he couldn't wait for his day in court. I withheld judgment because he faced federal charges, which in my view is never a good sign. Because everyone else on the Council threw their support behind him, I stood out as a spoiler.

Then at a Council meeting on Monday, October 19, 1982, with the press crowding the chamber, Orlinsky gaveled us to order. It was then that he surprisingly called our attention to a terse note of resignation that he had delivered to the mayor the day before. As part of a plea bargain in federal court, Orlinsky announced suddenly that he was stepping down. I sat there listening, expecting at the very least an explanation for Orlinsky's nearly yearlong charade and sidestepping. But with his family sitting somberly in the rear of the chambers, the weary-eyed Orlinsky didn't address any of the details behind his conviction or his recommended sentence of fifteen months in prison. Instead, he launched into a diatribe about the worthiness of Council vice president Clarence Du Burns, a black man, as his successor. Urging a color-blind voting process, Orlinsky said, "The members must remove from the body politic questions of race. It is my hope Du will be given the kind of cooperation and support he deserves." Orlinsky concluded, "He's one hell of a guy."

I sat there in complete disbelief at what I was hearing. Wally had gone from being the sober, dispassionate conscience of the Council to being an admitted liar in one breath—and now we were supposed to follow his advice for a successor. I was prepared for a lot of things but I was not prepared to do that. I still couldn't get over the fact that he had vehemently denied any wrongdoing day in and day out. Didn't he feel that he owed us an explanation? At the very least, couldn't he offer an apology for the dishonor he had brought on us all? Orlinsky had abused the public trust and the powers of the office bestowed upon him. Now he was spouting platitudes about Du Burns, and we were supposed to offer our support. As he gaveled the meeting to a close, my Council colleagues all rose and gave him a standing ovation.

I sat riveted to my seat. I could not bring myself to stand. Wally, no matter how much I liked him, had violated his oath of office. Unable to bear the sight of a sustained standing ovation, I remained seated. With folded arms I spun my chair around so that my back faced Orlinsky. When a reporter rushed over to me and asked why I refused to applaud, I told him the truth about how I felt.

"He committed a shameful act," I responded. "It's a sad day. Orlinsky had a lot to offer. Now it's all for naught."

I'll never forget the manner in which Wally Orlinsky left office that evening, grinning and waving and joking with reporters. When a television camera began focusing in on him, he pressed his nose against the lens and made a silly face. It saddened me that Orlinsky, a man in whom so many had placed their trust, seemed now to be making a mockery out of the people and his position.

The following day, newspapers ran photos of Orlinsky's resignation announcement, some of which showed me sitting down as my colleagues stood and applauded. It was a big story, and my unplanned act of independence bolstered my image as something of a rebel. It also brought me more credibility within the Council than ever. My not cheering for Orlinsky proved to some that my bluster wasn't simply for show after all, and that I was willing to take a stand for what I believed in, no matter how unpopular it made me. It would be almost ten years before Wally would speak to me again.

On Monday, October 25, 1982, Du Burns was indeed elected to succeed Orlinsky as president of the City Council, the first black person ever to assume the post. A former jazz saxophonist who grew up on the tough streets of East Baltimore, Du Burns was the son of a ward operative for the city's white political machine. In recognition of his family's political importance, Mayor Thomas D'Alesandro had given the young Clarence a job as a public baths attendant at the old battered Dunbar High School. The humble position became a perch for him to launch a career as a community activist. In fact, since he always seemed to get things done, people started calling him "Du."

Du Burns cemented his cooperative leadership style by becoming a diehard ally of Schaefer's, a tie that also made him a questionable figure to some in the black community.

Because of what I felt was Du Burns's virtual obsession with pleasing the mayor, I was not among his admirers. Like others, I appreciated that during his eleven years on the Council, five of which were spent as vice president, the sixty-three-year-old Du Burns had overcome most of his deficits. Du was not a riveting speaker or a publicly charismatic leader, but his personal resilience and pride had quickly earned my respect. While his ascension to Council president may have conveyed a laudable message of hard work rewarded, some wondered aloud whether he had finally wandered into waters too deep for his abilities. "Mr. Burns has earned the Council presidency, which is not the same as being in all respects well qualified," a local paper sniped in one editorial.

Even I couldn't deny Du's rich track record for delivering on key issues. What bothered me most was the backroom manner in which he often liked to cut his deals. I also believed that his rise to Council president was no exception. I was convinced that he had traded away key committee chairmanships in behind-the-scenes maneuvering for votes to gain support.

During the voting process, I looked directly at Du to let him know how incensed I was by his actions. "I rise to do something that is very difficult for me as a member of this Council," I said. "I've grown fond of Mr. Burns's tenacity and his ability to turn the other cheek. But I'm going to have to pass on the vote to confirm him."

In the end, I was among only three members who did not vote for Du. I looked on as the dark, round-shouldered Du Burns beamed victoriously across the chambers as he read from a prepared statement. "I am proud, pleased, but most of all humbled," he said, his voice wavering with pride. "When a soldier falls, as our man Orlinsky has," he said, "it is incumbent on us to move onward and upward."

Then his voice rose forcefully. "Here I am, a black man, standing before you as president of the City Council. But I don't believe I was elected because I am black, but because I am the best person qualified. This is just another example of the way this city is pulling together."

Afterward at a jam-packed victory party, Du was on a roll. "I'm a firm believer in the system, which wasn't devised by me," he told reporters. "When you're out there, and you know you need ten votes to win, and you've only got seven, you go out looking for them. So I made a commitment. I gave my word, and I intend to stick by it. That's what I did to win. I didn't do anything that hasn't been done for years."

As loath as I was to admit it, Du Burns was right. The system had worked that way for years, and would continue to work that way. I may have wanted to believe that I didn't need the mayor's support, or anyone else's for that matter. But the real truth was that I did. Running against the grain may have earned me respect in the community, but I wasn't delivering much else. Everything I put on the table was roundly defeated, and it was done with great delight by my colleagues.

For the first four of my seven years as a councilman, I got no legislation passed and very few favors. When there were projects or events held in my district that I could take pride in, I wasn't invited to the ribbon cutting, or my name would be left off the program. When an issue arose that was of great concern to me and my district, and I wanted to ensure that the City followed through on it, that issue would go to the bottom of the priority list. If I took one position in the Council on a piece of legislation, the majority would vote the other way. If I developed a proposal that required the mayor to sign off on it, he just ignored it. There were so many defeats that none even stand out. The Council wanted to show me that unless I played their game by their rules and became part of the club, all I would ever generate was a blur of defeats.

After three years of my butting my head up against the wall, Du Burns pulled me aside once after a Council meeting.

"Look," he told me. "You don't mean shit down here. I don't care how you got here because it doesn't matter to me. You have one vote and you can scream against the mayor all day long. You can't count votes so it doesn't matter and you don't matter because it ain't worth shit."

I wanted to punch him right in the mouth. He was viewed as an Uncle Tom, and I couldn't believe he was talking down to me like that. I thought he had a lot of nerve. But I also understood what he meant. Having lost on everything I sponsored, it was time to learn how to play to win, or get the hell out of the game. When you can't get a majority, you aren't doing anything but pushing water. I was embarrassed by his bluntness, but I knew he was right. I was tired of going to community meetings in my district and being asked about what I had accomplished, when all I could reply was that I'd raised hell and challenged the mayor.

Leadership is not about a single deed or quest. It's a process of evolution, of keeping your values and vision intact while honing your overall skills. Working in the City Council helped me understand that I had the power to effect how events would affect me. While I often did not possess the power to change the events and challenges thrust upon me, I did possess the power to shape my responses to fit them.

As time passed, I often butted my head against the wall and lay in wait while I learned the rules of the game. So much of one's effectiveness in politics, whether local or national, is rooted in a mastery of timing. When the time for action is right, you must move quickly and strike swiftly, because if you don't you have a real problem waiting to happen. Once the moment has passed, it may never come again.

Part of my learning process in the City Council was discovering how to deliver for the people in my district. To deliver, you must find a way to get the people to support you even when they do not want to do it. When compromises are necessary, you learn how to be persuasive. I believe in making a case in such a way that people feel there's something in the compromise for them and that they're also winners. You change things when

you're able to win on issues. Change takes place when you
develop the skills of diplomacy and negotiation. This means
understanding that you must often take one step back in order
to take two steps forward. That's the true art of the political
compromise.

One person who knew that best was a man named Dominic
"Mimi" DiPietro. A self-made man, Sicilian born, with a third-
grade education, Mimi was an old man when I met him. But you
couldn't have told him that. Crusty and outspoken with broken
English, he always said what he meant and meant what he said.
"I'm going to outlive all of youse," Mimi would often bark at the
suggestion that he was growing old.

I liked Mimi because he came out of the old school, where a
man's honor meant everything and your word was all you had.
He had emigrated to this country as a child after the turn of the
century, and worked on the waterfront as a teen. In the late
1920s and early 1930s, Mimi had gotten involved in Baltimore's
machine politics as a fluke. When the machine decided it needed
somebody to run for one of the grunt positions but lacked a
natural candidate, it tapped Mimi. Since the day of his election
to the City Council, Mimi's greatest claim to fame was that he
never broke his word, and that he always found a way to deliver
for his constituents.

Because Mimi was a social throwback, many blacks viewed
him as racist. They were constantly offended by his language,
which was peppered with phrases like "youse people" and "little
girl" and "little boy." The politically correct era had dawned, and
that kind of talk was considered disrespectful. I didn't believe
Mimi was a racist, though I can certainly understand the
assumptions that he was. His mistakes were so obvious, and so
were his lapses of grace.

Few ever confronted Mimi on this or anything else. Some
believed that in his early days he was part of the Sicilian mob in
town. Mimi seemed to know everybody. He was an icon in the
Italian community, and was a true Sicilian to boot.

Like me, Mimi worked hard and long, never backed down
from a fight, and always spoke his mind. During my rants in the
City Council meetings Mimi never said much to me or attempted

to mold me to his point of view. In his own way, Mimi respected me and the fact that I fought for what I believed in. This is not to say that he understood me or always agreed with my views. But he respected me nonetheless. I was part of a wave of vocal young black men coming out of the struggles of the '60s and the crusade for civil rights. Mimi just got out of my way.

I'll never forget the day Mimi walked up to me and quietly, almost sheepishly, admitted that he couldn't read or write my name. I was amazed at the confession and marveled inside at how far he had come without strong reading skills.

"I can't read it, so I can't say it, goddammit," he explained. "How do youse pronounce it?"

I said my name slowly and clearly for him. Mimi was the kind of person who had to memorize words because he couldn't always easily read them. He couldn't see the syllables or consonants but he could hear and remember the inflections. "Oom-Foo-May," he bellowed. "Oom-Foo-May."

"That's right, Mimi," I answered back.

"You little cocksucker." He smiled, placing his hand behind my neck. "You got balls."

"So do you, Mimi." I nodded and smiled with approval. "So do you. Just don't ever try to cross me." He began calling me Mfume from that point on and never attempted to pronounce Kweisi.

Over the next two years, Mimi and I became friends in the City Council. The greatest bonding force between us was that he looked out for his people, and I looked out for mine. It was that simple. We were both straight and both honest, and we lived under the singular, overriding principle that your word is your most valuable possession. As he realized that I operated under this assumption, while other members wavered in their integrity, he grew to appreciate me as a colleague. We didn't always agree on issues and most times voted differently, but we established a bond of trust much like the codes we had learned in our youth.

In the early 1980s, we were facing the redistricting of the city. Because the districts are the building blocks of power, there was a high level of interest in how they would be redrawn. Within the City Council, a number of plans were being drawn up—the mayor had a plan, the Council had a plan, and various people in the community had plans. But Mimi and I sat down one day and in a very basic way asked each other: What do you want, and what do I want? What do your people need, and what do my people need?

With all the elegant speeches put away, that was where we started. In the quiet dimness of our offices we proceeded to draw the city's districts over. From that point on we came up with a redistricting plan that we thought was extremely fair, the product of dual authors. It represented a compromise between two extremes. It helped me because it helped empower the growing black community more, while helping Mimi keep Little Italy together, and the neighborhoods of South Baltimore.

Our collaboration was significant for a few reasons. First, many power brokers had cut their own deals and were developing their own plans. Second, nobody thought ours would ever pass. And third, nobody believed that an odd couple like Mimi and me could hold together on anything. But in the end, our plan proved to be superior to all the others put on the table. We got the ten votes we needed and we won.

Perhaps more important than getting the redistricting plan through was that working with Mimi taught me a crucial element of leadership that I had failed to learn in the street. It was the first time that I really, truly understood the concept of taking one step backward from what you want in order to take two steps forward to get what you actually need. And once I learned that, life on the Council improved. I began winning on a series of amendments, winning on votes, and most of all winning the applause from the people I represented.

Meanwhile, I could always be counted on to be the loyal opposition to any legislation not in the community's interests. The fact that I was a maverick created its own share of tensions on the floor of the City Council. At one point, I was leading marches against the mayor and City Hall, while Schaefer was blasting me in the press.

Even in the City Council, attitudes were starting to soften toward me, though. I was beginning to garner respect for my political astuteness, instead of wrath. Opponents may not have agreed with me on certain issues, but they admired my determination and steadfast sense of conviction about them.

In 1986, I succeeded in doing what I once believed to be improbable: I successfully co-authored legislation that brought about divestiture of city investments in South Africa. The pension board had been pouring millions of dollars into the Apartheid economy without giving it a second thought. It had been fourteen years now since I started local activism in the Free South Africa movement as a freshman in college. Efforts to divert pension funds from use by the Apartheid government were springing up all over America. There was no reason why the City Council should not also act. In a manner that blended my newfound skills of diplomacy with my instinctive passion to fight back, I made a strong case to my colleagues that the city's moral integrity should always overshadow its fiduciary responsibility. "How can we condemn the racist and then quietly give fuel to his racism," I asked. "The government in South Africa is corrupt and illegal and we carry blood on our hands when we support them with investments."

One by one, Councilman Tim Murphy and I quietly put together ten votes in a way that made even Du Burns envious. Our backers all had different reasons for voting with us—it was just a matter of giving them some of what they wanted, or assuring them that we would in the future. We were just trading horses, I'd remind them. They would trade on my bill, and I'd be there for them on theirs.

On one of those heady afternoons when I was riding high in my newfound success in local politics, I happened to run into Arnette Evans outside of a downtown open-air market. I hadn't seen my old mentor and leader of the Falcon Drum and Bugle Corps since the year of my mother's death. It was Arnette who let grief nearly break his demeanor that day in 1965 when I had to leave the unit after Mama's funeral to find a way to survive. Now here he was, my favorite curmudgeon, standing before me. It was clear that things had changed for him over the years and that he had hit hard times. His face was unshaven, his clothing was disheveled, and I glimpsed a pint bottle jutting from his back pocket. But it took only a few seconds to realize that even if Arnette Evans's luck may have soured, his spirit remained intact. Rather than the warm, congratulatory greeting that I'd become accustomed to as an elected official, the Arnette Evans I knew fired away.

"So you think you're hot shit, don't you?" he began. "I saw you in the paper talking that shit. Yeah, I've been watching you. And let me tell you something, girlie. I've been through all that before, and that ain't nothing there—and you ain't nothing there."

"But I thought . . ."

"To hell with what you think. You ain't shit there 'cause you're just like all the rest of 'em—and if you weren't like all the rest of 'em, I wouldn't be here saying this to you."

I could feel myself getting a little irritated now, as I had when he was my drillmaster. I thought I was happy to see him at first, but now I was starting to wonder.

"What are you talking about?" I asked as innocently as I could.

"I'm talkin' about what you do, goddammit, that's what I'm talkin' about," he said. "You ain't doing anything new or anything significant. You're average, just like everybody else down there at City Hall."

I was really upset now and feeling insulted as well.

"Arnette, what did I do to you? I'm happy to see you."

"You ought to be happy to see me. That's right, you just oughta be happy, because I'm one of the few fuckers out here who will stand here and tell you the truth. And I'm telling you that your shit doesn't smell as sweet as you think it does."

"I admit I've made a few mistakes. I could have done some things better."

"Yeah, like that zoning ordinance last week." Arnette started rattling off a number of current issues before the City Council, and I realized that he knew what he was talking about. He had, in fact, been keeping up with me over the years, although he'd never bothered to call and let me know it.

"This little shit you're doing challenging the mayor, that ain't nothin'. It ain't nothin'. When you're the mayor, then come see me. Anybody can call the mayor a name. Hell, I call him names all the time. I was around the corner a minute ago calling him all kinds of names. So that ain't shit. You know what I mean, girl-friend? When *you* are the mayor, then come talk to Arnette."

He paused, and then lashed out again. "And I'm doin' all right, before you ask, dammit. I'm all right 'cause Arnette Evans is always all right."

"How come you've never called me all these years?" I asked. "I thought something had happened to you. I wondered for a long time even if you were still alive."

"Things have just been fuckin' with me," he said. "Shit's fuckin' with me right now, and I'm going to deal with it."

I knew, in Arnette's own way, he was admitting he was having hard times finding employment. I could see it in his eyes, and his unkempt gray hair, and the small bottle in his pocket. But Arnette was a very proud man, and would never admit defeat. As much as he could piss me off, I loved him. He pushed my limits as a teenager and helped me become a man. Yes, it was good to see him, even though he had never changed a bit.

"Look, I'm going to be all right, so don't waste your time won-derin' how I'm doin'. Shit, you might not see me for another ten years until you do something that's important, because I don't think what you're doing now is worth shit. You're just like all the rest of them down there, that's why I don't even get involved with that ole politics shit.

"Besides, I don't even know why you're even fuckin' around on the City Council anyway, that ain't no big deal. I told you about messin' around with little chump stuff. You always gravi-tate toward something that's not real. Do something real for a change, girlfriend. Go out and kick the ass of the President of the United States. When you do that, then you'll be doin' some-thing. Then you can come talk to Arnette."

In so many ways, Arnette was right. I knew that the City Council was a dead end for me, even though it had been an invaluable learning tool. I waited, bided my time, because I knew that one day I had to get out of there and move on to something else. The City Council was far too narrow, far too parochial for my growing interests. Increasingly, I felt that while it served a critical function, it was too limited in scope to solve the broad problems facing this country. I was outgrowing my role here. I no longer felt fascinated by it. So for the time being, I just sat there, waiting, learning, biding my time.

12

MR. MFUME GOES TO WASHINGTON

*O*N a bright October day in 1986, the Reverend St. George I. B. Crosse III stood in front of the Laurence G. Paquin School for Girls in a tough section of East Baltimore, surrounded by cameras and microphones. Crosse was my black Republican challenger in the general election for a seat in the United States Congress. Back at my campaign headquarters, I sat grimly in front of a television set, watching Crosse take his place behind the mike at the Paquin School. Deep in my gut, I knew that Crosse was just about to pull a dirty trick out of his sleeve.

As most people know, the setting for a speech can be just as important as the speech itself. Crosse, I suspected, was ready to strike out at what he considered the weakest link of my campaign—my character. By setting his speech at the Paquin School, a high school for pregnant inner-city girls, he figured he could attack me on the issues of morality and drive a stake right into the heart of my campaign. As a former teenage father, I was the perfect target for character assassination. Trailing miserably in the polls, Crosse had reduced himself to grabbing at straws. I wasn't that surprised. In this race for Baltimore's Seventh Congressional District, political hardball had become standard procedure.

After serving for sixteen years, Parren Mitchell was retiring. He had represented the district, and the black community at large, with unparalleled distinction. Now, at age sixty-four, he was stepping down from the prized seat, worn out by Beltway battles that were growing more futile by the day, and countless struggles, too numerous to remember. Rumors swirled that Parren's failing health was the real reason he was leaving Congress. Others speculated that he was incensed by his timorous Democratic Party colleagues who were trying to sound like Republicans in hopes of riding the coattails of the Reagan administration. Indeed, there was little doubt that Parren was becoming disgruntled with the party. During his final term, he kept warning that far too many Democrats were taking Republican positions.

Despite this, I've always believed Parren left office because he simply felt that eight terms in office were enough, and that Baltimore would benefit from fresh, new leadership. On many occasions, he had spoken to me about the perils of overstaying your time in elected office. "If you go to Washington to make a career out of it, you probably don't deserve to be there in the first place," he'd told me. It was a matter, I thought, of knowing when to hold them and knowing when to fold them, something I would one day come to understand for myself.

But the Democratic primary contest for his congressional seat had become a blood sport early on. The field was crowded with fresh candidates, including State Senator Clarence M. Mitchell III, Parren's ambitious nephew, and State Delegate Wendell Phillips. Unlike my initial ragtag foray onto the Baltimore City Council, my congressional campaign was enjoying a formidable mix of grassroots and political organizational support. Attorney Eddie Smith and community activist Rodney Orange, my campaign co-directors, had put together a wonderful band of volunteers, and we were out working the streets every day. I was still running behind Mitchell and Phillips in fund-raising, but Eddie and Rodney were finding new ways to make up ground. I had the best group of core supporters and workers that I ever had.

Also working in my favor was a relentless media attack on Clarence Mitchell, a blitz that accelerated during the final stretch of the primary. Most damaging was a series of scathing articles published in the Baltimore *Sun*. He was further crippled by revelations of a grand jury probe linking his business concerns to a convicted felon.

While Phillips didn't have a scandal to contend with, some voters were wary of his ties to Mayor Schaefer. He and I had been allies who liked each other and had worked together on any number of struggles, but now we were in opposite camps, vying for the same prize. The issues were hot and emotions ran high.

The result was an incendiary campaign of vicious mudslinging and character assassination. Mitchell attacked Phillips as a lackey of the white political establishment, while the well-funded Phillips aired a barrage of radio ads blasting Mitchell's integrity. As they savaged each other with sour accusations, my response was to stand firmly and take the high ground throughout the primary race, keeping my message tightly focused on the critical issues of education, employment, and economic development.

In the end, people responded more to my upbeat, positive campaign than to the free-for-all battle being waged by my opponents. I ended up with 47 percent of the vote, twice Phillips's draw, with Mitchell a distant third.

But on primary election night, the joy of winning was clouded in crises. Even after I was declared the winner, the celebration was cut short. The surprise of the night came from Clarence Mitchell. Amid the festive clink of champagne glasses, a reporter approached me after my acceptance speech and stuck a mike in my face. "I need to get your response to this, Mr. Mfume. Do you know that at this very moment Clarence Mitchell is about to make a statement? Would you look at the monitor?"

The press had their live cameras trained on me, so I complied, not knowing what to expect. I took a deep breath and listened to the reporter say, "We go live now to the Mitchell headquarters at the Palladium."

Clarence Mitchell was on the screen and livid—it was obvious from the tension around his eyes and mouth. "I'm challenging this election tomorrow!" he announced tersely. "We will be filing a challenge in court because this election was stolen. We are not conceding to Mr. Mfume. There is no way that many people could have voted for him."

"What is your response to those charges?" the reporter asked me.

"I am saddened that Senator Mitchell feels compelled to make such accusations. However, I believe that any inquiry into the election will support tonight's results.

"If he wants to challenge the election, fine," I concluded. "These are not my results. These are the results of the people. If he should change his mind, and even if he doesn't, we must find a way to reach out to heal the community. I'm reaching out to Senator Mitchell now. If he's watching, I want him to know that. One way or another, when this is all over, we all have to live and work together," I said. "And to the Reverend Phillips I offer my hand in friendship, in hopes that we too can help build a new tomorrow."

My supporters cheered me on as I made my way through the crowd. I have always liked Clarence, so his accusation put a damper on the evening. But the following day the matter was resolved in short order when his legal counsel advised him that he couldn't win the challenge because the three-to-one vote margin was too wide to overcome. I understood that it was a matter of pride and frustration for him. But at the time, Clarence, regrettably, was sinking deeper into a federal investigation of his involvement in the Wedtech scandal, a hodgepodge of government corruption and kickbacks.

Now, with only six weeks to go in the general election campaign, I was watching my Republican opponent, the Reverend Crosse, gearing up to block my attempt to break into national politics. A congressional seat had been a heartfelt goal of mine for some years, ever since I began to realize that many of the ills that affected black people were of national scope. I saw clearly that the best way to save the people in my district was to work to enact legislation that would help all Americans. While I hoped to coast to victory against my wily Republican opponent, I also knew that Crosse was not the kind of guy to take lightly. A tenacious and unpredictable campaigner, Crosse was pushing to advance a lackluster political career that had stalled ever since he'd been appointed special ambassador to the islands of St. Kitts and Nevis. He was nominated by the GOP for city comptroller but lost miserably in the 1979 general election. In this congressional race, Crosse seemed poised for another defeat. He was desperate to save his failing campaign with a boost in the polls, and I knew his next move would surely be an attack to my jugular. Sipping a glass of ice water, I watched TV and waited as Crosse somberly faced a barrage of media microphones, with a giggling audience of clearly pregnant teenage black girls at his back.

"I'm standing in front of this school building, which all these darling young ladies attend," said the Methodist preacher, gesturing toward the girls. "They attend this school not because they necessarily want to. No, they are pregnant and the fathers of their children are nowhere to be found."

It was a brilliant yet dishonest tactic. I could only hope it didn't spell disaster for my campaign. I sat listening with a sense of dread and outright contempt as he continued his slanderous speech.

"Now, we have somebody who could have had several girls forced to attend classes in this building and he wants to be your congressman," he continued with icy sarcasm. "But he's just like those other fathers, derelict in his duties and responsibilities. Even worse, he didn't learn his lesson, because he didn't do it once or twice. For heaven's sake, he didn't even do it three times. This man did it five times! Five!"

Now I was angry as hell. My youthful errors were not the major issue of the campaign, but he was trying to make them just that. All may be fair in war and politics, but this ploy of Crosse's was low-down and dirty. And he didn't stop there. In his best preacher style, he proclaimed, "We don't need that kind of person representing us in Congress. I am a minister and I know that God heals. But God also helps those who help themselves, and it's time for this district to help itself. We don't have to condemn Councilman Mfume, but we can't lift him up and give him this reward. Every time I walk by this school, and I look at my little girl as she walks by with me, I know that she could be in there with her life upset, waiting to have a baby."

Over the years, I'd learned the hard way that there are no guarantees in politics. But I've also learned that the voting public is much smarter than candidates tend to think. Long before the primary, the electorate had a fairly clear idea of who I was, both as a man and as a dedicated representative. They had witnessed me repeatedly going toe-to-toe against Mayor Schaefer and the city's power establishment on behalf of community interests. I never let anyone bully or intimidate me and I backed up my strong views with action. My record proved me to be among the most committed public servants in the state. Even so, I was still deeply worried that the bold-faced lies and innuendo of this one desperate man might put an end to my usefulness as an independent voice in government. Although I had never turned my back on my children for one second of their lives, how could I be certain the voters knew this? It was Crosse who had the stage, and I was defenseless against his attacks. Ironically, although the Baltimore *Sun* had recently dubbed me "an orator with electric timing and a rhetorical knack," I knew that no speech, no matter how sizzling, could erase the crude image Crosse was painting of me.

That night, I took a long drive alone. I drove for hours through the city. I drove through the blighted, run-down streets where I'd spent much of my youth, then along the avenues of glass and steel high-rises downtown, and I ended up in the rolling green countryside of horse and crop farms out in Woodstock. I was hurting inside, for myself and for my children. How long would the mistakes I'd made so early in life continue to haunt us? Ever since the night I'd seen the image of my mother's face, I had worked hard in both heart and deed to become a person whose life reflected the highest possibilities of change and redemption. I wanted to prove to myself, to anyone who had ever believed in me, that I had become someone to be proud of.

I believed my life was no longer anything to be ashamed of. I even hoped that it offered a glimmer of hope to the angry, frustrated, struggling people in my community, encouraging them to summon the strength and courage they needed to turn their own lives around. I wanted to be a voice for these people, a crusader for their causes.

Was it a fool's dream to expect my life to be interpreted by others as one of strength rather than weakness? Would people ever forgive me for the mistakes and transgressions I'd made during the lowest point of my youth? Even more, was it fair to make my children suffer through the humiliation of having their value as human beings reduced to the mean-spirited sound bites of a minister of the gospel labeling them as illegitimate?

All these questions swirled in my head as I drove alone through the darkness. And while I couldn't come up with answers, I decided that night that even though none of it was fair or just, I would simply have to let my spirit guide me through this. And right now, my spirit was telling me that I was on the verge of making a real difference in the lives of black people, that my journey was just beginning, and that there was no way I could let it be derailed by the defamatory work of a smear artist.

My children, as I see it, were far from being what some choose to call "illegitimate," and I resent and refuse to accept any such projection onto them. All children are legitimate and all are from God. This antiquated cultural stigma that allows society to adhere to a false code of behavior that penalizes children for their parents' actions is barbaric. It denigrates the value of every human life.

Fathering children out of wedlock was not a goal of mine. It would be dishonest to say that as a young man without a high school education, working menial jobs, and living in one room, I was eager to assume the duties of parenting. Hardly! I was angry and becoming more and more disillusioned with each pregnancy. But I never once considered abortion as an option, never once shirked my responsibility as a father, never willingly turned my back on the mothers of my sons.

Any confused and negative feelings I may have harbored initially, gradually evolved into something else: the singular desire to be a good father to each of my children. To be the kind of father I never had—a father my sons could love, respect, and even admire. It was a commitment I made to myself, as well as to them, and I have done the very best I know how.

As it turned out, Crosse's strategy backfired—and it cost him precious votes. The truth was that I had never been a bad father, and had never denied or neglected my children. The people of my district knew this—they had always seen me in the community with my boys. We'd walked the streets together, dined in fast-food restaurants, and knelt in church pews. As a result, Crosse's charges produced outrage, especially among women voters, who felt they were off the mark. Infuriated by the Reverend's slander, they rallied in my behalf, saying they knew too many other men who didn't support their children and that they resented a candidate making false attacks on someone who did!

Dented but not destroyed, Crosse still wasn't finished with me. As the days before the general election waned, he surfaced again with another ill-conceived rearguard action. Once again I watched the television screen as Crosse stood before the esteemed Johns Hopkins Hospital. He was throwing down the gauntlet in his latest attempt to seize the low ground with another moral issue, daring me to play his game by his rules.

"This is my urine," Crosse proclaimed in his Jamaican accent. "I want you to know that if you send me to Congress, you won't ever have to worry about whether I use drugs or not. I challenge Mr. Mfume to come and give his urine."

I didn't even dignify this challenge with a reply. I didn't need to, because the press jumped all over him, slamming him for resorting to dirty unrelated tactics and not debating the issues. I understood why he didn't want to discuss the issues—it was because he had no real grasp of how to solve the problems confronting our district.

My strategy against Crosse was essentially the same one I'd used in the primary, and that was to take the high road and keep my focus on the bread-and-butter issues of the district. Sadly, many of the issues hadn't changed much since I'd first been elected to the City Council.

My emphasis was on the fact that the city's renaissance was still not reaching deeply enough into the impoverished black communities, where physical suffering and moral anguish were still soaring.

To dramatize my point, I took the press with me on a walk through the old neighborhoods where broken curbs, sidewalks, and potholes were commonplace, and where abandoned buildings and empty lots were much too plentiful. In these neighborhoods the majority of the city's citizens lived in substandard housing, and the grip of high unemployment was felt in almost every home. At rallies and campaign stops, I reached out to the people who lived here, asking them to give me a chance. I asked for the privilege of being their voice in Washington. They cheered when I rejected the trickle-down notion of economics voiced by some who deliberately misused a quote of John F. Kennedy: "A rising tide lifts all boats."

Such rhetoric may have sounded good, but it was clearly not always true. I explained to the voters that only a small share of the federal urban-development money was coming their way, but that meanwhile, city taxes were continually going up. Some black officials were saying that this was a great time for minority businesses, that black entrepreneurs could do anything in Baltimore if they only showed some ambition. But what they weren't saying was that the white-controlled banks were making virtually no loans in the black communities for business start-ups or expansion. This was partly because there was no pressure being applied to them by local government, because black citizens were not represented in any significant number on the city's key boards and commissions.

"But it's a new day," I exulted, campaigning hard in the final days throughout the heaviest-populated areas of the district. "Our time has come. Seize your destiny. Vote for change. Give me the chance to serve you."

In the end, the voters responded to my call for change en masse, and I won the election handily with a comfortable 84 percent margin. Crosse's bag of dirty tricks had been no match against the truth. Still, the burden of being a continual target of character assassination, coupled with the routine hard work of campaigning, had taken a heavy toll on me. That election night, I was emotionally and physically drained.

While others celebrated our victory with champagne at a downtown hotel, I slipped away with my sons to go back to our suite. Carl Swann, George Buntin, and attorney Billy Murphy came with us. Carl in particular knew what I was thinking now. We had come a long way together since the days in Turners Station when we first learned how to win. My sons were happy and smiling. They were bubbling over with pride and raucously cheering my triumph. But I was feeling somber and reflective and more in the mood to talk to them about the moment, in the manner my mother used to talk to me.

"I want to talk to you about losing on this night of winning, and what losing is all about," I told them. "I want you to think about this whole campaign, the way the other candidates handled losing the primary when only one or two could bring themselves to say congratulations, and the nasty campaign that the Reverend Crosse ran because he could see he was losing. Their anger, bitterness, and lack of grace in defeat speak more about their character than the debates we had ever could. I want you to know that if I had lost this election, it would not have been the end of the world."

"But, Dad, you never thought you were going to lose, and neither did we," Michael cut in. "Let's talk about winning."

I was adamant. "No, let's talk about losing."

"What about it, Dad?" Kevin asked. "Nobody likes to lose."

"That's true. But if I'd lost, I would have tried to understand why," I began slowly. "I would have taken inventory of myself and the campaign I'd run. There would be questions to be answered, coldly and honestly. Losing is the hardest thing to do, especially for people who have only known winning. But to truly be a good winner, you have to know how to lose. To have the patience, self-control, and forbearance that it takes to be a true winner, you must understand the anguish of losing."

"The best thing is not to lose in the first place," Ronald said, grinning.

"So what's up with St. George Crosse?" Michael asked. "Why isn't he being a better sport about losing?"

"He can't accept the reality that the people rejected him and the old order he represents because they were ready for something new," I said. "He made the biggest mistake that a politician can make. He took the people for granted. It would have been better for everyone if he could have been gracious in defeat. Losing is nothing to be ashamed of. As long as you fight tough, hard, and fair, you can lose and still hold your head high. Everyone respects a clean, hard fight."

"We know that fool doesn't know what a fair fight is," added Carl.

"Yeah, Dad," Michael said. "That stuff about you not taking care of us was a real low blow."

"That's right," Kevin chimed in, as Keith nodded in support.

"Hey, Dad?"

"Yeah, Donald?"

"I've been doing some thinking, and I have a question to ask you."

"And just what might that be," I asked.

"Now that the election is over, Dad, can we go kick Mr. Crosse's butt?"

We all cracked up laughing, especially Ronald. "Sorry," I said. "Somehow I don't think that's a good idea. You know," I said, "in a sense, all of our lives are about to change drastically. Ever since I got elected to the City Council I've been watching how people scrutinize leaders under a microscope. They seem to be searching for flaws and shortcomings, while at the same time hoping not to find them. Yes, my life is about to change, but so are yours."

The boys looked at me curiously. Probably imagining all kinds of intrigue and surveillance, Ronald chimed in.

"What do you mean, Dad?" he asked. "You're the one who got elected, not us."

"Sure, I'm the one who got elected, but people are going to start looking at you differently now too," I explained. "They'll be watching you a little closer and perhaps judging you more harshly. It's not fair, but they will compare you to me and then to each other."

"So what are we supposed to do?" Donald asked. "I mean, it's not fair for people to want us to change just because you're going to Congress."

"Nobody's asking you to. All I'm saying is that you'll be in a kind of fishbowl, and that means understanding up front that your actions will reflect on all of us in the family in a way they never have before."

"Oh, I get it," Keith blurted out. "You mean, don't embarrass you."

"You guys could never embarrass me," I said. "I'm just saying, be as wise as you can about how you live your lives. Avoid the obvious traps. Choose your friends wisely. But most of all, don't embarrass yourself. Your grandmother died in my arms twenty-one years ago, in a world that now seems like a galaxy away. She went to her grave praying to God that I would one day make something out of myself. Even more than tonight's victory, she would be so proud of all of you, and what you've all become. Once, when I was just a little kid, sick and in pain, your grandma saved my life using old slave remedies and the power of prayer. This night was supposed to never have come. But God sent his deliverance then, and he is doing so again. We are still a family."

With those words, I ended my reflection, and the six of us huddled together in prayer.

Later that same night, I would kneel again by my bed and offer a longer prayer of thanks. Somehow, I was managing to do something everyone had said was impossible in assuming the mantle of leadership first worn by Congressman Parren Mitchell.

Parren was someone I had respected for so long. Ever since our meeting on Hankin's Corner, he had been largely responsible for my eventually taking this political path. A veteran of the civil rights movement in the '50s and '60s, Parren had headed an antipoverty program long before he'd made it to Capitol Hill.

From him, I had learned the importance of economics to our community. It had been one of my major themes in this first congressional campaign. "Our immediate concern," I told the voters, "is jobs, jobs, jobs. If a man has a job, he can support his family. If a woman has a job, she doesn't need welfare. The more opportunity people have, the more likely they will be to prosper, and for some that prosperity will lead to taking their skills and going into business for themselves. W.E.B. Du Bois once said, 'To be a poor man is hard, but to be a poor race in a land of dollars is the very bottom of hardships.' " Parren always said that racism rested on an economic base. He and I both knew that economic power was the solution to our ills! Since you don't get political power until you've acquired economic power, we stressed that developing our own black banks and businesses was crucial to our survival because it meant the money would be reinvested in the community. Parren's concern for the private sector meant that he was beloved by the business community.

I wanted to nurture those ties, too. But I also wanted, and perhaps needed, something else to bring fullness to my evolution. I wanted to have a strong presence in every sector of our community, both black and white. Perhaps because I'd been born in a small, rural community where everyone knew one another, maintaining that kind of personal touch has always meant a great deal to me.

I'll never forget the day I was shopping in a supermarket and an old black woman, walking with a cane, tugged on the arm of a young boy I assumed to be her grandson. "Look, Aaron," I heard her say, "that's Mr. Mfume, our congressman, out here getting his groceries just like one of us." She waved at me and I walked over and talked to her and the boy for a while. When I started to leave, she grabbed my arm, smiled, and said, "I'm mighty proud of you. Yessir!"

Several months after the election, I was finally sworn in ceremoniously, with all the pomp and circumstance accorded to such an event. "I do solemnly swear that I will protect and defend the Constitution of the United States from all enemies foreign and domestic, and that I will bear true faith and allegiance to the same. I take this obligation freely, without any mental reservation or purpose of evasion, and that I will well and faithfully discharge the duties of the office on which I am about to enter, so help me God." As I lowered my right hand I whispered, "Thank you, God," and then congratulated the others around me.

The freshman congressional class of 1987 was invited to meet with then-President Ronald Reagan in the Lincoln Room of the White House. It wasn't until that meeting, as I sat quietly amid some of the brightest, most ambitious people in the nation, that I began to realize what a tremendous challenge it was going to be to make a name for myself in this daunting crowd. It would be a much tougher job than my years on the City Council.

There were fifty-one of us newcomers—twenty-six Democrats and twenty-five Republicans. Many of them possessed a unique claim to fame, over and above the drive and determination it had taken to get here, that automatically gave them a prominent place on Washington's radar screen. There was Joseph P. Kennedy II of Massachusetts, exuding the kind of confidence you might expect from a man whose father was Robert F. Kennedy, and whose uncle was John F. Kennedy, the man I had once glimpsed as a teenager after slipping out of the house and into a crowded armory.

Sitting a few rows away from me, his head towering above us all, was Tom McMillen, the legendary pro basketball player who starred with the University of Maryland and later with the Washington Bullets. Across the aisle from him was Jim Bunning, the first major-league baseball player to be elected to Congress since Republican representative Wilmer D. "Vinegar Bend" Mizell of North Carolina. Bunning had been the only major-league pitcher to win a hundred games in both leagues. As a pitcher for the Detroit Tigers and the Philadelphia Phillies, Bunning had a blazing fastball that few fans will ever forget. Back in 1964, he pitched a perfect game for the Phillies, retiring all twenty-seven New York Mets batters.

And there were many more freshmen with impressive backgrounds. There was Joe Brennan, who had been governor of Maine. John Lewis had come from humble beginnings to rise to national prominence as a great civil rights warrior. Floyd Flake, a well-known AME minister, had come to Congress with a reputation for community service in New York. Mike Espy, the first black congressman from Mississippi since Reconstruction, was a part of that group, along with Ben Cardin, my friend and former Speaker of the Maryland House of Delegates, and actor

Fred Grandy, who played Gopher on *The Love Boat* TV series of the 1970s and 1980s.

Of them all, I was the only one in the Lincoln Room that day who had grown up on the streets, the only one who didn't have an illustrious background that would gain me attention. It hadn't taken me long after I arrived in Washington to notice that the media were flocking to my classmates and taking an immediate interest in their views. Reporters were kind and polite to me, but it was clear that my views on the issues were not valuable to them.

President Ronald Reagan was gracious and disarmingly personable as he stood behind a podium and spoke for about ten minutes about how good it was to have us here and why it was important that we have an opportunity to talk often. At first sight, I couldn't help thinking how true he was to his image on TV, the only place I'd ever seen him before. Some of the guys on the other side of the aisle knew most of his Warner Bros. films from the 1930s and 1940s. They could recite lines by heart from such movies as *Santa Fe Trail*, *Brother Rat*, and *Kings Row*, in which he played an amputee. The one I remembered best was *Bedtime for Bonzo*, where he'd shared the billing with a chimpanzee.

After his presentation, the President asked if we had any questions. Sitting there, I thought about what the years under Reagan had done to African Americans. Three months after his inauguration, he had proposed deep cuts in the budgets for programs aiding the poor. Four months later, he weakened the enforcement powers of the Justice Department in affirmative action cases involving African Americans and other minorities. By 1983, more than thirty-three state agencies responsible for overseeing civil rights law had signed a letter criticizing Reagan for "a dangerous deterioration in federal enforcement of civil rights." However, the President quickly dismissed the charges, replying that he was "color-blind."

In response to Reagan's request for questions, Joe Kennedy's hand flew up. He jumped on the President's case about the dearth of government action on housing issues in America.

"Our people desperately need shelter. I'd like to know if there

will be any new initiatives from the White House in this area?"
asked the young congressman. "Do you, Mr. President, have any
new solutions, because the lack of affordable housing affects all
of our districts."

Reagan looked down at the three-by-five index cards before
him on the podium. I suspect that he couldn't find one labeled
"housing," because he stood there for a few moments, quietly
shuffling through the cards, smiling and dipping his head at an
angle as he had frequently done before. I watched him closely in
those few moments. But he was cool about the situation and
wasn't nervous at all. He made small talk as he searched.
Finally, he decided to improvise and talk off-the-cuff, offering a
response that didn't make much sense. A few others asked questions, and then we broke up into an informal gathering. As it
turned out, President Reagan and I wound up in the same circle,
discussing baseball rather than politics. He told me he had once
been a big fan of sports announcers. I in turn invited him to
throw out the first pitch in Baltimore that year.

In the middle of our conversation about America's national
pastime, he somehow veered off into an odd dialogue about his
days as an announcer and the *General Electric Theater* on TV.
That's when I realized the President's concentration was very
limited, and that his thinking seemed not as structured as it
should be.

Nevertheless, while Reagan and I were to later have a hundred
battles, I learned to respect him because at least he had a vision
and a cause. Although I didn't agree with his conservative
agenda, I did admire his ideological toughness and his ability to
map out an issue with unshakable conviction and stick with it
until it became law. Any effective leader must possess that
quality. I respect the fact that he wasn't a man who waffled in the
face of opinion poll swings, as so many politicians do today.
With Ronald Wilson Reagan, the reformed liberal and staunch
anticommunist, you knew exactly what you were getting.

During the two years I served under President Reagan, he
clobbered us on the Democratic side on issue after issue, as
he wielded his veto power with a vengeance. Reagan got much
of what he wanted from the Congress, despite the fact that the

Democrats held their majority in the House during the 1980s and regained control of the Senate in 1986. He wooed moderate Democrats in both houses and charmed the loyalty of conservative Democrats in the South and West. Unlike Bush, he relentlessly worked the phones with the lawmakers and skillfully courted others on coveted jaunts to Camp David. The Democrats were never able to mount a stiff opposition to the Reagan forces. Our only real victory was blocking a big cut in Social Security benefits.

Was Reagan a racist? People often ask me this, and I have never been able to give a definitive answer. Ronald Reagan was a politician first and foremost. I believe Reagan was a man who had very little knowledge of or contact with poor people or African Americans. He spoke out in 1966 against the Civil Rights Act of 1964, denouncing it as "bad legislation." And he opposed the 1965 Voting Rights Act as a slam against the South. He was looking for white votes, much as Nixon had with his "Southern strategy" of courting Dixiecrats in 1969. Reagan never truly counted on African American voters because he felt he could win the Oval Office without their support. And yet, he understood the blue-collar heart of white smokestack America and plugged into it in a way that Nixon and George Wallace wished they could have.

Such heady experiences as meeting the President were constantly tempered by the cold reality that all freshmen are looked upon and treated as insignificant by veteran members of Congress. There's a subtle hazing process that begins early on and persists until you've been reelected. From the moment I walked into my new congressional office—smallish, nondescript, and tucked away on the first floor of the old Longworth Building on Independence Avenue—I could almost imagine Arnette Evans standing beside me, his face aglow with perverse pleasure, yelling in my ear, "That's right, little girl! It's tiny, like the rathole you climbed out of!" I imagined my old Drum and Bugle Corps leader screaming at the top of his lungs, "You don't even deserve an office! Tell me, goddammit, what have you done for this country, for black people, to deserve better than this? Tell me!!"

Fortunately, over the years I had spent enough time with Parren Mitchell to know that, contrary to the common misperception, members of Congress don't work in plush, luxurious environs. Behind Capitol Hill's great stone facades and wide marble corridors that reflect prestige and power, there's a world teeming with cluttered file cabinets, overflowing bookshelves, and the frenzied staffers who are the lifeblood of any bureaucracy. Each office generates a voluminous amount of paper, and as a result large offices are at a premium and the coveted prizes of a quiet competition among members. In this contest, freshmen always lose because congressional office space is acquired solely through seniority—the longest-serving members get first pick in a lottery system. I was among the fifty-one new members banished to serving my first few years in Longworth, the oldest and least desirable of the three House buildings that include the Cannon Building and the much desired Rayburn Building. Of my eight Washington staffers, only four could fit into my main office, while the others toiled in an annex.

Of all the obstacles facing new members, poor office space was the least of my concerns. While I couldn't change my freshman status, I wanted to at least come across as a sharp and seasoned politician—someone to be taken seriously. I wanted to make a name for myself quickly among my colleagues so I could be an effective representative for my constituents. From the moment I was sworn in by newly elected House Speaker Jim Wright, I made every effort to distinguish myself from the crowd. I stayed up late into the night, memorizing the names and interesting details about the background of key members of the House and Senate. Establishing personal relationships is important on the Hill, and people appreciate those who know more about them than merely what committees they sit on.

I restudied the history and origins of the Congress, going back to its creation as a safeguard against the establishment of a monarchy in the fledgling American republic. As a student at Morgan State, I had learned that the Founders had enacted these checks and balances because they feared trading one king for another. That concern was paramount during the debates of the Constitutional Convention of 1787. Benjamin Franklin found the idea of a Congress to be the perfect remedy, noting, "I am apprehensive that the Government of these States, may in future times, end in a monarchy." Establishing checks against the abuse of power by the President was the first subject on the agenda of those who drafted the inner workings of this new democratic system. The first duly elected Congress of the United States of America met in Philadelphia in the spring of 1789. It was white, male, and exclusive.

I spent hours reading about the African Americans who had served in high office before me. The rich tradition of black representation in the position touched something deep inside me, striking a resonant chord in my soul. It was a legacy forged in an environment of bigotry, adversity, and continual challenge. My finger traced the fiercely intelligent features of Jefferson Long on an engraving of this congressman who had represented a backwoods district in Georgia during the Reconstruction period of de jure segregation after the Civil War. Local whites thought they knew how to put him in his place, but he was full of surprises. They attacked black voters at polling places on Election Day, killing seven and forcing then-candidate Long to escape the mob by hiding in a sewer. In his first speech before Congress, the courageous black representative struck back at the corrupt Georgia political system that protected the Ku Klux Klan members and bigots who violated the constitutional rights of Negroes.

Long was one of a number of African American congressmen who banded together to use their collective power to sway the political tides and enforce the newly passed Fourteenth Amendment to the Constitution, which provided for equal treatment of blacks as citizens under the law. This particular group of representatives during Reconstruction was full of first-rate leaders, each articulate, capable, and intellectual. In one book, there was a group drawing of these men who held their seats in the U.S. House of Representatives and U.S. Senate amid stiff white opposition. They in essence really were the first Congressional Black Caucus. None of these black leaders were cowards. Some of their names still linger with me: Hiram R.

Revels, U.S. senator from Mississippi; B. K. Bruce, U.S. senator from Mississippi; John R. Lynch, representative from Mississippi; Robert Brown Elliott, representative from South Carolina; and Joseph H. Rainey, representative from South Carolina. The *Congressional Record* of that time is packed with accounts of Rainey. His scathing wit and brilliant legal mind often angered his white peers, who kept troubling their heads to find new ways to silence him.

One of my favorite black leaders of that era remains Alonzo J. Ransier, a representative from South Carolina and a major player in the debate on the civil rights bill of 1875. When I hear some of our young people talk about the system coopting our leaders, I recall the following reply by Congressman Ransier to Congressman James Beck of Kentucky, a noted white racist, during a heated exchange on granting blacks equal rights.

"It is feared by the gentleman from Kentucky that if colored people are put down upon a plane of civil equality in law—going into the same schools, hotels, places of amusement, and in the jury-box and cemetery—we by virtue of our intellectual superiority and our moral and physical force will absorb the race to which he belongs," Ransier then answered the bigoted remark. "Let me thank him, in the name of the colored people, for the compliment he has, perhaps unconsciously, paid them, but I must deny that there is a serious intention on our part to thus destroy those for whom he speaks."

The congressman paused for effect, then continued. "The bugbear of 'social equality' is used by the enemies of political and civil equality in place of argument. I would certainly oppose the Civil Rights bill if I believed that its operation would force upon me the company of the member from Kentucky, for instance."

When I read words like these in their historical context, I began to realize that being a congressman was far more than just a job. It touched on the cherished values that my mother had struggled so hard to impart to me—the values that had enabled our forefathers to survive and thrive under the heel of great oppression. Work hard, play by the rules, love your country, and cherish your faith, they taught us. Respect your elders. Remember that all life is sacred. Never forget that the gift of life comes with an awesome responsibility. My mother taught me never to run away from the responsibilities of life; that it is always wiser to accept what life has to offer and to work to change what is unacceptable to you. All of these things came back to me with crystal clarity as I began my first year on Capitol Hill.

Like those early black congressmen, I, too, was accustomed to being the underdog, and I realized it wasn't going to be easy breaking out of the pack. The only way to accomplish this was to be effective and not to lose the one thing that had gotten me there: my ability to challenge. I figured I wouldn't worry about overcoming the obstacles. If I did my job right, those barriers would fall, one by one.

13

"SHAME ON YOU, MR. PRESIDENT."

*M*Y first year in Congress is something of a blur—not because it was so long ago, but because the pace of Washington politics is dizzying. My home was in nearby Baltimore, so I did not establish a residence in Washington, as do most members who live farther away. But that meant an hour's commute each morning and evening on the Baltimore-Washington Parkway. Whenever I anticipated a long, busy night of meetings or House floor debates, I checked into a Washington hotel. Perhaps for reasons more psychological than practical, I tried to leave it all behind me at night.

On the Hill, you're always walking—more walking than I ever imagined before taking office. Most of the walking was done heading back and forth from my office to the Capitol to vote. Most members don't want to sit on the floor of the House all day listening to debates. There's always pressing work for constituents that needs to be done.

My debut was hardly that of the wistful Jefferson Smith, the character played by Jimmy Stewart in the 1939 film *Mr. Smith Goes to Washington*. There was no sauntering through the streets, gazing reverently at the Jefferson Memorial, the White House, or the Capitol building. Whenever I walked toward the massive expanse of the U.S. Capitol with its majestic dome, I was usually absorbed in thought, pondering the customs and language of this new culture. I was eager to learn the business of government, knowing that if I failed to learn the ropes quickly I'd get lost in the shuffle, or even worse, bounced out of office by my district. There was no manual to pore over, no gurus to consult. What you had to do was keep your eyes and ears open, and spend as much time as possible with the veteran members of Congress who knew the process backward and forward. This was the way you swiftly learned who had insider status, who were the gatekeepers for bills, who were the designated hitters for certain agendas, and who were known to be bomb throwers who could damage an amendment's chances of survival.

There are a lot of unwritten rules in the House. Among them: Don't try to be an expert on everything—instead, become an expert on something. Being perceived as a know-it-all on every issue gets you speedily disliked by your colleagues, because everybody knows it's impossible to know everything about everything. More realistically, you're expected to find niches, specialties, and become expert in those fields. The foundations for learning these areas are the twenty-two standing committees, the 147 subcommittees, and the five select or special committees in the House. House members are limited to one exclusive committee or one major and one nonmajor committee. Generally, members bid for three subcommittee assignments on their major committees, and two on their minor committees. Recommendations for these positions are in the hands of the Democratic Steering and Policy Committee to the Democratic Caucus.

After getting sworn in, I ended up sitting on the same two committees that Parren Mitchell had served on previously— Banking and Urban Affairs, and Small Business. I worked hard to become an expert in those areas, and over the years my colleagues would consult me on any issue dealing with finance, insurance reform, or capital standards for banking institutions.

As I monitored the route that a bill follows to become a law through the land mines of vetoes, filibusters, killer amendments, and other forms of legislative gridlock, I learned, in large part, what it was like to be a little fish in a big pond.

In varying degrees, all freshman congressmen, no matter their background, face the same obstacle: Nobody takes you seriously. The slight is nothing personal—it's a check on whether a new member may have been elected on a fluke. "Go out and get reelected, and then I'll take you seriously, then I'll remember your name," I once overheard a senior legislator ribbing a group of enthusiastic newcomers. It frustrated me to hear such condescension, but I understood the logic of it. Congress is based on a system of seniority, so two years of service mean very little in the scheme of things.

Early into my first term, I realized what a problem I was having in getting other members to correctly pronounce my name. I don't know what the source of the problem was, but whatever it was, only a few made an effort to get it right. By far the worst offender was Frank Annunzio. Frank was the chairman of the powerful Banking House Committee, and he'd do a hatchet job on my name whenever he called me for questions, even after I'd been sitting on his committee for two years. He called me every possible variation of my name, from Mr. Macfum to Mr. Meefoom to Mr. Fumee. He called me anything but my correct name. It was very embarrassing, and everyone on the committee would cringe whenever Annunzio looked in my direction because they knew he was going to commit the offense once more. I really don't think that Frank meant any harm. It's just that Annunzio was an old-school Chicago politician in his seventies, who figured he had more important things to do than to master my name. Besides, he liked me and there was nothing personal in his attempts to pronounce it, except that try as he might, it never came out of his mouth correctly.

One day, I decided to give Frank a personal pronunciation

lesson. While hammering out the details on a major bill, we were seated in a room packed with media, lobbyists, and staffers scurrying all over the place. When it was time for him to yield to me for questions, everybody cringed because they knew Annunzio was going to mispronounce my name again. When he did, I didn't react at all. I simply leaned into my microphone and began to speak.

"Thank you very much, Chairman Annunciation," I said calmly. "I thank the gentleman for yielding."

The entire chamber cracked up laughing. Annunzio glanced at me, rather embarrassed, but he started laughing as well when he realized that the cameras and the joke were on him. From that day on, Frank Annunzio pronounced my name perfectly. That subtle strategy made my peers take notice, because I had finessed the situation without a lot of rancor or hostility. As a rule, I try to live by the old African proverb that says, "It's not what you call me—it's what I answer to."

Of course, in those early years, all of my actions were measured against those of my predecessor, Parren Mitchell. In my district, everyone believed that nobody could replace Parren. He had been their champion for so many years, and an exceptional representative. My admiration and respect for him and his achievements for our district and our nation gave me the feeling that not only could I not fill his shoes, but that any attempt to do so would be a dishonor to both of us. This is why I set about doing things my way from the outset.

I learned early from Arnette Evans that if you want to win, you'd better first assess a situation fully. The second part of his lesson was that success requires some trial and error. One's tactical strategies must be carefully tested against other strategies to see if they have any validity, he'd say. Success in any field also comes with a price—hard work. Being a good fighter means learning not to act on your first impulse. Always weigh your options. Never play the card that your opponent expects, he'd say. A true leader leads. You must remember that knowledge without courage is meaningless. The capacity to lead comes only when you have developed a certain maturity of judgment, clearness of thought, and firmness of will.

I believe that one key component of leadership is to truly understand the times in which you live. It is through that understanding that you start to know your role, your mission, your purpose. As one wise axiom goes: "Not everyone finds the time he deserves, and even when he finds it he does not always know how to utilize it."

The worst thing you can do as a leader is to surrender to your passions, to your ego. When these elements are involved, defeat cannot be far behind. Some African American leaders have been stereotyped in the past as being ruled by their emotions, of talking a good fight but not being able to deliver. It's not enough to say "Let me speak," and then have nothing to say. Or to falsely lift expectations and promise things that can never be delivered.

I confront issues with a more varied approach today than I did years ago. Often, the words of old Mr. Smitty would come into my mind: "It's easy to kill a bird that flies straight, but not so easy with one that twists and turns." Habit and predictable action can neutralize one's effectiveness. Study your adversaries to find their weaknesses, both obvious and unseen, he would say. In direct confrontation, you would often lose your advantage, he'd remind us, because when you go straight at a foe, your adversary quickly sees your weaknesses.

When I think of the great African American leaders, I think of such people as Dr. King, W.E.B. Du Bois, Paul Robeson, Harriet Tubman, A. Philip Randolph, and Malcolm X. They were brilliant strategists who understood that the needs of the many outweigh the needs of the few. You got the sense that they could assess a situation, no matter how grave, and find a way to move toward its resolution. They were true leaders, people who were so comfortable and secure with who they were that they didn't have to flaunt it. What also made them effective was that they took action and never made excuses. They never ran out of energy or belief in their cause. When I was a freshman congressman, these examples of leadership would serve as guideposts for the work that lay ahead.

Personally, I have always loved the legislative process. I respect its rules and strictures, and I'm a strong believer in carrying out that process with a high degree of decorum and respect. During my group's freshman orientation, House Speaker Jim Wright spoke in glowing terms about the importance of procedure in maintaining a sense of fairness and efficiency in government. Recalling his speech, I approached Wright one day and asked if I could do more to support the party.

"What do you want to do?"

"Mr. Speaker, I've chaired the House once or twice, but I'd like to do it more often," I said. Everybody gets a chance now and then. But in order to chair on a regular basis, you really need the blessing of the Speaker.

Jim Wright didn't even hesitate. "By golly, if you want to do that I suspect the Speaker can help you out," he drawled. Most senior members don't want to take on a task like chairing the House because it's too time-consuming, and they're busy pursuing other leadership duties. I wanted to chair the House so I could master the basics of parliamentary procedure.

The objective is simple: You're there to move legislation through the process with the least possible disruption, and to control the proceedings and see that they remain orderly and efficient. As Speaker Pro Tem, I earned a reputation for being a straight shooter who moved the process forward with precision and authority, which won me respect and recognition from Democrats and Republicans alike. Assuming the role also helped me cement my position in the House. The proceedings are carried nationally on TV, and it gave many people a chance to watch a black man with an African name wielding the gavel of government. Unthreatened by it all, many wrote and told me they thought I was doing a good job.

I was a keen admirer of Jim Wright as Speaker of the House. The tough, swashbuckling Texas Democrat had risen from House Majority Leader to serve as Speaker of the House from 1987 to 1989. Unfortunately, Wright was forced to resign following an Ethics Committee probe of rules violations. He was succeeded by Tom Foley, a respected Democrat from Washington, and many GOP leaders thought the Democrats would be totally routed after Wright was deposed. It's easy to understand why. Jim Wright led the House, while Tom Foley merely presided over it.

Jim Wright led by example, with a total commitment to the Democratic agenda, and a firm finger of the pulse on the House membership. He knew what it took to pass a bill or to scuttle it. He caused trouble for the Republicans because he never hesitated to do whatever was needed to reach his goal, whether it was twisting arms or breaking them. With Wright, it was nothing personal, merely a matter of not letting anything deflect or sidetrack him from his mission.

Tom Foley carried the same title, but never the same clout. His name never inspired the same fear from the other side of the aisle. During his tenure as Speaker, he merely presided over the legislative process. The flow of legislation was never determined solely by him, always by a committee of others.

While I learned a great deal during those early years in the House, I didn't do it quietly. I consistently spoke out against the creeping ultraconservatism of representatives on both sides of the aisle, often finding myself alone or one of the group who was still able to vote from conscience. I also championed a number of causes, including youth employment, educational programs, minority business issues, more supplies for schools, civil rights, stronger sanctions against the Apartheid regime in South Africa, labor and consumer issues, and total bans on assault weapons. If I discovered any similarity between Congress and the Baltimore City Council, it was that both were legislative branches with a tough conservative core. But the same fearlessness and persistence that allowed me to survive in the City Council were still very much alive in Congress.

I tried to choose my battles well, and make every word count.

The "gridlock" phenomenon—in which partisan politics block every effort of both parties, and which plagued the Bush administration during its final days—is a malady that has struck Congress before and will no doubt afflict it again. I worked hard to avoid being a part of the self-defeating process that often allowed good and effective legislation to wither and die on the vine.

Whenever possible, I focused my efforts on areas that not only interested me, but also offered the possibility of fostering societal change and growth. Housing was one of my main areas of concern because I understood from my trying experiences as a youth how much having a decent home means to both individuals and families. If people managed to own or rent a house, there was always a chance for them to regroup and bounce back from whatever difficulties life sends their way. People and families living on the street have far fewer options. What happens to them is at the mercy and whim of others, and this destroys self-esteem and lowers their ability to cope, much less succeed.

In my early days as a congressman, I vigorously studied the areas of private and public housing, learning the history of both, the trends and tides of availability. It became very clear to me how racism and class often decide who lives how and where. President Kennedy had promised to issue an executive order to end bias in housing during his 1960 campaign. But he delayed action on the matter until after the 1962 congressional elections. On November 20, 1963, just days before his untimely death, President Kennedy signed an executive order prohibiting racial discrimination in housing built or purchased with federal assistance.

While the housing situation for African Americans did not improve significantly, there was some action taken to remedy the problem. On April 11, 1968, President Lyndon B. Johnson signed the Housing and Urban Development Act, a provision of the Civil Rights Act of 1968, prohibiting racial discrimination in renting or selling houses and apartments. The housing legislation was based on a proposal hammered out during discussions between the Texan chief executive and Dr. Martin Luther King, Jr.

Despite well-meaning legislation, the lack of housing for minorities continued. By 1980, census data revealed that only 44 percent of black households owned their own homes, compared with 68 percent of white households. A 1990 study by the private Center on Budget and Policy Priorities indicated that adequate housing was not attainable by nearly half of the nation's black families. Census information for that year uncovered the fact that 77 percent of black Americans were living in substandard housing and could not afford a midpriced home even with conventional financing. Very little has changed since then.

With all of this in mind, I was determined to play a part in overcoming this growing problem. I offered an amendment to the reauthorization of the Housing and Community Development Act. It required the Secretary of the Department of Housing and Urban Development (HUD) to submit a report to Congress on its activities since the provisions of the Housing and Urban Development Act had been written in 1968. I needed to see what HUD had been doing for low-income people in the last ten years. Was the agency doing its job?

My amendment was attached to the housing bill, H.R. 4, introduced in March 1987 by Senator William Proxmire (D-Wisconsin). The bill authorized over $30 billion for fiscal years 1988 and 1989 for public housing assistance, rural housing, and community development.

Bill Proxmire was extremely positive when I suggested an amendment to monitor the use of the funding to improve housing stock in the city and on the farm. "I understand you wanting to make sure that HUD has been doing its job and that the funds get used properly," he said as we walked from his office. "Just let me know how I can help."

When we received the HUD report on its Section 3 program, we learned that the federal agency was not fulfilling its mandate to assist the poor in obtaining adequate housing. Armed with this information, I was able to include several amendments to upcoming housing bills that required HUD to perform its mandate more efficiently, while adding more lower-income persons to its field staff.

One of my more effective amendments was attached to the National Affordable Housing Act, which stipulated a change in how rents were calculated for tenants living in public housing. Under the old system, tenants estimated their income and paid 30 percent of that revenue for their rent. Under my amendment, the tenants could exclude wages, tips, alimony, or child support supposedly earmarked for them but not received. We wanted only actual income, cash in hand, counted as money to be used toward rent.

Experience was quickly becoming a great teacher. I followed the bill, which Senator Alan Cranston (D-California) introduced in March 1989, as it moved slowly through the Housing Committee's bipartisan talks and wrangling. Both Democrats and Republican members had their say about the formation of a new corporation to oversee local efforts to create more affordable housing and home ownership. While it is tedious, this give-and-take process can lead to a consensus in which no one feels that their agenda is getting a bad deal. With the budget constraints we were facing, it was imperative that we get the most bang for our bucks. My amendment was one of several attached to the bill before its passage and signature into law by President Bush in late 1990.

Also while supporting a 1989 Youth Employment Services Act authored by Senator Howard Metzenbaum (D-Ohio), I once made an impassioned plea for its passage to a largely skeptical audience: "This legislation is desperately needed by many of our young people throughout the nation," I argued, "particularly in our cities, where youth unemployment has surpassed 40 percent. Lacking the employment opportunities and proper skills to achieve employment, many of these young people are caught in an ever-enduring cycle where upward mobility seems as remote as the stars over their head."

Also, that same year, ultraconservatives became fidgety when I pointed out that the hand-picked Supreme Court had reversed five affirmative action cases in a six-month period. My voice was steady when I uttered tersely, "The Court seems to be possessed these days by a political agenda which seeks to overturn laws which have changed America's course away from public and private racism and segregation." Nobody wanted to hear any of this. It would have been so much easier to have such a discussion become a part of the nondebate. As such, I concluded that those of conscience must "mobilize and march" on the ideological Court.

If there is anything I learned during my time as a congressman, it is that the Democratic Party is not a monolith either in ideology or ideals. Reflecting its varied constituency, the party includes a wealth of special interests and factions devoted to safeguarding their own individual concerns. This potpourri of views did not serve Democrats well during the Reagan years in the White House, because a sizable number from the more conservative wing of the party defected to the GOP in the 1980s.

Some of this trend was evident when I coauthored H.R. 1, the Civil Rights Act of 1991, during one of the most turbulent periods for African Americans. We couldn't get all of the Democrats in either house of Congress on board to back this antibias jobs bill against a possible veto from President George Bush. With the presidential elections only a year away, Bush was trying to position himself as a tougher candidate with a deep concern for the more conservative wing of the party. Some of the leaders in his own party were blasting him as a president who did not want to lead, heading a rudderless administration now adrift. Bush figured one way to get back in the running was to side with the far right on a growing number of social issues.

"I don't think America is in favor of reverse discrimination or quotas," President Bush replied when asked about the pending civil rights bill in Congress in the late spring of 1991. "This bill could lead to more quota hiring of minorities and women. We can't do that at a time when we are working so hard to achieve a color-blind society, a society based on merit, not on race or gender."

We knew we had a fight on our hands. Bush had vetoed a similar bill in 1990. The new bill, a revamped edition of the rejected version, offered workers more protection against discrimination by undoing a number of Supreme Court decisions that limited the power of antibias laws. One feature of the bill freed up previously restricted money damages for victims of harassment and other intentional discrimination based on sex, religion, or disability.

As Democrats huddled to plan a House strategy to find a two-thirds majority to offset any presidential veto, someone reminded us of the obstacles that both previous significant civil rights bills had faced in a divided Congress before their passage. The Civil Rights Act of 1957 had been signed by President Eisenhower in September of that year, after the tense months of Dr. King's Montgomery bus boycott. Although the Act declared that limiting the voting rights of blacks was illegal, it had little real effect other than granting the Justice Department the power to intervene when the right to vote was being hampered. After the Act was passed, there was less than a 3 percent increase of black voters in the South.

Congressional districts around the country had staunchly resisted passing any legislation to aid "the Nigra" and they battled against the bill to the very end. Congressman Strom Thurmond (R-South Carolina) earned the praise of every white bigot below the Mason-Dixon Line with his amazing one-man filibuster that lasted twenty-four hours and eighteen minutes. Thurmond thought he could talk the bill to death, but in the end the legislation passed.

In 1964, it was President Johnson's political savvy that got the next civil rights bill through Congress. It banned discrimination in public accommodations and jobs. Johnson's predecessor, John Kennedy, had long promised such legislation to Dr. King and the other civil rights leaders, but he had failed to deliver. Johnson cajoled, twisted arms, threatened, and got what he ultimately wanted: a bill that mandated that no federal funds could be used to aid segregation. A renegade Southerner and shrewd politician, Johnson personally knew every member of the Dixiecrat bloc in Congress and reached out to them one by one. He talked their talk and got the job done.

At the signing of the bill, Johnson tried to soothe both friend and foe alike: "Let us close the springs of racial poison. . . . The purpose of this law is simple. It does not restrict the freedom of any American so long as he respects the rights of others. It does not give special treatment to any citizen. It does say that the only limit to a man's hope for happiness and for the future of his children shall be his own ability."

In many ways, we faced a similar opposition to our 1991 bill because of the added complication of an upcoming presidential election. There was an endless amount of political posturing going on during the congressional debate. Republicans tried to turn the bill's noble intent to their advantage by playing up a threat that more employers would be forced to use quotas to sidestep costly lawsuits. They claimed that, if the measure passed, more qualified whites would lose their jobs to minorities and women. This didn't take a hard sell—the economy was weak and job security had become a priority for many Americans.

Democrats had been stunned by Bush's veto of the 1990 version. It had marked the first defeat of a major civil rights bill in twenty-five years. Senate supporters of the bill—an odd coalition headed by Edward Kennedy (D-Massachusetts) and John Danforth (R-Missouri)—had lacked one vote to override his veto. Quotas, quotas, quotas. A month after the Bush veto, Senator Jesse Helms (R-North Carolina) had used the quota issue to defeat his black opponent for one of the state's Senate seats. GOP strategists knew a good thing when they saw it.

Then our side fired back. Congressman Don Edwards (D-California) called the quota approach by its real name: "Politics and racism." To prevent the rejection of the 1991 civil rights legislation as simply another job quota bill, Democrats stressed that the new version of the bill would aid working women in breaking the glass ceiling of corporate America, so the battle heated up once again.

"If Democrats want to keep pushing the same old bill, bring it on," insisted Senator Richard Lugar (R-Indiana). "As a matter of fact, we think we have more going for us now than we did at the time of the 1990 fight." Charlie Rangel (D-New York), Ron Dellums (D-California), Lou Stokes (D-Ohio), Cardiss Collins (D-Maine), and Bill Clay (D-Missouri) led the effort within the Black Caucus. John Conyers (D-Michigan), dean of the CBC, had the toughest task—working it through the committee process.

Despite a Republican full-court press, however, the bill passed two committees by mid-March and the Bush administration was forced to move forward with its more conservative alternatives to the job bias bill.

Civil rights lobbyists attempted an end run by entering into talks with the business community to break the logjam. Their thinking was that if some progress could be made with the large Fortune 500 firms, they could use it as leverage against the bill's

stout opposition. They haggled for nearly five months with nego-
tiators from the Business Roundtable, a group of chief executive
officers from two hundred powerful companies. The consortium
then informed the lobbyists that they wanted to fashion the new
bill to their liking, or no deal.

To complicate matters, Bush decided to play hardball. He
called in his reserves—hundreds of small and midsized businesses—inciting them with talk that they would suffer under
any deal worked out with the richer, bigger firms. The little
guys responded with a withering assault on the big corporations, threatening to sabotage any agreement reached with the
lobbyists. Finally, Big Business blinked and announced that
they were pulling out of the talks. Bush had won another
round.

House Democrats, realizing that they were on the road to
defeat, conceded to several Bush demands and concocted a
weaker bill with limits on proposed money damages and
harsher standards for determining indirect bias. I was furious.
Many of the bill's supporters were completely dissatisfied with
the compromise, but the House leadership was willing to do
anything to prevent another Bush veto.

In the days before the weakened bill came up for a House
vote, the lobbyists for both sides were operating in full gear, and
the debate on the floor became fiery and full of accusatory
rhetoric. I had taken part in the negotiations with the opposition, struggling to prevent a rout while trying to preserve as
much of the bill's original intent as possible. But in the end, several of our supporters, including a few of those from the 1990
fight, went over to the other side.

Two days before the June 5 vote, I went to the well and joined
in the floor debate. I kept my voice calm and solemn, and did
not betray the frustration and anger stirring within me as I
faced the warring factions.

My first target was President Bush, who had vetoed our first
effort in 1990, and had seen the Senate fail to override it with an
elated David Duke, the former Grand Wizard of the Ku Klux
Klan, looking on from the gallery. I called it "the darkest day of
the 101st Congress." I questioned why the President continued

to fight the bill a second time, labeling it a quota bill and attacking it by any means necessary.

"Mr. Speaker, I believed that when the President was given a second chance, he would, in fact, do the right thing," I said. "So the sadness in my heart this evening, for all of you around this country watching this discussion, is not because there are persons advising the President who may be sinister influences in the area of civil rights, it is not because there is a body of misinformation and disinformation that is inflaming newspaper headlines and the news programs all across this country, because none of that really matters."

There was some shuffling of feet on the other side of the aisle before I went on, lowering my voice a notch. "My sadness is due to the fact that this President, who knows better, continues to argue—erroneously—that this is a quota bill. Shame on you, Mr. President. You know better. And you know I know you know better."

I was not finished. "I defy anyone in the White House to come to this body and prove beyond a shadow of a doubt that the bill we have before us is, in fact, a quota bill. I defy you. And I know you are watching this debate, all of you who have advised the President, all of you who, in your own way, recognize the virtue of the merits of this bill. Yet you have chosen to make political capital by continuing to confuse and divide and separate the public, by having them believe that women and persons of African and Hispanic ancestry are going to somehow benefit to the detriment of others. Shame on you. You know better. I know you know better."

Bush worked hard in the days before the House vote, making speech after speech attacking quotas and reverse discrimination. Many Republicans backed him, saying the legislation would only further divide the nation. Several members of the Congressional Black Caucus spoke out, stressing the fact that we were still striving to protect fellow Americans from bigotry, still fighting socially sanctioned, legally protected discrimination some thirty years after the bloody battles of the 1960s.

Before the final vote, both sides got in their punches, defeating one another's best proposals. Both the unadulterated Democratic plan and the unyielding White House bill bit the dust. The last tally was 178 for the bill to 158 against, just 15 votes short of the two-thirds majority needed to stave off another presidential veto. Nine Republican members who had voted with us in 1990 rejoined their party in opposing the compromise bill. One black member, Congressman Gary Franks (R-Connecticut), also sided with the opposition. In the case of Franks, he could have done what he knew was right and voted for the bill. However, he seemed hellbent from the time he got elected to prove to his Republican colleagues that he could vote against the positions of most black people in order to gain their acceptance.

Following the House vote, presidential hopeful Pat Buchanan spoke for the far right of the GOP in a June 5 syndicated column attacking the bill: "The new civil rights law has failed to attract the support of Americans because it is not equal rights as most Americans understand the term. It is about stacking the deck in civil suits where black plaintiffs and lawyers confront white businessmen."

In the Senate, supporters submitted a compromise bill in the hope of avoiding a major battle. Senator John Danforth pushed three proposals that allowed opponents to focus on the more controversial elements in a package that was separate from the tamer segments. He worked to hone the legislation during the summer, trying to convince Bush to end his assault.

Some pundits credit the confirmation of Clarence Thomas as Associate Justice of the Supreme Court as the turning point in the battle. Republicans were worried about the possibility of an extended fight with race as a centerpiece, which would create a split in their ranks. An override fight against a presidential veto could have led to a bloody conflict. In the end, the moderate Republicans, led by Danforth, finally won an agreement from Bush, who claimed victory, while Democrats pointed to the key concessions made by the administration. Bush respected Danforth for defending his nominee during the hotly contested Thomas struggle in the Senate, so he dodged a final confrontation with him. The President also knew the timing was not right for another veto of a civil rights bill.

"We didn't cave," Bush told reporters, boasting of having defeated any quota intentions in the bill. "We worked out, in a spirit of compromise, a negotiated settlement where I can say to the American people, this is not a quota bill." Of course it wasn't. It had never been a quota bill. And George Bush knew it.

Bob Dole (R-Kansas), the former Minority Leader, had served as the middleman between Bush and Danforth, seeking to keep the compromise on track. He understood that very little was to be gained by fighting with Danforth in an override conflict. Also, there were other Republicans who warned the President that they might not back him in a veto fight. The Senate approved the compromise bill by 93 to 5.

The Rose Garden signing, which was boycotted by all Democrat lawmakers except Senator Edward Kennedy, showed there was still continued politicking for advantage. Hours before, the White House had released a blistering statement underlining its opposition to affirmative action. This sucker punch infuriated our side—we knew the administration was speaking out of both sides of its mouth. I did not attend. My conscience wouldn't let me.

However, a smiling Bush put his own spin on matters at the signing, saying, "This historic legislation strengthens the barriers and sanctions against employment discrimination." Although I had fought and won the battle of keeping my amendment in the bill and even though some of the most significant language of the bill remained, the two-year fight for its passage had been brutal.

In Washington, you quickly learn that things are often not what they seem. An official may strike a public pose on an issue, blasting it at every opportunity. But he may take an entirely different route privately in the committee room. For this reason, the passage of particularly tough bills often might require hours of talks and ultimately additional amendments so that all sides feel appeased. In congressional politics, you sometimes have to give to get.

I had learned one key element in negotiating way back in Baltimore in the dogfights in the City Council. You start with a seemingly intractable position, stating that nothing is negotiable. You will not budge on any major point. But once you've staked out the territory, the real talking begins. By starting with a harder position in congressional negotiations, you lose fewer of the essentials as the give-and-take goes on. Conversely, if you start soft on a position, the final result will be extremely watered down.

With President Bush, there was often no room for negotiating, especially as the elections approached. In 1991, he kept coming at the Democratic Party from every angle. It seemed that as long as the media taunted him with the "wimp" tag, he felt compelled to intensify his attacks. Just before the election, he transferred $22 billion in federal aid from the cities to state control. In this way, he rewarded those governors and state legislatures who were predominantly white and largely Republican and punished the Democratic mayors, who headed the big cities, which were chiefly populated by blacks, Hispanics, and poor whites.

Eyebrows were raised in January 1991, when I opposed the passage of the Solarz-Michel resolution giving the green light to war in the Persian Gulf, Operation Desert Storm. I questioned the use of force over sanctions to dislodge Saddam Hussein from Kuwait to reinstall the Kuwaiti emir. President Bush's policies in the region were inconsistent and opportunistic, given the impending presidential election. "Let us not rush headlong into chaos and uncertainty," I said. "America has many pressing domestic economic problems. The cost of this war and its concomitant effects will only worsen our economic situation, which shows no visible signs of relief. I urge those who want to go to war with Iraq to remember that although the Middle East is strategic for its oil, I do not wish to see the Saudi desert become the symbol of unclarified policy and the massive loss of brave American lives." Needless to say, the war did nothing to save Bush's bid for reelection, and Saddam Hussein remains in Baghdad.

On July 10, 1991, President Bush removed the sanctions against South Africa. Conservatives cheered his action, remembering how a joint congressional effort had overruled President Reagan's veto five years earlier and imposed economic sanctions on the Apartheid government. Bush defended his moves with a

statement proclaiming that the white-led South African government had satisfied all of the demands of the 1986 Comprehensive Anti-Apartheid Act, and that President F. W. de Klerk was
proving to be a true reformer.

"This is a moment in history which many believed would
never be attained," said Bush, explaining his new order, which
had become effective immediately. "I really firmly believe that
this progress is irreversible."

The uproar from all of us who had fought so long and hard to
keep the pressure on the South African government was intense.
We reminded the public how some in the Republican Party had
continually tried to do whatever possible to aid the rulers of
Apartheid. We knew the Bush initiative had come too soon and
that it would only help the conservative Afrikaaners re-entrench
economically. There was some talk that the President had acted
illegally by removing the sanctions without the consent of Congress. We weren't about to let Bush get away with this possibly
improper action. We understood that the easing of the sanctions
would only add to the tremendous suffering of the black population of South Africa. I quickly moved, along with other members
of the Congressional Black Caucus, to write resolution H.R. 126,
challenging the President on his decision to dissolve the sanctions while black leaders in South Africa were still conducting
talks with the ruling party on government reforms. We knew
perfectly well that with the November elections coming up,
Bush's repeal served a twofold function. First, it was an attempt
to drive a wedge into the Democratic Party, pitting the liberals
against the conservatives. Second, it tossed a bone to representatives of Big Business, who were eager to get back into South
Africa to open up the markets.

John Conyers, Jr., didn't mince words when he addressed
Bush's latest ploy. "This is great news for General Motors and
everyone that was doing business in South Africa," said
Conyers. "What we're doing is shoring up the economic basis of
a system of Apartheid that can have fateful consequences in the
very sensitive period that is now going on."

In essence, Bush had set out to destabilize the reform process
under way in South Africa. I disagreed somewhat with then CBC

Chairman Ed Towns (D-New York), who was worried about the lack of broad support for our challenge in Congress. True, some of the most vocal supporters for the sanctions were now doing a flip-flop or remaining silent. The Congressional Black Caucus, along with Randall Robinson's TransAfrica, had been giving the conservatives hell on the South Africa issue for a long time, and we weren't about to throw in the towel now. Some civil rights groups called for us to write a new sanctions bill to counteract Bush's repeal, but there was serious doubt that a groundswell of public support could be generated.

Bush sent Herman J. Cohen, assistant secretary of state for African Affairs, to the Hill to defend his action. Cohen pointed out that the remaining pillars of Apartheid were collapsing, and reiterated Bush's contention that the process of change there was irreversible. Although he admitted that the South African government was still in violation of some provisions of the 1986 sanctions act, he said that President de Klerk had assured him that two major racial segregation laws would be repealed during the next parliament.

In interviews with the press, I continually attacked Bush's repeal, calling it hasty and premature: "A great deal more work needs to be done in South Africa before the claims of irreversible change can be substantiated." I added that I wanted to see solid political progress and the legislative dismantling of the Apartheid system before I could be as optimistic as President Bush. I denounced his notion that there was a speedy move under way toward full and free political participation for South Africa's blacks.

Sometimes in a battle, victory is not immediately obvious. We never converted Bush to our way of thinking. In many areas, he was still firmly committed to the old Reagan policy of "constructive engagement" toward South Africa. This meant that he gave lip service to a distaste for the evils of Apartheid—but there was never a full, genuine dedication to putting policies into place that would have hastened reform in Johannesburg. The Bush stance on South Africa was to give aid and comfort to a system that maintained the social oppression of blacks. However, he was right on one point: Nothing can stop change.

Apartheid did not survive. With the release of Nelson Mandela, head of the ANC, after twenty-seven years in prison, it would only be a matter of time before the white-led government was rocked back on its heels. At last, in May of 1996, the final nail for freedom was hammered into the coffin of white supremacy and bigotry in South Africa when the nation adopted a new constitution that guaranteed equal rights for blacks and whites. The new charter also offered everyone, black and white, full freedom of speech, movement, and political activity. And it established a hearty federal system with a powerful presidency and a two-chamber legislature. When the news that the new constitution had been passed reached the people, black South Africans danced in the streets, tears of joy in their eyes.

Two years of debate had gone into the creation of the 150-page charter, which guarantees a majority-rule government that will provide everyone with the right to adequate housing, food, water, education, and health care. The Zulu nationalists and their white Afrikaaner counterparts abstained from the final vote on the constitution, which passed 421 to 2. Ex-President de Klerk quit as deputy president, charging that whites were not being given an equal say in the sharing of power.

When he signed the constitution, President Mandela said eloquently, "Never and never again shall the laws of our land rend our people apart or legalize their oppression and repression. I would like everybody to think in terms of their country as a whole, black and white."

When I think about what Nelson Mandela has done in such a short time to move his nation from Apartheid, a lethal form of Jim Crowism, I'm filled with an overwhelming sense of awe, respect, and optimism. Sometimes, when I see how black and white in South Africa have been able to overcome their deeply felt differences and seek a road that would avoid total destruction, I wonder why here in the United States, the greatest country in the world, we cannot, as well, embrace change across racial lines and achieve our full potential as a democracy. At the Clinton inauguration, Mandela and I discussed the hard work ahead for him in his country—all the challenges and obstacles—but there was never any doubt about the outcome in any of his words.

I asked Mandela how he could be certain. He smiled warmly and looked me squarely in the eyes, and said, "Because our struggle is right. And we will never abandon our fight. We will never falter. If we do our part, then nothing, no guns, no hate, no ill will, will stop change. It will come, you will see. Kweisi, it will come."

Nothing can stop change. I have never forgotten those words of hope from Nelson Mandela, the great black warrior.

During the congressional debate on crime and punishment in 1994, I argued the unfavored position that building prisons and giving stiffer sentences doesn't necessarily reduce the crime rate unless we allocate more money for rehabilitation programs, including the return of Pell Grants for prisoners. I pointed out the disproportionate sentencing of minorities, with people of color often receiving harsher penalties than whites for the same crimes. My comment on the death penalty as "the most atrocious display of government-sanctioned racism in America today" caused some arch-conservatives to shake their heads.

Describing the Republicans' Personal Responsibility Act of 1995—the GOP's version of welfare reform—I called it a "wolf in sheep's clothing." I criticized the removal of welfare mothers and their babies from the rolls to fund a proposed tax break for the wealthy. I reminded my peers that welfare reform must be looked at against the backdrop of our nation's overall economic condition.

The more outspoken I became, the more praise I began drawing from colleagues, staff, lobbyists, constituents, and the media. However, such praise can become addictive, and it's very important not to believe all the talk of your alleged greatness and brilliance. You have to keep reminding yourself that you're no better than anybody else, that there's nothing special about you, and that you are only there to serve others. A congressional seat really belongs to the people in the district you represent—it's not yours. It's only on loan for a limited time.

Those who fall into the trap of believing in the illusion of their own power and invincibility often wind up getting sucked into the Washington maw and promptly spit out.

Black elected officials must be continually aware that Washington is not a friendly place. There are many who believe that African American and minority officials are especially targeted in the nation's capital. To avoid falling into the Washington power trap, I spent a great deal of time working in the trenches of my district at home. Baltimore's Seventh District ranged from the poorest of the poor to the supremely wealthy, from those existing in the decaying row houses of East Baltimore to those living in comfortable estates on the tony outskirts of the city. Tending to a racially and economically diverse constituency such as this required versatility, patience, tolerance, and compassion. It was important to learn how to listen to everyone, to assess their concerns and needs, and to deliver on them.

I considered this work the bedrock of my role in government. Compared to some of the tasks I faced in Baltimore, the work I confronted in the House was gravy. Working in your district is never glamorous. It's hard and tedious, and requires a lot of very patient listening. People have real problems and they want quick solutions. If you're in Congress and can't do constituent work, or don't like doing it, you should be doing something else. And you are likely to be, come the next election.

It's important for your constitutents to know that you're really listening to them. The problems of my constituents would run the gamut—mainly dealing with their inability to cut through government bureaucracy and red tape.

Take Mrs. Jackson, whose son is having legal problems in Guam. He's a military officer stationed there and she can't get any information from the armed services. They're getting ready to court-marshal him and she's trying to get an idea of what's happening to her son.

Then there's Mr. and Mrs. Smith, who are involved in buying a home, only to find out that their FHA loan is being withheld because of a lack of documentation.

Or somebody else's son is in jail in Ohio. His family wants him to serve his sentence in Baltimore so he can be closer for visits.

Or someone needs housing, but there are no Section 8 certificates available.

Or another person has an extreme handicap and is trying to prove eligibility for a government program that provides assistance.

Case after case needed solving, from employment discrimination to education and Social Security issues. That was my basic role as a congressman. People expected me to straighten out their problems, no matter what they were. And that's exactly what I did.

14

THE CBC: A FORCE TO BE RECKONED WITH

*L*IKE millions across the globe, I sat at home in front of my television set and watched with great emotion that Sunday, February 10, 1990, as Nelson Mandela strode out of Victor Verster prison after a twenty-seven-year incarceration. My biggest fear had been that he would die in jail, which would have triggered political and social unrest in South Africa that could not be contained. But the moment he stepped out into the bright sunlight of outdoors that afternoon, all my concern faded and was replaced only by an overwhelming desire to be there beside him and welcome him with a tight embrace, to tell him that I was among the masses who had been praying that he would one day enjoy freedom and finally reunite with his wife, Winnie, and his four children, Zindziswa, Zenani, Makaziwe, and Makgatho. Since I wasn't yet the chairman of the Congressional Black Caucus, I wasn't sure how I would meet this great freedom fighter. But my soul was calm. I knew that somehow our paths would cross, and that the day would be soon.

For the past two decades, so much of my world had been centered around the struggle for South African liberation. I had organized protests and informational campaigns at the Community College of Baltimore and Morgan State University, led annual candlelight vigils, passed a South African divestiture bill while on the City Council, and continued my crusade in Congress. Nobody was more joyous than I on February 2, 1990, when F. W. de Klerk stood before Parliament and announced that he was lifting bans on the ANC, the Pan African Congress (PAC), the South African Communist Party, and thirty-three other illegal organizations, as well as freeing political prisoners and lifting other restrictions that were at the foundation of Apartheid. It seemed only natural to me that I would meet Mandela, the heart and soul that embodied this epic struggle.

Months after his release, Mandela came to the United States to meet with members of Congress from both parties and particularly members of the Black Caucus. During my years on the Baltimore City Council and in Congress, I had become accustomed to meeting many of the world's most important leaders. Whether it was Lech Walesa, Mikhail Gorbachev, Fidel Castro, or Margaret Thatcher, I knew well the potent mixture of excitement and humility that accompanies standing face to face with greatness.

Yet, I must admit that I was not prepared for the piercing emotions that surged through me as I stood within feet of Nelson Mandela in a reception area in the Cannon office building. Simply put, I was awestruck and moved nearly to tears at the sight of this man. Tall and trim, with thick graying hair, Mr. Mandela was talking with Representatives Maxine Waters (D-California) and Harold Ford (D-Tennessee) when our eyes met. As I stepped over to introduce myself, I was startled to discover that Mr. Mandela already knew my name. A scholarly man, Nelson Mandela would later tell me that he read voraciously during his final couple of years in jail, after the ban on his reading material was lifted. It was during this time that he learned not only the names but the backgrounds of Caucus members.

"Kweisi Mfume," he said, smiling, in his clipped, precisely enunciated English. "It is a great pleasure to meet you."

"I am honored."

I reached out to shake his hand, and it was at this moment that our friendship was cemented. Instead of simply shaking my hand, Mandela leaned forward and held me in a long, sincere embrace. It struck me that with all this man's influence and nobility, he was a person of such genuine warmth and affection. While he exuded a king's aura, there was nothing intimidating about him. He was like a warm and gentle grandfather, rugged and wise, fierce and loving. From all my reading about him, I had correctly imagined Mandela to be a humble man. But even I was startled at how earnest he was in his affection toward me. With that hug, my feeling of awe bloomed into a sudden and remarkable closeness with this man.

Over the next fifteen months, my relationship with Mr. Mandela grew. During his visits to the United States and my travels to South Africa. There was an immediate and natural connection between us, as though we had known each other for years. By the time I took over the CBC in 1993, we had spent a lot of time together, one on one and with other Caucus members, as well as with officials of the Clinton administration. Mandela was in the United States frequently, raising money for his organization, the African National Congress, and for the election, so I got a chance to spend many hours in his company, to observe his brilliant reasoning process, to study his mannerisms, to enjoy his quick wit and wry sense of humor, and to even glimpse his frailties, his shortcomings, the few that he had.

By September 1993, South Africa's first national, nonracial, one-person-one-vote elections were approaching and the atmosphere was tense and violent in his homeland. I flew to South Africa to visit him, against the backdrop of shooting sprees that were erupting throughout Johannesburg, with factions trying to disrupt the upcoming elections. I had gone there with several members of the CBC and a few staffers. Mandela was feeling upbeat, and we wanted to ensure his safety during the restive weeks prior to the election. We had gone over to meet with the election commission and help them with their humanitarian effort of moving the country toward the election as smoothly and peacefully as possible. While there, we met with President

F. W. de Klerk, as well as traveling to Durban to confer with Chief Mangosuthu Buthelezi, the head of the Inkatha Freedom Party and the chief minister of the KwaZulu, a key player on the South African political scene, with an estimated seven million members. We also went out to Soweto and Cape Town to spend time with township residents and government leaders.

The day prior to our arrival had been full of sporadic gunfire. As we rode a bus toward the ANC headquarters, we were all looking through the windows, hoping not to spot a problem or incident that might spark a riot. I'll never forget the moment our bus neared the headquarters and the sharp crack of gunfire rang out from a rooftop, followed by more gunfire from another rooftop.

"Snipers," I heard Carl Swann cry out from on the floor of the bus, the same cautious voice I remembered from way back in Turners Station. "Get down," he yelled.

But Carl was the only one on our bus smart enough to hit the deck. We could have been shot that day with the automatic weapons sputtering crossfire around us. Amazed at warfare we had only witnessed on nightly television news, we gawked at the action like sitting ducks. The bus driver was trying to rush us out of there, but traffic was snarled. Fortunately, the shooting ended quickly—only ten minutes after it erupted. The driver found a break in the gridlock, sped away, and delivered us safely into the driveway of the ANC headquarters.

"You okay?" I asked Rep. Donald Payne (D-New Jersey), who looked a little shaken, just like the rest of us.

"Yeah, just fine," he said, pointing to Congressman John Lewis as if to suggest that John might not be okay. But John was all right, and it was soon clear that no one on our bus had been hit.

The following afternoon, Mr. Mandela invited us to his home. Located just outside of Johannesburg, it isn't grand or palatial, as many might expect, but it is comfortable, with modest, suburban charm. It sits up a sloping incline that over-looks Johannesburg and offers a beautiful view of greenery and countryside. The rooms are large with high ceilings. The living room window opens onto a small veranda, which is where we sat.

Mr. Mandela, dressed casually that day in a sweater, slacks, and loafers, pulled me aside to express his concern over what he perceived as a threat to financial aid to South Africa, as many members of Congress were pushing to reduce the aid that President Clinton had proposed.

I understood his concern. It seemed that racism in my homeland might cripple his efforts to restore democracy in his. It has always been U.S. policy to support emerging democracies with foreign aid. But in this case, some of my congressional colleagues wanted to reduce Clinton's budget for aid to South Africa. Ironically, these same colleagues had been quick to sign off on providing millions in guaranteed loans to Poland when Lech Walesa became President, or stepping up foreign aid to Egypt to make sure that President Mubarak could maintain a stable government. We had given money everywhere, except now we were talking about trying to support a fledgling democracy in Africa, where the citizenry is predominantly black. It was clear to me that the notion of a black government coming into power struck a discomforting chord among some members of Congress. But it was just as clear to me that during Mandela's early period in office, sufficient funding would be critical for everything from keeping electricity in houses to keeping public schools open.

"I spoke recently with Maxine Waters and she gave me a sense of the problems you are facing with the budget for foreign aid," he said. "I would appreciate it if you could get for me a fuller sense of whether we can prevent this threat from becoming a reality. Assuming I win this election, expectations will be quite high. Our borrowing authority, as well as foreign aid, will be absolutely crucial."

We discussed this issue for a while, and I assured him that I would do everything I could to keep U.S. aid flowing to South Africa. We then settled back into our seats, where John Lewis (D-Georgia), Donald Payne, Craig Washington (D-Texas), Carl, and a few other staffers were drinking tea and mellowing out after a long day. As the daylight faded over Johannesburg, we thanked Mr. Mandela for his hospitality and decided it was time to head back to our hotel.

"Mr. Mandela, it was a great pleasure to meet with you again," I said.

He grimaced. "Kweisi, haven't I asked you not to call me Mr. Mandela? I want you to call me Madiba."

"But sir, I can't do that," I said.

"But you must do that. That is my clan name. And now I give your permission to forever address me that way, for now you are a son."

On May 2, 1994, after a four-day election, F. W. de Klerk made his concession speech, ending more than three hundred years of white minority rule. News of the ANC's victory celebration at the Carlton Hotel in downtown Johannesburg quickly made its way back to Washington, where I was following events closely. To a packed ballroom whose guests included Coretta Scott King, Mandela beamed proudly as he spoke of a new beginning now that power had been turned over to the black majority. He proclaimed, as Dr. King had, that South Africa was "Free at last! Free at last!"

On May 10, 1994, I was among the U.S. delegation arriving in Pretoria for Mandela's inauguration. Colin Powell, Ron Brown, Quincy Jones, Senator Carol Mosley-Braun (D-Illinois), Mayor Kurt Schmoke, Rev. Jesse Jackson, and NBA Commissioner David Stern were among the many who crowded the President's plane for that trip. It was the largest gathering of world leaders in South Africa's history, and I was bursting with joy to be able to witness it. I took time to speak with Yasir Arafat and his wife who were both generally pleased that the hour had arrived. Fidel Castro, whom I had not seen in over five years, invited me to come back to Havana in my new role as caucus chair. In the Union Building's majestic sandstone amphitheater, I sat beside Maxine Waters and Ron Dellums (D-California) as de Klerk was sworn in as second deputy president and Thabo Mbeki was sworn in as first deputy president. Among so many survivors of so many struggles, I sat like all the others and waited. When the bells in the tower overlooking the majestic square began to ring, all eyes focused on the stage before us. That stage was soon to become a place of history. Nelson Mandela, a manchild in his promised land, had come to fulfill his destiny. Tears welled in my eyes as I watched him pledge to obey and uphold the constitution. Then he turned to the masses under the brilliant blue sky:

"Today, all of us do, by our presence here . . . confer glory and hope to newborn liberty. Out of the experience of an extraordinary human disaster that lasted too long, must be born a society of which all humanity will be proud.

"We, who were outlaws not so long ago, have today been given that rare privilege to be host to the nations of the world on our own soil. We thank all of our distinguished guests for having come to take possession with the people of our country of what is, after all, a common victory for justice, for peace, for human dignity.

"We have, at last, achieved our political emancipation. We pledge ourselves to liberate all our people from the continuing bondage of poverty, deprivation, suffering, gender and other discrimination.

"Let freedom reign. God bless Africa!"

As I sat there with Maxine and Ron, we couldn't hold our tears back. We had never experienced a moment so powerful, so transcendent in our lives. As we basked in the glory of witnessing a transition from decades of colonial rule to absolute liberation, we heard a roaring in the sky and looked up to see a formation of jets wheeling in perfect precision as they streamed a smoke trail with the black, red, green, blue, and gold of the new South African flag.

When the inaugural was over, a rainbow of thousands of people poured out on the streets of Pretoria. Colin Powell, Ron Dellums, and I got caught in the sea of people celebrating and moving in all directions. As we moved toward the Presidential Palace, we bumped into a group of school kids who looked like sixth graders. More than anything else, these kids symbolized what the struggle was about, because they were Dutch, Afrikaaner, colored, black. Dressed neatly in their school uniforms, they were screaming jubilantly over what had taken place in their country. Upon spotting us, they ran over and tried to make us feel at home by singing a few songs. The big surprise, though, was that they didn't sing tunes of their native land. These kids sang old American doo-wops that many of us had sung in our youth. They sang "In the Still of the Night," "Blue Moon," and several more. Flattered by their hospitality, Colin Powell and Ron Dellums decided we should return the favor and serenade our newfound friends. So, standing side by side, looking like the Temptations or the Four Tops, we crooned several doo-wop tunes with all the harmony we could muster as a crowd gathered around us. Soon, the kids had joined in, and we were all singing together in the great new democracy of South Africa.

An hour or so later, as the crowd began dispersing, I stood talking with Dellums and Maxine about all that had transpired. Despite all the great joy, we also shared a strange feeling of bewilderment. With Apartheid now a system of the past, we were left without a movement.

"It is remarkable, almost unbelievable to get to this point," Dellums said. "The pain and the passion. Getting to this point though, is, tough you know. You are out of the struggle after all these years. What do you do or say to yourself now?"

That's when the three of us looked at each other and, in unison, uttered one word: "Haiti."

My frustration over Haiti had peaked just a week after Bill Clinton's presidential inauguration in 1993. I had attended the ceremonies in the best of spirits. Nelson Mandela was my guest on that cold January day, and we sat on the steps of the Capitol as Clinton stood a few yards away, taking his oath of office. Thousands of people had traveled to Washington to watch this momentous shift of power, and you could see the pride in their faces as they listened to his speech of hope and prosperity.

Moments before, writer Maya Angelou had electrified the crowd with a moving rendition of her poem, "On the Pulse of Morning," which resonated with the promise of change in a United States weary from neglect suffered during the Reagan and Bush eras.

Mandela, too, was in an upbeat mood. Two years out of prison, he was not yet a head of state and therefore had not been officially invited by the White House to attend the inaugural ceremonies. My first gesture as the new chair of the Congressional Black Caucus was to extend him an invitation to come as my guest. He accepted graciously, expecting to accomplish several goals during his trip to the United States. At the time, Mandela was in the process of galvanizing support for the African National Congress so that it could become a powerful force in South African politics. Being in the United States gave him an opportunity to visit several major cities to raise money for his fledgling political campaign. It was important for him to meet with President Clinton and the new secretary of state, Warren Christopher, and other administration officials.

In January 1993, as Bill Clinton assumed the presidency, I found myself holding an enviable political hand as chairman of the Congressional Black Caucus. The CBC, founded in 1970, originally had thirteen members, including the fiery Shirley Chisholm, who would run for the White House the following year. They seized national attention after the 1972 election when they boycotted President Nixon's State of the Union address after he refused to meet with them on the issue of police brutality and the 1969 killings of Black Panthers Fred Hampton and Mark Clark. After the boycott, Nixon met with them. In 1972, during the height of the infamous Watergate scandal, a CBC member, Michigan congressman John Conyers, who was sitting on the House Judiciary Committee, became one of the first lawmakers to call for the president's impeachment. An eloquent Barbara Jordan, representative from Texas, was also a part of that committee. By the late 1970s, the CBC had seventeen members, including William Gray, Julian Dixon, Mickey Leland, Charles Diggs, Cardiss Collins, John Conyers, Jr., Harold Ford, Augustus Hawkins, Louis Stokes, and Walter Fauntroy.

Throughout the 1970s and 1980s, the CBC was an active group. In 1979, the Caucus, headed by Parren Mitchell, alarmed many in Congress when it lobbied for a probe into a possible federal takeover of the oil industry at a time when there were long gas lines, soaring fuel prices, double-digit inflation, and a recession. Parren went out on a limb but insisted the CBC's actions were necessary because unemployment figures were skyrocketing in minority neighborhoods.

This was the strong activist legacy inherited by me at the helm of the Caucus. For two straight years, I tried to lead the forty-member Caucus through a period of dynamism and influence that would forever change how people view the organization both inside and outside the Beltway.

Once simply a loyal rubber stamp of the Democratic Party, the Caucus ultimately evolved into a group of tough-minded activist legislators willing to challenge everyone from Bill Clinton to Louis Farrakhan. It was our time to shine. While some basked in the rays, others only felt the heat.

I had worked hard to reach this position in the Caucus. Starting in 1987 when I was elected to Congress, I served as treasurer of the Caucus for two years under Merv Dymally of California. During my second two years in office, I served as second vice chairman under Ron Dellums, also of California. And the following couple of years, I served as first vice chairman under Ed Towns of New York. Not only had I been chairman of the Caucus Executive Committee, which organizes the popular CBC Legislative Weekend, I had also been a member of the Congressional Black Caucus Foundation the entire time. The members of the CBC, who select their leaders through a kind of pecking order, knew it was definitely my turn.

One person didn't agree, however. Craig Washington, of Houston, Texas, wanted to run for the chairmanship and decided that the position should no longer be decided by seniority or pecking order, but through a competitive election process. This was virtually unheard of in the Caucus's twenty-three-year history. But we decided to take up Washington's challenge.

As in any campaign, Washington painted a distorted and unflattering picture of me. He took me to task in the press, ironically labeling me as an Establishment type who wouldn't challenge the status quo. He claimed I would be a go-along, get-along, business-as-usual kind of chairman. Of course, he offered himself as a fighter who would challenge the system. In the end, there weren't many Caucus members who bought into Washington's line, and I defeated him 27 to 9.

In the months ahead, nationwide congressional redistricting added sixteen new members to the Black Caucus, swelling our ranks to forty strong. When the dust cleared, I found myself at the helm of the largest Congressional Black Caucus ever. We all knew we were now a power to be reckoned with. I hoped that I was wise enough to leverage the Caucus as a voting bloc so that we could make a tremendous difference on legislation.

Barely one week after Clinton's inauguration, the CBC experienced its first challenge from the White House. The President decided to reverse his campaign promises about Haiti. Throughout his campaign, Clinton had assured voters that he was going to end the Bush policy of sending Haitian refugees back to the country they had risked their lives to escape. The Haitians, he had told us, were fleeing their native land seeking a safe haven and political asylum. Black people all across this country gravitated to Clinton's message because he was moving beyond Bush's inhumane policy, which turned a blind eye to conditions in Haiti—men being tortured and maimed, women being raped, and the bodies of children found washed up on shore. Yet, in Clinton's first week in office, he announced that he would continue to maintain the Bush policy of repatriation, mumbling some kind of poor excuse for his decision.

In my opinion, Clinton could not have done such a thing without taking the black vote and the Caucus for granted. He obviously hadn't bothered to consider the threat of upsetting forty members of Congress who wielded enough votes among them to put his legislation in jeopardy. He didn't consult us on the matter, or even warn us that this was coming down the pike. I heard about it on the *CBS Evening News*. As chair of the Caucus, I was instantly ambushed by the larger black community, who were wondering why Clinton had breached his promise, and by the press wanting a reaction to this news. Clinton had broken his covenant with the black community. It was obvious that there would be no honeymoon between us.

In mid-January all hell broke loose with the Haiti situation. Thugs roamed the streets of the country, killing anybody suspected of being a supporter of its exiled president, Jean Bertrand Aristide. Schools were closed and health care services were almost nonexistent. According to a study by public health experts at Harvard University, nearly 1,000 children were dying each month from lack of food and proper medical care. Haiti, the first black republic in the world, seemed to be coming apart at the seams.

The next challenge to the CBC's power came on the House floor in the push to pass legislation in favor of a line-item veto. This would allow the President to pick and choose which of the items attached to a bill he wished to accept and which to reject, instead of okaying or vetoing a bill whole cloth. It was a tricky issue for many of the new Caucus members. Several of them had come to Congress from state legislatures where they had voted to give their governors line-item veto, only to be burned later on when projects in their districts started to be zeroed out. They knew better than anyone else the dangers of giving the executive branch this power. Then there were other Caucus members, like myself, who were strict constitutionalists and believed that the legislative branch should never cede power to the executive branch. Each time you give up power, you never get it back, and the result is that you don't have equally balanced branches of government anymore. Under such circumstances, all Americans suffer.

Despite the Caucus's expressed reservations, the administration moved forward with this bill. Even though the House leadership was aware of the Caucus's problems with the legislation, they decided it was tough luck. The feeling was that the Caucus would just have to knuckle under on this one because the House wanted to give Clinton these powers to prove to the country that we could break the gridlock that had characterized Bush's presidency.

While the Republicans had approved the line-item veto for Reagan and Bush, suddenly they were hesitant about signing off on one for Clinton. They were evenly divided for and against, and even the Democratic side was only about two-thirds for and one-third against the legislation. The result of this split was that the balance of power rested on the forty votes of the Caucus.

Maybe House Speaker Tom Foley didn't think the Caucus could count. I'm not sure. All I know is that the Caucus was holding a meeting when we were informed that the House was voting on the line-item veto. It was in this meeting, in my opinion, that the Congressional Black Caucus redefined itself.

Unanimously, we refused to accept this flagrant lack of consideration of our opinions and input on this legislation. The House leadership knew we were opposed to the bill, yet they didn't take the time or show us the courtesy of listening to us and discussing the issues involved. They simply announced that we had fifteen minutes to get over there and vote.

At that moment, we decided that we didn't care if it was the President or the Speaker of the House, we were no longer going to be put in a position where we were expected to just deliver votes and preserve harmony with our Democratic colleagues. We were no longer going to put up with being ignored or consulted after the fact.

I looked at my colleagues and asked, "Do I have the consensus of the group to go out and announce to the House that if they move forward with this vote, the Caucus is going to oppose it and attempt to kill it?"

Almost to a person, they said, "You have that power."

I rushed out of the meeting and walked out on the House floor. I asked for unanimous consent to proceed out of order for one minute. It was granted by the Speaker Pro Tem.

"The Congressional Black Caucus has, for many reasons, been opposed to this bill in its present form," I said. "We have had no negotiations or consultations with the Democratic leadership. We have had no consultations or input from the White House. And we are not going to vote for the bill in its present form. We know that our votes can make or break this bill. You can move forward with it if you choose, but the bill will die. You must ask yourselves whether you want a major piece of Democratic legislation defeated by Democrats, or whether it's time to change the way we do business around here."

There was dead silence in the House gallery when I sat down. Speaker Foley wasn't in the Chair at the time; he was in his office. But the Majority Whip, Majority Leader, and everyone else just sat there staring at me. Finally, Foley walked briskly onto the floor and asked me if I would meet with him, immediately, in his office. I went to his office, accompanied by Caucus members Maxine Waters and Julian Dixon (D-California). While very polite, Foley was visibly upset. His face was flushed and he seemed to be shaking with anger. Gesturing for us to take a seat, he leaned across his desk.

"Apparently we have a problem," Foley began. "What can we do about it?"

"Mr. Speaker, with all due respect, there is nothing that can be done," I told him. "Either pull the bill or it will go down in defeat. It's just that simple."

"What's wrong?"

"There has not been any consultation. There has not been any reaching out. There has not been any discussion. There has been no input from forty members of Congress, who you expect to march out like soldiers and vote for something they do not approve of and have not seen. So there is no option. You either pull the bill and get it off the calendar, or you move forward with it. Either way, you can't keep that vote open much longer."

It was supposed to have been a fifteen-minute vote. But the vote had been kept open for thirty-five minutes and was becoming an embarrassment for the Speaker.

"Can't we solve this right here?"

"Let me be very straightforward with you," I went on. "First of all, it's foolish to think that you can be Speaker of the House and have a forty-member Caucus that you don't communicate with, don't have dialogue with, and don't meet with as a group.

"There are two hundred and sixty-seven Democrats in the House, forty of whom are members of this Caucus. But you don't meet with us, you don't consult with us, you don't ask us for our input. From this point on we insist that, as loyal members of this party, we must be included. You have a choice: either we help to shape the legislation that the Democrats bring to the House, or we will fight on every issue that comes before this Congress in the next two years. If we're not included, then we're going to be your worst nightmare. It's really up to you."

Foley sat back in his seat, and studied our faces for a moment. "I see," he said. "Then let's sit down and talk first thing tomorrow. In the meantime, I'm going to go pull the bill."

Foley marched onto the floor, and announced that the final vote would not be taking place then, it was being deferred. This was the defining moment for the Caucus in the 103rd Congress and among the first signs that we could, and we would, be taken seriously.

In late March of that year, I left for a trip to Aruba. It was my first break in several grueling months of round-the-clock politics. The general congressional campaign and election had kept me busy through November. Following that, I was flying around the country meeting with newly elected Black Caucus members, trying to win their support. In December, I was elected chair. And then, right after President Clinton's inaugural, the Haiti situation had exploded. I desperately needed a few days to relax and unwind.

When I departed Washington, the Lani Guinier affair had been percolating. Guinier, a noted law professor and NAACP civil rights attorney, had been slated for an assistant attorney general post, but questions about her views on affirmative action were raised. Clinton was under pressure from conservatives to withdraw her nomination. The Black Caucus tried to get out front on the issue, but was having difficulty getting media coverage. The right wing of the Republican Party saw this as an ideal opportunity to settle an old score by savaging her reputation and views, much as the Democrats had done years earlier with the nomination of Judge Robert Bork. At sparsely attended press conferences, we raised hell about the precedent being set and denounced the bitter whispering campaign that had been launched against her. But the press didn't report it because, after all, we were only the Congressional Black Caucus. Clinton would not let her publicly defend herself. Conservative columnists lashed out at Guinier on a daily basis, labeling her the "Quota Queen."

When I arrived in Aruba, I figured the Guinier flap had already blown over, as so many Washington issues do.

But one afternoon, while sitting in my hotel room, I got a call from Amelia Parker, the executive director of the Caucus.

"Mr. Chairman, you may have to come back right away because the President looks like he's getting ready to withdraw Lani Guinier's name."

"C'mon," I said in disbelief. "Tell me you're kidding."

"No, I'm very serious. And there's nobody in Washington."

Congress was on a four-day recess, and everybody in Washington knows that the best time to announce bad news is when nobody is around to react.

"Any of the Caucus members around?" I asked.

"None of the officers are here," she said. "And none of the real supporters of Ms. Guinier in the larger white community are here either. You have to come back because this may happen in a day or two."

I dropped everything and hopped on a plane to Washington. Unfortunately, everything Amelia told me was true. Indeed, the Guinier nomination was starting to unravel in the worst of ways. When I got into my office, Craig Washington was the only member of the Caucus who was around that day. I told him that I was going to hold a national press conference, that I thought it was important to send a message to the White House to hold firm on this nomination, and to remind other people who wouldn't cover us before that the Caucus took this as a very serious matter.

That afternoon, in the House Radio and Television Gallery, I held a press conference, with Craig Washington standing beside me. There was more than a touch of irony in the fact that not long before, Washington had called me part of the Establishment and warned that I would sell out under pressure. My statement that day was fairly terse and straightforward. I essentially urged the President to hold firm and not to withdraw the nomination or to back out, and assured him that the Caucus supported him completely and expected him to stand strong, and that we would fight along with him and the administration on this issue. My second point was that every person who is accused has a right to meet their accusers, and that Lani Guinier deserved a hearing at the very least. Don't pull her name out before the hearing, before American people hear her present her side of these issues face-to-face with her detractors. My third point was a very stiff warning to what I called the "nameless, faceless, and spineless" members of the Senate who through innuendo and a vicious whisper campaign were trying to discredit Lani Guinier and her character.

"We know who you are," I said, "and you will not get out of this unscathed. The Congressional Black Caucus challenges you not to whisper to reporters, but to come forward right now and stand before a microphone like I'm doing if you have problems with her."

Craig weighed in after me, and he was just as forceful. It was a strong press conference with good media coverage.

Lani Guinier was not a personal friend of mine at the time. I had met her socially on a couple of occasions, but our exchanges were mostly polite and brief. What I did know about her was that she was a brilliant civil rights attorney with an impeccable record within the larger civil rights community, and that her work with the NAACP and other groups was spectacular. She had a reputation for having a sharp, incisive mind and strong cognitive skills. I also knew that this nightmare was happening to her because she was a woman, and a woman who happened to be black. That put her in a kind of double jeopardy.

Women were catching hell in the Clinton White House nomination process. Zöe Baird's name had been put forward, for Attorney General, and the administration had been forced to pressure her to withdraw after information came out that she had illegal immigrants working for her. Kimba Wood had been nominated next, and the White House wiggled away from her. Now it appeared that Clinton was backpedaling on Lani Guinier as well. Somebody had to challenge the administration, and the criticism had to come from within the Democratic Party. Challenges from Republicans were being eschewed as partisan politics.

In Lani Guinier's case, it didn't matter what she said in the press or how she answered the charges. The die was cast. The conservatives wanted blood. Again and again, Guinier tried to explain her views on affirmative action. In July 1993, she told a group of reporters in Washington, "I became the 'Quota Queen' because I talked openly about existing racial divisions. . . . It did not matter that I, a democratic idealist, had suggested race-neutral election rules such as cumulative voting as an alternative to remedy racial discrimination. It didn't matter that I never advocated quotas."

On Friday morning, two days after the press conference, I was in my office in Washington when I got a call from President Clinton.

"Kweisi, I just wanted to bounce some things off of you regarding Lani Guinier," he said. "I'm not sure how I'm feeling right now about this whole thing. I think I need to read some of her stuff."

This was strange. Here was the President, telling me that he hadn't done his homework on his nominee.

"What do you think about it?" he asked.

"Mr. President, first of all, let's take Lani Guinier out of this. Let's just say it's Jane Doe. We have a system in our country that says you have the right to face your accusers. That's why the Senate has this role of advise and consent. That's why the Senate holds confirmation hearings, so the public can weigh the nominee's merits pro and con openly and make a decision on whether or not somebody should be confirmed.

"Sir, your job is to appoint, and to appoint the best people you can. But the confirmation process has to go forward. Pulling Lani's name out of this process would be the worst possible thing because it denies her that opportunity. Sir, I hope that I'm never accused of something without the opportunity to present my side of it."

"That's fair," the President said. "I understand. She's a brilliant woman, you know."

"May I ask, sir? What are you planning to do about this situation?"

"Nothing right now," he said. "I'll be sure to call you when I've got something further on this, certainly before I make any moves."

As I thanked him and hung up, bells were going off in my head. My next move was to call President Clinton's confidante Vernon Jordon and tell him that I'd just spoken with the President. I asked him how things were going with the Lani Guinier situation.

Jordan said that he thought things were good, that the President was taking some beating on this nomination, but that he was probably going to hold firm. I told him that I was a little concerned after my conversation with the President, and asked if there were some people we could call at this late moment to feed into the White House. He said no, that he'd already talked to the President about this and that he thought it was going to be okay.

When we hung up, I still didn't feel good about it. I called Janet Reno, who had held extremely firm on Guinier's nomination. "Madam Attorney General, I just talked with the President, and I'm feeling a little concerned about Lani's nomination. I think the whispering campaign, her detractors and her opponents, may be starting to have some impact on the White House."

Reno didn't have any inside knowledge on the matter, but agreed that Guinier needed a chance to present her story.

"I'll call you back if I hear anything more," she said. "You know, I've made some office space for her to work out of as the nominee over here at the Justice Department. I can give you her number and you can call her yourself, and see what she knows."

I took the number from Reno, and dialed Lani Guinier.

"Lani, I just spoke with the President and I'm not feeling good about what's going on. He didn't sound as firm as I think he should right now. And by the way, I thought you did an excellent job making your case on *Nightline* last night."

"Well, thank you, Kweisi," she said. "No, I haven't heard anything except what I've been reading in the papers. I know the President fairly well, you know—I mean, the man was at my wedding. I'm sure that he'd tell me if he were concerned."

"You're not getting ready to withdraw, are you?"

"Oh, no. I'm in this till the end."

She didn't come across as nervous at all. In fact, she sounded in good spirits. I told her that I was going to be in Baltimore that evening, and I gave her my home number and asked her to please call me if anything changed, and that I'd call her if I heard any news.

I hung up, packed my briefcase, and headed back to Baltimore. As I was driving on the parkway listening to the radio, the five o'clock news came on and the lead story was that the President had summoned Lani Guinier to the White House. The speculation was that he was going to withdraw her nomination.

I was floored. Clinton had told me that if he changed his mind, he'd get back to me, and I had taken him at his word. When I got home, I immediately got on the phone and called both Vernon Jordan and Janet Reno. I couldn't reach either of them, so I called Amelia at the Caucus office and asked if there was new information. She said no, that Lani was at the White House, but no one knew what was going on, and that there was all sorts of speculation.

In Baltimore, I was hosting a weekly television talk show called *The Bottom Line*. That night I had a taping scheduled, so I headed over to the station, went into makeup, got briefed for the show, and went on the set to start taping. Just before 9 P.M., while the show was in progress, I got a call from the White House. We halted the taping, and I explained to the audience that I had an urgent call and needed to be excused momentarily.

I went into the control booth, where my assistants put me in a secured room and closed the door. When I got on the line, the President said, "Hello, Kweisi. How are you tonight?"

"Well, Mr. President," I said. "I really don't know, getting this call. How are you?"

"Not too good. I want you to know that I've read some more of Lani's writings, and some of them concern me. I've tried to weigh what's best for the country, and what's best for her in all this. And because I told you that I would call you, I want you to know that I've decided to announce shortly that I'm withdrawing her nomination."

"Mr. President, I think that you're making a very serious mistake," I told him. "I hope you'll think about this some more."

"I've thought about it. I've been thinking about what's in the best interest of the country and what's in her best interest. And my decision was to withdraw her nomination. I have to be President of all the people and do what I think is right."

"Well, I understand, but I still think it's wrong, sir."

"I understand your position, Kweisi. I know you have to do what you have to do. But on this matter, I have to do what I have to do."

"I understand, Mr. President, I'm sorry that we've come to this point."

I thanked him for keeping his word and calling me. We said good night and hung up. A few minutes later, at about 9 P.M., I sat in the control room and watched President Clinton walk into a press conference and announce in a written statement that he was withdrawing Lani Guinier's nomination.

The Guinier fiasco was a breaking point for me, as well as for the Caucus. The day after Clinton's decision, I held a press conference, berating the President and his administration for its approach to a very serious problem. The American people deserved, at the very least, a public hearing of complaints against Guinier, and she deserved an opportunity to present her views and face her accusers. While she was gracious and respectful of the President's decision, I knew that she was feeling deeply hurt and abandoned by Clinton, who had purported to have her and the nation's best interests at heart.

It was clear that Clinton was afraid of an embarrassing political bloodbath, and that he'd placed his political interests above all else in the decision. Whatever trust and goodwill I harbored for Clinton was greatly diminished by how he handled the Guinier situation. "Wounds that deep take a long time to heal," I told reporters at the press conference, "and this is a very, very deep wound."

For the next few weeks, the President tried to make amends with the Caucus by extending invitations for us to meet with him at the White House. Each time, we flatly turned him down. We saw no reason to meet with him, or to pose for holy pictures at a social event with the President. It was a mockery to invite us to the White House after the damage had already been done. Within the Caucus, a more serious attitude had begun to take hold, particularly among the veteran lawmakers. They were tired of going over there and being serenaded. They had served under many presidents, and had been feted at the White House countless times. Now all they wanted was respect, and that desire was flowing strongly through the organization.

We rejected the President's invitations on three separate occasions. Holding firm to our position not to meet with Clinton may have struck some Beltway insiders as cutting off our noses to spite our faces, but it also won the Caucus a newfound respect on the streets. Folks from their districts were writing letters congratulating the Caucus for a valiant fight over such a serious issue. Indeed, the Caucus had been earning new spurs as a force in Washington politics with each issue after that line-item veto legislation.

When the Clinton administration introduced its five-year budget deficit plan, I was appointed the chief negotiator and met for weeks with (Democrats) Dan Rostenkowski of Illinois, Jack Brooks of Texas, Charlie Stenholm of Texas, Henry Waxman of California, and Dave Bonior of Michigan. We hammered out what eventually became the $500 billion deficit reduction plan for which the administration took credit. Up to that point there had been a lot of wrangling over how to reduce the budget deficit. The administration's original plan, however, had been totally contrary to what our constituencies wanted, in that it proposed an absolute freeze on Medicaid and Medicare. It also wiped out funding for a number of bread-and-butter programs, including women's services, infants' and older children's nutritional programs, and the Head Start program.

In the end, we negotiated empowerment zones, $20 billion worth of earned income tax credit, the Mickey Leland Child Hunger Relief Package, and several other issues that the Caucus put its stamp on as nonnegotiable items. It had required a lot of give and take, but every piece of legislation coming down the pike was negotiated with Caucus consultation. House Speaker Tom Foley agreed to confer with us on a regular basis at breakfast meetings, and have direct dialogue and input from us on bills that were coming up before the House. We forged a completely new relationship with Foley because he realized that in order to be an effective Speaker of the House, he needed our support.

It was a new Caucus and a new day. I didn't shy away from national debate in confronting my opponents and in facing urgent issues and hard questions. I held regular press conferences. There wasn't an issue that came up that the Caucus didn't address in a press conference.

When AT&T used a caricature of a gorilla on its company magazine as a depiction of symbolic reference to Africans, the

Caucus called AT&T President Robert E. Allen onto the carpet. We worked out an agreement that called for the company to issue a public apology, to increase their contracting with minority enterprises, and to increase their efforts in hiring and promoting blacks.

When the Black Coaches Association ran into the problems with the NCAA, over Proposition 48 and financial aid and recruiting, threatening to boycott the championships, they turned to the Caucus. I met with Georgetown basketball coach John Thompson and several others, and we put together a solidarity statement that told the NCAA, this is larger than black coaches, now you are talking about black legislators, who ultimately have a sway over legislation.

As the Caucus began to broaden its scope far beyond its traditional platform, I set up meetings with at least half of all national black organizations. I met with John Jacobs, the head of the Urban League, and agreed on a new working arrangement over the next two years. I established a dialogue with Dr. Benjamin Chavis, who had just taken over as executive director of the NAACP. While the NAACP and the Caucus mutually respected each other, up to now there had been no working relationship, and I believed it was important to begin one. I met with the National Black Police Officers organization, and a slew of other organizations who had been supportive of the Caucus but not linked in any productive way to our efforts.

Similarly, while it was fine for the Congressional Hispanic Caucus and the CBC to remain separate and distinct entities, there were many crucial issues that affected both groups. We needed a mechanism for discussing and standing together on critical issues—such as immigration, minority business, and affirmative action. We held a joint press conference stating as much, and announced that the two Caucuses were going to work closely together on issues from this point on. Congresspersons Jose Serrano, Nydia Velasquez, Louis Guiterez, Lucille Roybal-Allard, and others understood instinctively the power of working together. This sent shivers of fear through the hearts of a number of members of Congress who didn't look forward to contending with forty Black Caucus members who were strategically aligned as a united front with the nearly twenty members of the Hispanic Caucus.

Our message was finally getting out. Realizing C-SPAN's tremendous reach and its ability to fill in the blanks often left by the daily media, I decided to become a regular voice on the network. If an issue was distorted, I knew C-SPAN could help correct that misperception by airing our forty-minute press conference in its totality, which allowed viewers to make up their own minds. As the head of the Caucus, I was also being invited to appear on national news programs including *Nightline*, *Face the Nation*, *Meet the Press*, *Crossfire*, the *Today* show, *Good Morning America*, and *60 Minutes*.

While my media blitz was partly driven by a desire to let the American public know that there is another perspective to all these issues and to increase the Caucus's visibility, I also wanted to force the print media to cover the issues of African Americans. To some extent, airing our positions on the broadcast media made it more difficult for major print organizations to ignore us.

The Caucus members knew it was critical that the black perspective be included in any economic or social debate in Washington. While the Congressional Black Caucus strives to represent all the minorities in the country—blacks, Hispanics, Jews, whites, Asians, and other citizens—our primary motivation is to have a platform to discuss national issues from a black perspective. In order to do that, you have to go through the media. You cannot, in my opinion, be chairman of a group with that kind of numerical power and with that kind of legislative ability, and remain silent.

In 1970 the Congressional Black Caucus had thirteen members with zero committee chairmanships. By 1994 the CBC had forty members with seventeen chairmanships of some of the most powerful committees. With that kind of leverage, we'd have been fools not to take advantage of the system and make sure that it delivered for all our people, giving us equal treatment, equal opportunity, and equal access under the law.

Over those decades some issues had arisen that had deep and

grave implications for black people, yet there was no unanimity on how to vote on them. One such case was the 1994 crime bill, and habeas corpus reform. The generalities were that habeas corpus reform, if legislated wrongly, would inadvertently affect minorities, and that if you are going to have a major omnibus crime bill, that bill can't all be about punishment. There must be some measures covering prevention. The Caucus's role was to work toward putting in place a $9 billion prevention program (which ultimately was scaled back to $7 billion).

The other premise was that the Constitution is still the Constitution, and you can't just throw away search and seizure laws under the guise of wanting to arrest people. Search and seizure laws are crucial because in the name of trying to arrest people, doing away with a basic guaranteed constitutional right suggests that one day in the future, if you are white or black, and you happen to rub somebody the wrong way, they can simply come into your home or onto your property and trash the place. The Caucus tried to suggest to the American public that, while the impetus of the crime bill may have been "lock those black folks up," the long-term effect might have a very negative impact on the freedoms of all people in this country.

That is a difficult argument to get across when you're a black man, because the general case promulgated by detractors and opponents is that you're just making the system soft on criminals. This assertion, however, is false. We represent people living in crime-filled neighborhoods. We want to punish perpetrators of crime as much as or more than anyone. However, we also know that in many instances we're dealing with young lives. Prevention, therefore, must also be part of the solution. You can't just scrap certain constitutional rights, because those rights are there to protect all people. One day in the not too distant future, the absence of those rights may work to the disadvantage of all Americans. We nearly lost them in the Nixon years. We cannot let this happen again.

The Caucus also emphasized that in order to fully address the problem of crime, we must ban assault weapons, insure passage of the Brady Bill, as well as take a deeper look at how we license people to have guns, and how we sell bullets and other armaments in this country—and who profits! That argument proved to be very divisive because that assault weapons ban cost the seats of some Democrats in very conservative and rural districts, where the National Rifle Association's propaganda campaign made people believe that giving up your assault weapon today meant giving up your shotgun tomorrow, and your handguns soon after. Our contention was that while people ought to have a right to bear weapons in this country, nobody should have a right to bear an assault weapon. You don't need an assault rifle to hunt deer. Assault weapons are used to hunt people.

The Caucus was trying to bring a different perspective to the crime bill. On the one hand, we supported President Clinton's idea of adding 100,000 new policemen to the streets, and some of his other initiatives. On the other hand, we wanted to broaden the debate and temper the rush to solve the crime problem through solutions that had a disproportionate effect on African Americans and Hispanics.

Still, the Caucus did not walk in lockstep on all issues. Rather than being annoyed by this, I actually found it one of the most refreshing aspects of running the organization. During my campaign for chairman, part of my platform was that I was not seeking to run an organization of unanimity, because the days of unanimity had passed. I felt strongly that the best way for us to govern ourselves as a body would be through consensus. This creates an atmosphere of debate and dissent, but it avoids getting stalled in gridlock.

In some ways, the Caucus was as diverse in its political views and ideology as Congress itself. The freshman class of the 103rd Congress brought in members from the South and Midwest who harbored a strong rural perspective that had not previously existed within our ranks. Traditionally, Caucus members hailed from California and parts of the East Coast, and a few from the upper Midwest. So while the new members offered a new conservatism and regionalization to the mix, they also challenged us to expand our thinking on the issues that affected their constituents as part of our efforts to reach consensus.

Eventually, I could look at virtually any issue before it developed and know instantly whether it would cause problems within the Caucus based on regional or ideological differences. For example, an issue involving building the space station or a military compound was likely to draw favor from representatives from highly industrialized districts in Houston and some parts of California, where technology translates into jobs. Look at the B-2 bomber issue in the 103rd Congress, where seventeen members of the Caucus voted in support of the B-2. That would have been inconceivable years ago.

Opinions vary widely on the death penalty as well. Some hard-line traditionalists believe any form of killing is cruel and inhuman punishment, while others believe it could help reduce violence on city streets. On issues of gun control, Democrats Mike Espy of Mississippi and Sanford Bishop of Georgia both voted with the NRA. So you cannot assume that the Congressional Black Caucus is monolithic. That's a great fallacy. Black organizations have never been monolithic, and there is no reason to ever believe that our organizations should be.

15

POWER POLITICS

*O*N a sweltering August day in 1992, members of Trans-Africa held a demonstration against U.S. policy in Haiti in front of the White House. It was a great day of marching and chanting, and it attracted a broad range of activists from across the country. For several hours, I marched along with Trans-Africa president Randall Robinson, Congressman Charlie Rangel (D-New York), the late tennis pro and humanitarian Arthur Ashe, and film director Jonathan Demme. Even though the sun was hammering down on us, I was enjoying every moment of the demonstration, especially my long conversations with Arthur Ashe.

Looking quite cool that day, Arthur was sporting a white cotton shirt, white slacks, and a great big straw Panama hat. As we strolled together in the picket line, we spent a great deal of time discussing health care reform, from his own perspective as a person suffering from AIDS. He spoke about others who are infected with HIV who are running up against a health care system that can't provide for them because they lack the money and resources for proper care. He had some very good ideas about how to break through this, and asked me if I would take those ideas back to Dan Rostenkowski. Even though I didn't serve on the Ways and Means Committee, Arthur wanted me to use my clout as chairman of the Caucus to push Rosty. I assured him that I would.

As late afternoon approached, Randall Robinson cut into our conversation.

"Okay, that's going to do it," he said. "I think we made our point. Now, who's going to jail?"

When you participate in demonstrations in front of the White House, you can't stop moving. Once you stop moving, you're in violation of federal law, and the Park Police haul you off to jail.

Jonathan looked at Randall, who looked at Charlie, who looked at me.

"Look at Arthur," I said. "We have to go vote on the floor in about twenty minutes. So I guess you're going to jail."

"I guess I am," he said, smiling.

So Arthur stopped moving, violated the law, and went to jail that day. About a year later, I got arrested in a similar march, along with Ron Dellums, Donald Payne, Major Owens, Joe Kennedy, and Alcie Hastings. At various marches that year, several members of Congress were locked up for demonstrating against the U.S. policy of repatriation in Haiti.

To understand why I adopted such a strong confrontational posture on the issue of Haiti, it's important to know something about its history. In the last half of the twentieth century alone, the people of Haiti have been forced to live under the iron-fisted rule of one family, the Duvaliers. François "Papa Doc" Duvalier was overwhelmingly elected president in 1957, but by 1964, when he revised the Haitian constitution to make himself president for life, it had become very clear that he was simply another one of the autocratic despots who have dominated Haitian history.

Papa Doc had used military force to undermine the previous government and install himself in power. Then, to ensure his absolute power over the military, the police, the populace, and Haiti's resources, he created his own private army—the Tonton Macoutes, which means "bogeymen" in Creole—an elite, clandestine force of cold-blooded assassins who used violence, intimidation, and superstitious fear to maintain control. While the Haitian businesspeople supported the Duvalier regime because they thrived under it, the Haitian masses caught hell. After Duvalier's death in 1971, his nineteen-year-old son, Jean Claude "Baby Doc" Duvalier, took over.

By 1985, after nearly three decades of bloody Duvalier terrorism and corruption, the Haitian masses had had enough. It took an entire year of violent protests and demonstrations, backed up by international threats and the cutting off of foreign aid, to bring down the regime. In February of 1986, with the country near economic collapse and the government under siege, Jean Claude Duvalier fled into exile.

With Baby Doc out of the picture, Haiti was suddenly free of totalitarian rule, and the central question was whether democracy could finally take root and flourish in this troubled island nation. An aggressive grassroots push led to an election in November of 1987, but it was turned into a bloodbath by the Tonton Macoutes, who had not been forced to leave the country with the Duvaliers, and by the leaders of the army, who perceived themselves as Baby Doc's successors and refused to relinquish power. They mounted a campaign of murder and terror, and finally ambushed the polling stations, spawning a terrible massacre of Haitian men, women, and children. Yet again, the larger question arose—would Haiti ever become a democracy?

Few people are aware of Haiti's long historical struggle for peace and democracy. The Haitians were the first people in the Western Hemisphere to rise up against slavery, and Toussaint L'Ouverture, Haiti's great black liberator, is still worshiped by his people. After the French Revolution in 1789, there was growing unrest among the slaves in Haiti until, finally, Toussaint rose to lead his people to freedom against the French in 1794. Unfortunately, he was captured and died in a French prison. However, when Napoleon dispatched an army under General Charles Leclerc to put down the Haitian rebellion and restore the lucrative sugar trade in 1802, the French were defeated once and for all by the Haitians under Jean-Jacques Dessalines and Henri Christophe.

After the French were driven out, the whole island of Hispaniola was renamed Haiti, and declared its independence on January 1, 1804, making it the second-oldest independent nation in the Western Hemisphere, after the United States. Despite some two hundred years of oppression, in 1987 the Haitian people once again attempted to establish democracy. Trapped between two warring factions, they were slaughtered at polling places, and the election never took place. It was a sad, sad day for Haiti.

Finally, in December of 1990, after three years of coups and military rule, their economy collapsing amid political chaos, the Haitians found new hope in Father Jean Bertrand Aristide, a thirty-seven-year-old Catholic priest who preached a fiery message of liberation. A fascinating folklore surrounds Father Aristide. Because of his overwhelming popularity, the army kept trying to assassinate him during the fervent underground push to register citizens to vote. During the campaign, Aristide's presence at a secret voter registration site was betrayed, and the army showed up with machetes and machine guns and besieged the building. Many people in attendence were slaughtered, but somehow Aristide managed to escape—and to this day, nobody knows how. The myth that surrounds him says that, facing certain death in the crossfire of blaring machine guns, Aristide transformed himself into a rooster and darted off untouched. The people still believe that he possesses magical powers and the symbol of the rooster still holds sway in Haiti.

On December 16, 1990, Aristide was democratically elected President of Haiti, with 77 percent of the vote, which is more than any U.S. president ever received. However, during his first year in office, Father Aristide's manner and speech were so rash and impulsive that he alienated the establishment and the wealthy business community. Fearing that Aristide was fomenting an uprising against the elite class and promoting the redistribution of wealth, the wealthy and the military united in a campaign of gradual political destabilization. It culminated eight months later in a coup by a military junta, which forced Father Aristide into exile.

The world responded by condemning the military government and imposing trade sanctions in 1991. In early 1993 an arms and oil embargo was imposed, but it was lifted later in the year when the junta agreed to relinquish power to Aristide. After the junta reneged in April of 1994, the Clinton administration asked the UN Security Council to tighten the net around the Haitian regime—extend international sanctions, freeze overseas assets, and impose an international trade embargo. These deprivations, added to the violent repression of the regime, made life more and more unbearable, and thousands of Haitians were forced to flee their country.

For some years the Haitians had been taking to the sea in tiny boats, without proper food, water, or protection from the sun, and heading for the coast of Florida. Now there was a floodtide of refugees. Despite his campaign promises to the contrary, President Clinton decided to continue the Bush administration's policy of repatriation—of sending all these desperate people back home. He eased this a little in the summer of 1994 by enacting a policy of intercepting Haitian refugees at sea, and interviewing them aboard U.S. ships to decide whether they were candidates for political asylum.

At about the same time, there was growing pressure in Congress on Clinton to send U.S. troops to Haiti to establish peace and order, and to restore Aristide to the presidency. However, the political right was fighting such a move tooth and nail. They believed that Haiti held little strategic, political, or economic importance to the United States, and they viewed the Caribbean country as simply our hemispheric neighbor. Ignoring the fact that U.S. Marines occupied Haiti from 1915 to 1934, arch-conservatives in this country have blocked all subsequent notions of our intervention for years. Their attitude has been that they're just some crazy black folks down there, leave them alone. Haiti holds no economic or military interest for us; why waste taxpayer funds or endanger American lives?

This policy is deeply flawed and hypocritical. Poland was not in our strategic or military interest, but we invested a lot of money, time, blood, sweat, and tears there because we recognized that the success of democracy in Poland boded well for democracies everywhere. The best advertisement for democracy is the creation of a new democracy.

This was the case with Haiti. But there were racial overtones to the way this country viewed the situation in Haiti, and it created a thorny situation for me as chairman of the Caucus. In my heart of hearts, I knew that race was playing a key role in U.S. policy in Haiti, but I also knew that stating this fact would have triggered a chorus of critics screaming, "Race, race, race! Why does everything have to be cast as a racial issue? Can't we just discuss the politics in this?"

Meanwhile, GOP conservatives were having a field day on Haiti. Senator Jesse Helms, the senior Republican on the Foreign Relations Committee, read a litany of sins supposedly committed by Aristide. Aristide the madman. Aristide the closet communist. Republican senator John McCain of Arizona compared the priest to Hitler. Senator Dole of Kansas warned against spilling American blood to force a democracy on Haiti. Some Washington pundits said Clinton's Haitian policy was an olive branch to the Caucus and the African American community in the wake of the Guinier disaster. The papers were full of leaks. One report had the CIA bankrolling the political foes of Aristide. The CIA and the conservative congressional wing countered with a release saying that Aristide was emotionally unstable and consumed daily more than ten different types of medications to control his moods. This was political hardball at its worst.

At press conferences, reporters would ask me, "Congressman, do you think that this is just happening because they are black people?"

I would respond by saying, "Well, I don't know. But it's my guess that if we had a nation of white people in Haiti, the U.S. would probably have a different posture." I'd let them draw their own conclusions, but I certainly wasn't going to be the one to bring race into the debate only to wind up on the defensive.

However, if you were a Haitian who put together a little raft, stayed out on the sea for three weeks and got baked and parched, and crawled up on the shore of Miami half-alive, you got turned around and shipped back out—it was called repatriation. You can draw your own conclusions.

In September of 1994, the Clinton administration finally sent U.S. armed forces to Haiti. President Clinton faced the dilemma during that period of whether to accept my invitation to attend a Caucus dinner. There were some in his administration who didn't think it was appropriate for him to come out during the intense strategic military planning negotiations that had Jimmy Carter, Colin Powell, and former congressman Bill Gray working over in Haiti. Our troops were on alert. We had ships all around Haiti. The Marines were on alert. The feeling was that Clinton should appear presidential and reflective to the American public during this foreign policy crisis. It wouldn't be politic for him to be seen hanging out at some big gathering.

However, Clinton accepted our invitation to attend. In two months, my two-year term as head of the Black Caucus would end, and I was pleased that the President attended this culminating event of my tenure. In my speech that night, I directed my remarks to him.

"We've had our battles, Mr. President," I said. "We've not agreed on a lot of issues, but I've always tried to be a straight shooter. I came directly at you. I was at times your biggest detractor and your biggest supporter. I look forward to working with you in the future. But I'm always going to speak out against what I think is wrong. And even though we argue, as family members sometimes do, the Caucus wishes you the best of luck, as our President."

I went back and sat down with him. We shook hands, and he thanked me for my remarks. What I remember most about the night, though, is that the President didn't do a lot of smiling. I'm sure he had been instructed to avoid being photographed with a smile on his face, because of the tremendous foreign policy crisis in Haiti. Now and then, he'd lean over and talk to me and flash a quick smile. But when he took the stage, and while he was greeting people, he wore a solemn, respectful look. On the other hand, I smiled most of that evening, knowing that the people of Haiti might finally get a shot at democracy.

A couple of weeks later, in early October, the President addressed the nation one evening from the Oval Office to announce that he had given the order for our Armed Services to invade Haiti. The planes had just taken off, as all of America held its breath.

When the televised address ended, I immediately called the White House. The President came on the line minutes later.

"Mr. President," I said, "what you've just done took a lot of courage and leadership. I pray to God for the safety of our troops and their families. And I pray tonight for you as well."

"Yeah," he answered in a haunting and subdued voice, "God bless us. . . . God bless all."

While minorities will only benefit from fostering a broad base of political views, I strongly believe certain issues demand that we move together in a decisive and cohesive fashion toward a resolution. We must know when to put aside our differences and develop a single, unified strategy that will benefit all the people of our race. One of those issues is the killing that plagues our neighborhoods.

In 1994, I began organizing a leadership summit that would focus on one simple issue: "Stop the Killing." It's hardly a novel concept—many black organizations have attempted to launch programs that address the issue of violence in our communities. The problem has been that the efforts were unconnected. It was important that real and perceived differences in the black community be put aside so that we could finally form the kind of alliances that I knew we needed to be able to make a difference. I saw a lot of splintered efforts. Not that they were weak, but they weren't connected with one another. The NAACP was working over here, the Urban League was pursuing their agenda over there, while the Congressional Black Caucus had its own program. Add to this the efforts of the Nation of Islam, the Rainbow Coalition, African American fraternities and sororities, and the black churches.

There were all these power bases emitting separate and distinct energies toward the same objective. I figured that we could make more headway on the issue of violence if all these groups joined together for a common goal, while agreeing to let each group maintain its general and separate autonomy. The majority of people are looking for direction and wondering why there is so much conflict and disunity at the top of the leadership ranks.

I wanted to prove that we could cast aside all of our differences and recognize that, at least on this one critical national issue, we could move together as one.

A summit was held in September of 1994 in Washington, D.C., as a part of the CBC's annual Legislative Weekend. A month prior to that had been the thirty-first anniversary of the historic March on Washington for civil rights. The anniversary celebration had been cloaked in controversy because the Nation of Islam had been invited and then disinvited. The word on the street was that the Nation of Islam had been asked not to attend the march because the Jewish community had put pressure on the NAACP, which in conjunction with a number of other groups was a major sponsor of the event. Whether you agreed with the Muslim philosophy or not, when the Nation of Islam was disinvited, people were upset. Many decided not to participate because they believed the event was not truly designed to uplift the larger African American community, but that it was staged and contrived.

There was a certain irony to this flap because the first March on Washington had had its share of infighting, too. In one of Malcolm X's speeches, he talks about how Roy Wilkins and others were going to pull out of the march because certain parties were trying to dictate how, where, and why they ought to march. Thirty years later, the same controversy reared its head all over again—different organizations and different players, but the same charges. The Rainbow Coalition was off in its direction. The Congressional Black Caucus, bigger and badder than ever, was off in its direction. The idea of the summit conference was to galvanize all our efforts into one problem-solving strategy.

I invited Maxine Waters of California, Louis Farrakhan, Jesse Jackson, and Ben Chavis to participate on the second day of the summit panel. I wanted Angela Davis and Anita Hill, but neither could attend. *ABC News* anchor Carole Simpson was our moderator.

Many have asked me whether it was difficult convincing Farrakhan, Jesse Jackson, and Ben Chavis to all agree to sit together. It was not. I invited them all in my position as chairman of the

Congressional Black Caucus. And while the CBC never had a great working relationship with the Nation of Islam, there was at least a respectful relationship. Minister Farrakhan understood the overall thrust of the summit, while he also recognized that many members of the Caucus disagreed passionately with some of his positions. But that wasn't the issue with him. To his credit, on that day, he was focused on the larger issue of taking an opportunity to put aside those differences, and dealing with the tremendously high homicide rates in our communities.

But if that was our collective motivation when the summit began, it quickly changed the moment panel members got their turn at the microphone. Tensions began flaring across the table. Farrakhan and Jesse were verbally jousting, while Chavis was essentially denying that the NAACP had disinvited Farrakhan and the Nation of Islam to the anniversary celebration. He offered an apology to the Nation of Islam, then turned around and accused Farrakhan of wrongheadedly suggesting without evidence that the NAACP had done that. He insisted on an apology from Farrakhan. It started out a mess, but Carol and Maxine helped to keep things focused. In the end, tempers cooled and we managed to generate some constructive dialogue, particularly with the large audience in attendance.

However, the real trouble was just beginning. I got back on the microphone in summation and announced that from this point on, just as the Congressional Black Caucus had entered into a sacred working covenant with the NAACP, we would now enter that same covenant with the Nation of Islam, with the Rainbow Coalition, with black churches, fraternities, and sororities, with synagogues throughout our nation, and with anybody else who would be willing to come forward and work with us to stop the killing in our communities.

The only part of my statement that the press heard that afternoon was that we were entering a covenant with the Nation of Islam. I thought I had gotten some reactionary press on Lani Guinier and Haiti, but this was a different kind of reaction— angrier and more explosive than I would ever have imagined. I've played the tape of my speech back at least two dozen times and listened to my full statement, and each time I wondered how it was that reporters failed to mention the desire to have that same covenant with churches and synagogues or black fraternities and sororities or the NAACP or the Rainbow Coalition. They focused only on the Nation of Islam.

I got all sorts of bad press. *The New York Times* claimed on its editorial page that the Congressional Black Caucus had had its pockets picked by Louis Farrakhan. Other columnists and editorials in papers across the country denounced us for lying down with the devil and selling our souls. The interesting aspect of this, though, was that the masses of black people across the country were quite pleased with what had happened. They cheered the display of unity, and the public airing of problems that paved the way for a new willingness to work together, even though most rejected any hint of anti-semetic rhetoric.

Despite this barrage of criticism, I held firm to my position that the summit did not mean that the Caucus embraced or endorsed the policies of any group. I reminded people that many of us have publicly taken completely different positions and have criticized the policies of Farrakhan, but that the summit was not about our differences. It was about stopping the killing and restoring our communities, and how we could best achieve that. The Caucus continued to work on that issue with the Nation of Islam and other groups, and I caught a lot of hell for it. The Black Caucus was blamed by people who thought that we were out here only working on their mainstream agenda, and not understanding that we were working on our own issues and trying to figure out a way to deal with the problems in our communities.

The cooperation continued for several months until Khalid Abdul Muhammad, a national spokesman for the Nation of Islam, made some comments which were absolutely racist, sexist, anti-Semitic, anti-Catholic, and anti-black. All of us involved in the summit thought these statements were completely deplorable, and Chavis of the NAACP was the first to condemn the speech publicly. I too responded and said that Muhammad's remarks were racist, sexist, anti-Semitic, anti-Catholic, anti-black, and anti-human.

Khalid Muhammad was an angry man whose unbridled hatred of anyone who did not agree with his positions made him persona non grata even with many of those who supported the Nation of Islam. Farrakhan then announced that he was taking action against Muhammad and would be demoting him from his perch as a national spokesperson.

Shortly after Khalid Muhammad's speech, I wrote to Farrakhan asking, quite frankly, for his take on all this. Personally, I did not buy into the media's saying that Muhammad was speaking for Farrakhan. I wanted Farrakhan, in his own words, to tell me what was going on. I really needed a response because my Caucus members were upset, and quite a few had begun blaming me for entering into this covenant with the Nation of Islam. They accused me of speaking on my own. They were washing their hands of the situation and taking the position that the Caucus had never endorsed this to begin with. I was left to carry the burden of this one.

After several days, Farrakhan had still not responded to my letter, and this only added fuel to the fire raging around me. Caucus members were asking me why he hadn't written back, and how much time were we expected to wait for a response? Farrakhan is not tough to get on the phone, but I didn't want a phone response—I needed something in writing. That's the official way you handle matters as important as this, and I knew the membership needed a written statement.

Eleven days passed before Farrakhan's response arrived. Even worse, his response was far from satisfactory to many Caucus members. Basically, the letter told us to watch his press conference the following day to learn his response to this situation. In the minds of some, that was a nonresponse, and they were livid. I was told that as chairman of the Caucus I should hold a press conference and announce that there was no covenant with the Nation of Islam, and no relationship from here on out. I couldn't argue with my members, because that was the consensus. And I govern by consensus.

That afternoon in February, I went out and held a nationally televised press conference all alone. None of the Caucus members showed up for the reading of the statement or the questions that followed. The Caucus never had one-person press conferences, but on that day and on that issue, it was just me.

In the end, Farrakhan came out and stated in a Washington, D.C. press conference that he was disappointed with what had transpired and that Muhammad's comments were *not* the positions in keeping with the teachings of Allah.

Some have asked me whether I felt abandoned by the Caucus. I cannot say I did because there was tremendous pressure brought to bear on that issue by the Jewish community, the larger white community, and some in the black community. I was inundated with requests for information from the media. My workdays were being gobbled up by this one issue.

I met with national Jewish groups from around the country, from the Anti-Defamation League to the National Jewish Congress to the rabbis in my district. I told each of them how I felt, that the Congressional Black Caucus had not turned its back on them, that we hold a strong belief that anti-Semitism is wrong. We deplore it. I told them that they didn't have to take my word for it—just check our record. It was replete with instances of our support for Israel. I explained that in this particular instance we have a problem in our community, that our young children are dying, our seniors are fearful for their lives. We are losing an entire generation of our children. I told these groups that, as a race, black people in the United States have to deal with this. There is nothing you can do about this issue, I reminded them. You are our allies, and we get along. But this is our problem and we have to deal with it ourselves. If that meant working with the Muslims in our community, then so be it.

I emphasized that the fact that black people are trying to develop a degree of unity in our communities does not mean that we buy into any specific organization's position. It's simply that we recognize that there are many powerful groups that affect people in our community and that if we can pull all of them together on this one issue, we might have a better chance of success. While I think many of the Jewish groups understood this, they complained that the summit legitimized Farrakhan. My position was that Farrakhan was already legitimate in the black community, whether we wanted him to be or not. All Americans came to recognize as much on October 16, 1995, with the Million Man March.

On November 8, 1994, the lights suddenly went out. That day, the Republican Party won control of the Congress.

In almost cataclysmic proportions, the convergence of angry white men, low voter turnout, and the "new nigger syndrome" caused the earth to move off its axis. "Republican Landslide" was how *The New York Times* labeled it. "Republicans End 40 Years of Democratic Control" bannered the *Los Angeles Times*. "Republicans Win Back House" wrote *The Washington Post*.

For Newt Gingrich, Dick Armey, and their camp of hard-line conservatives, it was soon to become the best of times. With all the pomp and circumstance they could muster, the Republicans announced their "Contract with America." Not long before the election, a Democratic publication had circulated around congressional offices featuring a full-page black-and-white photo of Gingrich and Armey on a liquor bottle in the style of the Wild West with the caption "Snake Oil Salesmen" below it. America needed another promissory note. Who would have expected the American public to buy their brand of mischief? I certainly did not.

The GOP wasted little time flexing its newfound muscles. Shortly after taking office, the party voted to end funding for the Congressional Black and Hispanic Caucuses. Two weeks later, the effort to abolish affirmative action suddenly became a de facto "Contract" item for the Republicans. Two months after that, welfare reform became a catchall for every negative stereotype the GOP felt it was worth saving the taxpayer from.

The Republicans were finally having their day in the sun, and I was neither surprised nor thrown off guard by their full-throttle push to dismantle the long legacy of Democratic rule. I had expected them to kick butt and take names. When you're holding the winning hand in Washington, it's not the time for modesty or second-guessing. The point is to use your clout to play your opponents right under the table. You don't apologize for it. You don't make excuses for it. You don't even have to think about it. For this small moment in history, at least, you are running the table in the rough and tumble of power politics.

The new Republican majority decided early on that they didn't want forty renegade Caucus members impeding their legislative initiatives. Before the 1994 elections, seventeen of the Caucus members were chairmen of either full committees or subcommittees. When the House switched overnight to Republican rule, the repercussions were profound. We lost all seventeen chairmanships in the process. African Americans had worked so hard to elect black members of the Congress over the preceding four decades, and had rewarded the performance of their representatives by reelecting them time and again. Congressmen like John Conyers, Jr., Lou Stokes, Charlie Rangel, Ron Dellums, and Bill Clay (D-Missouri) shot straight up the seniority pole, not unlike their white counterparts such as Strom Thurmond or Jesse Helms. If you get reelected enough times, the seniority system begins to work for you and your community.

The fact that the Republicans were in the majority and that we had lost our seventeen chairmanships wasn't enough. Somebody got the bright idea that if you create and pass new rules saying no legislative service organization can occupy space in a federal building, and that members of Congress cannot contribute out of their official accounts to run such an organization, that would mean the death of the Caucus.

They were wrong. The GOP did manage to wipe out our five staffers, take away our office space, and strip our funding. But they forgot that the Caucus had established a foundation. The Congressional Black Caucus Foundation was the body with the money, not the Caucus itself.

But the fight wasn't over. Someone got the bright idea that they should go after the Foundation. The House passed a rule that no member of Congress could work with or be a member of any outside foundation that they had created. It looked as though they were really going to wipe us out this time. But the trouble with their new approach was that the Congressional Black Caucus Foundation hadn't been created by the members of the Caucus, but rather by an outside group that wanted to be supportive of the Caucus. So the Republicans had spent all this time passing new rules, only to discover that the rules didn't apply to us. At a press conference, held jointly with the Hispanic Congressional Caucus, I had to remind Republicans that they couldn't destroy us because they didn't create us.

While this was all relatively humorous, the new political reality we were facing was quite troubling. Once again, we had become the minority within the minority, and all our efforts lost, no matter what the legislation. If I'd learned anything growing up on the streets, it was that the fight isn't over until it's over. My hands have yet to be raised in surrender. Although bloodied, I remained unbroken.

"When God closes one door," Mama would say, "He always opens another."

● ● ●

At the dawning of a new day, the young man sees it as just another day, but the mature man sees it as another chance. On this cool October morning in 1995, with the symbolic and picturesque grandeur of the Mall in Washington, D.C., as the backdrop I, like a million others, instinctively knew that this breaking day would be different.

A slight chill hung in the air while the early morning dew glistened on the grass and the sun arched upward over the marble memorials to Washington, Jefferson, and Lincoln. A cloudless sky heralded the promise of an almost perfect day, and, in many respects, it would be.

That day, the massive reflecting pool would reveal the faces of men, inquisitive and thoughtful, black and real. The converging of the brethren had begun even earlier than most had imagined. Soon there would be a sea of bodies locked together by fate—old and young, weak and strong. What had drawn them was their love of each other and love for our communities.

No scriptwriter could have written the scenario for the Million Man March. Its characters were real, their emotions were powerful, and their energy was high. I stood there, freely absorbing the feeling that rushed through my mind and soul. In just a few hours, more than a million men would converge here for what was to become one of the largest demonstrations of solidarity and commitment in the nation's history. In my address to those gathered I would refer to them as the "problem solvers." There, in the deep morning stillness, I could almost hear the rumbling of their footsteps. They had come to the nation's capitol from every city, town, and hamlet across America—marching, walking, riding, flying. For the next twelve hours they would bask in the curiosity of the world's spotlight, and be forever changed because of it.

My sons Donald, Michael, and Keith had accompanied me. Like their father, they had sensed the history of the moment and had chosen not to miss it. We'd spoken for months about the march and the need for black men to come together under the banner of commitment. They, like I, anguished over the deep problems that continued to beset our communities. The dangerous waters that some of us had managed to navigate in our respective generations continued to wash too many others overboard. Standing there with my sons at my side, I thanked God for making a way out of no way, for delivering them as he had delivered me, through the uncertainty of childhood and the risks of adolescence. Now they stood as men, rooted in purpose and connected to the moment.

But an even more powerful symbol of this moment was the miracle of the man who sat quietly near me. I felt the entire spirit of the march resonating from Julius James. He was 109 years old, and he had traveled to the march from Ocala, Florida, brought here with tender care by a great-great relative. As he lifted his wrinkled eyelids to glance into my eyes, the history of a century flashed quickly but clearly before me. From the day he was born in 1886, Mr. James's life had been one of pain and endurance. His hands were rough and gnarled from nearly a century of farming okra and peanuts. His back was bent from decades of tending to hogs and cattle. He had grown up on the fifty-nine-acre farm that had been acquired by his grandparents shortly after they were freed from slavery. Outliving his brothers and sisters, his wife and his only son, this extraordinary man—

known affectionately as "Uncle Gud"—still lived in the same flat-board house that he was raised in.

Now here he was before me. Breathing slowly, yet content-edly, with the help of an oxygen tube that curled around his ears and rested just under his nose; his wheelchair was like a chariot, a throne, and he was like an ancient god. In that moment, Julius James embodied the legacy of struggle, courage, and triumph for us all. He sat erect, his lanky, angular body almost hidden in the blankets that protected him from the crisp morning chill. Although the journey to Washington had taken a toll on him, his eyes said something else. Through the blue haze of cataracts, Mr. James peered intently at the throngs of black faces that swelled just below us, then across the mall toward the Lincoln Memorial.

The sun broke through and warmed his dark, leathery face, and he managed to smile with a pride unbroken. "He is so happy," said the man who had brought him. "On the way here, he told me, `I just want to be there. I just want to be there before I die.'"

It is men like Julius James who have kept our struggle alive. His long journey—our long journey—for equality has been marked by roadblocks and detours. But we continue to find our way. My own journey had begun in poverty and had taken me through aimlessness, trouble, and pain. However, I now realized that it was the journey itself that made me the man I have become. Standing in the shadow of Julius James, with my sons at my side, the connection I felt with this gathering of brothers was awesome. It was all hitting home in a dozen different ways. The emotions came fast, but the memories came faster. How I wished that my friend Gary, now a successful businessman in Florida, and Mr. Smitty, and Arnette Evans could be here. How I longed for my father's assurance.

For some reason now I was remembering how God's deliver-ance had found me one night, long since forgotten, racked with fever and twisted with pain. I remembered Mama praying to God for a miracle. I recalled that Dr. Wade—with the mysterious black bag he carried like an extension of his arm—found nothing to break my fever. Once again I sensed the shadow his hulking figure cast over me as he put on his hat to leave. Slowly turning to look down at me, he all but declared my death imminent.

That was the night the spirits of the ancestors spoke to Mama of slave remedies and slave cures, the night when sliced potatoes and prayer somehow brought forth a miracle. For whatever reason, I, her firstborn, was spared. I had received the blessing of life and, along with it, the struggle to make it work. There would be no free ride.

With the crowd expanding around me and fanning out from the forbidding stone steps of the Capitol, the words of historian Carter G. Woodson echoed and reverberated within me: "The race needs workers," he said. "If we can finally succeed in translating the idea of leadership into that of service, we may find it possible to lift the Negro to a higher level."[7]

I knew that beneath the pageantry of a million black faces gathered together lay a deep yearning within us all to be of service to our community. While many would try to divide us, none would succeed. On that day we had come to heed the lessons of the past. In the spirit of 109-year-old Julius James, and generations still unborn, we marched passionately.

We cheered. We listened. We talked. We hugged. And for the first time in years, many of us cried. As the Bible foretold: "The old men did prophesy, and the young men dreamed dreams." We affirmed the values in our own lives and in the lives of our children. And we promised to work together for a better world.

Later, as the autumn sun descended over the Potomac and the crowd began to disperse, I savored this gift of renewal. The seemingly unending evolution of time had brought with it yet again a possibility of great hope. Like the others who had come together that day, I clutched it, and knew I would never let it go.

16

A NEW DAY BEGUN

*O*N the night of December 8, 1995, I checked into the Wyndham Bristol Hotel in Washington, D.C., under the assumed name of Charles Newday. The name reflected the culmination of Operation Newday, a strategic campaign that was orchestrating the next evolutionary shift in my life. Two months earlier, on a blustery October evening, I had gotten yet another call from Charles Tribbett, an executive with the New York–based international search firm of Russell Reynolds Associates.

Tribbett had first called me in the late summer to ask if there was anyone in particular I would recommend as a candidate for the long-vacant position of executive director of the NAACP. The organization had been leaderless since the 1994 ouster of Dr. Benjamin Chavis following charges of sexual and administrative impropriety.

Benjamin Chavis had been a friend, and I was all too familiar with the pain and agony that matter had caused both him and the organization. It was clear that finding a successor of merit and caliber would prove to be a daunting task given the dire straits the NAACP was in. The civil rights organization was struggling with a deficit of close to four million dollars; there had been two retrenchments of staff at the national headquarters; and meeting the monthly payrolls was becoming increasingly difficult. For over a year, the national media had been chronicling this prestigious organization's downward spiral, and people across the nation were openly questioning its relevance and continued viability.

To the NAACP's credit, however, the board of directors had elected Myrlie Evers-Williams as its new chairperson earlier that same year by one vote. Her election signaled a break from the past and provided one last hope for those who believed in the organization's historic mission and purpose.

Since I was aware of all this, my response to Tribbett's earlier question had been guarded. I couldn't think of anyone outside the organization who would be willing to leave a secure position for the uncertainty of the NAACP. But I could think of someone inside the organization who I knew, without reservation, would be an ideal choice. I told Tribbett that I thought Wade Henderson, director of the NAACP's Washington Bureau, would be perfect to run the organization. We had worked closely on Capitol Hill, and I knew he was balanced in his approach, thoughtful on the larger issues of governance, and possessed of a temperament that was suited to compromise yet had the tenacity he would need to endure struggle.

I thought little more about its search until I received Tribbett's second call. This time he didn't have a question; he had an offer. It seemed that throughout the months of his search, my name had continually come up in his discussions with focus groups and government, religious, and business leaders.

He'd called to request a meeting—not to seek a commitment, simply to lay out the facts. "That's very kind of you," I responded, "But I already have a job, and one that I like. Although I love the NAACP and would do anything to help save it, there are at least a dozen people more qualified and more available than I am," I said.

"We've met with twice that number already," he replied. "And

I wouldn't be doing my job if I didn't at least attempt to meet with you."

Then he said something that made his request almost impossible to turn down. "I think it's important for you to know that Judge A. Leon Higginbotham is the person appointed to head this search team, and the meeting is his idea as much as it is mine."

Judge Higginbotham heads the list of individuals I hold in the highest regard. He represents the epitome of excellence and the manifestation of sheer will. The son of a domestic servant and a laborer, he escaped a Trenton ghetto to emerge as a giant of jurisprudence. His passionate pursuit of justice and equality is legendary. He had been an assistant district attorney and special deputy state attorney general, and he had risen through the ranks and sat on the bench as a federal district judge, a U.S. Court of Appeals magistrate, and finally the chief justice of the Court of Appeals. Early in 1995, having completed a three-decade tenure as the nation's longest serving federal judge, Judge Higginbotham had been awarded the Presidential Medal of Freedom, the nation's highest civilian honor. Less than a year later, in appreciation of his integrity, vision, objectivity, generosity, compassion, and eloquence, the NAACP would bestow upon him its highest honor, the Spingarn Medal.

After hearing that the judge had requested this meeting, I quickly agreed. A few days later, we met at the St. James hotel in Washington, D.C., to begin what would become a series of talks that took place in Washington, New York, and Baltimore. Lenny Springs, chairman of the NAACP's Special Contribution Fund, and Charles Tribbett joined Judge Higginbotham at that first meeting. The later ones would include Myrlie Evers-Williams and Earl Graves, publisher of *Black Enterprise* magazine.

Earl and I were alumni of Morgan State University. In our work together on university projects I had developed an appreciation of his candor and honesty, and I considered him a friend. Once the discussions picked up, it was clear to me that I needed an honest broker outside of the process to offer assessments and opinions. Earl was my choice for that role. "Big brother," as I affectionately called him, was to spend many more hours than he ever imagined working to close the negotiations.

Myrlie, on the other hand, was a page of living history. A woman of great strength and dignity, she would bring to bear her great powers of persuasion, rooted in her deep sense of her own destiny.

At that first meeting, Judge Higginbotham addressed me with unrestrained candor. "We all have the utmost respect for you, and none of us want to mislead you or to misguide you about this," he said in his dramatic voice. "We feel very strongly, very strongly, that not only can this organization survive but that it can thrive again. This is an American institution, and it can become the premiere organization it once was."

I listened intently, watching the impassive faces of Tribbett and Springs.

"The NAACP must survive," said the judge in thundering tones that stirred something in my chest. "We also believe that there are very few people who could lead this organization in a way that could take it into the next century; who could assure its ability to exist while making it the sort of organization that all Americans— black, white, Hispanic, and Asian—could be proud of."

He took a sip of water from his glass, then continued. "I'm not trying to give you a big head, but you're the person we want."

Hearing these words come from a man I so admired was a humbling experience. And the others said, "We concur."

However, the judge wasn't done yet. "When I got married," he continued, "I sat down with my wife and said, `Look, I know that you're good for me. The question is, Am I good for you?' " A pause for effect. "I know, my friend, that you would be good for the NAACP. But you also have to ask yourself whether the NAACP would be good for you. And if the answer is yes, then we can make that happen because we believe that you're the person for this position."

I was impressed with the Judge's candor during this round of talks, which lasted close to two hours. There had been an overall willingness to share information while framing the context of the offer in a frank, honest manner, all of which suggested a grave seriousness in the desire to turn this beleaguered organization around.

Most impressive was the larger historical context in which the offer was being made—at a time when African Americans were facing a reactionary Supreme Court and a mean-spirited Congress that was aggressively attempting to dismantle the gains made by minorities and others in this country over the years. On a closer-to-home scale, the offer came at a time when crime, low self-esteem, drug abuse, and health problems were running rampant in our communities across the country.

Judge Higginbotham's words echoed in my mind that night as I considered their offer. Would this move be good for me? Was it the right time for such a move? Leaving Congress and taking myself out of the congressional loop was a very tough decision to make. Many of my congressional colleagues had left to pursue opportunities in lobbying or in the corporate or business realms. In any of these arenas, our skills and contacts were considered valuable and were much sought after.

Some of my closest friends looked at this offer as a roll of the dice. Many also wondered if moving to the NAACP would take me out of the halls of power where policy-setting decisions were made. Although as head of the NAACP I would still be dealing with Congress and the White House, I would nevertheless be sacrificing the ability to make things happen—for a situation with no guarantees.

But then, when had I ever lived with guarantees? Through storms, passages, and sunlight, mine has been a life of blessings, not a life of guarantees—a life of second chances and of going that second mile.

The issue about whether I would be sacrificing power was relative, for I now had to define it against a different reality. Power is earned or given, you can't lose it as if it were a coin. While serving in Congress had offered me a chance to help enact legislation on a national scale, I still represented my Baltimore constituency. The NAACP would offer me the opportunity to fight for the rights of all people of color, free of partisan wrangling. This would allow me to make the kind of impact I wanted to leave as my legacy to those who would come after.

I felt myself racing toward a new door that was opening just as an old one was closing. This offer to step out on faith called me, and I could not easily dismiss it. Leaving Congress for the unknown future of the NAACP was the mother of all challenges. But I saw it as a way for me to follow the path that had been set before me years ago and from which I had once strayed. I would not stray again. How could I continue my lifelong stand for justice and equality for all people and not answer this call, no matter what the risks? My life has always been fueled by challenge, by taking risks. Guiding the NAACP back to its own true path as a voice of truth and clarity, as the power point of unity for our embattled communities, would be a Herculean task, but one I could not refuse.

I became convinced that, at this point in time, I could best affect social, economic, and political change on the broader capacity that the NAACP represents.

Over the next two weeks I devoured every book I could on the NAACP's trials and triumphs, especially the memoirs penned by its former illustrious directors: *Along This Way* by James Weldon Johnson; *A Man Called White* by Walter White; and *Standing Fast* by Roy Wilkins. Many of my future challenges would be very similar to the ones faced by my predecessors. Over the years I had learned to profit from the lessons of history.

The accomplishments of the NAACP during some of the bleakest moments in this nation's racial history are still remarkable. From its origins in 1905 as the Niagara Movement to its official emergence in 1909 as the National Association for the Advancement of Colored People—the nation's first civil rights organization—this coalition of black intellectuals and white progressives always tackled the toughest issues, such as lynching and race riots. W.E.B. Du Bois's scathing editorials in *The Crisis* never flinched when telling the truth about America's reluctance to guarantee its black citizens the rights promised in the Constitution and the Bill of Rights. In 1917, two years after D. W. Griffith made his blatantly racist film, *The Birth of a Nation*, the NAACP led a march down New York City's Fifth Avenue to protest segregation and Jim Crow laws. During World War I, it successfully opposed segregated boot camps. Possibly the organization's crowning moment came in 1954 when a group of NAACP attorneys, headed by Thurgood Marshall, won the *Brown v. Board of Education of Topeka, Kansas* decision in the U.S. Supreme Court that put an end to "separate but equal" Jim Crow laws.

In almost ninety years of existence, the NAACP has never abandoned its mission or mandate. During the dangerous days of the civil rights movement, the NAACP was on hand, in the person of Executive Director Roy Wilkins, whenever it was needed. Under the leadership of Ben Hooks, the organization often slugged it out with the Reagan-Bush regimes as a major player in the Leadership Conference on Civil Rights. The NAACP worked hard to secure the Voting Rights Acts of 1982, despite stiff opposition from hard-line conservatives. It also did its part in the campaign to buttress the cause of affirmative action with the passage of the Civil Rights Act of 1991. In 1994, the association won a $100 million settlement from the government in a Minneapolis public housing discrimination lawsuit.

Critics have accused some of the organization's recent efforts on Capitol Hill of being tame and timid and too focused on legislative matters. Another criticism is that the NAACP is out of touch with today's social and racial challenges and that it is not speaking for the widest range of people within the African American community. Unlike many of these critics, I never thought that the NAACP's efforts were too legislative, although I thought some of its problems may have come from being too disconnected from our young people and a bit complacent about a number of critical issues.

However, these problems were inevitable, considering that the organization in many respects had become a rudderless ship. There had been no one at the helm since Chavis's ouster. Earl Shinhoster had been named acting executive director, but he was given little power to facilitate real change. Operating by committee the organization had no sense of direction. It was floundering, often paralyzed and unable to reach consensus.

Over and over again I replayed the seemingly endless series of meetings and conference calls of the past few weeks and the tension and urgency of those early encounters. I had not been looking to leave Congress, and I had made that clear from the start. Still, I understood that the NAACP desperately needed to restore its sense of purpose, credibility, and vitality. Even more, I realized that many of the converging social and political forces that had spurred the organization's formation nearly ninety years ago in a Manhattan apartment were not all that different from the forces currently at work in America. Racism, sexism, and anti-Semitism were on the rise. Xenophobia against immigrants, religious intolerance, and hate crimes had given way to a new and more malevolent form of bigotry.

The members of the search team understood that they needed to find someone who was outside of the association's traditional leadership pool and that they needed to find someone who would act as a unifying force to heal the widening rift between the national office and the branches.

This was no public relations ploy—either for me or the NAACP. The fate of the troubled organization was at stake. After my name was advanced I met with the judge and Myrlie Evers-Willliams in Baltimore, where a very frank exchange took place. She gave me a no-nonsense explanation of why she thought the organization could not afford to accept a mediocre candidate and why in her opinion I was the best person for the job. Mrs. Evers-Williams was firm and focused, but honest and caring. She said that, of all the things she had fought for, the salvation of the NAACP was the most important.

Myrlie had secured the services of two outstanding treasurers and had to put together a core group of supporters on the board. But she wanted more and was determined not to rest until every problem had been addressed. Now she needed a CEO, and she felt I was the right person for the job. We agreed to carry on the discussions quietly, out of the long reach of the press. Following the bloodletting in the Chavis affair, it was concluded that more could be accomplished without the scrutiny of the media. Unwelcome publicity could cripple the search process. I was thankful for the confidentiality factor because I was still a sitting member of Congress and because I hadn't sought out the NAACP, although as a life member and a strong supporter, I was deeply concerned about its future. All my life I had held only respect for the organization, and during my career in public service I had supported its causes in every way possible.

. My family was supportive throughout the entire decision . process, my sisters in particular stood by me. I discussed the NAACP offer with Donald, my oldest son, and he, like his brothers, Ronald, Kevin, Keith, and Michael, said he was behind me 100 percent if I decided to take the position.

If anything, I was most concerned about what my departure from Congress would mean to my constituents—the people whose interests I had promised to protect and serve. All through my seventeen years in public office they had never abandoned me. On the other hand, unlike some of my colleagues in Congress, I did not go to Washington to stay forever in public office. I went to get a job done. I understood that the seat I held was never mine to own, that it belonged to the people that I represented in Maryland. I could always seek elective office again, but for now a different task was at hand.

As I sat in Judge Higginbotham's D.C. office with Earl, Lenny, Myrlie, and Charles, I knew that our weeks of discussions had now reached the moment of truth.

"Madame Chair," I said turning to face Myrlie squarely, "since I'm going to have to learn to address you in that way, I might as well begin doing it now. . . ."

"Oh?" she responded, her eyebrows arching slightly. "That sounds like a man who's made up his mind. Do I sense that the NAACP has a new president and CEO?" she asked cautiously.

"That's correct, Madame Chair, and this soon-to-be-former congressman has a new home."

As Earl, the judge, Lenny, and Charles cheered their approval, I turned again to face Myrlie. With her arms now extended, she and I embraced, smiled, and shook hands on a new future.

During the previous weeks, I had quietly prayed to God for direction and insight, and now I was certain he had given it. The easy part of saying new hellos had begun, but the hard part— saying good-bye—was yet to come.

As I called my congressional staff together the day before the official public announcement, new emotions were stirring within me. These seventeen familiar faces were more like my family than a staff. Most of them had been with me for half my congressional career. Breaking the news to them of my decision to leave Congress was very emotional. Tears flowed freely down everyone's face. They were genuinely happy for me but heartbroken at having to say good-bye. Aside from creating uncertain futures for them, I knew that I would miss their counsel.

The afternoon before, I had placed a call to the White House and had spoken at length with President Clinton about my decision. He took the news quietly, reflectively, although he was somewhat shocked. But after a moment's contemplation, he became very excited.

"This is wonderful," the President said, a lilt coming into his voice. "You're the right person for the job. I can't think of anybody else to do it. We're going to miss you, but you have great possibilities in front of you. You can help this nation do more and become more, in terms of relations between the races and other issues. Whatever the vice president and I can do to help, we will do. A strong NAACP working with all of our people is good for America."

There was a genuine warmth in his words as he spoke of how pleased he was, how he thought the decision was the right one. In the end, he wished me luck and offered to attend my inauguration.

House Speaker Newt Gingrich was also surprised by my news. I had been with him the day before, but I had said nothing about it. Now, as I sat across from him at a coffee table in his office and announced my intention to lead the NAACP, he was speechless for a moment. We stared at each other for a second or two before he realized I was serious.

Sitting back in his chair, he took a deep breath. "I don't need to tell you this," he said slowly, "but you've got respect on both sides of the aisle. Everybody in this institution has appreciated the way you've conducted yourself because you've been an example of the House at its best. We will miss that. We'll miss you because if there was ever anybody who was a straight arrow around here, it was you. You shot from the hip. You didn't play some of the games that take place on the Hill from your party or mine."

At that moment there was no partisan gamesmanship. I felt his words were sincere. We'd known each other for years, long before he became Speaker. We'd often find ourselves on the floor of the House by the rail or sitting and talking about issues. While I didn't agree with most of his ideas, or he with most of mine, we managed to maintain a good working relationship. As I thanked him for his kind words, there was still concern on Newt's face.

"I have to say this," he added, his hand going through his white mane. "You know the organization is not at its best, but you're the right person for the position. The right person. You're going to make it a great organization again. And let me tell you this, Kweisi—I will do whatever I can to help you succeed because I want you to succeed and I want the NAACP to succeed under you."

I caught up with House Minority Leader Dick Gephardt on the campaign trail. Several other Democrats had announced their plans to retire from Congress, and Dick had been concerned about the exodus. Now he was hearing the news firsthand about another Democratic retirement, only this time it was me, one of his lieutenants.

"It's probably the best thing that could happen to the country, and you're going to do the right job because it's your time," Dick said. "We're all going to miss you around here, but what you can do in the streets and around the nation in terms of energizing people to get involved again is so much more than you could ever do here because *that* potential is unlimited."

During my years in Congress, I had tried to make sure I didn't lose track of what was going on back home. I kept my finger on the pulse of the streets because I wanted to stay in touch with the people I represented. But, as much as I loved the people of Baltimore, it was clear that my universe was about to widen to include the fifty states. Even my representational duties would be forever changed. Now it was time for me to move beyond the boundaries of passing bills and delivering speeches of outrage about the plight of my people. I would now be able to fight freely for the causes of those without hope or help. I could fight for those interests across the board now, without being hampered by partisan concerns. My life was only one among the millions who had benefited from the tireless struggles of the NAACP. I owed them a debt that I was eager to repay.

Consensus. Coalition. Both concepts would become vital building blocks in my vision for the reinvigorated NAACP. I saw it as an organization poised for action on the threshold of the new millennium. In order to do this, it would be important to mend some fences, to recapture the moral high ground, and to rise above the emotional rhetoric of days past. I knew that as long as old wounds were constantly being reopened in a divisive climate, we'd never make progress on many of the major issues confronting the African American community—or the nation as a whole.

As I saw it, coalitions would become the most potent antidote to the rapidly increasing wave of bigotry and intolerance infecting both our society and its politics. Building successful coalitions meant finding the broadest common denominator among all people of color. I had never viewed the National Association for the Advancement of Colored People as an organization concerned solely with black issues. In my own definition, "colored people" means all the races of the human rainbow. The NAACP's vitality rests in its numbers, and it would be folly not to take advantage of the power and strength of other minorities affected by many of the same problems.

I knew the time was ripe to reach out to other groups to make overtures, and to listen to their concerns. I would now have to become familiar with their specific issues and needs and would have to work to align them with those of black people. I would now proceed to operate on the basis that we were one another's natural allies. Broadening its traditional definition of itself is the next evolutionary step for the NAACP and must be a top priority. Clearly, the issues of African Americans remain of foremost concern for the organization, but Hispanics, Native Americans, and Asians face similar issues. Like us, until the day they die, they too live under the social limitations of not being white. Their communities, like ours, have needs and concerns and a desire to have the same legal protections as the rest of this society.

Historically, there has always been a role for sympathetic whites and Jews within the NAACP, and that will not change. A strong and effective NAACP is as critical for white co-existence as it is for black progress, and I knew it was now up to me to strengthen the tone of that message. I knew that America would benefit from the efforts of any movement that seeks to make the nation better, fairer, and more responsive to the needs of all its citizens.

African Americans in particular must now unify in a way that reflects how serious we are about transforming our communities. One of the most crucial messages we can send is to galvanize our collective strength into an effective economic and electoral force to put extra pressure on the decision makers to address a broad range of our concerns.

The young men and women among us must also feel that they have the capacity to shape their future. My generation, like the generation before it, was the first to think there was no more time to wait. Today's generation was born knowing it—yet, too many of our young people feel that they are powerless to make change happen. An invigorated and united NAACP must reach out to this new generation as well as to the older one. But we also need to remind everyone that there are no overnight solutions to resolving the pathologies rampant in too many of our communities.

Ignorance is the enemy of self-reliance, and we must choose to become as self-reliant as possible. One of the major shortcomings of integration was that it destroyed our powerful sense of social and economic self-sufficiency. Working together to create a new attitude of self-reliance might allow us to shed our anger and bitterness and low self-esteem. Too many among us have been succumbing to defeatism—blaming everyone and everything for our woes rather than taking the future into our own hands and doing something about it ourselves. This restructuring of our mission requires purpose and clarity of mind.

The first element we need for this restructuring of the qualities that enable us to persevere is honest communication—telling the truth. The time for having others tell us what we want to hear is past. Now we must tell ourselves and each other the unadorned, unadulterated truth about where we are and where we're headed—as a community and as a people in today's America.

For us truly to start an honest dialogue about our national ills and begin the long, slow journey of progress toward our renewal and reconstruction as a community, we must refuse to be side-tracked by ego and celebrity. None of these things will alter the horrid conditions plaguing those among us who are trapped in the bleak killing fields of our inner cities or those who are struggling to exist in the poverty and deprivation of rural America. Those who lead must take on the nettlesome task of going into those areas, talking with people, listening to their concerns, and working with them to overcome and change the conditions of their individual lives and communities.

As part of this honest communication, we must frankly acknowledge that we have not yet utilized the best of ourselves, we have not fully developed, among the largest number of us, the skills and talents necessary to acquire the power we need to shape our future. How often have we left this task to others? How often have we been bitterly disappointed? Because we have failed to apply our creativity, strength, and imagination to finding these solutions ourselves, how many of us have found it easier to throw our hands up in despair and allow ourselves to become mired in hopelessness, believing that nothing will ever change?

Honest communication is built step by step as we begin to face hard truths with integrity and respect for others and ourselves. A quick look at these key areas of our lives shows us that although we may have come up short in the past, we can change. Educational excellence, economic empowerment, political leadership, legal redress, and development of our young are areas of urgency into which we must now hurl our every effort. And bolstered by each other's hope, support, and determination, we are changing. We must find a way to rise beyond ourselves, beyond our conditions, and find the courage to make the painful but crucial sacrifices that will not only nourish our human spirit but elevate our communities and empower our nation. As those qualities become part of our daily lives we will no longer be prisoners of the false barriers of class, skin color, and gender.

People all over the country have come to see the crises now plaguing our land as intractable, unsolvable, and epidemic. And yet my life continues to be a testament that as long as hope is the driving force, anything is possible. The greatest obstacle to our renewal and reconstruction as a people is the absence of hope—and the lack of belief that our lives can get better.

It is very important that we do not adjust our will to fit these times by accepting our plight or succumbing to our fears. For ours is still a nation divided against itself, in need of the clearest thinking we can collectively and individually muster. That need predated the founding of this Republic and it continues to drive our agenda for social change. At the same time, we're still laboring under the master-slave ontology and the doctrine of white supremacy that also predated our founding and have kept this a nation of two societies: one black, one white, separate and unequal.

In two centuries this country has grown from a small band of impoverished colonies to become the strongest, wealthiest, most powerful and influential nation on the face of the earth. But despite our achievements, we have yet to solve our oldest, deepest, and most vexing problem—the issue of race.

Hate speech, hate radio, hate groups, and hate crimes are widening the divide in our nation as never before. And yet it is the very people who are made to stand on either side of that divide who must stand up and speak out.

We have every right to fight against what's wrong in America. Because we are American. Our parents begged on bended knee to be accorded the most elementary of human rights. We have peacefully assembled and petitioned our government for the redress of our grievances. We have stood in, slept in, studied in, and prayed in. We've waged our struggle nonviolently, in the spirit of love; appealed the fundamental morality of the nation and of the nation's conscience. The result has been bloodied hands and broken limbs. Burned churches and bombed homes. Assassinated leaders and murdered followers. Broken spirits and crippled hopes.

Jim Crow Senior is dead. But Jim Crow Junior is alive and well.

Unlike his father, who just loved to segregate, who loved to discriminate, who got his joy from our pain and his pleasure from our lynching, Jim Crow Junior is different. Yes, he likes to discriminate. And if he had his way he would even try to segregate. But unlike his father he gets his joy from watching us lynch ourselves, black against white, Jew against gentile, old against young.

Today, our charge has been renewed by a plague in America, an old plague that has resurfaced with great abandon—a national scourge of insensitivity and intolerance. Whether it is the repugnant act of burning churches or desecrating synagogues, whether it's increased violence from militia groups or demonstrations against immigrants, tolerance has become a dirty word.

So, then, when people ask, "What does the NAACP stand for?" I feel we must answer proudly that we stand for the eradication of that hatred, of that bigotry, of that second-class citizenship, and all those other evil and ugly things that have always worked against this great country.

In an era when so many have diminished visions and hopes, when apathy is rampant and mediocrity is celebrated, we desperately need to keep fighting for what is right and speaking out against what is wrong. Truth in its purest form is not a polite tap on the shoulder, it is a howl of reproach.

It is time we stand up to say again—"The battle begins here."

Where once it was poll taxes and literacy tests, now it is cries of reverse discrimination and a rollback of voting rights.

When we once were subject to the noose and the torch, we are now plagued by the gun and the needle and crimes against each other.

If we cannot remind ourselves of the challenges overcome in the past, we will never overcome the obstacles set in our future.

We can vote in greater numbers . . .

Speak in louder voices . . .

Write with sharper pens . . .

Walk with bigger strides . . .

Act with firmer conviction . . .

In leaving Congress to head the NAACP, I am returning full

circle. I am coming home—back to the place where my zest for the impossible was first formed, the place where my courage was first tested, and the place where my mother taught me that there is no dishonor in defeat, only in surrender.

Although the road less traveled is less certain, it is the road that we must take. Taking this road demands courage, the courage to hope, the courage to take risks, the courage to turn possibilities into realities.

I am a believer. I believe in life, I believe in love, and I believe in tomorrow. I will never give up my faith in mankind, nor will I ever stop believing that the surest test of a person, or a nation, is not where he has been but where he is headed.

ACKNOWLEDGMENTS

Shaping the story of one's life is a demanding and humbling task. Just as accomplishing one's goals in life requires the support of many individuals—the creation of a book involves the labor of many hands.

First, my heartfelt thanks go to my co-writer, Ron Stodghill II, for his invaluable contribution in helping me realize my vision for this book. Thanks also to my agent, Joel Fishman, for his foresight and guidance.

I also owe a special debt of gratitude to Ballantine president Linda Grey, and to the extraordinary staff at One World Books, including my editor, Cheryl D. Woodruff, and Gary Brozek, Robert Fleming, Barbara Shor, Leah Odze, and Nora Reichard. This team's unflagging commitment to this project was nothing short of miraculous.

Many thanks are also extended to several former and current staff members including Ruth Simms, Veronica McKnight, Dan Willson, Tammy Hawley, Carl Swann, and Nancy McCormick.

KM

My deep appreciation to Kweisi Mfume for taking me on the remarkable journey told within these pages. Many thanks also to my families, my agent, Joel Fishman, and my supportive colleagues at *Business Week*.

I am most grateful to my wonderful wife, Robyn, who is always there beside me.

RS

KWEISI MFUME is the new President and Chief Executive Officer of the NAACP. Before that, he was a five-term United States Congressman for the 7th District, Maryland, and served on Congressional Committees for Finance, Banking, and Urban Affairs. He lives in Baltimore, Maryland.

RON STODGHILL II is an award-winning journalist on the staff of *Business Week*. His work has appeared in such publications as *Black Enterprise*, *Emerge*, and most recently *Brotherman: The Odyssey of Black Men in America*. He lives in Chicago with his wife, Robyn.

Extraordinary Lives, Powerful Stories from

ONE WORLD/Ballantine Books

Now that you've read Kweisi Mfume's inspirational
NO FREE RIDE
You'll also want to read:

The Autobiography of Malcolm X, as told to Alex Haley. In this national bestseller that has become a classic of modern America, we hear the voice of the one man who articulated the anger, the struggle, and the beliefs of African Americans in the 1960s. This book expresses like none other the crucial truth about race and racism in our time.

A One World paperback
ISBN 0-345-37671-4 $12.00

Days of Grace by Arthur Ashe and Arnold Rampersad. This number-one *New York Times* bestseller is the remarkable story of a man who was the true embodiment of courage, elegance, and the spirit to fight: Arthur Ashe—tennis champion, social activist, and person with AIDS.

A One World paperback
ISBN 0-345-38681-7 $6.99

Available in paperback in September '97
JOURNEY TO JUSTICE
by Johnnie L. Cochran, Jr.
0-345-41367-9 $6.99